THE NEW NATURALIS

A SURVEY OF BRITISH NATURA

BADGER

*

The aim of this series is to interest the general reader in the wildlife of Britain by recapturing the enquiring spirit of the old naturalists. The editors believe that the natural pride of the British public in the native flora and fauna, to which must be added concern for their conservation, is best fostered by maintaining a high standard of accuracy combined with clarity of exposition in presenting the results of modern scientific research.

THE NEW NATURALIST LIBRARY

BADGER

TIMOTHY J. ROPER

Collins

To
Larissa, Vanja, Conrad and Laurence

This edition published in 2010 by Collins,
An imprint of HarperCollins Publishers

HarperCollins Publishers
77–85 Fulham Palace Road
London W6 8JB
www.collins.co.uk

First published 2010

A CIP catalogue record for this book is available from the British Library.

Set in FF Nexus, illustrated and designed by Tom Cabot/ketchup

Printed in Hong Kong by Printing Express

Hardback
ISBN 978-0-00-732041-7

Paperback
ISBN 978-0-00-733977-8

Contents

Eurasian badgers *Meles meles*. (H. Clark)

Editors' Preface

BADGER IS A NEW DEPARTURE for the New Naturalist Library: a volume on a single species in the main series. As Professor Roper also points out, it is the replacement for the very first volume in the original monograph series – Ernest Neal's *The Badger*. We aim to produce further volumes on single species, but only where they are the sole representative of their group in the UK, or where there is a considerable scientific interest and information available for the species.

The badger *Meles meles* is a perfect example of a species that qualifies on both counts, so is the ideal subject to start with in this new departure for the main series. As the largest naturally occurring carnivore currently found in the UK, it is perhaps surprising that it is not seen more often in the British countryside, but its cryptic lifestyle means that it often goes unnoticed. It is also one of the most social of UK mammals, a lifestyle that makes it attractive to nature lovers. This combination of scarcity and popularity means that members of the speciality Badger Groups are the most likely people to see these fabulous animals and probably accounts for such groups being the most numerous single species groups in the country. As a social animal, the badger has also been intensively researched for many years. Recently, its implication in the transmission of bovine tuberculosis has increased interest in and scientific study on this species and has resulted in the badger becoming the centre of a controversy surrounding the control of the British and Irish populations.

There is thus no better moment than now for an in-depth description of the species' lifestyle to be published by the UK's leading badger scientist, someone who has shared the badger's position at the centre of the controversy. As a considered view of the facts behind this fascinating animal's life, this book is a timely contribution to the history of its study and a worthy replacement for Ernest Neal's original volume in the series.

Author's Foreword and Acknowledgements

Most badger lovers would agree that the first 'proper' badger book was the New Naturalist Monograph written by Ernest Neal and published by Collins in 1948. It is a privilege to be allowed to follow in Ernest's footsteps, for several reasons. First, his was the first single-species volume in the original New Naturalist series, just as this is the first single-species volume in the new series. Second, Ernest's knowledge and love of badgers were unrivalled. Third, and by no means least, he was one of the kindest and most modest people one could ever hope to meet – a real authority but one who wore his erudition lightly and was always willing to share it. I have thought about him often during the writing of this book.

Ernest wrote three books about badgers, the most recent of which, co-authored with Chris Cheeseman, was published in 1996. Why, then, do we need another? The main reason is that during the last 15 years an enormous amount of new research on badgers has been published that not only adds, quantitatively, to what we know about the species but also materially changes our view of what badgers are like. In some respects, it is almost as though the old badger that we knew and loved has been replaced by a different animal. For example, whereas we had always assumed that badgers live in relatively large social groups, as they do in the UK, we now know that they exist in quite small groups or pairs over much of their geographical range. Similarly, whereas early studies had suggested that badgers were strictly territorial, we now know that movements between social groups are quite common and that, in some populations, territoriality is much less evident. Again, whereas we used to think that badgers fed mainly on earthworms, we now know that their diet is much more catholic and that in some parts of their range they eschew earthworms altogether. And whereas we used to think that breeding outside the social group was rare, we now know that it happens all the time. Even the basic taxonomy of badgers is being questioned.

These latest insights about badgers have come partly from the application of new techniques, particularly in the field of molecular genetics. More importantly, however, they have originated from research conducted in countries other than the UK, which has given us a wider, richer and more representative view of the species. Outstanding studies of badgers in the Doñana reserve in southern Spain, in the Serra de Grândola in Portugal, in the Białowieża Primeval Forest in Poland, and even in the suburbs of Tokyo and Yamaguchi City, Japan, have fundamentally changed our ideas about many aspects of badger behaviour. The picture that emerges is of a remarkably adaptable and resourceful animal that, despite now being one of the world's best-studied mammals, can still regularly surprise us.

My purpose has been to review, as completely as is feasible in a book of this type, the existing scientific literature on badgers. I have taken this approach rather than a more anecdotal or descriptive one, because, as a scientist, I want to explain why things are the way they are. This means being interested in hypotheses and interpretations as well as in natural history per se. The difficulty, of course, is in conveying the nuts and bolts of hard scientific information and the excitement of ideas in an intelligible manner, without oversimplifying and, even more importantly, without losing the sense of wonder and delight in nature that motivates every enthusiastic naturalist and every professional biologist. This is what I have tried to do.

Many people helped to make the book a reality. David Streeter first suggested that I write a badger book and I could not have done so without the support and facilities of the University of Sussex. Chris Cheeseman and Peter Lüps read the entire manuscript, while John Davison, Maren Huck and Noel Smith read parts of it. Their comments were invaluable and resulted in many improvements to the text. The responsibility for any remaining errors or omissions rests, of course, with me.

The Badger Trust kindly put out a call for photographs, and the following people very generously supplied me with images or other illustrative material: Alexei Abramov, Brian Andrews, Marc Baldwin, Keith and Colleen Begg, Karen and Martin Blackman, Nick Brickle, the Centre for Ecology and Hydrology, Hugh Clark, Michael Clark, Elizabeth Close, Dan Collins, Miranda Cowan, Tim Crawshaw, Barry Crowley, Dan Danahar, Aparajita Datta, Dassenwerkgroep Brabant, John Davison, Dez Delahay, Ray Dixon, Emmanuel Do Linh San, Michael Edwards, Carol Evans, the Food and Agriculture Research Agency, Tony Goodchild, Kurt Grossenbacher, Julia Hurst, Valerie Hutchin, Ian Hutchison, Md,

Anwaral Islam, Gareth Jones, Yayoi Kaneko, Andrew Kelly, Rafał Kowalczyk, Richard Lawrence, Roland Lowery, David Malins, Simon More, Paul O'Donoghue, Sue Old, Mike Rendle, Eloy Revilla, Luis Rosalino, Thomas Scheppers, Lesley and Peter Schofield, Scottish Badgers, Graham Shepherd, Chris Smal, Noel Smith, Lynsey Stuart, Michele Taylor, Willy Thÿssen, the University of Sussex, Hans Vink, VLA Weybridge, Alastair Ward, Simon and Jane Wild, and Neil Yeo. Michael Clark also generously allowed me to reproduce some of his drawings of badgers and Keith Hunt produced electronic versions of these and other hard-copy illustrations. Oliver Keuling kindly provided data on badger population densities in Germany and elsewhere, and Emmanuel Do Linh San data on hunting bags in Switzerland. The following publishers allowed me to reproduce material without charge (others were less charitable): Elsevier, the Finnish Zoological and Botanical Publishing Board, Koninklijke Brill NV, the Editors of *Lutra*, Nature Publishing Group, the Polish Academy of Sciences, the Public Library of Science, Royal Society Publishing, the Editors of the *Russian Journal of Theriology*, the *Societas Europaea Mammalogica*, the Editors of *Wildlife Biology* and the Mammalogical Society of Japan.

I thank all of these for their generosity and help, and for the enthusiasm with which they have supported this project.

Introduction: Badgers in Britain

THIS IS NOT PRIMARILY a book about British badgers. On the contrary, it seeks to provide a global view of a species that has a huge geographical range and that can adapt itself to a correspondingly impressive variety of climates and habitats. Nevertheless, badgers do occupy a unique place in the British consciousness. Surely, the rest of Europe can only wonder at the number of UK organisations that use the badger as a logo or trademark (Fig. 1); the number of websites featuring information about badgers; the number of voluntary badger protection societies that flourish here; the extent to which the scientific literature on badgers is dominated by British studies; and the vigour with which the public has defended badgers against the threat of culling for purposes of disease control. And where else, other than in Britain, can one book a holiday with badger-watching as the primary attraction?

FIG 1. The badger as a marketing device. (E. Do Linh San)

In some respects, however, this passion for badgers is not as general as appears at first sight. For 15 years I lived in a village at the bottom of the South Downs, in an area where the population density of badgers was high and where there was ample evidence of their presence. Yet when I told people that I was interested in badgers, the most common response, even from those who had lived in the country all their lives, was surprise that there

FIG 2. 'Badgers by moonlight' – an outstanding example of badger photography. (B. Crowley)

were badgers in the locality. It is tempting to think that this lack of awareness must be a recent phenomenon, reflecting the extent to which we have now all become divorced from nature. However, Ernest Neal encountered precisely the same unconsciousness of badgers, even among country people, more than half a century ago (Neal, 1948).

The truth is that the attitude of most ordinary people towards badgers is complex and contradictory, involving a combination of familiarity and ignorance, concern and indifference. On the one hand, virtually everyone nowadays must be aware of what badgers look like and know something of their habits, if only from television documentaries and children's books. In addition, there is no doubt that most people feel well disposed towards badgers in a general way and are strongly opposed to any form of deliberate persecution. On the other hand, few have ever seen a live badger and most are not particularly interested in doing so. Only for a minority of enthusiasts do badgers constitute a real and important source of interest and pleasure, whether it be through watching them in their gardens or in the wild, photographing or filming them (Fig. 2), sharing badger-related knowledge and experiences with others via the internet, or defending badgers against threats to their welfare. To a considerable extent, the apparent British obsession with badgers results from the activities of this relatively small but highly committed minority.

How did badgers come to Britain and how has our attitude towards them evolved? Fossil evidence shows that the ancestors of modern badgers originated in Southeast Asia but then expanded their range northwards and westwards so as to reach western Europe about 3 million years ago (see Chapter 1 for details). It seems likely, then, that badgers reached Britain (or, at least, the part of the European landmass that subsequently became Britain) at about that time. The earliest British remains of the present-day species *Meles meles* are, however, much later. They were discovered at Boxgrove, West Sussex, and have been dated to the Cromerian Stage of the Early Pleistocene – that is, to about three-quarters to half a million years ago (Yalden, 1999). A few human bones have also been recovered from the same site, providing the earliest indication we have of the long association between humans and badgers. However, we can only speculate as to the nature of the association at this distant point in history.

Regardless of when they first arrived, badgers were forced to retreat temporarily from the whole of northern and central Europe, including Britain, during the most recent glaciation, which lasted from about 110,000 to 11,500 years ago and was at its maximum about 18,000 years ago. However, recolonisation of Europe following the retreat of the ice seems to have been rapid, enabling badgers to return to Britain (which was still connected by land to the rest of Europe) about 10,000 years ago. Remains from sites such as Plas Heaton Cave, Clwyd, probably date from about this time and show badgers coexisting with species such as Arctic foxes, wolverines and reindeer (Yalden, 1999). However, climate warming in the post-glacial period was rapid and within a few hundred years the fauna of Britain came more to resemble that of a temperate forest. For example, the Mesolithic site of Star Carr, Yorkshire (dated to about 9,500 years ago), reveals, besides remains of badgers, those of wolf, brown bear, red fox, pine marten, beaver and wild boar (Yalden, 1999). By this time, then, badgers were probably living in Britain much as they still do today in the forests of central and eastern Europe, and Scandinavia.

During the most recent 5,000 years, records of badgers from British sites are surprisingly sparse. A badger mandible from the early Bronze Age (4,000–3,500 years ago) was discovered in the Outer Hebrides (Fairnell & Barrett, 2007) and badger remains have been found in Roman Exeter; but in neither case is it clear how the remains came to be there or what they signify. Remains are equally scarce from the Anglo-Saxon period (about AD 500–1,000). However, the species seems to have been a familiar part of the landscape during this period, since an estimated 140 Anglo-Saxon place names have their origin in the term *broc* (badger) (Yalden, 1999). Clearly, then, the absence of badger remains from archeological sites does not necessarily mean that the animals themselves were rare.

So much for the history of badgers in Britain: what about the relationship between badgers and us Brits? Here we are on even shakier ground, at least until medieval times, because scarcely any of the physical remains that have been found (and there have not been many of them) provide clues as to their cultural significance. One exception is the discovery of remains in the Outer Hebrides (see above), which is interesting because this is outside the present range of the species. Consequently, these finds suggest deliberate transportation of badgers, probably in quite small numbers and presumably as carcasses.

We can only guess as to why Bronze Age humans might have taken badgers to their settlements on remote Scottish Islands. However, badgers provide several valuable commodities including meat, leather, pelts, bristles and fat, and it seems likely that they have been hunted for these commodities since ancient times (Griffiths, 1991). As regards the hunting of badgers for food, there is documentary evidence that badger meat was eaten by Roman legionnaires, including those garrisoned in northern Europe; and badger bones with cut marks suggestive of butchering, dating to the 16th or 17th century AD, have been recovered from two sites in Scotland (Davies, 1971; Fairnell & Barrett, 2007). There are also written records of badger recipes, and descriptions of what badger flesh tastes like, dating back at least a few centuries (Jaine, 1986). Such sources suggest that badger was mainly a food of the poor, as it still is in some parts of eastern Europe. The part of the animal most often referred to is the ham, which could be brined and roasted, or smoked for more prolonged preservation (Davidson, 1999). Its taste has been likened to that of mutton but when I once ate badger meat myself, in Switzerland, I found it tasted of the forest from which it came, with flavours reminiscent of earth, leaf mould, pine needles and fungi. In any case, it was not very palatable.

As regards the other commodities that badgers provide, fat was used in cooking, for medicinal purposes, for the manufacture of soap and for the waterproofing of clothes; bristles were used for brushes; pelts were used for clothing, rugs and carpets; and leather for various purposes (Griffiths, 1991). All of these uses have continued at least until recent times in parts of eastern Europe and Asia.

A far less defensible kind of badger hunting – namely, deliberate persecution for reasons other than commodity value – seems to have developed in medieval and Tudor times. One factor in this was a series of 'Tudor Vermin Acts', dating from 1532, which sought to identify certain species as vermin and to encourage their control by offering a bounty for carcasses. The best known of these pieces of legislation is the 'Acte for the Preservation of Grayne', implemented in 1566 and not repealed until 1863, which designated as pest species not just granivores such as rats and mice but also a wide range of carnivores and other non-cereal-eating species, including badgers (which earned a bounty of 12 pence per head). Although this legislation seems to have impacted especially heavily on pine martens, polecats and wild cats, it also encouraged the slaughter of badgers. Even less justifiable, however, was the digging and baiting of badgers purely for reasons of 'sport', which seems to have begun in medieval times and is still practised in Britain today, despite its illegality and manifest brutality (see Chapter 1).

Deliberate persecution of badgers as pests became more intense and widespread in the 18th and 19th centuries, owing to the various enclosure acts passed between about 1759 and 1850. These gave landowners exclusive rights to game on their land, leading to the development of 'sporting' estates managed by professional gamekeepers (Yalden, 1999). Thus began a systematic campaign of snaring, poisoning and shooting of carnivores, mainly in order to protect the eggs and chicks of ground-nesting game birds. Badgers, however, were doubly unfortunate, because they also suffered persecution from fox-hunting enthusiasts on the grounds that they competed with foxes for earths (e.g. Blakeborough & Pease, 1914). As a consequence of these twin sources of harassment, badgers had become rare in some parts of Britain, and were nowhere abundant, by the mid-19th century. Indeed, some authors, writing at about this time, predicted that the species would become extinct (Cresswell *et al.*, 1989).

The British badger population probably reached its lowest point in the early 1900s, by which time the number of gamekeepers had risen to about 23,000 (compared with about 17,000 in the early 1870s: Yalden, 1999). However, after World War I, which produced a sharp decline in the number of gamekeepers, populations of carnivores, including badgers, began to recover (Langley & Yalden, 1977). By the early 1930s, badgers were reported to be 'fairly common in suitable areas all over England and Wales' (Neal & Cheeseman, 1996), while in Shropshire an increase in the number of setts, from 10 to 37, was recorded during the period 1900 to 1934 (Pitt, 1935). Similarly, Ernest Neal concluded that badgers were widely distributed and locally numerous by the 1940s (Neal, 1948).

More formal national badger surveys, begun in 1963 and 1985, confirmed these impressions and produced estimates of 36,000 and 43,000 badger groups, respectively (Clements *et al.*, 1988; Cresswell *et al.*, 1990). Since then, there has been no further nationwide survey but it seems likely that the population is at least stable and may well have experienced a further increase. In addition, British badgers now, for the first time in their history, enjoy a considerable degree of legal protection (see Chapter 1). Nevertheless, they still face serious anthropogenic threats from increasing volumes of road traffic, urbanisation and agricultural intensification (see Chapter 2). They are also still under threat of localised culling for purposes of bovine tuberculosis control, especially in Wales, Northern Ireland and the Republic of Ireland (see Chapter 10).

Given this history, it is not surprising that our relationship with badgers is complex. Now that people have become more humane in their attitudes towards wildlife in general, our concern for badgers may be partly a wish to make amends for the appalling and unjustified persecution that they have suffered in the past. In addition, we have learned, not least through the work of Ernest Neal and also from sources such as wildlife documentaries, that badgers are harmless and fascinating creatures. But we also admire badgers because we see in them characteristics that we regard as laudable and perhaps even quintessentially British. We can sympathise with their curmudgeonly manner, their liking for privacy, their unwillingness to take offence and their tenacity when threatened. And if ever there was an animal whose home is its castle, it is the badger. Of course, this kind of anthropomorphism should not be taken too seriously, but if it helps us to feel sympathetic towards another species, then it has its uses.

For me, however, badgers deserve respect for two additional reasons. First, they are our largest remaining carnivore species – serious animals with the capacity, should it be required, to do serious damage. It pleases me to know that in our excessively civilised and overcrowded country, such creatures are still going quietly about their business at night, probably not far away from where I am sleeping safely in my bed. And second, I cannot help but admire the combination of flexibility and robustness that has enabled badgers to withstand millennia of environmental change and deliberate persecution while remaining true to themselves. Badgers are survivors, not just in the sense that the species is still with us but also in the more specific sense that in many places, hidden away throughout the land, individual social groups still cling to the sites that their ancestors have occupied for decades or even, perhaps, for centuries. Uniquely among mammals, badgers attach themselves to the very landscape. They remind us that it is possible to survive change without surrendering to it.

CHAPTER 1

Classification, Evolutionary Origin, Geographical Distribution and Conservation Status

CLASSIFICATION AND EVOLUTIONARY ORIGIN

Badgers as mustelids

THE GREAT SWEDISH NATURALIST Linnaeus, the founder of the science of taxonomy, thought that the species we now call 'Eurasian badger' was a kind of bear. And you can see his point. Badgers do exhibit a number of superficially bear-like characteristics, such as their shaggy, loose-fitting coats, short tails, long claws, rolling gait and winter torpor. They even share with bears a liking for honey. Linnaeus had some justification, therefore, for naming the badger *Ursus meles* ('honey bear') in the 1758 edition of his great work, *Systema Naturae.*

However, appearances can be deceptive and Linnaeus was mistaken. Four years later, the French naturalist and philosopher Mathurin Jacques Brisson correctly assigned badgers to the mustelid family (Mustelidae). This means that their closest relatives are not bears at all but rather weasels, stoats, polecats, martens, mink, otters and wolverines. Brisson also deserves credit for giving badgers their present Latin specific name, *Meles meles.* Nevertheless, because Linnaeus was the first to recognise badgers as a distinct species and to describe their appearance and habits, he remains the ultimate authority when it comes to defining what a badger is. Consequently, the badger's full, formal, scientific name is given as '*Meles meles* (Linnaeus 1758)', or '*Meles meles* (L. 1758)' for short.

To taxonomists, the defining features of mustelids are the size and shape of some of their teeth and the presence of a pair of enlarged scent glands, situated either side of the anus, that produce a pungent secretion responsible for giving

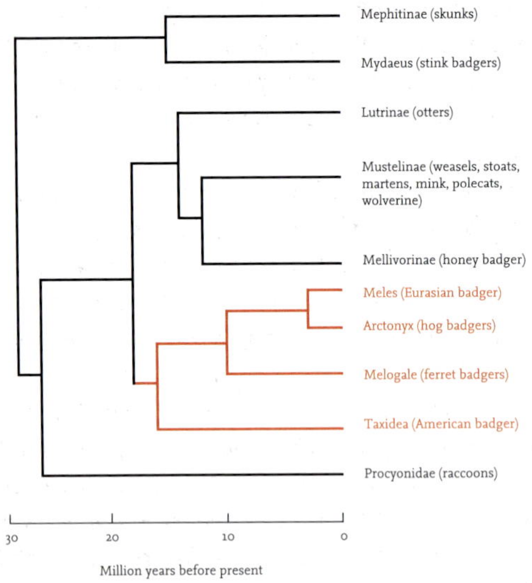

FIG 3. 'Traditional' phenetics-based phylogeny of mustelids and related carnivores. Red indicates the lineage of the 'true' badgers (Melinae). (Based on Dragoo & Honeycutt, 1997)

them the reputation of being rather smelly animals. Badgers share these features. More obvious to an ordinary observer, however, is the basic body plan, characterised by a long spine and short legs, which gives all members of the family a distinctive elongated shape and an unmistakable sinuosity of movement. This body plan has proved extraordinarily adaptable over the course of evolutionary time, enabling different branches of the Mustelidae to become specialised climbers (martens), swimmers (otters and mink), hunters of small burrowing mammals (stoats and weasels) or burrow-dwellers (badgers).

The badger subfamily

During the last few years, taxonomy, never a very exact science, has been in a state of flux. Traditionally, the classification of living organisms has relied on what are called 'phenetic' criteria: that is, differences in physical characteristics such as, in the case of mammals, coat colour or the size and shape of bones and teeth. Recently, however, a completely different approach to taxonomy ('phylogenetic' classification) has become possible, based on comparing the DNA of different taxonomic groups; and this has sometimes produced radically different results from those based on phenetics. In principle, phylogenetic classification should more accurately reflect the genetic, and hence evolutionary, relationships between different species, but in practice there remain doubts about the relative merits of the phenetic and phylogenetic approaches. In addition, the mustelids have always been a difficult family for taxonomists to classify, owing to their great diversity and the relative rapidity with which different genera and species diverged from one another over the course of evolutionary time. The reader will perhaps not be surprised to learn, therefore, that there is no generally accepted taxonomy of the mustelids in general, or of badgers in particular.

The most widely accepted taxonomy, based mainly on phenetic criteria, classes the 'true badgers' as a subfamily (Melinae) (Fig. 3). However, the common name 'badger' has been applied more widely than this, referring to a loose assortment of what are generally regarded as ten but may be as many as fourteen different species. All of these are mustelids but in other respects have little in common beyond a tendency to dig and a more or less striped coat.

For present purposes, we can dispense fairly rapidly with three of these ten 'badgers': namely, the African honey badger *Mellivora capensis* (Fig. 4, left) and the two species of Oriental stink badger, the Indonesian (or Sunda) stink badger *Mydaeus javanensis* (Fig. 4, right) and the Palawan stink badger *Mydaeus marchei* (formerly known as *Suillotaxus marchei*). The African honey badger, although it resembles the true badgers in some aspects of its morphology and behaviour, belongs in a different subfamily (Mellivorinae). Most authorities regard it as being related to the weasels, stoats and martens (Mustelinae), from which its ancestors diverged 10–11 million years ago (see Fig. 3). However, a recent phylogenetic study suggests that the Mellivorinae split off on its own from the main mustelid line about 12–13 million years ago (Koepfli *et al.*, 2008: see Fig. 5). The two species of Oriental stink badger, although until recently regarded as true badgers, are now generally considered to belong to the skunk subfamily (Mephitinae). If this is correct, then their evolutionary ancestors have been distinct from those of the rest of the mustelids for at least 30 million years (Dragoo & Honeycutt, 1997).

FIG 4. (above left) African honey badger *Mellivora capensis*. (Keith & Colleen Begg); (above right) Camera-trap photograph of Indonesian stink badger *Mydaeus javanensis*. (Nick Brickle, Wildlife Conservation Society – Indonesia Programme)

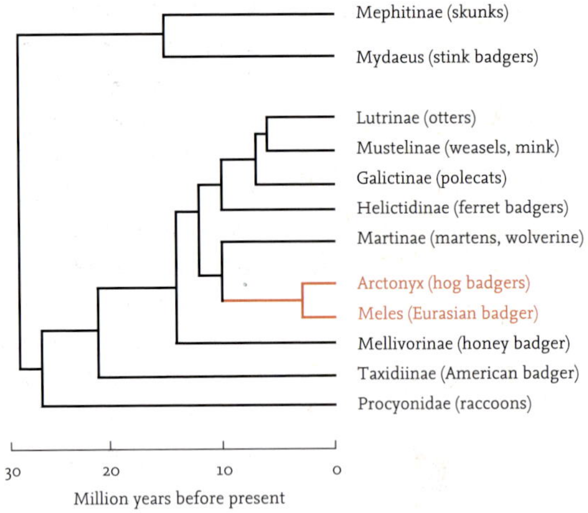

FIG 5. DNA-based phylogeny of mustelids and related carnivores. Red indicates the lineage of the 'true' badgers (Melinae). (Based on Koepfli *et al.*, 2008)

The remaining seven 'badgers' are traditionally regarded as constituting the subfamily Melinae or 'true' badgers and belong to four different genera: *Taxidea, Meles, Arctonyx* and *Melogale*. The first of these genera contains only a single species, the American badger *Taxidea taxus* (Fig. 6a). The second genus, *Meles*, is also generally supposed to contain only one species, the Eurasian (or European) badger *Meles meles* (Fig. 6b). However, as we shall see, some authorities distinguish three species: the European badger *Meles meles*, the Asian badger *Meles leucurus* and the Japanese badger *Meles anakuma*. The third genus, *Arctonyx*, was also until recently considered to contain only one species, the Asian hog badger *Arctonyx collaris* (Fig. 6c). However, recent evidence suggests that there are in fact three species of hog badgers: *Arctonyx collaris, Arctonyx hoevenii* and *Arctonyx albogularis* (Helgen *et al.*, 2008). The fourth genus, *Melogale*, is now thought to contain four species of ferret badgers: the Chinese (or small-toothed) ferret badger *M. moschata* (sometimes erroneously referred to as *M. mosquata*); the Burmese (or large-toothed) ferret badger *M. personata* (Fig. 6d); Everett's ferret badger *M. everetti*; and the Javan ferret badger *M. orientalis*. (Some authorities regard *M. orientalis* as a subspecies of *M. personata* but most consider it a species in its own right.)

Of these 'true' badgers, the Eurasian badger is the most widely distributed, occurring across Europe and Asia from Ireland in the west to Japan in the east (Fig. 7). The American badger is found throughout the western and central states of the USA and penetrates into Mexico as far south as Puebla, while the hog badgers and ferret badgers are found in east and southeast Asia.

In morphological and behavioural terms, the American badger and the hog badger have quite a lot in common with the Eurasian badger, insofar as all three

FIG **6.** (a) American badger *Taxidea taxus* (US Fish and Wildlife Service); (b) Eurasian badger *Meles meles* (H. Clark); (c) Asian hog badger *Arctonyx collaris* (Namdapha Wildlife Monitoring Programme, Nature Conservation Foundation, India); (d) The large-toothed ferret badger *Melogale personata*, one of four species of ferret badger. (Md. Anwarul Islam, Wildlife Trust of Bangladesh)

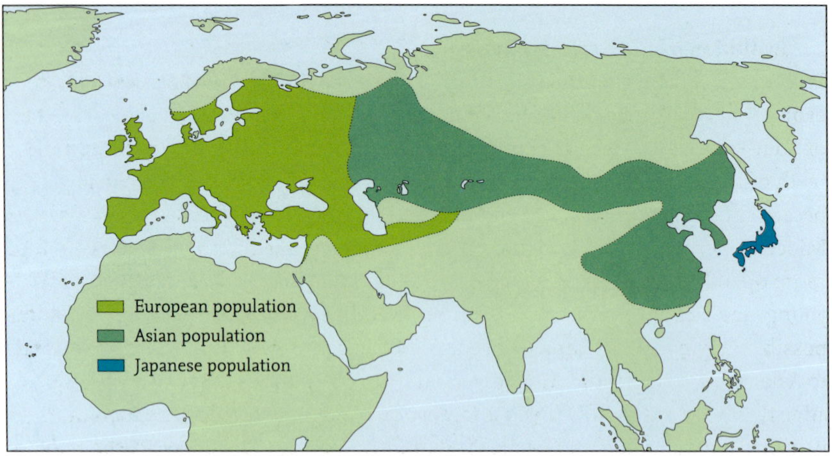

FIG 7. Map showing worldwide distribution of badgers of the genus *Meles*. Authorities differ as to whether the European, Asian and Japanese populations are different sub-species or different species. (Original from Abramov *et al.*, 2003)

species are about the same size (5–12 kg) and shape, are terrestrial and are burrow-dwellers. The ferret badgers, by contrast, are small (1–3 kg), nimble, tree-climbing predators with thin bodies, long bushy tails and sharp, pointed snouts. In many aspects of their habits and morphology, therefore, the ferret badgers resemble martens or weasels more than they do the other true badgers. Nevertheless, from an evolutionary point of view, it is the American badger that is the least closely related to the Eurasian badger. Its ancestors represent a distinct lineage that probably parted company from the other true badgers 16–17 million years ago (Marmi *et al.*, 2004: see Fig. 3) and may even have parted company from all of the other mustelids as much as 20 million years ago (Koepfli *et al.*, 2008: see Fig. 5). The ferret badgers diverged as a separate evolutionary line perhaps 10–11 million years ago, while the Eurasian badger and Asian hog badgers shared a common ancestor until about 3.5–4.5 million years ago.

The Eurasian badger and Asian hog badgers are therefore the most closely related of all the so-called 'badgers'. Indeed, a recent DNA-based study argues that the genera *Meles* and *Arctonyx* should be regarded as the only 'true' badgers (Melinae) and that the American badger and ferret badgers should be assigned to different subfamilies (Taxidiinae and Helictidinae, respectively: see Koepfli *et al.*, 2008 and Fig. 5). In short, the taxonomy of the 'true' badgers is by no means settled and the subfamily Melinae could contain either two or four genera, and anything from 2 to 11 species.

Evolution of the Eurasian badger

It seems likely that the true badgers, including the Eurasian badger *Meles meles*, evolved originally from a marten-like ancestor that inhabited the tropical forests of Southeast Asia – an agile climber and active predator, with a long tail and the teeth of a typical carnivore (Long & Killingley, 1983). These animals probably became gradually less arborial and more terrestrial during the Early to Middle Miocene, perhaps 20 million years ago, at the same time leaving the forests for more open habitat, starting to dig burrows for shelter and for the rearing of young, and adopting a more omnivorous diet. The ancestral form of *Meles*, which possibly originated in China from the Pliocene genus *Melodon*, was still confined to Asia when *Arctonyx* and *Meles* diverged from one another. However, shortly after this it spread rapidly north and west into Europe, reaching the Iberian peninsula by the Middle Pliocene (Madurell-Malapeira *et al.*, 2009). At the same time, it increased in body size and evolved anatomical, physiological and behavioural attributes to enable it to cope with colder climates – for example, a thicker coat, deeper burrows and the ability to store large amounts of fat as a defence against harsh winters. At some point, the ancestor of the present-day badger must also have become more tolerant of other members of its own species, enabling it to live in pairs or larger groups, rather than solitarily as do most of the other mustelids (see Chapter 7).

Fossils bearing a recognisable resemblance to modern Eurasian badgers date back about 4 million years: that is, to about the time when *Meles* and *Arctonyx* became distinct genera. Fossils classified as belonging to the genus *Meles*, 2–3 million years old, have been found in countries as far apart as Spain and China, suggesting that the genus was not only established by that time but was widely distributed. By the Early to Middle Pleistocene (1.5–0.5 million years ago), the species *Meles meles* is distinguishable in the fossil record, albeit in the form of a different subspecies *Meles meles atavus* (Petter, 1971); and fossils of the Japanese badger *Meles meles anakuma*, dating back to the late Middle Pleistocene (about 100,000 years ago), have been found in southern Japan (Kawamura *et al.*, 1989). The earliest badger remains found in Britain are from Boxgrove, West Sussex (probably from the Cromerian Stage of the Late Pleistocene, about 0.75–0.5 million years ago), and from Barrington, Cambridgeshire (from about 250,000 years ago) (Neal & Cheeseman, 1996; Yalden, 1999).

Although, as we have seen, ancestral badgers were distributed widely across Europe by the Middle Pliocene (about 3 million years ago), they were forced to retreat again during the ice ages, surviving only in a few southern refugia. Subfossil evidence (i.e. incompletely fossilised remains) indicates that these refugia included parts of Iberia, Italy, the Carpathians and, possibly, the Balkans and the northern Pontic. However, a recent DNA-based study shows that present-day badgers are genetically rather homogeneous, suggesting that the post-glacial recolonisation of Europe by badgers was from a single population and, hence, from a single refugium (Pope *et al.*, 2006). Be that as it may, recolonisation seems to have occurred rather rapidly following the final retreat of the ice about 15,000 years ago. Thus, badgers reached Britain (across the land bridge that then connected it with the continent) about 10,000 years ago, and Scandinavia about 8,000 years ago (Sommer & Benecke, 2004).

There still remains, however, a puzzle as to how badgers recolonised Ireland. A variety of evidence suggests that a land bridge or bridges existed for short periods of time between Ireland and Scotland, in which case badgers may have migrated across it. However, this hypothesis is called into question by the fact that present-day Irish badgers are genetically more similar to those of central England than to those resident in Scotland (Pope *et al.*, 2006). One theory is that humans took badgers to Ireland about 10,000 years ago; another is that they were not driven out of Ireland completely during the ice ages but, rather, survived in an ice-free refuge in southern Ireland.

Classification of the Eurasian badger

Modern Eurasian badgers exhibit considerable variation, across the species' geographical range, in characteristics such as body size, coat colour, bone morphology and dentition (for references, see Kurose *et al.*, 2001). The taxonomic interpretation of this variation is, however, controversial. Depending on which authority you believe, the genus *Meles* contains from 1 to 6 species, from 2 to 8 subspecies and up to 24 different geographical types (Long & Killingley, 1983; Kurose *et al.*, 2001).

The most widely accepted classification recognises one species (*Meles meles*) and four subspecies: *Meles meles meles* (Europe), *M. m. leptorhynchus* (Siberia and China), *M. m. amurensis* (Manchuria and Korea) and *M. m. anakuma* (Japan). However, a group of Russian taxonomists led by Alexei Abramov has recently challenged this view, suggesting instead that anatomical differences (for example, in the skull, teeth and penis bone: see Fig. 8) justify dividing the genus into three separate species: European badgers *Meles meles*, Asian badgers *Meles leucurus* and Japanese badgers *Meles anakuma* (Fig. 7). In addition, the Russians argue for the existence of two distinct forms of *Meles meles* (European and Transcaucasian) and two forms of *Meles leucurus* (Siberian and Far Eastern) (Abramov & Puzachenko, 2005). At the other extreme, Lynch (1996) has argued that the morphological variation across Eurasia is in fact continuous (i.e. it constitutes a single spectrum

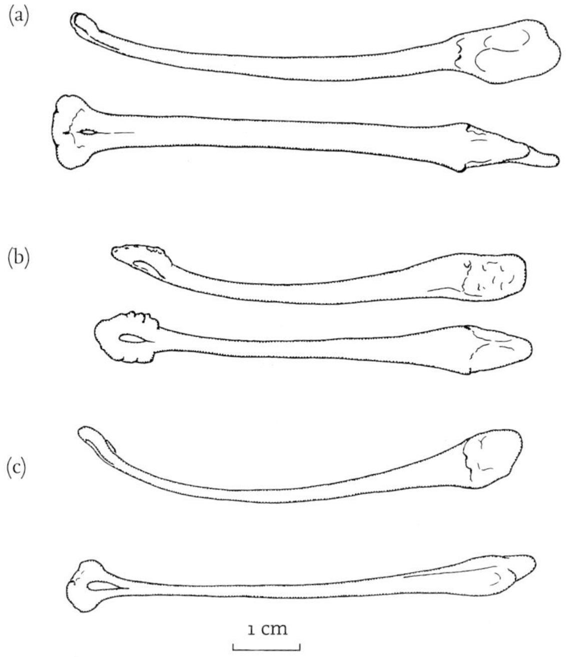

FIG 8. Lateral and dorsal views of the baculum (penis bone): (a) European badger *Meles meles*; (b) Asian badger *Meles leucurus*; (c) Japanese badger *Meles anakuma*. (Abramov, 2002)

or 'cline'), except in the case of Japanese badgers, which are anatomically distinct (Fig. 9). Accordingly, Lynch argues for a single species *Meles meles* containing two subspecies: *Meles meles meles* (Eurasia) and *Meles meles anakuma* (Japan). All of these classifications are based on phenetic criteria.

A recent DNA-based analysis by Josep Marmi and others divides Eurasian badgers into four main groups corresponding to Europe, Southwest Asia (Crete, Israel, Georgia and Tajikistan), North and East Asia (Russia, Kazakhstan, Mongolia, China and Korea) and Japan (Marmi *et al.*, 2006). This classification is reassuringly similar to the phenetic taxonomy of Alexei Abramov and his colleagues. Thus, Marmi's 'European' population corresponds to Abramov's 'European' form of *Meles meles*; his 'Southwest Asian' population corresponds to Abramov's 'Transcaucasian' form of *Meles meles*; his 'North and East Asian' population corresponds to Abramov's *Meles leucurus*; and his Japanese population corresponds to Abramov's *Meles anakuma*. The only difference, therefore, is that Abramov recognises two different forms of *Meles leucurus* whereas Marmi distinguishes only one.

FIG 9. The Japanese badger *Meles (meles) anakuma*. (Y. Kaneko)

As regards time of origin, the DNA data suggest that the European, Southwest Asian, and North and East Asian groups have been diverging since the end of the Pliocene (i.e. since about 2.5 million years ago), probably because they became separated by major geographical barriers. The Japanese group, by contrast, diverged from the North and East Asian group more recently.

To summarise, recent work is converging towards a taxonomy of *Meles* involving three, or perhaps four, geographically distinct forms. However, important questions remain as to the status of these. Should the European and Asian populations be classified as different species, as Abramov has argued, or merely as different subspecies? What is the taxonomic status of the two different 'forms' of European badger and the two 'forms' of Asian badger identified by Abramov; and why does Marmi's DNA-based analysis not support the existence of these different forms in the case of the Asian population? And, finally, should Japanese badgers be regarded as a different species, as Abramov suggests, or continue to be classified as a subspecies?

In addition, more general questions remain about the relative ability of the phenetic and phylogenetic approaches to reveal the true taxonomy of any animal group, and about the accuracy with which genetic data can reveal the date at which different taxonomic groups became distinct. These are exciting times in taxonomy and although much progress has been made in recent years, we have certainly not yet arrived at a definitive classification of badgers.

A note on terminology

Although Abramov and his colleagues have developed a strong case for recognising three different species within the genus *Meles*, this classification has yet to be officially sanctioned. For the purposes of this book, therefore, I shall stick to the traditional view that all members of the genus *Meles* belong to the single species *M. meles*. The generally accepted common name for this species used to be 'European badger' but in recent years 'Eurasian badger' has become more popular, no doubt because it is clearly more descriptive of the species' wide geographical distribution. In addition, 'Eurasian badger' avoids any suspicion of parochialism on the part of western European writers. For these reasons, I shall use 'Eurasian badger', or just 'badger' for short, to refer to all badgers of the genus *Meles*.

However, we need not discard the term 'European badger', because, as we have seen, most attempts to classify badgers distinguish a more or less separate population inhabiting the parts of Europe that extend from Ireland and Portugal in the west to the Ural mountains, the Volga river and the Caspian Sea in the east (see Fig. 7). Furthermore, this population is disproportionately important from a scientific point of view, because most of what we know about badgers comes from studies carried out within this geographical area. Henceforth, therefore, I shall use the term 'European badger' to refer specifically to members of this western, central and eastern European population.

DISTRIBUTION AND POPULATION DENSITY

As we have seen, the Eurasian badger is widely distributed, occurring across the western Palaearctic region from Ireland and Portugal in the west to Japan in the east, and from Finland in the north to Israel, Iran, Afghanistan, Tibet and China in the south. Within this vast geographical range, badgers occupy an equally remarkable variety of habitats, from the Białowieża Primeval Forest on the border of Poland and Belorussia to city suburbs in the south of England; from the coastal sand dunes of southern Spain to the alpine forests of Switzerland; and from the lush pastures of Ireland to the semi-desert of Israel (Fig. 10). Within Europe, badgers are more or less ubiquitous, being absent only from Iceland, northern Russia, northern Scandinavia and various small islands (Fig. 11). Less is known about their distribution in the vertical dimension but they occur at altitudes ranging from sea level to at least 2,300 m. If proof were needed of the species' adaptability, here it is.

On the other hand, this broad picture of the species' range masks very significant variation in population density (Fig. 12). For example, more than half of the European population of badgers resides in just three countries: the UK, the Republic of Ireland and Sweden. Within Britain, population densities range from close to zero in parts of East Anglia and the Scottish Highlands to more than 20 adults/km^2 in Woodchester Park, Gloucestershire, and more than 30 adults/km^2 in Wytham Woods, near Oxford. Clearly, then, badgers do very much better in some places than in others. This raises the question as to what factors favour badgers and, conversely, what factors discourage them.

FIG 10. Contrasting badger habitats: (a) Białowieża Primeval Forest, Poland (R. Kowalczyk); (b) Whitehawk Estate, Brighton, UK (J. Davison); (c) Doñana reserve, Spain (E. Revilla); (d) Swiss uplands. (E. Do Linh San)

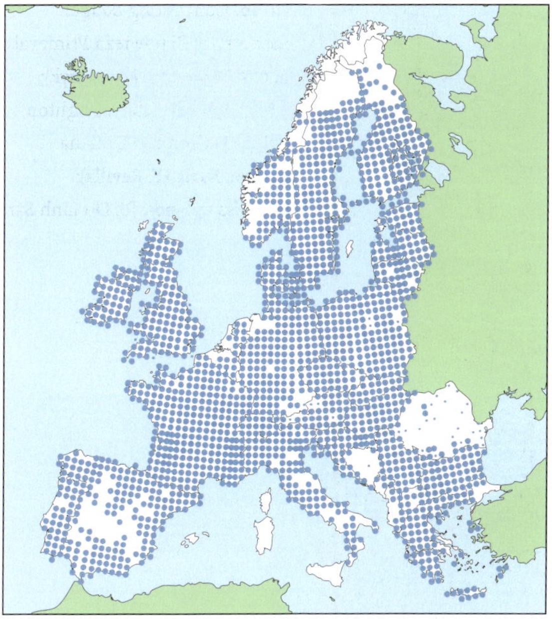

FIG 11. Distribution of badgers within Europe. (From Mitchell-Jones *et al.*, 1999, reproduced by permission of the Societas Europaea Mammalogica)

FIG 12. Map showing population density of badgers in different European countries.

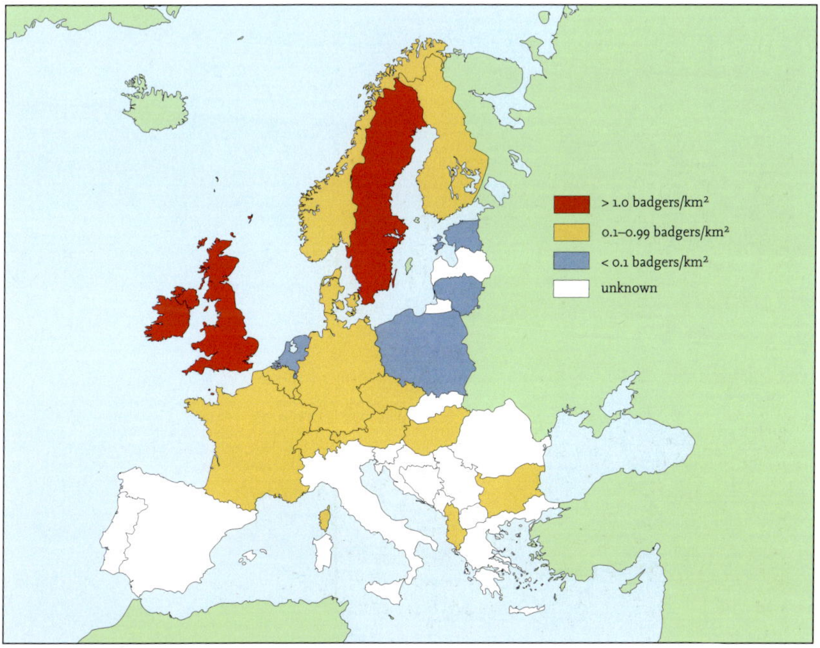

Population size and density across Europe

Badgers, like most mammals, are difficult to census and few European countries have undertaken systematic badger surveys. Consequently, data on national population sizes and population densities are often not much better than educated guesses (see Appendix for further details). The total population of badgers in Europe is believed to number about 1.5 million (Table 1), the countries with the largest populations being probably Sweden (350,000), the UK (about 340,000, including 38,000 in Northern Ireland) and Germany (142,000). As regards population density, the UK wins, with 1.46 badgers/km^2, followed by Sweden (1.35 badgers/km^2) and the Republic of Ireland (1.19 badgers/km^2). Although little is known about national population densities in eastern Europe and Asia, such evidence as is available suggests that these are generally low. It seems safe to conclude, therefore, that badgers do best in the far northwestern corner of their geographical range.

TABLE 1. Population size and population density of badgers in different European countries.

Country	Pop. Size	Badgers/km^2	% Total Pop.	Source
Albania	12,500	0.43	0.83	Griffiths & Thomas (1993)
Austria	30,000	0.36	2.0	Griffiths & Thomas (1993)
Belgium	3,500	0.11	0.23	Do Linh San (2002)
Bulgaria	35,000	0.35	2.3	Griffiths & Thomas (1993)
Czech Republic	21,000	0.38	1.4	Griffiths & Thomas (1993)
Denmark	25,000	0.58	1.7	Griffiths & Thomas (1993)
Estonia	2,000	0.04	0.13	Griffiths & Thomas (1993)
Finland	70,000	0.32	4.7	Griffiths & Thomas (1993)
France	80,000	0.15	5.3	Griffiths & Thomas (1993)
Germany	142,000	0.40	9.5	O. Keuling (pers. comm.)
Great Britain	300,000	1.39	21.3	Wilson *et al.* (1997)
Hungary	20,000	0.22	1.3	Griffiths & Thomas (1993)
N. Ireland	38,000	2.75	2.5	Feore & Montgomery (1999)
Republic of Ireland	84,000	1.19	5.6	Sleeman *et al.* (2009)
Lithuania	3,000	0.05	0.2	Griffiths & Thomas (1993)
Luxembourg	2,000	0.78	0.13	Schley *et al.* (2004)
The Netherlands	3,000	0.07	0.2	Das en Boom (unpubl.)
Norway	45,000	0.23	3.0	Griffiths & Thomas (1993)
Poland	12,000	0.04	0.8	Griffiths & Thomas (1993)
Sweden	350,000	1.35	23.3	Griffiths & Thomas (1993)
Switzerland	7,500	0.18	0.5	Do Linh San (2002)

Factors affecting population density

In general terms, if badgers are to thrive, they need a suitable climate, adequate food resources, somewhere to dig their burrows, a sufficient level of immunity from disease and safety from persecution by humans or predators. Population density in any one place most likely reflects the combined impact of all of these variables. However, the relative importance of different factors seems to depend on the geographical scale at which comparisons are made – that is, whether we are talking about differences in population density at global, national, regional or local level.

Limits on the global distribution of badgers

Obviously, the distribution of badgers is limited to the east and west by the Pacific and Atlantic oceans, respectively. To the north and south, however, climatic factors are almost certainly of primary importance. For at least a century, the badger populations of Scandinavia have been creeping gradually northwards, probably mainly owing to climate change (Fig. 13). This has resulted in a lengthening of the summer and, hence, of the time available to cubs to put

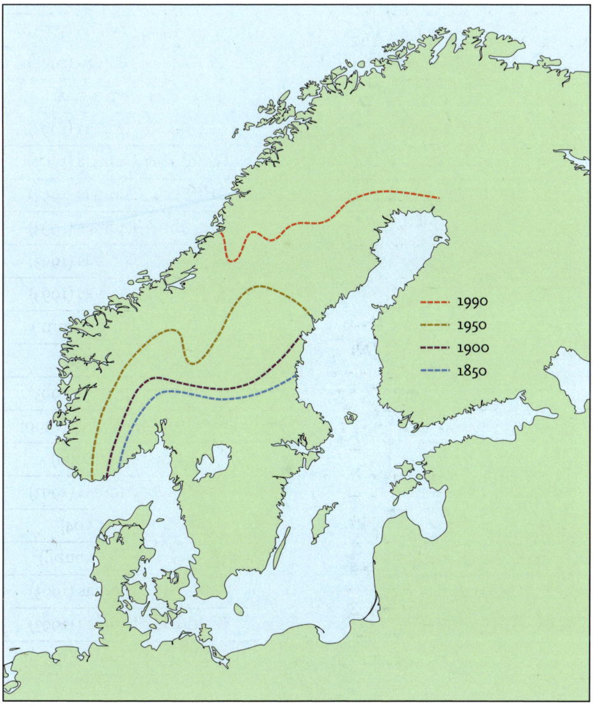

FIG 13. Map showing northward expansion of Scandinavian badger population. (Original from Bevanger & Lindström, 1995)

on enough fat to survive the winter, though a reduction in predation by grey wolves *Canis lupus* may also be a factor (Kauhala, 1995; Bevanger & Lindström, 1995). To the south, by contrast, the relevant climatic factors are heat and drought, which probably impact on badgers primarily via their effects on food availability (Virgós & Casanovas, 1999)

International variation in population density

The factors underlying international variation in population density are poorly understood. It seems likely that badgers do well in the UK and Ireland at least partly because a temperate climate, together with the heterogeneous nature of the landscape, means that plentiful food is available more or less all year round (see also Chapters 4 and 7). In the Netherlands, on the other hand, the overall paucity of badgers is surely at least partly related to lack of suitable habitat for burrowing. Much of the land in the Netherlands is simply too flat and wet to enable badgers to dig viable setts. Similarly, badgers are confined to the southeastern part of Belgium, where the countryside is relatively hilly (Scheppers, 2009: see Fig. 14).

In Europe in general, however, human persecution may be the single most important determinant of differences in badger population density. Across most of continental Europe, badgers are, or have been until recently, hunted, either for

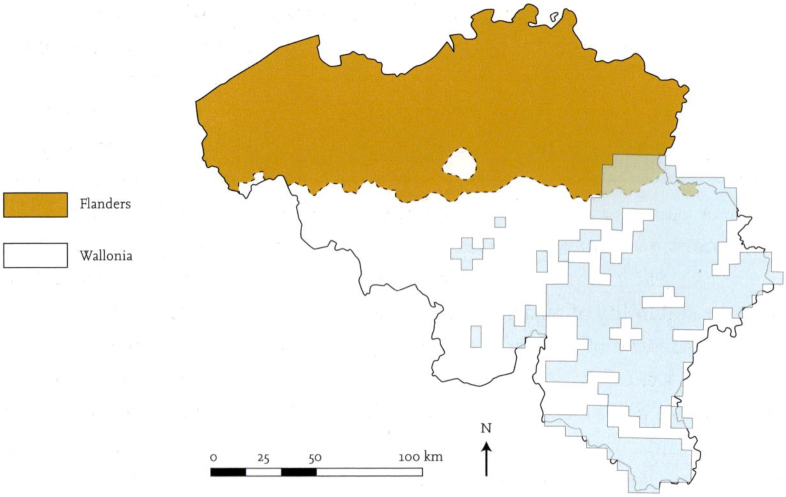

FIG 14. Distribution of badgers in Belgium, based on presence in 5 × 5 km squares. Yellow area: Flanders. White area: Wallonia. (Original from Scheppers, 2009)

reasons of sport, because they damage crops, for their commodity value or just because of a deep-rooted conviction among hunters, gamekeepers and farmers that carnivore numbers need to be controlled. In addition to this kind of more or less casual persecution, populations across much of continental Europe underwent a significant decline in the 1960s and 1970s, when large numbers of badgers were killed, either deliberately or as a consequence of the gassing of fox earths, in order to control rabies (Griffiths & Thomas, 1993). In Ireland and the UK, by contrast, rabies has mercifully never been a problem; a comparable tradition of hunting with guns, as a pursuit of ordinary people, has never developed; and badgers are now well protected by legislation. These may be the main reasons why badgers are more numerous in Ireland and the UK than elsewhere in Europe.

However, significant anomalies remain, the most obvious of which is the high population density of badgers in Scandinavia and, especially, in Sweden. Seasonal variation in climate is pronounced in Scandinavia, badgers are still legally hunted and there are no large areas of what would normally be regarded as 'good' badger habitat, either from the point of view of food availability or as regards suitability for digging setts. Just what makes Scandinavia such a good place for badgers remains, therefore, a mystery.

Regional and local variation in population density

A significant amount is known about the factors associated with regional variation in badger population density, by which I mean variation from locality to locality within a single country (for example, in Belgium, differences in population density between the southeast and the rest of the country, or within different parts of the southeast region: see Fig. 14). The first study to investigate this issue using rigorous statistical methods was conducted by Penny Thornton (1988), who surveyed about 100 setts in the southwest of England and recorded, for each one, 18 separate land-use and habitat variables. Some of these variables (e.g. soil type, slope, presence of cover) were chosen because they were thought to reflect the suitability of an area from the point of view of sett construction, others (e.g. amount of pasture or arable land) because they were thought to reflect food availability. Statistical analysis was then carried out to determine which of these variables were the best predictors of sett density. Interestingly, the only significant variables to emerge from the analysis reflected soil 'diggability', hilliness and availability of cover – that is, factors related to sett construction. This suggests that what makes a particular locality favourable to badgers, at least in the southwest of England, is usually the availability of suitable conditions for burrowing rather than the availability of food.

The same conclusion has subsequently emerged from comparable studies elsewhere in the UK and in other European countries, including Denmark, Ireland, Italy, Norway, Poland, Spain and Switzerland, and even from two studies involving urban badger populations (Wright *et al.*, 2000; Huck *et al.*, 2008). Admittedly, some of these studies have also indicated the availability of pasture as a factor influencing sett density, which has been interpreted as evidence that population density is also affected by food availability. However, one of the most recent and most careful studies of this type, which not only examined the influence of various habitat factors but did so at different spatial scales, concluded that what matters most to badgers is the type of habitat at and in the immediate vicinity of the sett, rather than what is available elsewhere within the relevant territory (Jepsen *et al.*, 2005). Altogether, then, there is strong evidence that badger distribution and population density are primarily controlled, at what I would call a regional or local level, by the availability of terrain suitable for burrowing (see also Chapter 3).

Extremely local variation in population density

At a very local level, however, yet another factor seems to operate. In Wytham Woods, badger population density has increased to a remarkable extent during the last few decades. One consequence of this has been that the Wytham badgers have had to dig additional setts in order to provide themselves with enough burrow space. Thus, both the number of main setts and the number of secondary setts have approximately tripled in the last 20 years. In view of this phenomenon, David Macdonald and his colleagues at Wytham quite reasonably argue that the availability of sett sites cannot previously have been limiting the growth of the population (Macdonald *et al.*, 2004).

If Wytham Woods is typical, then the implication is that at a very local level, within a small area where the terrain is generally suitable for burrowing, badgers can dig as many setts as they need. What alternative factor has allowed the Wytham badger population to undergo such dramatic recent growth in numbers is unclear, but an increase in food availability seems the most likely candidate. David Macdonald and Chris Newman have suggested that food availability has increased for the Wytham badgers owing to a combination of changes in agricultural practice and global warming (Macdonald & Newman, 2002).

However, if food availability has increased, it may have done so for an additional reason. The Wytham population has been studied very intensively during the last three decades and the research carried out there has included regular trapping and bait-marking operations. Both of these require feeding bait to badgers, usually consisting of peanuts or a mixture of peanuts and golden syrup (Fig. 15). Bait has also frequently been provided for other purposes,

FIG 15. Badger eating peanuts in Wytham Woods, near Oxford. (M. Baldwin)

such as to attract badgers to a particular area for observational purposes or to investigate social dominance. It is possible that the extraordinarily high population density of badgers in Wytham Woods owes at least something to this type of artificial provisioning.

CONSERVATION STATUS

As the preceding discussion shows, badgers are widely distributed on a global scale and are present in substantial numbers in most European countries. Consequently, they do not seem in obvious need of protection. This is reflected in their absence from both the Convention on International Trade in Endangered Species of Wild Fauna and Flora (CITES) and the International Union for the Conservation of Nature (IUCN). Badgers are, however, included in Appendix III of the Bern Convention (Council of Europe, 1979), which permits hunting but requires signatory nations to conserve the species in question and to protect it from over-exploitation.

From the point of view of conservation, however, what really matters is not so much the absolute population size (though very small populations are intrinsically vulnerable) as whether this is increasing or decreasing. Here,

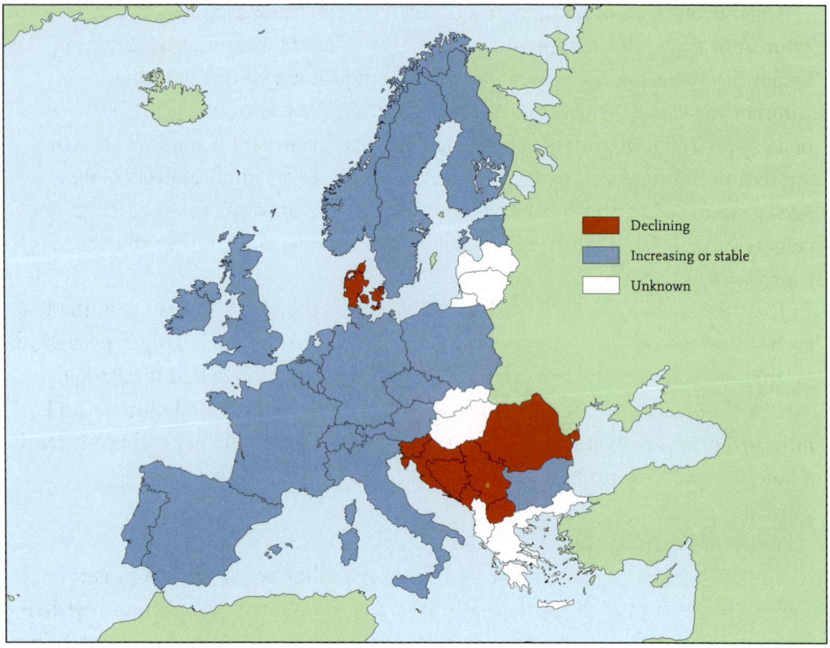

FIG 16. Map showing conservation status of badgers across Europe.

therefore, I consider what is known about the direction of change of population trends in different countries across the European badger's geographical range (Fig. 16). Unfortunately, I have been unable to track down any information about changes in population size in countries outside Europe.

The UK

Some of the most accurate data on changes in population size come from the UK, where systematic sett surveys have been undertaken at a national level. These estimate that the population of badgers increased by 77 per cent (from 250,000 to 400,000) between 1985 and 1988 and 1994 and 1997, owing mainly to increases in the size of existing social groups but also to colonisation of previously unoccupied areas (Wilson *et al.*, 1997). No national sett survey has been undertaken since the 1990s but data from long-term capture–mark–recapture studies at Woodchester Park and Wytham Woods show that at least in these localities, badger populations are either stable or increasing. Most naturalists would agree that the same is true of the national badger population.

Legal protection of badgers has probably been the single most important factor underlying these population increases. Badgers were first protected by the Badger Act 1973, which was subsequently strengthened by various other Acts, culminating in the Protection of Badgers Act 1992. As a result, the badger is now the best-protected mammal in the UK. This may seem odd given that the UK population has not been endangered, at least in recent times. However, the legislation in question was motivated by a desire to prevent cruel persecution of badgers (mainly in the form of badger-digging and baiting), rather than to improve their conservation status.

Laws themselves, however, are no good unless they are enforced, and the UK has been fortunate in having a well-organised network of local badger protection groups, currently represented by an umbrella organisation called the Badger Trust. Other factors, such as changes in agricultural practice and climate, and a more responsible attitude towards wildlife on the part of the general public and of landowners, have probably also made life easier for badgers.

The Netherlands

In the Netherlands, an enormous amount of effort has been put into badger conservation, with the result that setts are more closely monitored than anywhere else in Europe. In a classic monograph published in 1964, Van Wijngaarden & Van de Peppel provided evidence of an alarming reduction in badger numbers and distribution that had been going on since at least the 1930s and that was threatening the Dutch population with extinction. In their own dramatic words, the history of badgers in the Netherlands prior to 1960 had consisted of 'a rather monotonous and sad story of traps, snares, poison, shooting and killing'. Their report led to badger censuses being undertaken every decade, the instigation of protective measures and the approval of a 'Badger Management Policy' by the Dutch Parliament in 1985. The latter involved a 15-year action plan intended to halt the decline in, and then increase, the badger population (Mulder, 1996).

There were about 600 setts in the Netherlands in 1960, but this had declined to about 400 by 1980. Thereafter, things began to improve as protection measures took effect, such that by 1990 the number of setts had returned to about the 1960 level. Since then, sett numbers have increased still further: for example, an isolated population between Hilversum and Utrecht has increased dramatically from 4 to 41 badgers, and from 1 to 11 social groups, during the period from 1983 to 2001 (Apeldoorn *et al.*, 2006). In this intensively studied area, and probably in the Netherlands as a whole, the population increase has resulted from recolonisation of previously vacated areas rather than from an increase in the average number of badgers per social group.

FIG 17. Badger underpass beneath a road in the Netherlands. (Dassenwerkgroep Brabant)

In the Netherlands, badgers and their setts enjoy a comprehensive level of protection under the law of 25 May 1998 for The Protection of Flora and Fauna. In addition, considerable efforts have been made to reduce badger mortality and to increase the species' range: for example, providing badgers with underpasses beneath roads and bridges across canals; artificial setts to encourage colonisation of new areas; specially planted crops to provide food; and wildlife corridors to connect separate populations (Fig. 17). Badgers have also been deliberately reintroduced to some parts of the Netherlands (for further details, see Chapter 9 and Mulder, 1996). The Dutch badger protection group Das & Boom, which has been formidably effective in lobbying for badger conservation and welfare, deserves much of the credit for these actions.

The rest of Europe

Elsewhere in Europe, the conservation status of badgers is much less clear. A heroic study by Huw Griffiths and David Thomas (1993, 1997), involving the collection of a vast range of information from numerous sources, attempted to assess population trends in every country in Europe in the early 1990s; but much of the evidence on which they based their assessments was of questionable accuracy, either because it was anecdotal or because it provided only an indirect indication of population trends. In addition, even the best of this information is now over a decade out of date. However, no subsequent review of the conservation status of badgers has been attempted, so their work remains the best guide we have to the situation in many countries. In some cases, however, more recent relevant information has become available, enabling their conclusions to be reassessed.

Griffiths and Thomas classified national badger populations as 'unknown', 'declining', 'stable' or 'increasing'. As regards the 'unknown' category, they were unable to obtain any information about the badger populations of Crete or Rhodes and called for the status of these to be investigated urgently.

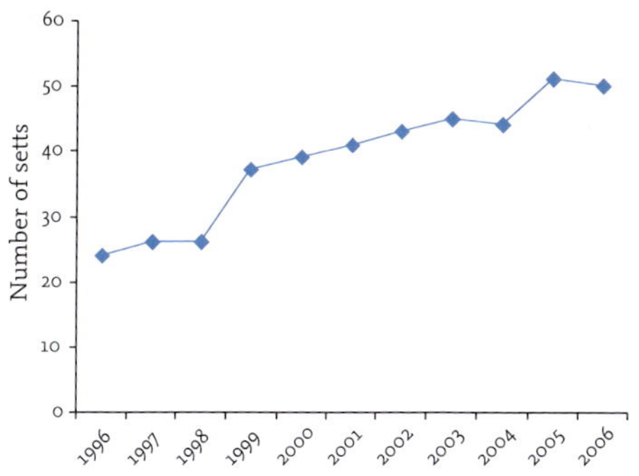

FIG 18. Number of occupied main setts in the Haspengouw area of Belgium, 1996–2006. (From Scheppers, 2009)

Unfortunately, this has still not been done, despite the fact that these populations are intrinsically vulnerable owing to their small size. We also lack information about badger populations in the Baltic states of Estonia and Lithuania.

Griffiths and Thomas considered the populations of Albania, Bosnia and Herzegovina, Croatia, Kosovo, Macedonia, Montenegro, Serbia and Slovenia to be in decline, and the troubled recent history of this region suggests that the situation for badgers is unlikely to have improved in the intervening decade. There is also concern about the Danish badger population, which is reported to have declined by 50 per cent during the last 50 years (Aaris-Sørensen, 1995). In addition, there are said to be hardly any badgers left in Romania owing to poaching by villagers in order to obtain badger fat (Hans Vink, pers. comm., 2008).

This leaves a large part of Europe in which badger populations are probably stable or increasing. As we have seen, populations are now known to be increasing in the Netherlands and are at least stable in the UK; and badgers are also thriving in at least one part of Belgium (see Fig. 18), Luxembourg (Schley *et al.*, 2004), Finland (Kauhala, 1995) and Latvia (Ozolinš & Pilāts, 1995). In Germany, game-bag data show a steady increase in the number of badgers killed per year over most of the last 20 years, suggesting an increase in population density; but the fact that this has levelled off in the last few years suggests that the population may now be stable (Fig. 19). There is some concern about Irish badgers, as culling is being carried out on a significant scale in an attempt to control the spread of bovine tuberculosis (see Chapter 10). However, Ireland generally offers good habitat for badgers and the available evidence suggests that were it not for culling, the Irish population, after increasing throughout most of the 20th century, would now be stable (Sleeman *et al.*, 2009).

As regards the rest of Europe, including Norway, Sweden, Belarus, Ukraine, Poland, Austria, Hungary, the Czech Republic, Slovakia, Italy, France, Spain and

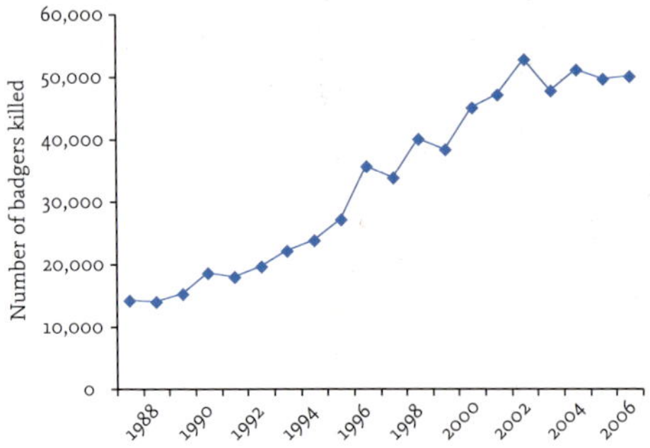

FIG 19. Number of badgers killed per year by hunters in Germany, from 1988 to 2006. (Deutscher Jagdschutzverband and O. Keuling, unpublished data)

Portugal, we are on uncertain ground. However, these are mostly large countries that have at least moderate populations of badgers and still contain significant amounts of suitable habitat. In addition, apparently healthy badger populations have now been studied at a local level in Spain, Portugal, Italy and Poland. The likelihood, then, is that badger populations in these countries are at least stable and may, in some cases, be increasing.

THREATS TO BADGERS

Roads and railways

Roads and railways are detrimental to wildlife in three main ways: they take up physical space that could otherwise be occupied by wildlife; they act as a barrier to movement (the phenomenon known as 'habitat fragmentation'); and they result in the killing and injuring of animals by traffic (Fig. 20). Of these three effects, the least significant for badgers is probably habitat loss, for the simple reason that roads and railways occupy relatively little space in percentage terms, even in countries with dense road and rail networks. Indeed, badgers may sometimes profit from roads and railways by using them as commuting routes and by exploiting embankments and cuttings for purposes of sett construction.

One might expect that the impact of habitat fragmentation would be more significant, especially in countries like the Netherlands where badgers exist in small, isolated subpopulations. Also, it seems inevitable that as roads and railways get bigger, faster and busier, they must constitute increasingly impermeable barriers to animal movement. However, the evidence, as far as badgers are concerned, is equivocal. In the case of the Netherlands, a recent study shows that the population is genetically homogeneous, implying that spatially separate subpopulations are managing to interbreed with one another (Zande *et al.*, 2006).

FIG 20. Road-killed badger. (B. Crowley)

This may reflect the success of measures deliberately taken to encourage badger movement and recolonisation, such as the provision of road, rail and canal crossings, and the active reintroduction of badgers to some regions (see Chapter 9). In Denmark, by contrast, there is some evidence of genetic differences between different populations, and it has been suggested that these may result to some extent from habitat fragmentation (Pertoldi *et al.*, 2005; Zande *et al.*, 2006). However, the differences could also have a much more ancient origin, reflecting the pattern of recolonisation of the Danish peninsula by badgers following the most recent glaciation (Pope *et al.*, 2006). To summarise, there is no doubt that habitat fragmentation is a real phenomenon and that its impact on animal populations will intensify as transport corridors grow in size and number, and as the traffic that they carry increases in density. However, there is little evidence that habitat fragmentation is, at present, a significant threat to badgers.

When it comes to road mortality, hard data are available and they suggest that this is indeed a serious problem. In the UK, road mortality impacts primarily on adult badgers and affects both sexes about equally: and it tends to peak in spring and autumn, roughly coinciding with peaks in the fertility of females (Fig. 21). These findings suggest that most road deaths are caused when adult badgers, of both sexes, seek mating opportunities outside their own social group – males in order to increase their reproductive success and females in order to avoid inbreeding (Davies *et al.*, 1987; see also Chapter 5). Female deaths in early spring are especially significant, because at this time of year a sow may be both pregnant and lactating, so that her death also results in the loss of two litters of cubs. Nevertheless, badgers do get killed on the roads at all times of year, not just when they are distracted by the prospect of mating. It is often supposed that major

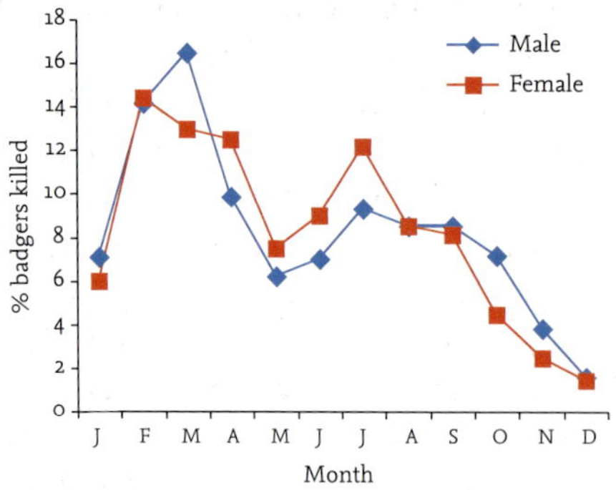

FIG 21. Seasonal pattern of road deaths for male and female badgers in the UK. (Davies *et al.*, 1987)

roads are more of a threat to wildlife than minor roads, but a recent Dutch study suggests that this is a misconception (Langevelde *et al.*, 2009).

A number of surveys in the UK, carried out both at a local level and more widely, suggest that road mortality is the biggest single cause of death in adult badgers. Nationally, it was estimated that road traffic killed about 50,000 badgers per year in the early 1990s, equating to a fifth of the adult population and constituting almost half of all adult mortality (Harris *et al.*, 1995). Local surveys have indicated even higher levels of mortality: for example, a survey in Surrey suggested that road deaths accounted for 60 per cent of all adult mortality, while they accounted for about 66 per cent of all adult mortality in the intensively studied population of badgers at Woodchester Park (Clarke *et al.*, 1998). Given that both badger numbers and traffic density have increased substantially since the time of these surveys, the number of deaths per year is now likely to be significantly greater.

In Denmark, a survey carried out in 1991 estimated total annual road deaths at 3,600 badgers, equivalent to 10–15 per cent of the total population (Aaris-Sørensen, 1995); while in Sweden, a questionnaire survey of drivers in the early 1990s indicated that about 30,000 badgers per year, equivalent to 11 per cent of the total population, were killed by traffic (Seiler *et al.*, 2004). Again, it seems likely that the numbers of fatalities will have increased significantly since the time of these surveys. In Switzerland, traffic is thought to have killed an average of 1,668 badgers per year between 1992 and 2002 (Do Linh San, 2004).

In terms of their sheer size, these death tolls make for astonishing reading. But what effect are they having on the relevant badger populations? In Denmark, the number of badgers killed annually on the roads is thought to be about equal to the number of cubs produced, in which case the population must be in decline. In the UK and Sweden, however, badger numbers are thought to be at least stable and possibly increasing, so it is clear that road mortality is not yet reducing populations at a national level. Nevertheless, traffic deaths are predicted to become sufficiently numerous in Sweden as a whole to bring about an overall decline in the badger population within the next few decades (Seiler, 2003).

At a more local level, traffic is thought to have been a major cause of a decline in badger numbers in Essex, UK (Skinner *et al.*, 1991), and in some parts of the Netherlands (Zee *et al.*, 1992) and Sweden (Seiler, 2003). In all these cases, the regions in question have never been especially favourable for badgers, suggesting that the impact of traffic is most critical for populations that are already low.

Much less is known about the impact of railways, but the construction of a new railway has sometimes resulted in locally significant numbers of badger deaths. Railways are particularly hazardous to wildlife in places like the southeast of England, where electrical power is provided at ground level by a high-voltage live rail.

Hunting

Badgers can still be legally hunted in most continental European countries, albeit subject to constraints such as a closed season or the requirement to show that the badgers in question are guilty of crop damage (see review by Griffiths & Thomas, 1993). In the UK, where there has never been a grass-roots tradition of hunting for game, the idea of respectable people going out at night and shooting badgers seems incomprehensible – about as incomprehensible as our tradition of fox-hunting on horseback seems to continental Europeans. However, hunting is a deeply rooted and fiercely defended aspect of culture in much of continental Europe, and in many countries the hunting lobby exerts a powerful political influence over decisions relating to wildlife.

In former times, badgers were hunted as a source of fur, hair, fat and meat (Griffiths, 1993) and some hunting may still occur for these sorts of reasons. For example, badgers in Romania are still (illegally) hunted for fat (Vink, pers. comm.) and there are hunters in Switzerland who shoot badgers (legally) because they consider the meat to be a delicacy (Lüps, pers. comm., 2009). Badger hair is also still used to make shaving brushes and paintbrushes (Fig. 22). Some of the hair used for shaving brushes originates (again, illegally) from European badgers (Domingo-Roura *et al.*, 2006) but most of it derives from China, where badgers are specially bred for this purpose. On the other hand, badgers have never been a trophy species and it seems likely that, nowadays, most are killed either because they are damaging crops or, more or less casually, because they happen to find themselves in the wrong place at the wrong time. For example, in one part of the Doñana National Park in southern Spain, poachers killed 46 per cent of badgers that had been radio-collared for research purposes. However, these animals do not seem to have been deliberately targeted. Rather, poachers were attracted to the

FIG 22. Badger-hair shaving brush.

park by the unnaturally high densities of deer and wild boar to be found there and sometimes their dogs would round up a badger by mistake. When this happened, the consequences for the badger were usually fatal. Ironically, deaths caused in this manner have meant that the population density of badgers is lower within the (supposedly protected) reserve than just outside it (Revilla *et al.*, 2001).

In a review of game-bag data from the 1980s, Griffiths (1990) concluded that about 110,000 badgers were being killed each year in Europe, representing about 6 per cent of the total population. However, this was probably an underestimate, as subsequent data reveal a current bag of about 50,000 badgers in Germany alone (see Fig. 19, above). Nevertheless, it seems likely that hunting pressure is declining, partly as legal protection of badgers has become more widespread, partly because of a greater appreciation of the value of wildlife and partly because the hunting culture itself may be weakening. Thus, data from Sweden show that whereas hunting and road traffic killed about equal numbers of badgers in the 1960s, deaths from traffic are now about twice as numerous as deaths from hunting (Seiler *et al.*, 2004).

To summarise, it seems unlikely that hunting constitutes a significant threat to badgers save in some exceptional localities, and in most places it is less of a threat than road traffic.

Disease control

The two main fatal diseases of badgers are rabies and bovine tuberculosis, neither of which is sufficiently serious to threaten badger populations at other than a local level (see Chapter 2). However, because both diseases pose a significant threat to human interests (to human health in the case of rabies, to domestic animal health in the case of bovine tuberculosis), rigorous attempts have been made to control them. These control measures have had a far more significant impact on badgers than have the diseases themselves.

As regards rabies, it is generally acknowledged that many badgers died in central Europe in the 1960s and 1970s as a result of rabies control measures (see Fig. 23). At that time, rabies, having expanded across Europe from the

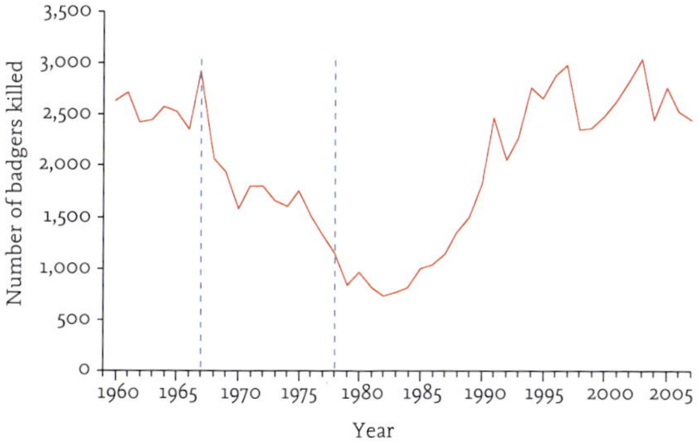

FIG 23. Effect of rabies control measures on the number of badgers shot by hunters in Switzerland, 1960–2007. Note the decline after rabies arrived in Switzerland in 1967 and recovery following the commencement of oral vaccination of foxes in 1978. (Data in Do Linh San, 2004)

Russian–Polish border, had progressed as far south as Italy and as far west as the northeastern quarter of France. Drastic action was therefore justified and it took the form of widespread gassing of fox earths and badger setts. However, following the development of an oral vaccination for red foxes, control of the disease by this new method began in Switzerland in 1978, followed by Germany, Italy, Belgium, France and Luxembourg during the 1980s. As a result of this vaccination campaign, the number of cases of rabies in wild mammals in Europe began to decline, such that most European countries are now considered rabies free. It seems unlikely, therefore, that culling for purposes of rabies control will ever again threaten badgers. In addition, a change in public attitudes means that there is increasing unwillingness to accept the widespread destruction of wildlife for any purpose, including that of disease control.

Bovine tuberculosis (TB) is an important and globally widespread disease of domestic cattle. Within the geographical range of badgers, however, it is only seriously problematic in the UK and Ireland. Badgers enter into the equation because there is evidence that they transmit TB to cattle (see Chapters 2 and 10). Here, I focus on how TB control measures have impacted on badger populations in the UK and Ireland.

Culling of badgers in order to reduce the incidence of TB in cattle commenced in the UK in 1973, when affected farmers were permitted to shoot badgers on their own land. This method was replaced in 1975 by the gassing of badger setts, which continued until 1982, when it was replaced for humanitarian reasons by live trapping followed by humane killing (usually shooting). Until 1998, culling of badgers was largely restricted to land used by cattle herds that had tested positive for TB (so-called 'reactive' culling). However, three larger-scale blanket culls ('proactive' culls) were also carried out during the 1970s and

1980s at Thornbury in Avon (104 km^2), Steeple Leaze in Dorset (12 km^2) and Hartland in North Devon (64 km^2), respectively (see Krebs *et al.*, 1997). In addition, badgers were culled from 20 100-km^2 areas in the southwest of England between 1998 and 2005, in a trial (the 'Randomised Badger Culling Trial') specifically aimed at measuring the effect of badger removal on the incidence of TB in cattle. Ten of these 100-km^2 areas were reactively culled and the other ten proactively culled (for details, see Chapter 10 and Bourne, 2007).

In the Republic of Ireland, meanwhile, two large-scale proactive badger culls have been carried out, one at East Offaly (738 km^2) between 1989 and 1995 and the other involving four separate areas (totalling 1,961 km^2) in Donegal, Monaghan, Cork and Kilkenny, respectively (Griffin *et al.*, 2005). Both of these culls, like the Randomised Badger Culling Trial in the UK, were scientific trials intended to assess the efficacy of badger removal as a TB control strategy. However, a further reactive culling programme is continuing in Ireland, with the aim of reducing the national incidence of TB in cattle. This programme involves the removal of badgers from farms in which tuberculosis has been detected in cattle and is considered to be attributable to badgers. In Ireland, the preferred method of culling is snaring, which probably results in the capture of more badgers than the live-trapping method used in the UK.

Although the scale of some of these culling operations is dramatic (for example, the East Offaly and 'Four Areas' culls in Ireland have involved removing badgers from over 5 per cent of the nation's total agricultural area), their effect on national badger populations is less so. In the UK, the Randomised Badger Culling Trial involved killing 10,969 badgers, which is equivalent to only about 3 per cent of the total population. In Ireland, the East Offaly and Four Areas culls together removed 4,157 badgers, equivalent to about 2 per cent of the national population. Nevertheless, these culls have resulted in severe local reductions in badger numbers: indeed, this was their purpose. More worryingly, the current removal programme in Ireland could, potentially, result in the extinction of badgers over significant areas. In the longer term, however, it is hoped that vaccination, either of cattle or badgers, will make the culling of badgers unnecessary (see Chapter 10).

Urbanisation

Worldwide, urbanisation causes higher local extinction rates and endangers more species than any other form of habitat modification. However, some species can thrive in urban environments and the badger seems to be one of them. A pioneering study by Warren Cresswell and Stephen Harris showed that badgers were well established in some parts of Bristol, attaining population

FIG 24. Badgers are intentionally fed by many householders. (R. Lowery)

densities of about four to seven adults/km^2 (Harris & Cresswell, 1987; Cresswell & Harris, 1988). This density is low by the standards of 'good' rural areas in the UK and Ireland but high in comparison with almost anywhere else in Europe (see Table 1 above).

Even more remarkably, a recent study by Maren Huck, John Davison and myself showed that badgers in one part of Brighton achieved a local population density of 30 adults/km^2, which is extremely high by any standards (Huck & Roper, 2008). This concentration of badgers resulted not from unusually large social groups but from the fact that territories were extremely small, enabling a large number of groups to co-exist in a relatively small area. Almost certainly, the small size of territories was in turn a consequence of unusually rich food resources, especially in the form of food deliberately provided by householders (Fig. 24). For example, the members of one social group hardly ever ventured beyond the confines of two small back gardens in which they were regularly and profusely fed (Davison, 2007; see also Chapter 7).

It is not clear to what extent urban badgers are a general phenomenon but complaints about the damage they cause are numerous and geographically widespread within the UK, and we now know that significant badger populations exist in many towns and cities (see also Chapter 9). Badgers apparently do best in the suburbs and it seems unlikely that they could survive in inner-city areas, except possibly as transient visitors. Overall, then, it appears that while intense urbanisation is deleterious to badgers, moderate levels of urbanisation need not be.

FIG 25. Landscape in eastern Flanders. Despite its inhospitable appearance, this area contained a surprisingly large number of setts, including one in the small patch of scrub in the centre of the photograph. (T. Scheppers)

Changes in agricultural practice

Since badgers are opportunistic foragers, able to consume both plant and animal material, they can find food in a wide variety of habitats (see Chapter 4). Consequently, changes in agricultural practice have probably not disadvantaged them as much as might have been expected. Although many studies suggest that badgers do best in a heterogeneous landscape containing a small-scale mixture of woodland, pasture and arable crops, they can withstand large-scale planting of arable crops surprisingly well.

One of my research students, Thomas Scheppers, studied badgers in a part of Belgium that appeared, at first glance, to consist of little except arable monoculture and roads (Fig. 25). Consequently, we expected badger population density to be low. However, this unpromising landscape turned out to contain a surprising number of setts, some of them evidently very old, situated in isolated patches of woodland, overgrown banks that were too steep to plough and the occasional hedge. Social groups contained, on average, five adults, which is about the same as in most rural populations elsewhere in Europe (Scheppers *et al.*, 2007). We did not investigate the diet of these badgers but studies in other arable landscapes have found that wheat, maize and oats can be eaten in large amounts (see Chapter 4). In general, then, the message seems to be that badgers can cope with anything other than extreme agricultural intensification – and the latter is only likely in landscapes that are so flat they would have been unsuitable for badgers in the first place.

Deliberate persecution

In the UK, deliberate persecution of badgers occurs in two contexts: the digging and baiting of badgers for reasons of 'sport' and the snaring, poisoning and shooting of badgers by gamekeepers and farmers.

Digging and baiting

Digging badgers out of their setts has a long history as a rural pastime. Sometimes it seems to have been attractive as an end in itself, but more often it was encouraged by the fox-hunting community because badgers were thought to compete with foxes for burrow space (e.g. Blakeborough & Pease, 1914). After being dug out, the badgers were usually killed in one way or another, often by setting dogs onto them.

In addition, and even more barbarously, badgers can be dug out of their setts explicitly in order to be 'baited'. Badger-baiting, which consists of enclosing a badger in a confined space and setting one or more dogs onto it, constitutes an ignominious and depressing chapter in UK and Irish cultural history. It probably dates back to medieval times and is responsible for the establishment in the language of the verb 'to badger', meaning to persecute or harass. Its appeal seems to have been as an excuse for gambling as well as constituting a 'sport' in itself, but nowadays the thrill of engaging in an illegal activity may also contribute to its attraction. In the past, special permanent arenas were constructed for the purposes of badger-baiting (see Long & Killingley, 1983), but now that baiting is illegal, it is often carried out at the sett itself, either in a temporary arena constructed of branches or in the open (Fig. 26). Eye-witness accounts of the injuries suffered by both badgers and dogs during the course of baiting make for horrific reading.

There is no doubt that badger-digging and baiting still go on and may even be subject to something of a revival. For example, photographs and videos of badger-baiting are available on the internet and there is a slow but steady trickle of successful prosecutions against diggers and baiters. But because badger-digging and baiting are highly illegal, anything other than anecdotal data are hard to come by. A systematic survey of UK setts carried out in the 1980s suggested that 9,000 setts, including 10.5 per cent of all active main setts,

FIG 26 (ABOVE). Badger-baiting. (Anonymous photograph, reproduced by permission of G. Shepherd)

FIG 27 (RIGHT). Illegal digging of a badger sett. (Dassenwerkgroep Brabant)

were being dug each year (Cresswell *et al.*, 1990: see Fig. 27). A more local survey of setts in the Bradford area, in the north of England, indicated an astonishing average of 10.7 'disturbance events' per sett during a seven-year period, about 20 per cent of which involved sett-digging. This same study showed that setts that were close to public rights of way were less likely to be disturbed, so long as they were not also close to large conurbations (Jenkinson & Wheater, 1998). Paradoxically, therefore, badgers may benefit from proximity to human activities in regions where deliberate interference with setts is common. Or, to put it another way, setts are more vulnerable if they are in remote places.

Digging is thought to have caused a dramatic reduction in the number of occupied setts in West Yorkshire during the 1970s, so much so that the county was designated a Special Protection Area under the Badgers Act of 1973. Although it seems unlikely that digging and baiting still endanger badgers on anything other than a very local scale, these activities remain issues of significant welfare concern. Unfortunately, the problem is not with the law itself, which provides for severe penalties, but with its enforcement, which relies mainly on the vigilance and courage of ordinary badger lovers, and on the willingness of bodies such as the Badger Trust and the RSPCA to pursue offenders through the courts.

Other kinds of interference with setts

Until relatively recently, fox-hunters were allowed to block the entrances of badger setts before a hunt, in order to prevent foxes from taking refuge in them – a practice known as 'sett-stopping'. The Protection of Badgers Act 1992 stated that stopping should be temporary and involve only the insertion of loose material, but cases were often reported of sett entrances being blocked with tree stumps, empty oil cans and so on. Thankfully, however, stopping was banned altogether by the Hunting Act 2004.

Farmers also sometimes interfere illegally with setts in an attempt to remove badgers from their land. Setts can be ploughed over or, in a particularly unpleasant form of persecution, slurry can be poured into sett entrances.

Snaring, poisoning and shooting

Gamekeepers sometimes snare, poison or shoot badgers on the grounds that they destroy the eggs and chicks of game birds. In fact, the consensus of informed opinion is that badger predation on game birds is insignificant (see Chapter 4), but the prejudice persists nevertheless.

Of these methods of 'controlling' badgers, snaring is particularly unpleasant and can inflict horrific injuries on the animals concerned (Fig. 28). Unfortunately, it is difficult to obtain convictions for snaring or poisoning, because gamekeepers can always claim that they were targeting foxes, even when snares are positioned explicitly on badger runs or when poison is laid at the entrances of a sett (Fig. 29). Shooting is even more difficult to police, because it usually takes the form of 'lamping' of badgers at night. As with digging and baiting, it seems unlikely that persecution by gamekeepers or farmers threatens

FIG 28. The effects of snaring: (above left) wounds caused by a snare around the neck (G. Shepherd); (above right) snares are often set beneath fences – this badger died trying to escape through the fence. (M. Edwards)

FIG 29. Poisoned potato left at the entrance of a badger sett. (G. Shepherd)

badgers at anything other than a local scale, but it is certainly widespread, may well be increasing as pheasant shooting becomes more popular and clearly constitutes cruel mistreatment of the animals in question.

SUMMARY

To summarise the situation as regards conservation, badger populations are probably stable or increasing over much of Europe. The main threats to the species are undoubtedly road traffic and hunting, of which hunting probably still kills more badgers overall, as traffic densities over much of central and eastern Europe are relatively low while hunting culture is still active. But hunting is in decline whereas traffic is increasing, and hunting is regulated whereas traffic is not, so traffic represents the more serious future threat. However, the example of the Netherlands shows that given the will and the financial support, traffic deaths can be significantly reduced, for example by providing wildlife tunnels beneath, or bridges over, new roads (see also Chapter 9). It is to be hoped that such measures will be employed in central and eastern parts of Europe if, as seems inevitable, they experience a significant increase in road and rail development.

Notwithstanding these threats and the continued deliberate ill-treatment of badgers, they are a robust and adaptable species, able to withstand a significant degree of interference whether from hunters, gamekeepers, transport corridors, agriculture or urbanisation. We can be fairly optimistic that badger populations will persist in many parts of Europe and Asia for the foreseeable future.

CHAPTER 2

Basic Biology

IN THIS CHAPTER, I describe the external appearance of the badger and review what is known about its size and body weight, internal anatomy, activity cycles, metabolic rate and body temperature, locomotion, and diseases and parasites. As we shall see, some of these aspects of the species' general biology are unusual, especially when viewed in the context of other members of the mustelid family. At the end of this chapter, therefore, I place the badger's anatomy and physiology within a more general functional framework, in an attempt to explain why it is so different from most of its close relatives.

EXTERNAL APPEARANCE: PELAGE

It is no coincidence that one of the colloquial English names for the badger is 'grey'. Although the badger's fur ranges from pure white to pure black on different parts of the body, the overall impression is of grey – not the uniform grey of, say, a mouse but a complex silvery grey that seems to sparkle in the bright light of a camera flash. This handsome effect is produced by long (7–10 cm) guard hairs that are pale except for a black band, about 1–2 cm long, that starts about 1 cm below the tip (Fig. 30). Beneath these guard hairs is a dense, felt-like under-fur, which is also white but is usually hidden, unless the

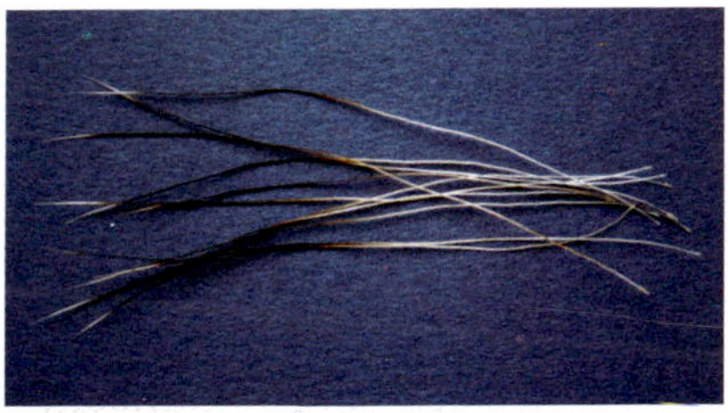

FIG 30. Guard hairs. Note the alternate light and dark colour bands. (R. Lawrence)

FIG 31. A wet badger. Note how the pale under-fur shows through the darker guard hairs. (K. & M. Blackman)

pelage is wet, in which case the paler under-fur shows through (Fig. 31). The guard hairs are straight and stiff and are oval in cross-section, as can be felt if you roll one between your fingers. The under-fur hairs, by contrast, are shorter, curled and rounder in cross-section. Histological examination shows that the two types of hair grow together in clusters, each cluster containing one guard hair and several under-fur hairs that emerge together from a single pore in the skin (Maurel *et al.*, 1986).

The guard hairs are an intense glossy black on the limbs and on the underside of the neck, chest and abdomen, which is unusual, because most mammals are lighter in colour on the ventral than on the dorsal side. However, because there is little or no under-fur on the lower chest and abdomen and the guard hairs are sparse, the badger's pale skin is clearly visible in these regions. To some extent, therefore, the animal is in practice lighter on its underside even though the pelage itself it darker. The upper side of the tail is also usually somewhat lighter than the rest of the body, and the underside is generally lighter still. The tail is often tipped with white (see Chapter 1, Fig. 6b).

The real surprise, however, is of course the head and neck, where the hairs are shorter and pure white, except for the black longitudinal stripes on each side that give the badger its unique and dramatic facial 'mask' (Fig. 32). These twin stripes of intense black pigmentation begin on the neck, some distance behind

FIG 32. The badger's face mask seen (above left) from the front (N. Yeo); and (above right) from the side. (H. Clark)

the ears. They encompass the ears except at the tips, which remain white, and then travel forwards towards the snout, narrowing as they do so but remaining wide enough to completely surround the eyes (which are also black). Just before reaching the nose pad, each stripe curves abruptly downwards around the circumference of the muzzle to meet the upper lip. Consequently, when a badger looks straight at you, what you see is a pattern of two black and three white vertical stripes, white ear tips, white circle surrounding the tip of the nose, and black nose pad. On anything other than the darkest of nights, this highly contrasting pattern is clearly visible and immediately recognisable. As if to emphasise the effect even more, elongated hairs on the side of the face provide a pair of distinct, bushy white 'sideburns'.

'Iconic' is an overused word but it is fully justified as a description of the badger's face mask. As well as constituting the logo of numerous wildlife and other organisations, the facial pattern is responsible for the very name 'badger' (from 'badge') and for its French equivalent 'blaireau' (from old French 'bler', meaning 'striped with white'). But what is its function? The most widely accepted explanation, usually attributed to Pocock (1911), is that it is a form of warning coloration. Pocock noticed that mammals with distinctive black-and-white pelage usually have some special way of defending themselves against attack, such as a noxious secretion in the case of skunks or an unusually powerful bite in the case of the badger. Therefore, he suggested, the function of the conspicuous pelage of such species is to warn a potential predator to keep its distance.

Chris Newman and others, working at Oxford University, have recently substantiated Pocock's hypothesis. They have shown that there is indeed a statistical correlation, across different mammal species, between the presence of contrasting facial markings and the possession of some sort of specialised defence mechanism (Newman *et al.*, 2005). In addition, the relevant species tend to be nocturnal, are not fast or agile enough to outrun predators, are not large enough to constitute an obvious threat in and of themselves (as would, say, a wolf or a bear), and are not especially cryptic in terms of their behaviour (i.e. they tend to be noisy foragers, crashing about in the undergrowth with scant regard to concealment). All of these features are not only typical of badgers but are also consistent with the 'warning signal' idea. In addition, when faced with an adversary, a badger adopts a distinctive head-down posture as if to display the mask to its best advantage; it erects the hairs on its cheeks so as to make the head seem broader; and it draws further attention to itself by emitting an abrupt snorting sound (see Chapter 6). Having had a badger display like this to me on a number of occasions, I can only say that if it is meant to be intimidating, it works.

Numerous other explanations for the facial mask have also been suggested, such as that the striped pattern provides camouflage by breaking up the outline of the head; is a sexually selected signal used in mating; or is used for purposes of communication within social groups. Some of these ideas can be dismissed out of hand (for example, if the mask is a mating signal, then it should be more prominent in males than in females), while others are plausible but lack any supporting evidence. However, before we get too carried away in the attempt to find a function for the facial mask, it is worth pointing out that some badgers, especially those from eastern parts of the Eurasian badger's range, manage perfectly well with much less dramatic facial patterning (see below and Chapter 1, Fig. 9). Thus, the mask could be a functionless by-product of whatever genetic changes have taken place over the course of evolutionary time, as different geographic populations of badgers have diverged from one another. If this is the case, the precise colour and form of the mask might be irrelevant from the point of view of individual survival.

Variation in pelage colour

So far I have described the appearance of a 'typical' European badger. However, there is considerable variation in pelage colour both within and between populations, owing to differences in the extent to which the black pigment (melanin) is expressed in individual guard hairs and also, possibly, to differences in the molecular structure of the pigment itself. Ernest Neal (1986) describes (white), melanistic (black) and erythristic (reddish) colour variants in the UK, of which albino seems to be the most widespread and melanistic the least common. Albino badgers are white all over, which means that they have no facial mask at all. In melanistic individuals, by contrast, the parts of the pelage that are normally white are still white, while the grey parts are darker than usual.

FIG 33. Erythristic (right) and normal-coloured (left) badgers. (A. Crowley)

Erythristic badgers are an attractive caramel colour on the back and sides, and pinkish on the parts of the body that are normally black (Fig. 33). Other colour variants, such as semi-albino and yellow, have also been reported.

Because hair colour is genetically controlled, particular colour variants tend to cluster in particular populations: for example, according to Neal, albinism is especially common in the badgers of Dorset, Kent, Berkshire and Essex. One could be forgiven for thinking that a pure white coat would constitute a significant disadvantage to a nocturnal animal such as the badger. However, one albino boar badger, appropriately named 'Snowball', is known to have bred successfully and to have survived for at least nine years in the company of normally coloured individuals (Neal, 1986; see also Løfaldi, 1980).

On a larger geographic scale, differences in coat colour are among the criteria that have been used to classify Eurasian badgers into different species or subspecies (see Chapter 1). The best description of these colour variants is provided by Alexei Abramov (2003), who inspected 266 skins collected from Russia and other more easterly parts of the badger's geographical range. As regards body colour, badgers from the Middle East and Mediterranean are paler and brownish rather than grey; in Asian badgers, the light-grey upper parts of the body are tinged with a sandy colour; badgers from the far east of Russia are very dark; and those from Japan are light and yellowish. As regards the facial mask (Fig. 34), the dark stripes are narrower and browner in Asian badgers than in European ones, and do not continue back beyond the ears; while in Russian badgers, the white parts of the mask are replaced with brown, reducing the contrast to such an extent that the black stripes are sometimes hardly visible. In Japanese badgers, the background colour of the head is yellowish rather than white and the black

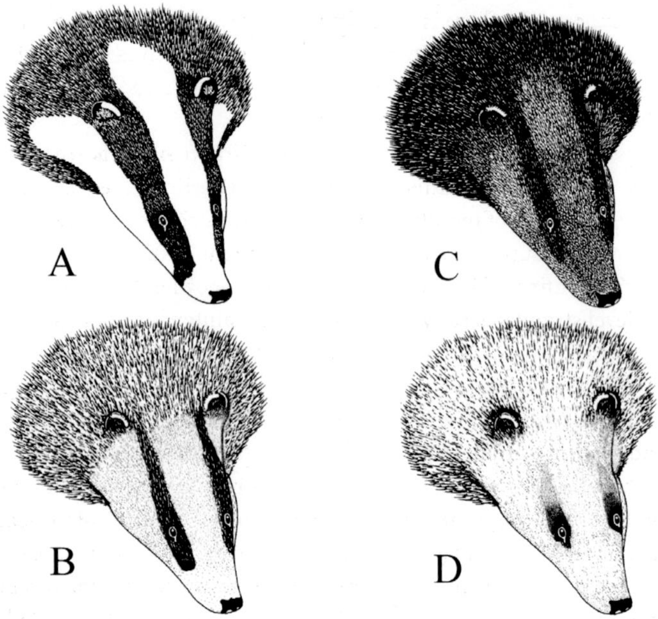

FIG 34. Geographical variations in the colour of the facial mask. (A) European badger *Meles meles*; (B) Asian badger *Meles leucurus*; (C) Far-eastern form of Asian badger, *Meles leucurus amarensis*; (D) Japanese badger *Meles anakuma*. (From Abramov, 2003)

stripes are little more than patches around each eye, giving the animal a melancholy, panda-like appearance. To summarise, geographical variation in the mask results both from differences in the background colour of the head, which varies from white through yellow to brown, and to differences in the colour (varying from black to brown) and extent (both length and width) of the stripes.

Moulting

Adult badgers moult once per year, starting in June or July and ending in November or December. In cubs, hair growth is more or less continuous and there is no moult, while in yearlings (i.e. animals in their second year of life) the annual moult occurs a month or two earlier than it does in adults (Maurel *et al.*, 1986; Stewart & Macdonald, 1997).

Shedding and the growth of new pelage starts in the shoulder region and progresses gradually forwards, backwards and downwards, ending with the hind legs and tail. The new coat appears glossier and feels less coarse than the old one but, perhaps surprisingly, there is no difference in the actual density of hairs. Badgers do not, therefore, moult in order to provide themselves with a thicker winter coat but merely in order to gain pelage that is newer and therefore in better condition.

Studies by Daniel Maurel and his colleagues in France have shown that in male badgers, the onset of moulting is triggered by a decline in testosterone level, while the cessation of moulting coincides with a decline in secretion of the hormone thyroxin (Maurel *et al.*, 1987). The involvement of these two hormones has been further confirmed by experimental studies showing that a reduction in testosterone level stimulates early moulting while maintenance of a high testosterone level delays moulting; and vice versa for thyroxin. In natural conditions, the timing of the moult is almost certainly controlled by changes in daylength, via hormones secreted by the pituitary gland (luteinising hormone, prolactin and thyroid-stimulating hormone) and pineal gland (melatonin).

Comparable studies have not been carried out on female badgers but there is a suggestion that moulting is delayed in lactating sows (Stewart & Macdonald, 1997). Since lactation is accompanied by the maintenance of high levels of prolactin, this constitutes further evidence that the hormone is involved in the control of moulting. It also fits with the idea, first suggested by Maurel *et al.*, that moulting in badgers is timed to avoid periods of major investment in reproduction, in the form of mating, pregnancy or lactation. This would make sense, as evidence from other species suggests that the growth of new pelage requires a significant energy investment.

OTHER EXTERNAL FEATURES

Long & Killingley (1983) aptly describe the overall appearance of the badger as 'shaggy, squat and powerful'. The impression of shagginess comes from the length of the guard hairs (see above) and also from the fact that the skin is loosely fitted to the body. This latter characteristic has been seen as an anti-predator adaptation, making it difficult for an adversary to get a firm grip on, or do serious damage to, underlying tissues. However, it is more probably related to the necessity of providing room for a thick layer of subcutaneous fat to be laid down in the autumn (Fig. 35). In a really fat badger, the skin is stretched as tight as a drum.

The impression of squatness and power comes from the compact shape of the body, the shortness of the legs and the degree of muscular development. Muscular development is especially evident in the neck (which is so well muscled

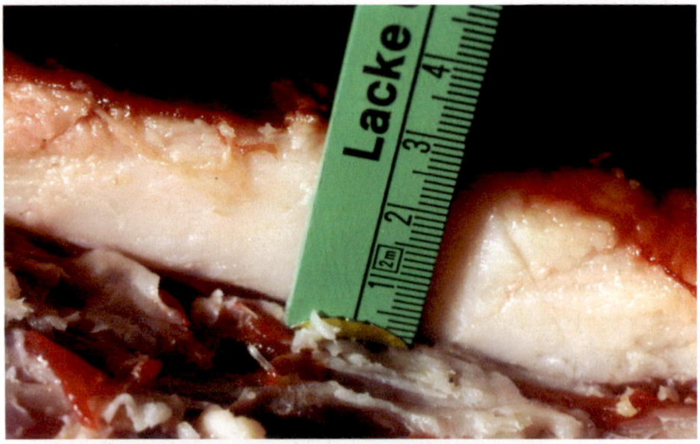

FIG 35. Subcutaneous fat in a Swiss badger. (P. Lüps)

FIG 36. Front paw, showing long claws. (E. Do Linh San)

as to be hardly narrower than the head), shoulders and front legs. This concentration of muscular bulk towards the front end of the body makes badgers extremely strong – strong enough, according to Chris Cheeseman, to tip up a 25 kg stone (Neal & Cheeseman, 1996).

The exaggerated musculature of the neck is probably concerned with self-defence: it enables a badger to hang on to an adversary that is twisting and turning (and which might well be bigger and stronger) without getting its neck broken. The front legs, by contrast, are primarily tools for digging, both in the context of burrowing and for rooting in the soil surface to obtain food (see Chapter 4). Dramatic evidence of their effectiveness is sometimes visible at setts in my downland study area, in the form of large lumps of solid chalk, occasionally bearing visible claw marks, that have been wrested from the subsoil and ejected onto a spoil heap.

A few other features of the external anatomy are worth a mention. The eyes and ears are quite small, suggesting that badgers rely more on their sense of smell than on vision or hearing. The snout is elongated and narrow: badgers as depicted in drawings and paintings, or in the form of stuffed toys, almost always have unnaturally short and rounded noses, making them look cuddlier than the real thing. The nose pad itself is flexible, enabling badgers to root in grass and soil in a pig-like manner. The tail is short and bushy, but not so short as to preclude its use for purposes of communication (see Chapter 6). The front feet have longer and thicker claws than the back feet, which is almost certainly an adaptation for digging (Fig. 36). However, there is also an anecdotal account of a badger using its front claws to slash, bear-like, at an adversary (MacNally, 1970).

BODY SIZE

People are often surprised, when they first see a badger in daylight, by how small it is. On the other hand, badgers can look deceptively large at night, so claims to have seen badgers the size of small bears should be treated with caution.

The truth is that while there are plausible reports of badgers weighing upwards of 20 kg (see Neal & Cheeseman, 1996), 10 kg or less is the norm, at least in western Europe (see Table 2). Males are 1–2 kg heavier, on average, than females, and 2–5 cm longer (see Table 3). However, the range of body weights and body lengths overlaps considerably between the sexes, meaning that it is impossible to sex an individual badger on the basis of its size alone. Indeed, in two of the studies listed in Table 2, the heaviest animal that was recorded was a female.

TABLE 2. Body weight (kg) of male and female badgers.

Country	*Male* Mean (Range)	*Female* Mean (Range)	Source
Spain (Donana)	7.3 (5.9–9.3)	6.9 (4.8–9.2)	Revilla *et al.* (1999)
Spain (Huesca)	7.7 (6.0–8.3)	7.3 (5.5–9.8)	Lüps & Wandeler (1993)
Japan	8.0	7.0	Kaneko *et al.* (1996)
Scotland (West)	8.4	6.7	Kruuk & Parish (1983)
Scotland (Central)	8.8	8.0	Kruuk & Parish (1983)
Scotland (East)	10.4	9.6	Kruuk & Parish (1983)
England (SW)	9.1	8.2	Fargher & Morris (1975)
England (SW)	9.3	8.1	Neal & Cheeseman (1996)
England (Central)	10.4	8.4	Kruuk & Parish (1983)
England (SW)	11.1	10.2	Neal & Cheeseman (1996)
England (SW)	11.6 (9.1–16.7)	10.1 (6.5–13.9)	Neal & Cheeseman (1996)
Denmark	11.3	9.6	Lüps & Wandeler (1993)
Switzerland	12.6 (8.4–14.5)	10.7 (8.4–18.0)	Lüps & Wandeler (1993)
Germany	12.6 (10.9–14.1)	11.3 (8.7–12.8)	Lüps & Wandeler (1993)
Netherlands	12.9 (9.7–17.1)	10.5 (8.0–12.9)	Lüps & Wandeler (1993)

TABLE 3. Body length (cm) of male and female badgers

Country	*Male* Mean (Range)	*Female* Mean (Range)	Source
Spain	68.1 (58–75)	66.1 (59–75)	Revilla *et al.* (1999)
England	68.5 (64–88)	66.0 (45–88)	Fargher & Morris (1975)
England	75.3 (69–80)	72.0 (67–79)	Neal (1977)
Switzerland	77.8 (74–80)	73.2 (65–78)	Lüps & Wandeler (1993)
Germany	81.3 (74–87)	78.5 (69–85)	Lüps & Wandeler (1993)

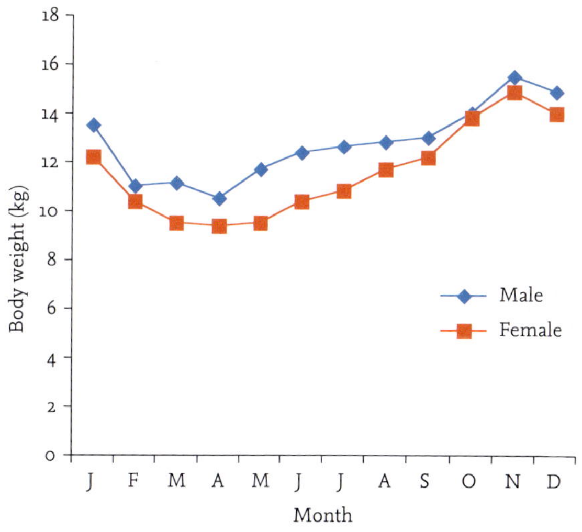

FIG 37. Seasonal changes in body weight in male and female badgers in Switzerland. (Based on data in Lüps, 1983a)

Geographical differences in body weight are evident at both a regional and an international level. At a regional level, Hans Kruuk and Tim Parish (1983) found that badgers on the west coast of Scotland were, on average, 2–3 kg lighter than those on the east coast. This difference was probably a consequence of variations in food supply, as the east coast offers a far richer agricultural habitat with, in particular, significantly higher availability of earthworms (Kruuk & Parish, 1983). Indeed, the weights of east coast badgers subsequently dropped by about 1 kg when changes in farming practice reduced the availability of earthworms (Kruuk & Parish, 1985). Similarly, urban badgers tend to be about 1.5 kg heavier than neighbouring rural badgers, probably because they are better fed (Davison, 2007).

On a larger geographic scale, it is clear that Japanese and Spanish badgers are unusually small (Tables 2 and 3); and Spanish badgers are also exceptional insofar as males are not significantly heavier than females (Revilla *et al.*, 1999). Some of this reduced size may be a result of poor nutrition. However, it seems likely that genetic differences also play a part, as Spanish badgers are sometimes regarded as a separate subspecies, while Japanese badgers are generally classed as a separate subspecies and sometimes as a separate species (see Chapter 1).

Body weight also varies seasonally. Studies in the UK and elsewhere show that maximum weight is reached in autumn and minimum weight in late spring or early summer in both sexes (see Fig. 37). The disparity between the highest and lowest weights in a single year can exceed 100 per cent and is attributable to differences in the amount of fat, most of it subcutaneous. Badgers fatten up in the autumn in preparation for a period of winter inactivity and for breeding, and they continue to utilise this stored fat during the ensuing spring and early summer when insufficient food is available to meet their energy needs. Once again, however, Spanish badgers are exceptional, as they exhibit no statistically significant change in body weight during the year and do not reduce their activity in winter (Revilla *et al.*, 1999). This doubtless reflects the fact that the main food of badgers in this part of Spain (young rabbits) is available year-round.

Where there is a seasonal rhythm in food intake and fat deposition, it is driven by internal physiological changes rather than by external food availability. This is shown by the fact that when badgers are kept in captivity, with food freely available throughout the year, they still become noticeably greedy in the autumn and anorexic in winter. A particularly informative study of the effect of food availability on autumn weight gain was carried out in Japan by Yayoi Kaneko and others (1996), who measured seasonal changes in body weight in two families of badgers, one of which was artificially provisioned. The provisioned badgers lived beneath the house of a Shinto priest, whose wife supplied them with about 500 g of food per day, including, for example, steamed rice, noodles and bread. From April to August, these badgers weighed about 2 kg more on average than the unprovisioned animals. In the autumn, however, the unprovisioned badgers put on weight more rapidly until, by December, the two groups of animals weighed the same. This suggests that there is a genetic 'set point' for winter weight and that animals go on feeding, regardless of food availability, until they achieve this weight.

INTERNAL ANATOMY: SKULL, TEETH AND DIGESTIVE SYSTEM

Skull

The striking feature of a badger's skull is its mass: even to a casual observer, it appears heavy and big-boned (see Figs. 38 and 47 below). Seen from above or below, the most conspicuous feature is the pair of wide, strong-looking zygomatic arches that project from either side, surrounding the hinged end of the lower jaw (Fig. 38a). Seen from the side, the most conspicuous features are a vertical ridge of bone (the sagittal crest) that runs from front to back along the top of the brain case, and the lower jaw itself (Fig. 38b). The latter, again, appears strikingly massive, with a large upward-projecting blade (the coronoid process) at the hinged end. Less obvious, but even more unusual, is the fact that from the age of about 13 months onwards, the lower jaw is permanently attached to the rest of the skull. The reason for this is that the 'socket' of the ball and socket joint

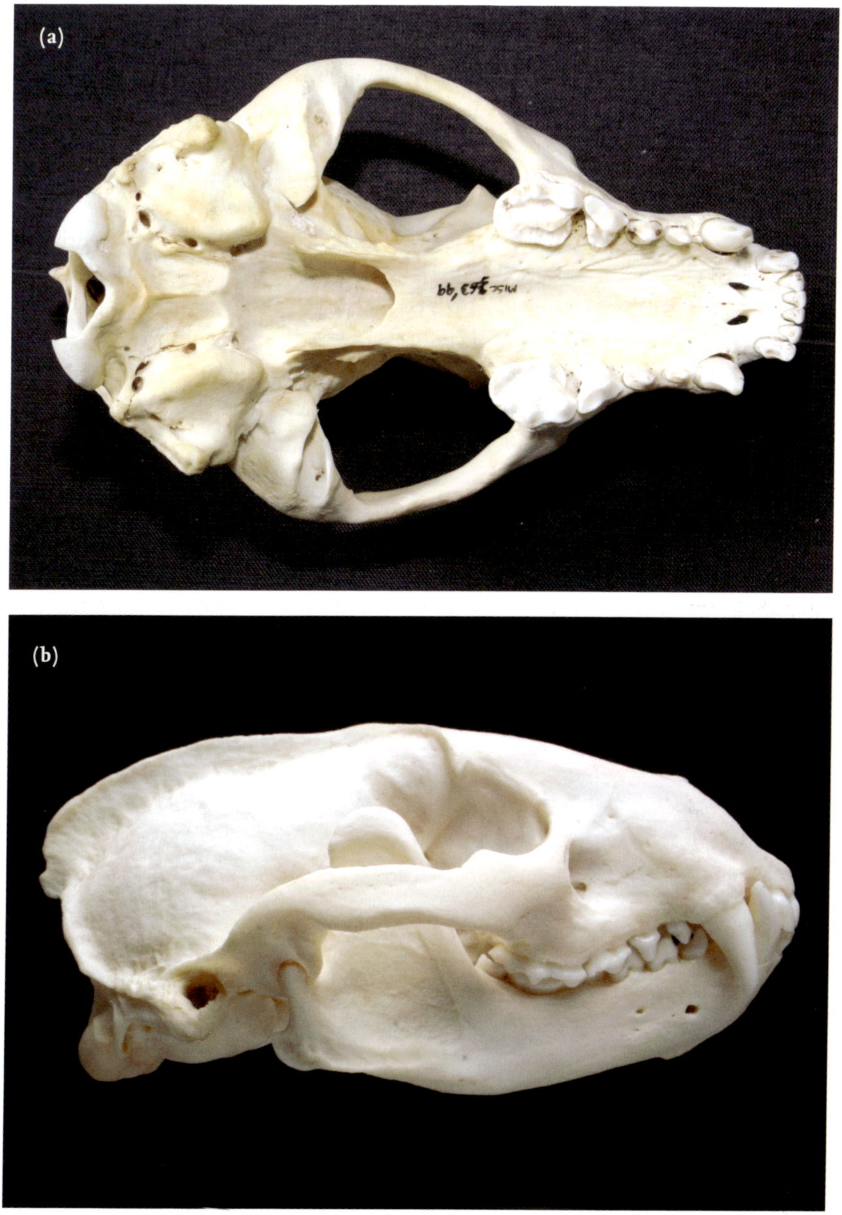

FIG 38. (a) Upper half of skull seen from below; (b) badger skull seen from the side. (R. Lawrence)

that constitutes the hinge of the jaw grows around the 'ball' (which is in fact more of a cylinder) to such an extent that the two cannot be separated without breaking one or the other.

It is generally agreed that these features provide the badger with an unusually strong bite. The sagittal crest and zygomatic arches provide anchorage for highly developed muscles (especially the temporal and masseter muscles) that open and close the jaws. At their other ends, these muscles attach themselves to the enlarged coronoid process of the lower jaw. The unusual structure of the hinge of the lower jaw probably makes it especially strong, reducing the possibility that it will dislocate when the teeth are crushing something that is held relatively far back in the mouth. However, it may also increase the accuracy of the bite by stopping the lower jaw from moving sideways in relation to the upper. This would prevent an adversary from slipping out of a badger's grasp by twisting its jaws apart and might also be important in maintaining the alignment of the upper and lower canine teeth, which slide past one another as the jaw is closed (Long & Killingley, 1983).

That badgers do have a strong bite, both in the dynamic phase when the jaws are closing on something and in the static phase when they are holding onto something that has already been grasped, is undisputed. Several people who have reared tame badgers can attest to the severity of the injuries that they can cause, and it is said that badger-baiters would sometimes break the lower jaw of a badger before setting dogs onto it, in order to give the dogs a better chance of survival. However, given that badgers mostly prey on invertebrates and eat fruits and seeds, one could be forgiven for asking why such a formidable bite is necessary.

Almost certainly, the structure of the skull has more to do with aggression and self-defence, against predators and against other badgers, than with capturing or consuming food. Although badgers have few or no predators now in most parts of their range, badger remains have been found in the scats or stomach contents of wolves *Canis lupus* in China, Finland and Italy; and radio-collared Eurasian lynx (*Lynx lynx*) have been observed to attack badgers in Switzerland. There are also anecdotal accounts of badgers or their cubs being attacked by brown bears *Ursus arctos*, wolverines *Gulo gulo*, red foxes *Vulpes vulpes*, eagle owls *Bubo bubo*, golden eagles *Aquila chrysaetos* and buzzards *Buteo buteo*; and in the evolutionary past, they would have had other predators. As badgers cannot run fast and often find themselves at some distance from their burrows, the ability to stand and fight is an important part of their defensive repertoire. As regards aggression towards members of their own species, badgers can and do engage in fierce fighting over territorial boundaries and, in particular, over mates (see Chapters 5 and 7).

We can assess the relative importance of these two sources of selection pressure (defence against predators and aggression towards other badgers) by looking at the degree of what is called sexual size dimorphism. Sexual dimorphism in general means a difference in appearance between the two sexes, and sexual size dimorphism means that males and females differ in body size: usually, males are bigger and stronger than females. This comes about because males generally compete with one another over access to females, whereas females rarely compete for males. Consequently, natural selection (or, more accurately, 'sexual selection') has operated on males to improve their competitive ability, for example by making them larger and stronger, and providing them with more effective weapons. It follows that if sexual selection has played a large part in the evolution of the badger skull, we should expect it to be larger and stronger in males than in females. On the other hand, if skull morphology has been shaped primarily by the need to fight off predators, we should see no difference between the sexes, since both males and females need to defend themselves against predators to an equal extent.

In the case of the badger skull, there is undoubtedly some degree of sexual size dimorphism, manifest especially in the width and height of the zygomatic crest, the overall width of the skull (zygomatic width) and the length and diameter of the canine teeth (Johnson & Macdonald, 2001; Abramov & Puzachenko, 2005). In all cases, the relevant measurements are larger, on average, in males than in females. This suggests that the formidable bite of the badger has indeed evolved, at least in part, as a weapon for use in competitive fighting between males. On the other hand, the degree of sexual dimorphism is relatively small in absolute terms, and in all cases there is significant overlap between the two sexes at the population level. From an evolutionary perspective, therefore, the characteristics of the badger skull and the size of the canine teeth probably owe comparatively little to sexual selection and rather more to the need for defence against predators.

Teeth

Among the badger's many unusual features, perhaps the oddest is that no one can agree how many teeth it is supposed to have. The dental formula (number of teeth of each type in the upper jaw and lower jaw, respectively) is variously given as:

Incisors 3/3	*Canines 1/1*	*Premolars 4/4*	*Molars 1/2*	*Total* = 38
Incisors 3/3	*Canines 1/1*	*Premolars 3/4*	*Molars 1/2*	*Total* = 36
Incisors 3/3	*Canines 1/1*	*Premolars 3/3*	*Molars 1/2*	*Total* = 34

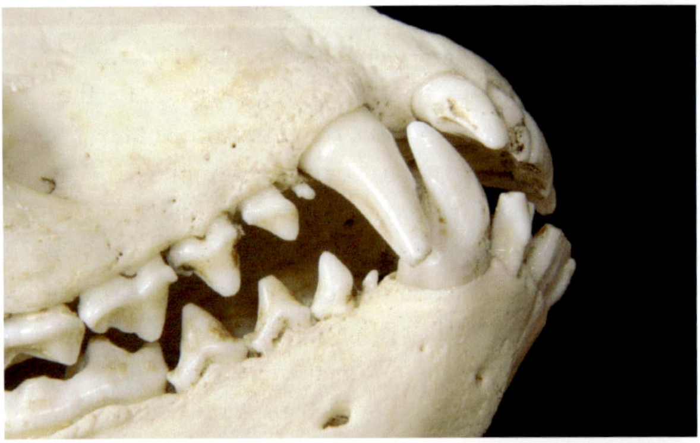

FIG 39. Front teeth seen from the right-hand side. Note the vestigial first premolars, which are the very small teeth immediately behind the canines. (R. Lawrence)

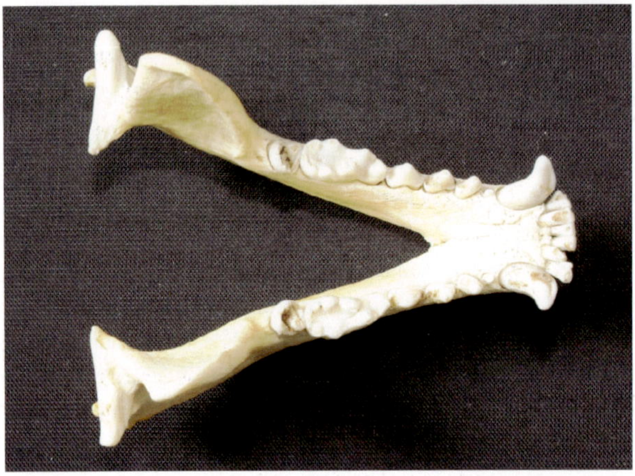

FIG 40. Lower jaw, showing teeth. (R. Lawrence)

The problem, clearly, is with the premolars, and it arises because the first premolars are vestigial (Fig. 39). In some individual badgers, all four of these premolars are present but very much reduced in size; others have the lower pair but not the upper pair; and yet others have none at all. Comparing Eurasian badgers across different geographical regions, there seems to be a more or less smooth reduction (a 'cline'), going from west to east, in the percentage of individuals that have first premolars, ranging from 2 per cent in Kazakhstan through 30 per cent in central Asia to 70–80 per cent in central and western Europe. In some individuals lacking first premolars, the teeth in question develop but soon drop out, while in others they are absent altogether. Even when they are present, the first premolars are too small (1–2 mm long) to have any function, so it appears, from an evolutionary perspective, that they are in the process of being lost altogether.

Two evolutionary forces seem to be at work here (Lüps & Roper, 1988). First, there is evidence of a continuing decrease in the overall body size of Eurasian badgers, causing a reduction in the size of the jaw and leaving less room for the present number of teeth. Second, the first premolar is being squeezed out by enlargement of the remaining premolars and, especially, the first molar. Since these latter teeth are located at the point of maximum masticatory force, an increase in their size fits with the idea that having an unusually effective bite is important to the survival of badgers. Alternatively, enlargement of the molars might be related to a long-term change from a primarily carnivorous to a more omnivorous diet.

Of the other teeth (Fig. 40), the most immediately conspicuous are the canines, which, as suggested above, probably function more in the context of aggression and self-defence than in relation to feeding behaviour. The incisors, by contrast, are relatively small and set closely together in a shallow arc at the front of the jaw, making them effective for nipping an adversary or grasping small prey. Hans Kruuk (1978a) describes how, when badgers are picking large earthworms (*Lumbricus terrestris*) off the surface of the ground on rainy nights (a behaviour that he calls 'worming'), they seize a worm with the incisors and engulf it with a backward toss of the head, sometimes nipping it again with the incisors as it is swallowed (for more details, see Chapter 4). I have found earthworms in badger stomachs that showed exactly this pattern of damage, as if someone had tried to chop them in half with a pair of scissors. Badgers also use their incisors when rooting for and seizing earthworms that have retreated beneath the surface, or searching for soil-dwelling insects such as leatherjackets (*Tipula* larvae). As a result, the incisors can be worn down almost to stumps in old animals (see Fig. 41). Indeed, the degree of wear of the incisors and other teeth may be employed as a rough guide to the age of a badger (Hancox, 1988b).

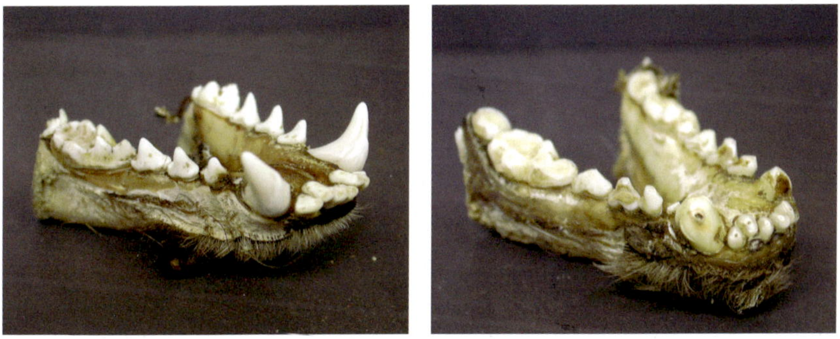

FIG 41. Lower jaw of (above left) yearling and (above right) an elderly adult badger. Note how the teeth are worn down in the older animal. (L. Stuart)

As regards feeding habits, however, the most informative teeth are the premolars and molars, which, by carnivore standards, are relatively broad and flat: they appear to be made for crushing rather than slicing. This is most evident in the upper first molar, which is the largest tooth of all in terms of surface area, is unusually firmly rooted in the jaw and has a complex multi-cusped surface adapted for crushing. The lower first molar has two parts: a front part (the trigonid) that is adapted for cutting and works together with the upper fourth premolar, and a rear part (the talonid) that is adapted for crushing and works together with the large upper first molar (Lüps & Roper, 1988). These teeth suggest that badgers are not just omnivorous now (see Chapter 4) but have been so for a significant part of their evolutionary history.

Digestive system

While the badger's teeth suggest omnivory, its gastrointestinal tract is more in line with what we would expect of a carnivore. The stomach is somewhat elongated in shape and consists of a single compartment; the small intestine is long (about 0.5 m); and the colon is simple and short (about 30 cm). The dimensions of these parts of the gut are about what we would expect to see in a 'typical' carnivore weighing the same as a badger. This fact, together with the absence of a caecum for the fermentation of plant material, suggests that the gut is adapted primarily to a meat-based diet (Stark *et al.*, 1987).

Nevertheless, as we shall see in Chapter 4, badgers do eat a significant amount of plant material including cereals, roots, seeds and fruits. However, there has been debate as to how well they can process such foods. Casual inspection of badger faeces suggests that some plant foods pass more or less intact through the gut (see Fig. 42); and although the teeth seem appropriately

FIG 42. Faeces containing maize residue. (E. Do Linh San)

shaped for crushing, they cannot grind, because the unusual way in which the jaws are hinged (see above) prevents them from moving laterally with respect to one another. On the other hand, it seems unlikely that badgers would eat plant foods if they were unable to digest them.

The only hard evidence in relation to this issue is from a study by Luis Rosalino and others (2003), who fed a captive badger on known weights of various different foods one at a time and then measured the weight of each food that was subsequently excreted in the form of faeces. By subtracting the amount excreted from the amount eaten, they were able to derive an estimate of the proportion of each food that was digested. The results show that soft fruits, olives, earthworms, insects and vertebrates were all 90–99 per cent digested, the only exception being acorns (64 per cent digested). Insofar as evidence is available, then, it suggests that badgers are no worse at digesting soft plant material than they are at digesting animal material.

To summarise, the badger's alimentary system remains a bit of a puzzle. The teeth suggest omnivory and it seems that most plant material can be adequately digested, while the gut resembles, anatomically, that of a typical carnivore. Consequently, although it is clear that present-day badgers eat a wide variety of foods of both plant and animal origin (see Chapter 4), it is less clear to what extent this is an ancient, evolved characteristic, as opposed to being a relatively recent, opportunistic response to the availability of domestic crops.

ACTIVITY CYCLES

It is universally acknowledged that badgers are nocturnal, though they are certainly capable of diurnal activity if undisturbed. I have met badgers foraging in wheat and maize fields at 15.00 hrs on a summer afternoon. Neal & Cheeseman (1996) provide similar anecdotes.

Like body weight, the activity cycle undergoes marked seasonal changes. However, the precise nature of these varies from place to place. One might expect a nocturnal animal to become active at dusk and cease to be active at dawn, in which case its activity period should be shortest in summer, when the nights themselves are short. And this is what seems to happen in the UK (Neal, 1977) and Scandinavia (Jensen, 1959). However, more recent studies in Switzerland and Poland show that the activity period is longest in summer and shortest in winter (Ferrari, 1997; Kowalczyk *et al.*, 2003a; Goszczyński *et al.*, 2005: see Fig. 43). All studies show that return times are less tightly linked to sunrise than are leaving times to sunset, suggesting that badgers remain active for as long as it takes for

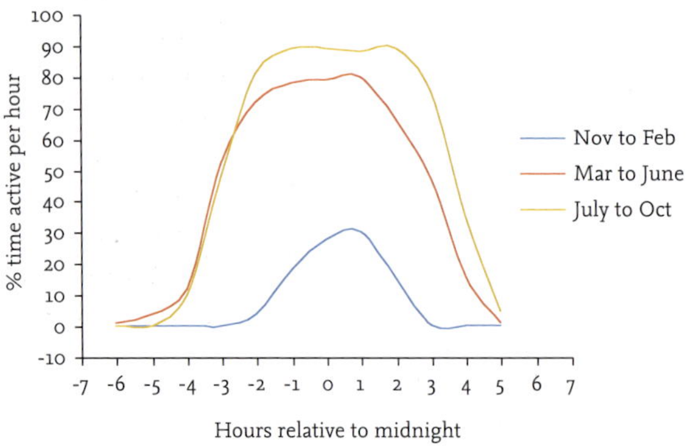

FIG 43. Duration and intensity of activity during different seasons of the year, for badgers in Poland. (Based on data in Goszczyński *et al.*, 2005)

them to find enough food, even if this requires them, in summer, to be up and about after dawn. In urban environments, however, badgers are more strictly nocturnal and delay emergence until late at night, presumably waiting until human activity has subsided (Harris, 1982; Davison, 2007).

Just as everyone agrees that badgers are nocturnal, so everyone agrees that they become less active in winter. Again, however, this means different things in different places. Although in southern England, badgers can be active for much of the night in winter, 'activity' at this time of year means a night-long sequence of individual badgers emerging above ground, pottering around the sett for a few minutes and then disappearing again. If an individual does leave the sett, it will not venture far or for very long. So, although English badgers may not sleep all night in winter, they are only 'active' in a rather limited sense. The same sort of behaviour occurs in Poland, except that here badgers are only active, even in this limited sense, for a few hours per night (Goszczyński *et al.*, 2003: see Fig. 43).

In more extreme conditions, however, badgers become 'inactive' in winter by any criterion, remaining below ground for periods of time ranging from days to months. For example, Rafał Kowalczyk lists Russian studies showing periods of winter inactivity ranging from 103 to 180 days (Kowalczyk *et al.*, 2003a). Conversely, badgers in Portugal and southern Spain remain as active, in all senses, in winter as at any other time of year. An interesting analysis by Kowalczyk *et al.*, bringing together results from 23 different studies covering most of the European badger's range, suggests that these differences are driven by winter temperature: the lower the mean January temperature, the longer the period of winter inactivity and the greater the difference between spring and winter body weight (Fig. 44). Of course, this makes sense, because the longer the period of winter inactivity, the more fat is needed for survival. However, these data provide a particularly elegant

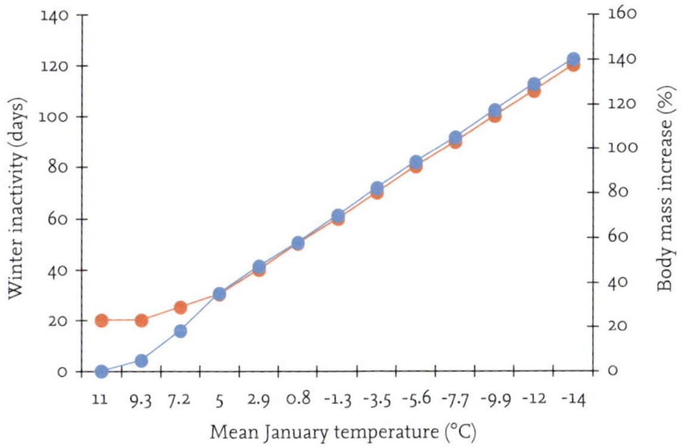

FIG 44. Effects of January temperature on the duration of winter inactivity (blue) and the gain in body mass between spring and the onset of winter (red). (Based on data in Kowalczyk *et al.*, 2003a)

illustration of how the deposition of fat and the cessation of activity interact to produce a coordinated strategy for dealing with harsh winters.

In all of these studies, 'activity' means activity above ground. However, it does not necessarily follow that badgers are always asleep when they are within the sett. My own radio-tracking experience suggests that there is little movement within the sett during the morning and early afternoon, so return to the sett is probably followed by several hours of unbroken sleep. However, badgers begin to move around within the sett towards the late afternoon, some time before they actually emerge.

METABOLIC RATE AND BODY TEMPERATURE

Metabolic rate has been measured only once in badgers, in a study conducted over 30 years ago on (probably) a single animal. This yielded a value for oxygen consumption of about 0.21 cm^3O_2/g-h, equivalent to heat production of about 200 kcal/day (Iversen, 1972). When differences in body weight are taken into account, this value is low by the standards of both mammals in general and mustelids in particular. Since burrowing mammals generally have lower metabolic rates than non-burrowers, the relatively low metabolic rate of badgers is probably associated with their semi-fossorial habit (McNab, 1979). However, further studies of metabolic rate, involving more badgers and using more up-to-date methods, are clearly desirable to confirm Iversen's result.

Three studies of badger body temperature have been conducted, in Scotland, Norway and Japan, respectively (Fowler & Racey, 1988; Bevanger & Brøseth, 1998; Tanaka, 2006). All show that during the period of winter inactivity, body temperature declines by a few degrees from its norm of about 37°C, reaching a minimum in December. Entry into the period of minimum body temperature, and recovery from it, is gradual, taking from one to three months. Data from the American badger *Taxidea taxus* suggest that a 1°C fall in body temperature results in an energy saving equivalent to 10g of fat per day (Harlow, 1981), in which case a sustained reduction in body temperature of 5°C would save about 1.5 kg of fat per month. Given the long winters experienced by Norwegian badgers, Bevanger & Brøseth argue that they could not survive without economising on energy expenditure by reducing their body temperature.

Body temperature reduction is one of the defining features of hibernation and some authors refer to badgers as hibernators. However, true hibernation results in larger reductions in body temperature than those so far recorded in badgers, and these occur in periodic bouts rather than being sustained over weeks or months as seems to be the case in badgers. In addition, badgers, at least in western Europe, are not totally inactive throughout the winter; rather, they 'wake up' and leave their setts if conditions become temporarily mild. For these reasons, it is more accurate to describe the overwintering strategy of badgers as involving 'torpor' or 'winter lethargy' rather than hibernation.

On the other hand, overwintering badgers do undergo physiological changes, such as depressed levels of the hormone thyroxin, similar to those described in deep hibernators (for references, see Fowler & Racey, 1988). The probable reality is that 'winter lethargy', 'torpor' and 'hibernation' are points on a continuum rather than distinct states, and that badgers lie somewhere in the middle of the spectrum. It is also worth remembering that we lack information about the physiological changes associated with overwintering in really cold places, where badgers can remain confined to the sett for months on end. Quite possibly, badgers in such regions undergo something more akin to 'true' hibernation.

SPECIAL SENSES

Naturalists universally agree that badgers have an acute sense of smell, pretty good hearing and rather poor vision. However, this view is based almost entirely on anecdotal evidence: very few experiments have been conducted to investigate the nature and limits of the badger's sensory world, and hardly anything has been written about the structure of the sense organs themselves or about the parts of the brain that serve a sensory function. Here, rather than repeating the many anecdotes that have been provided by other authors (see especially Neal, 1977, 1986; Neal & Cheeseman, 1996; Kruuk, 1989), I shall summarise the general impression that has emerged and add a few novel observations of my own.

Vision

In order to gather as much light as possible, the eyes of nocturnal animals need to be large. Badgers' eyes are relatively small, suggesting that the species does not rely heavily on vision when active at night (see Fig. 45). On the other hand, the eye does have a reflective layer (the tapetum) at the back of the retina, which is why a badger's eyes shine back at you if you direct a light towards its face at night. The purpose of the tapetum is to reflect back any incident light that is not absorbed by the retina, so that this 'leftover' light has a second chance to be detected. Thus, the tapetum endows the eye with greater sensitivity in low-light conditions. With respect to its size, therefore, the badger's eye does not seem well adapted to a nocturnal lifestyle; with respect to the presence of a tapetum, it does. This suggests that contradictory selection pressures have been operating during the badger's evolutionary history, so as to maximise the sensitivity of the eye while keeping it small in size. Possibly, this reflects a trade-off between a tendency for the eyes of burrowing animals to become reduced in size and the badger's need to retain some visual capacity for use on the surface.

Being nocturnal animals, badgers probably have little in the way of colour vision. In apparent confirmation of this, Neal & Cheeseman (1996) state that the badger retina consists mainly of rods; but the source of this information is not cited, so I have been unable to check its reliability. As regards visual acuity,

FIG 45. Badger head, showing the small eyes and ears. (H. Clark)

anecdotal evidence suggests that badgers can see shapes and silhouettes, perhaps from distances of up to 50 m, but cannot discern much in the way of detail, at least at night. My own experience bears this out. On one occasion, I was sitting on a hillside watching a badger foraging on blackberries about 25 m below me. It was a clear moonlit night, so I could see the badger well; and, because a breeze was blowing up the slope, the badger could not smell me. Eventually, when it finished feeding, the badger started trotting up the slope towards me but stopped about 15 m below me and peered intensely in my direction. After several seconds of this, it ran around to my right side in an arc and then, when on a level with me but still about 15 m away, it peered at me again. Still not satisfied, it ran all the way round below me in a semicircle until it was level with me once more, this time on my left side, and peered at me a third time. After this third inspection, it trotted off up the slope and disappeared. During all three inspections, it was clear from the badger's posture that it was looking at me, not trying to scent me.

My interpretation of this incident is that the badger had seen, on the hillside, a dark shape that it thought should not have been there. However, it required several inspections, from different angles, to convince itself that this was the case and, judging from the relatively leisurely way in which it eventually departed, it was unable to tell that the shape in question was human. Had I moved, it would have been a different story, because, like other animals, badgers can discern movement much more readily than they can discern static differences in contrast.

Neal & Cheeseman (1996) summarise the available evidence by suggesting that vision serves to alert a badger to possible danger, whereupon it brings its other, more acute, senses to bear in order to provide additional information. I see no reason to doubt this conclusion, though it is worth adding that badgers also seem to use vision for purposes of communication at close range (see Chapter 6). In this context, Hans Kruuk (1989) describes an experiment in which two adult captive male badgers were presented with four different cardboard models of badger 'faces', one painted with realistic vertical black-and-white stripes, one with horizontal stripes, one plain black and one plain white. The boars attacked the realistic face significantly more often than the horizontally striped or plain-coloured faces, showing that badgers have some ability to distinguish pattern. Unfortunately, however, Kruuk does not say at what distance the cardboard 'faces' were presented, or under what lighting conditions.

Hearing

Like its eyes, the badger's ears (at least, the externally visible part) are small (see Fig. 45). Anecdotal evidence suggests that badgers, at least when they are on the alert, react strongly to sudden sounds such as the click of a camera shutter or the rustle of clothing; but when foraging in undergrowth, they sometimes make so much noise themselves that it is difficult to imagine they can hear anything else. It is also clear that badgers can tell the distance from which a sound originates, because they will ignore loud sounds that come from a long way away while reacting to less intense sounds that originate in their immediate vicinity (Neal & Cheeseman, 1996). A variety of sounds are also used for purposes of short-distance and long-distance communication (see Chapter 6).

Smell

Many anecdotes, contributed by generations of badger-watchers, attest to the acuity of the badger's sense of smell and to the importance to the animal of this sensory modality. As Neal & Cheeseman (1996) remark: 'The sense of smell in badgers is extremely well developed and is undoubtedly their most important sense.' For example, when badgers emerge from the sett in the evening, or are alerted by a sudden sound or movement, they adopt a characteristic, nose-up posture in order to scent the air (Fig. 46). Consequently, there is no point in trying to watch badgers unless you are quite sure that you are downwind of them. In places where badgers are unused to humans, such as some of the forests of central Europe, the scent left by a person walking over a sett during the day is

FIG 46. Badger scenting the air. (H. Clark)

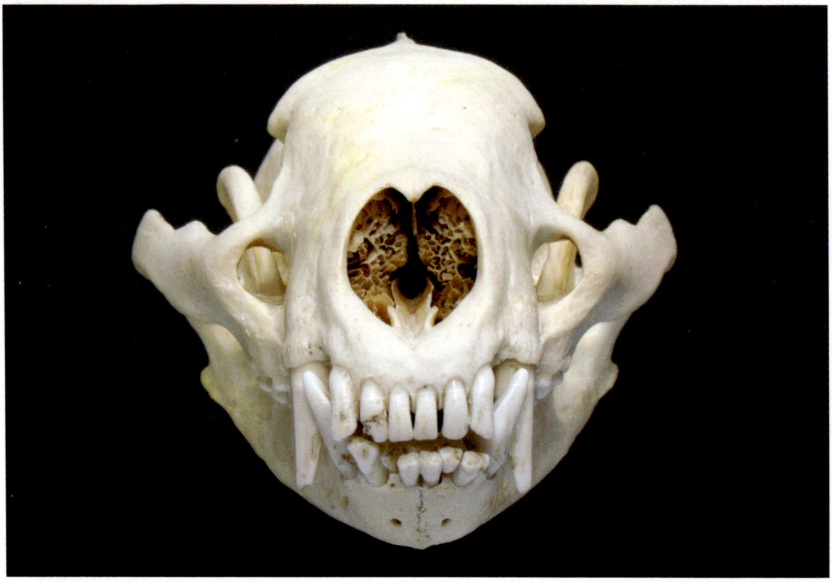

FIG 47. Badger skull from the front, showing the large nasal cavity. (R. Lawrence)

enough to prevent badgers from emerging the following night and, if repeated, can cause them to abandon the sett altogether. The large size of the nasal cavity provides additional, anatomical evidence of an acute sense of smell (Fig. 47).

Badgers do not just use their sense of smell to give notice of potential danger. They are also well endowed with scent glands, which they use for various purposes of communication with members of their own and other social groups (see Chapter 6), and they use smell to orient themselves within their territories. When badgers are moving rapidly from one part of the territory to another, they usually take the same route, following trails that they and their ancestors have created. Sometimes these trails are sufficiently well worn to become visible (Fig. 48), but the primary sense used for locating and following them is surely olfaction. Neal & Cheeseman (1996) describe a case in which a badger trail was ploughed over but was immediately re-established in the same place, presumably because the scent was still detectable; and I have made similar observations in my Sussex study area.

The extent to which badgers use smell for foraging purposes is less clear. Their primary mode of foraging, snuffling around in the vegetation with their noses close to the ground, or rooting with the nose in the top few centimetres of soil, strongly suggests that they do. It has not been demonstrated that badgers can detect earthworms by smell but this seems likely, as earthworms possess a distinct

FIG 48. Badger path crossing a field in the Netherlands. (Dassenwerkgroep Brabant)

olfactory signature. Foods such as ripe fruits, and the nests of bees and wasps, are other likely candidates for olfactory detection.

In addition to asking what badgers can smell and how they use their sense of smell, we may also ask to what extent they can distinguish different odours of the same general type. Neal & Cheeseman (1996) provide anecdotal evidence that badgers can discriminate individual humans by smell, and Hans Kruuk and his colleagues briefly describe an experiment in which captive badgers were trained to discriminate samples of caudal gland secretion that had been obtained from different individual members of different social groups (Kruuk *et al.*, 1984; Kruuk, 1989). According to Kruuk, his badgers could tell the scent of one individual from that of another, and could also distinguish between scents that came from other members of their own group and scents that came from 'strangers' (see Chapter 6 for more details).

LOCOMOTION

Badgers have three distinct gaits: they can walk, trot and gallop (Jensen, 1959; Neal & Cheeseman, 1996). In this they resemble most mammals. However, the long spine and short legs that are characteristic of the Mustelidae give the movements of all members of the family, including badgers, a kind of rippling sinuosity that is instantly distinguishable from the gait of any other mammal. Watch a badger running and what you see, in the flexing and rolling of its body, is a scaled-up stoat, polecat or otter.

Although they are not fast-moving by general carnivore standards, badgers move more rapidly and more efficiently than one might expect from their compact appearance. As I and other radio-trackers have discovered to our cost, they can easily outrun most humans, especially when travelling uphill. They can

FIG 49. Badger footprints in the sand at Doñana reserve, Spain. Note how the front and rear paw prints are partly superimposed, showing that the badger was walking. (E. Revilla)

also cover surprising distances. Jaap Mulder (1996) reports instances of badgers travelling several kilometres in a single night, and Emmanuel Do Linh San has reported a badger travelling 9.5 km in one night. Mulder also describes a case in which a sow covered a linear distance of 115 km during a two-week period.

Walking is used when a badger is not in a particular hurry to go anywhere, for example when it is meandering around looking for food. In walking, the legs move symmetrically, with the left leg (front or rear) repeating the movement of the right one half a stride later. Consequently, three legs are in contact with the ground at any one time. The tracks of a walking badger can be distinguished by the fact that the prints of the left and right paws (either front or rear) are more or less superimposed on one another (Fig. 49).

Trotting is probably the most frequent form of locomotion, seen when a badger is moving purposefully from one location to another (for example, to visit a latrine or to return to the sett). Two diagonal legs are in contact with the ground at any one time, the head is held low, and the head and rump swing from side to side in synchrony with movements of the legs, giving the gait a rhythmic, swaying character (Fig. 50). The distance between the tracks of the front and rear paws is greater in trotting than in walking, so that the prints of the front and rear paws are no longer superimposed. Trotting can be sustained for long periods and can carry a badger over at least a few kilometres in a relatively short time. The maximum speed of movement with this gait is about 7 km/hr.

Badgers gallop when frightened or when chasing one another. In galloping, only one foot at a time makes contact with the ground and, between paces, all four feet are off the ground simultaneously, so that the animal moves forward by a series of bounds. Consequently, the paw prints of a galloping badger are well spaced out and, because the legs are moved asymmetrically, individual footfalls

FIG **50.** Badger trotting. (H. Clark)

FIG **51.** Badger climbing a tree. (A. Kelly)

are separated by approximately equal distances. Ernest Neal reports a badger galloping at a speed of 25–30 km/hr but anecdotal evidence suggests that this sort of pace cannot be kept up for long (see Neal & Cheeseman, 1996).

When it comes to climbing, badgers are more agile that one might suppose (Fig. 51). Neal & Cheeseman provide anecdotal accounts of badgers climbing elder and beech trees to a height of about 5 m, usually in order to find slugs but also, in one case, to raid a bird-feeder. Badgers can also climb wire-netting fences, garden trellises and stone walls, and they can climb into cattle-feeding troughs (Garnett *et al.*, 2003).

Badgers can also swim well, holding their heads high out of the water and propelling themselves along by paddling like a dog. It seems unlikely that many swim habitually, but Ernest Neal tells of a group of badgers in Devon whose members regularly swam across the river Yeo in order to reach feeding places on the other side. Similarly, Jaap Mulder (1996) observed radio-collared badgers swimming across the river Regge in the Netherlands, at a point where it was about 20–25 m wide. He also reports that Dutch badgers are often found drowned in canals, presumably because they try to swim across but are prevented from climbing out by the steepness of the banks.

DISEASES AND PARASITES

On the face of it, one might not expect badgers to be especially healthy animals. Their foraging behaviour is hardly hygienic, consisting as it mainly does of grubbing around in (and to some extent, inevitably, ingesting) soil or sources of decaying organic matter such as leaf litter, cattle faeces, silage, compost and garbage. Also, conditions within the sett seem ideally suited to disease transmission, insofar as they involve badgers spending large amounts of time in close proximity to one another, in an environment characterised by high humidity and moderate temperature (see Chapter 3). Nevertheless, there are no reports of badger populations being decimated by disease on anything other than a local scale, suggesting that badgers on the whole have a robust ability to combat infection (Gallagher & Nelson, 1979). As we shall see, the reasons for this vary from disease to disease.

Hancox (1980) lists 19 fungal, bacterial and viral infections, 55 species of endoparasites and 45 species of ectoparasites that have been detected in badgers; and others have subsequently been discovered. Most of the relevant reports, however, merely confirm the presence of this or that parasite or pathogen in a particular badger population, leaving open the question of how prevalent the condition is in the species as a whole. In addition, little or no information is available about the effects, for example on physical wellbeing, reproductive success or mortality, of the majority of these conditions, though it seems reasonable to assume that the impact of most of them is negligible. Here, therefore, I shall concentrate on the diseases and parasites about which we know most.

Rabies

Rabies is the most important fatal disease of badgers. It is a viral infection (caused by an RNA *Lyssavirus*) transmitted mainly by exposure to infectious saliva, for example via bite-wounding or licking of one animal by another (Smith, 2002). As is well known, animals at an advanced stage of infection can behave in an odd and dangerous manner, leaving their territories, wandering around at unusual times of day and becoming highly aggressive and unpredictable (the so-called 'furious' syndrome) before finally succumbing to paralysis and death. However, some infected individuals progress to paralysis and death without showing other obvious symptoms (the so-called 'dumb' syndrome). Rabies is primarily associated with dogs, cats and foxes but badgers seem to be at least as susceptible to the disease as foxes and become at least as infectious. They also display 'furious' symptoms, though possibly less often than do foxes or dogs. There is no doubting that rabies is fatal to badgers: at a local level, it can result in the death of 90 per cent of the badger population (Wandeler *et al.*, 1974; Smith, 2002).

Nevertheless, badgers account for only 1–2 per cent of all cases of rabies in wildlife in Europe, while foxes account for about 90 per cent. Furthermore, during the course of a rabies outbreak, the infection rate in badgers waxes and wanes in proportion to the infection rate in foxes, and the disease dies out in badgers shortly after it disappears from the corresponding fox population (Wandeler *et al.*, 1974). It seems, therefore, that the badger is more a victim of rabies in foxes (a 'spill-over' host) than a reservoir or vector of the disease in its own right (Holmala & Kauhala, 2006).

The primary reason for this is almost certainly that over most of Europe, the population density of badgers is not high enough for the species, on its own, to initiate or maintain a rabies outbreak. In addition, the very high mortality rate associated with rabies in badgers, together with the badger's low reproductive rate, means that an outbreak rapidly burns itself out. In short, rabies can spread rapidly through a badger subpopulation and cause very high levels of mortality in a particular locality, but it does not decimate the species on a larger scale. In the UK, however, where badger population densities are higher, computer models suggest that badgers could both initiate and maintain a rabies outbreak (Smith & Wilkinson, 2002). In addition, as was noted in Chapter 1, rabies has had a major indirect effect on badger populations across much of continental Europe, owing to the gassing of setts in an attempt to control the disease in foxes.

Bovine tuberculosis

Bovine tuberculosis (TB) is a bacterial disease caused by the bacillus *Mycobacterium bovis*. It results in the formation, within the internal organs of the host, of 'tubercles' or 'lesions': small (1–4 mm), spherical, pale-coloured nodules within which the bacterium multiplies (Fig. 52). If these nodules rupture, they expel large numbers of live bacteria that not only spread the disease to other parts of the host's own body but also make the host capable of infecting other individuals.

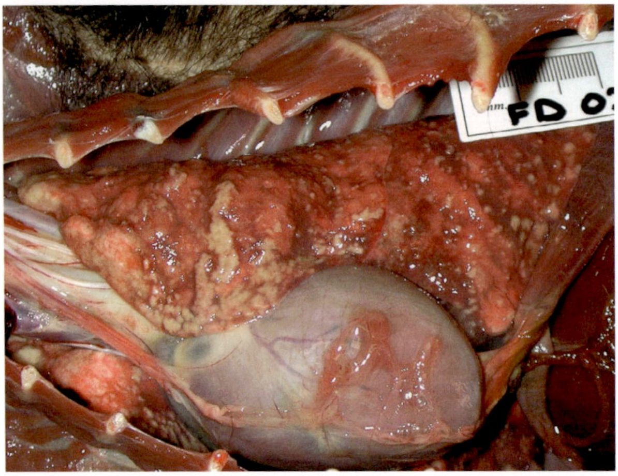

FIG 52. Tuberculous nodules or 'lesions' in the lung of a badger. (© Crown Copyright 2010, published with the permission of the Controller of Her Majesty's Stationery Office)

Lesions are found most often in the lungs and associated lymph nodes but can also occur in most of the other organs of the body, including the kidneys, digestive system, reproductive system, liver and skin. Depending on where the lesions are located, infection can be passed from badger to badger by coughing, sneezing, close physical contact, licking or biting, or via contact with infected faeces or urine. Given that about 80 per cent of infected badgers have lesions associated with the respiratory tract, aerosol infection is the most likely mode of transmission, especially within a social group where there are plenty of opportunities for close physical contact between individuals (Bourne, 2007). However, bite-wounding may be a significant source of transmission of the disease from one social group of badgers to another (Gallagher & Clifton-Hadley, 2000).

The pathogenesis of TB in badgers is complex. Not all badgers that are exposed to infection become diseased: many fight the infection off by mounting an immune reaction. Others may develop lesions as a consequence of infection but these lesions may remain dormant, in which case the animal shows no obvious signs of ill-health. If lesions rupture, badgers can become infectious but still do not necessarily show any obvious external symptoms, at least for a period of time. In a minority of cases, however, the disease progresses, leading to emaciation, general bodily weakness and death. Badgers in this state are a sorry sight indeed: they become very thin; develop overgrown fore claws, presumably because they are too weak to dig; are often severely infested with ectoparasites, presumably because they are too weak to groom; and their eyes become sunken owing to the depletion of suborbital fat. Often they become badly bitten, perhaps because they have been specifically targeted by other badgers or perhaps just

FIG 53. Badger in the terminal stages of bovine tuberculosis infection. Note sunken eyes, poor condition of pelage, extreme emaciation and bite wounds on the rump. (M. Edwards)

because they are unable to defend themselves (Fig. 53). Severely debilitated badgers may also behave oddly, leaving their social groups and taking up residence in farm buildings or gardens, probably in order to exploit the easy sources of food to be found in such places (Gallagher & Nelson, 1979; Cheeseman & Mallinson, 1981).

In view of this complex pathogenesis, it is far from straightforward to estimate the prevalence of TB in badgers or even to say what one means by a 'tuberculous' badger. Ideally, we would like to distinguish five classes of badgers: those that have never been exposed to TB; those that have been exposed to the disease but have successfully avoided becoming infected; those that are infected but not infectious; those that are infectious but do not show obvious symptoms; and those that are severely debilitated and highly infectious (Smith *et al.*, 1995). In practice, however, only the last state can be unambiguously diagnosed either in live badgers or in carcasses.

The best data on prevalence come from a long-term study of a population of about 300 badgers (about 30 social groups) at Woodchester Park, Gloucestershire. This study was set up in 1977 to monitor the progress of TB in an otherwise undisturbed badger population, and is still ongoing. It consists essentially of trapping as many members of the population as possible, every few months, and testing them for TB. The results indicate that a large majority of badgers (perhaps 80 per cent) never contract TB, with only about 5 per cent becoming infectious and only about 2–3 per cent super-infectious (Wilkinson *et al.*, 2000). The accuracy of these results can be questioned on the grounds that the tests used to diagnose tuberculosis in live badgers are known to underestimate the true prevalence. However, a second study, using a different methodology (namely, postmortem examination of a large number of badger carcasses), paints a broadly similar picture, classing 14 per cent of badgers as infected, 6 per cent as infectious and 1–2 per cent as severely infectious (Jenkins *et al.*, 2007). Nevertheless, yet another study, in which badger carcasses were subjected to more rigorous postmortem examination, yielded infection rates that were about double those of the preceding studies (Bourne, 2007), and in the Republic of Ireland the infection rate may be as high as 40 per cent (Corner, 2006). To summarise, up to about a third of badgers may be infected, up to about a tenth infectious, and up to about 1 in 20 severely infectious, but it is impossible to be certain about the first two of these categories. As regards the geographical distribution of TB in badgers, testing of road-killed animals suggests that the disease is widespread, but there are too few data to enable levels of disease prevalence to be compared in different parts of the UK or to know whether any badger populations are disease-free (Krebs *et al.*, 1997)

The Woodchester Park study has also provided valuable information about the effects of bovine TB infection on longevity. Once a healthy badger reaches the age of one year, it has a relatively constant probability, of 0.31 if it is a male or 0.24 if it is a female, of dying in any subsequent year (Wilkinson *et al.*, 2000; see Fig. 54). By comparison, that probability increases to 0.70 for males, and 0.51 for females, in super-infectious badgers: that is, advanced TB more than doubles the chance that the individual in question will die within any one year. However, since only a

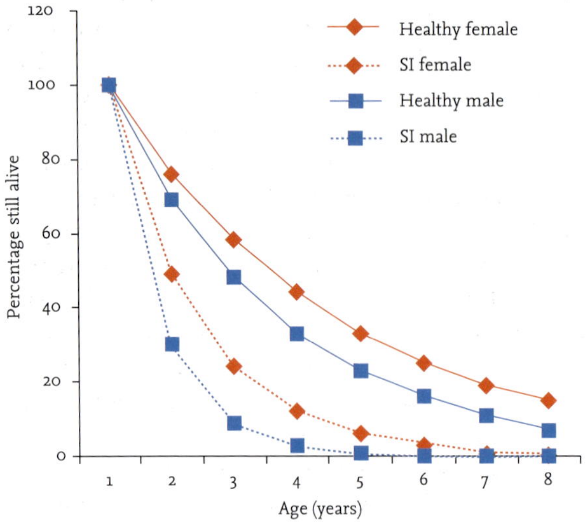

FIG 54. Percentage of badgers of each sex that survive for a given number of years, when either healthy or super-infectious (SI). (Based on data in Wilkinson *et al.*, 2000)

small minority of badgers reach super-infectious status, and since less advanced stages of the disease have little or no effect on mortality, the direct impact of TB on mortality in the population as a whole is slight (Wilkinson *et al.*, 2000). The indirect impact of the disease, on the other hand, has been much greater, because attempts to control TB in cattle have resulted in the culling of significant numbers of badgers in the UK and Ireland (see Chapter 10 for further details).

To summarise, not many badgers suffer from advanced TB but for those that do, the disease is fatal. In addition, males are more likely to become infected than females and are more susceptible to rapid disease progression (Wilkinson *et al.*, 2000). Why TB is not more prevalent in badgers, given their social lifestyle, is unclear, but it seems likely that they have evolved some degree of resistance to the disease. In addition, the fact that badgers are territorial (see Chapter 7) means that opportunities for the disease to spread from one social group to another are limited. Indeed, several studies have shown that the distribution of TB in badger populations is clustered, indicating that between-group transmission occurs at a slower rate than within-group transmission (Delahay *et al.*, 2000a; Bourne, 2007).

Ectoparasites

The main ectoparasites of badgers are fleas, lice and ticks. The most commonly reported fleas are the 'badger flea' *Paraceras melis* and the related species *P. flabellum*, both of which are rarely found on hosts other than the badger. They also have the distinction of being the largest fleas so far discovered. The two species are geographically separated, *P. melis* being associated with the European badger and *P. flabellum* with the Asian badger (Abramov & Medvedev, 2003). Japanese badgers carry a third form of *Paraceras*, the taxonomic status of which is unclear. The commonest louse is the biting louse *Trichodectes melis*, which is also specific to the badger, while the most frequent ticks are the sheep tick *Ixodes ricinus*, the dog tick *I. canisuga* and the hedgehog tick *I. hexagonus*.

In our study area in East Sussex, 88 per cent of badgers had fleas, 66 per cent lice and 75 per cent ticks, while about 38 per cent of badgers had all three types of ectoparasite and none was ectoparasite-free (Butler, unpublished). Hancox (1980) reports figures of 60 per cent, 80 per cent and 40 per cent of badgers having fleas, lice and ticks, respectively, while Emmanuel Do Linh San (2007) reports figures of 20 per cent, 58 per cent and 76 per cent for badgers in Switzerland. Thus, it seems clear that most, perhaps all, badgers carry ectoparasites of one kind or another. The parts of the body where ectoparasites are most commonly found are at the base of the ears, in the armpits and groin, and around the tail.

On the other hand, the ectoparasite burden is, in most individual cases, surprisingly small. Our study revealed that the mean number of parasites per

FIG 55. Grooming postures. (Copyright © Michael Clark. Reproduced by permission of the artist)

badger was only 3.0 for fleas, 11.9 for lice and 6.3 for ticks, while Do Linh San reports similar figures of 2.6, 17.1 and 4.8, respectively. Furthermore, these mean values were skewed by the presence in the sample of a few individuals that had exceptionally high parasite burdens.

As already noted, badgers that are severely debilitated by disease or starvation can be literally crawling with ectoparasites (see also Neal & Cheeseman, 1996). Healthy animals, therefore, must have some way of defending themselves from infestation. As we shall see in Chapter 3, badgers regularly switch from one nest chamber to another within a sett and also sometimes bring nest material out of the sett in order to 'air' it, both of which activities probably reduce the accumulation of ectoparasites (especially fleas) within the confines of the sett. However, the badger's main defence against ectoparasites is undoubtedly grooming (Fig. 55). As anyone who has watched badgers knows, prolonged grooming sessions are common, usually shortly after emergence from the sett but also at other times. For example, a badger will often suddenly sit down in the middle of a bout of foraging and start to scratch itself.

As well as grooming themselves (self-grooming), badgers also groom one another (allo-grooming). Stewart & Macdonald (2003) have shown that these two types of grooming occur equally often and last for about the same length of time (a few seconds on average, though bouts of up to 40 minutes have been recorded). Self-grooming tends to focus on the chest, belly and tail, while allo-grooming tends to focus on the back – which makes sense, because this is a part of the body that an individual cannot reach for itself. Self-grooming consists of vigorous scratching with the claws and occasional nibbling with the incisors, while allo-grooming consists mainly of incisor nibbling. It has not been shown in the case of badgers that grooming actually results in the removal of ectoparasites. However, convincing evidence of this is available from other species and it is implausible to imagine that badgers would spend so much time grooming to no purpose.

CONCLUSIONS

In some respects, the general biology of badgers resembles that of other mammals. For example, a nocturnal activity pattern, which in turn requires reliance on smell and hearing rather than vision, is a common mammalian trait. Nor is it unusual for mammals to adopt a burrowing lifestyle and to exhibit traits associated with this, such as small eyes and ears, and muscular forelimbs. In other respects, however, and especially by comparison with carnivores in general and the other mustelids in particular, badgers are unusual. For example, they are relatively large by mustelid standards, have a relatively low metabolic rate, become inactive during winter and have a less obviously 'carnivorous' dentition. At the risk of anthropomorphism, they seem rather heavy, sluggish and slow-witted animals by comparison with their nimble relatives the stoats, weasels, martens and otters. How should we best interpret these characteristics?

As a (very) broad generalisation, animals can survive either by being quick and agile or by being robust. This is a bit like the distinction, in human warfare, between a sniper and a tank: the former relies on the ability to strike rapidly and move on, the latter on brute strength and massive firepower. By analogy, the 'quick and agile' versus 'robust' distinction is relevant to animals in a number of different survival contexts. For example, in the context of acquiring food, active predators of live prey need to be able to run fast, whereas gleaners of slow-moving or immobile prey do not. This has consequences in the context of avoiding predation, because animals that have to run fast in order to catch prey can also run fast to avoid their own enemies, whereas those that are slow-moving must rely on muscular bulk and weaponry to protect themselves. In the context of metabolism and activity patterns, the capacity for rapid movement and agility requires a high metabolic rate and prevents the storage of large amounts of body fat, which would impede mobility. Therefore, 'quick and agile' species must remain active year-round, whereas a more sluggish species can lay down enough fat to see itself through the winter, hole itself up somewhere safe and warm, and reduce its metabolic rate in order to conserve energy. According to this line of argument, we can interpret various aspects of an animal's lifestyle – diet, defence against predators, metabolic rate and overwintering strategy – as fitting together to constitute what one might call a coherent 'survival strategy'.

This line of argument can perhaps make sense of some of the unusual aspects of the badger's morphology and physiology. Badgers are relatively large and slow-moving by comparison with their closest taxonomic relatives; their primary means of self-defence is to stand and fight, for which they have evolved muscular strength, their legendarily strong bite and, perhaps, their iconic face mask; they have a relatively low metabolic rate; and they overwinter by retreating into the fastnesses of their burrows, where they are protected from cold and predators and where they remain inactive, lowering their body temperature and living off energy reserves built up during the previous autumn. In short, if the distinction between 'quick and agile' versus 'robust' has any validity, then many of the badger's unusual anatomical and physiological attributes can be explained by placing the species firmly into the 'robust' category.

CHAPTER 3

Badger Setts

ONE OF THE MOST STRIKING characteristics of badgers is their habit of constructing underground burrow systems or 'setts'. Although a burrowing habit is not in itself unusual among mammals, badgers are distinguished by the sheer size, complexity and longevity of some of their excavations, such that the biggest and oldest badger setts rank among the largest and most permanent artefacts produced by any vertebrate. In their own way, then, badger setts are as unique a feature of the species as is the black-and-white facial mask of the animal itself (Fig. 56).

Badgers spend as much as 70 per cent of their time underground and this is reflected in many aspects of their anatomy, physiology and behaviour. For example, their short muscular limbs, strong claws, small eyes and ears, streamlined body shape and low metabolic rate are all adaptations or pre-adaptations to a burrowing habit. From a behavioural point of view, the sett constitutes a safe sleeping place, a focal point for social and reproductive activities, a refuge when threatened and a defence against climatic extremes, especially of cold and wet. For its occupants, therefore, a well-established sett is an extremely valuable resource, being both essential to survival and not readily replaceable. As such, it is well worth defending.

We should not be surprised, therefore, that it is extremely difficult to evict badgers from a sett by any means short of completely destroying it; and even then, the chances are that the erstwhile occupants will re-establish themselves in the same place if allowed to do so. I was once involved in the excavation of a sett close to Brighton, where a major new bypass was under construction. After excluding badgers from the sett, removing surface vegetation and completely excavating the burrow system, we bulldozed the area flat so as to prevent the badgers from

FIG 56. Well-established main setts in (left) a Scottish woodland (Scottish Badgers) and (below left) a bracken-covered hillside in England. (M. & K. Blackman)

returning. Nevertheless, it was clear from footprints and signs of digging that the badgers had returned the next night and had tried to re-establish their home. Many householders can provide similar evidence of the tenaciousness of badgers that they have tried to evict from problem setts (see Chapter 9).

Setts are not only valuable to their current occupants; they are a traditional resource, handed down from generation to generation within the same social group. As a result, they can be continuously occupied for centuries. Ernest Neal describes a sett at Ashlyns, Hertfordshire, which was known to be extant at the end of the 18th century and was still occupied 200 years later, despite strenuous efforts to destroy it in the late 1880s (Neal & Cheeseman, 1996). Indeed, it is still occupied now. A good way of identifying ancient setts is to look on a map for locations with badger-related names, such as 'Badger Wood' or 'Brock Bank', and

FIG 57. Outlier setts in (above left) the Netherlands (Dassenwerkgroep Brabant) and (above right) northern England. (L. & P. Schofield)

visit them in person. Unless the location in question has been developed in the meantime, the chances are that you will find a badger sett. If you do, it is probably the very one that was there in the distant past when the place acquired its name and, even more remarkably, its occupants may well be descendants of the badgers that originally founded it.

TYPES OF SETT

Most badger territories contain more than one sett but the actual number varies from territory to territory and from region to region. In areas of high population density, for example in the south of England, there are usually three to six setts per territory and rarely more than ten. However, in areas of low population density, where territories can be very large, a single social group can have access to as many as 40 separate setts (Revilla *et al.*, 2001b).

Various attempts have been made to classify setts according to their size and manner of occupation. In a classic paper based on his pioneering studies of badgers in Wytham Woods, near Oxford, where badger density is high, Hans Kruuk (1978b) defined three types of sett: 'main setts', 'outliers' and 'annexes'. Main setts are multi-entrance burrows that are permanently occupied and used for breeding; outliers are setts that are only intermittently occupied and usually have only one entrance; and annex setts are close to a main sett, have an intermediate number of entrances and are occupied much of the time. To these three categories, Penny Thornton (1988) added a fourth, that of the 'subsidiary sett', which she defined as a sett that was 'not always' in use, had several entrances but (unlike an annex) was some distance away from a main sett. A typical territory in England or Ireland, in an area of moderate to high population density, will have a single main sett, one subsidiary sett and two or three outliers. About half of such territories contain in addition a single annex sett (e.g. Cresswell *et al.*, 1989; Feore & Montgomery, 1999).

All four of these categories strike a chord, in the sense that anyone experienced in surveying for badgers in an area of moderate or high badger population density will recognise setts that correspond to Kruuk's and Thornton's descriptions (Figs. 56 and 57). However, in reality there is a substantial degree of overlap between the various categories. For example, Ernest Neal and others have reported main setts with only one entrance, while my study area in Sussex contained a sett that was permanently occupied by a single female and used successfully for breeding, but that was by other criteria a subsidiary. In addition, some social groups periodically migrate, en masse, from one sett to another within the same territory, in which case the territory can be said to contain more than one main sett. There are also practical problems in applying Kruuk's and Thornton's definitions in the field, owing to the imprecision and subjectivity of some of their criteria. These and other problems relating to the classification of setts, and their implications, are considered in more detail in the Appendix.

In the face of these difficulties, some authors simply distinguish between 'main setts', on the one hand, and 'other setts', 'non-main setts' or 'secondary setts' on the other. Here, I shall stick to the four-way classification developed by Kruuk and Thornton, because it has stood the test of time and largely fits with my own experience based on visiting hundreds of setts in several different countries, and observing the behaviour of groups of badgers over prolonged periods of time. However, the reality of the situation is that, even in areas of moderate to high badger population density, setts do not fall easily into a number of discrete categories, either in terms of their size or in the way they are used.

In areas of low population density, the classification of setts becomes even more problematic and may be positively misleading. In Norway, Henrik Brøseth and his colleagues report that territories contain on average 13 setts, all of which are generally small in size (between one and six entrances). All members of a badger group share the same sett for purposes of overwintering, but this sett is not necessarily the largest in the territory, nor is it necessarily the one used for breeding. During the summer, members of a group utilise many different setts, so no sett can be classed as permanently occupied (Brøseth *et al.*, 1997). In the Doñana National Park, southern Spain, where Eloy Revilla and others have studied a unique population of badgers, the situation is even more extreme. Here, setts are again small, with an average of only 2.6 entrances, and are extremely numerous, averaging 27 per territory. No sett is inhabited year-round or used consistently for breeding (Fig. 58). In such circumstances, the distinction between main setts and other setts, let alone between outliers, annexes and subsidiaries, is no longer tenable (Revilla *et al.*, 2001b).

FIG 58. Sett in the Doñana reserve, Spain. (E. Revilla)

Problems of classification of setts also arise in areas of extremely high population density. In Wytham Woods, which probably has the densest rural population of badgers in the world, a single social group can simultaneously occupy more than one main sett and no distinction can be made between outliers, annexes and subsidiaries (Macdonald *et al.*, 2004a).

THE ECOLOGY OF SETTS

Where to find setts

Naturalists have known for centuries that the best place to look for a sett is within, but fairly close to the edge of, woodland or forest; on a moderate convex slope; and in a region where the soil is easily dug and well drained. This latter factor is especially important. For example, in Wytham Woods, setts are largely situated in a relatively narrow band of calcareous grit sand that runs, like a contour line, around the hillside (Kruuk, 1978b: see Fig. 59). Similarly, in the Chilterns, setts are significantly more likely to occur in upper chalk than in middle chalk or clay and, within the upper chalk, are significantly more likely to occur in woodland than in the open (Neal & Roper, 1991). So good are badgers at exploiting the local geology that setts are sometimes located in tiny outcrops of sandy soil within regions that would otherwise not be suitable for burrowing. Indeed, the map of Wytham Woods (Fig. 59) provides an example of this. More systematic studies have confirmed the importance of the same three variables (cover, slope and soil type) but on a larger scale (see Chapter 1).

As regards cover and slope, the ideal is a wooded hillside, but 'cover' could just mean a clump of brambles or elders, or an overgrown hedgerow. Similarly, 'slope' could mean a railway cutting, a ravine, a bank alongside a field, road or

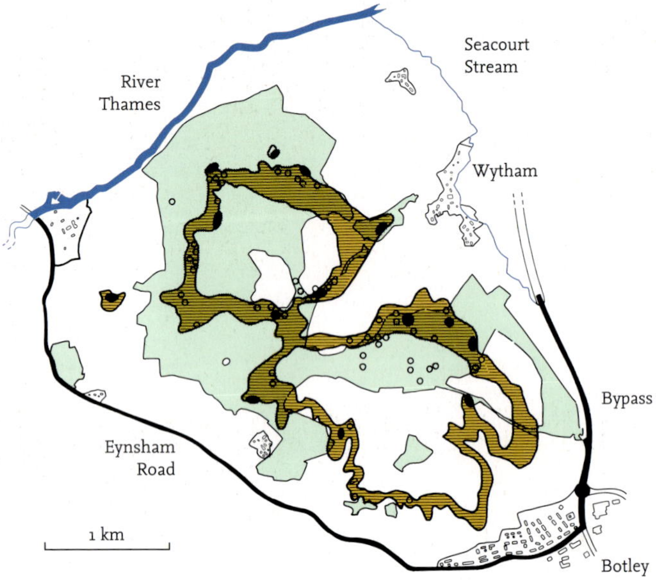

FIG 59. Map of Wytham Woods, near Oxford. Green area: woodlands. Yellow hatched area: belt of grit-sand. Filled black circles and ovals: main setts. Open circles: outliers. (From Kruuk, 1978b. Copyright © Wiley 1978. Reproduced with permission of Blackwell Publishing Ltd)

canal, or the base of a raised hedge (Fig. 60a–c). Indeed, in the Republic of Ireland, about half of all setts are built in raised hedges (Smal, 1995). Cover is generally assumed to be important because it makes the sett less conspicuous and enables its occupants to enter and leave in safety. However, it probably also offers a structural advantage, insofar as tree roots provide support for the tunnel system and assist with drainage, and a climatic advantage by shielding the sett from wind and frost. Sloping ground may be preferred for a variety of reasons: because it offers good drainage, because it is easier to remove soil from burrow entrances that are dug into a slope, or because suitable soil strata are more likely to be exposed on hillsides.

Nevertheless, preference is not the same as necessity, and badgers do dig setts in what would appear to be less than ideal conditions. In the South Downs, where cover is at a premium, setts are sometimes situated on open hillsides, enabling their white chalky spoil heaps to be seen from kilometres away. Setts can also be dug on level ground (see Fig. 60d) or, conversely, in sea cliffs that are

FIG 60. Setts in unusual places: (a–d, clockwise from top left) a river dyke; a field edge; a hedgerow; and flat land. (Dassenwerkgroep Brabant)

almost vertical. They can be found in clay soil (e.g. Cowlin, 1967; Frewin, 1976); in mountainous areas they are often located beneath rocks (e.g. Brøseth *et al.*, 1997; Virgós & Casanovas, 1999); and they can be constructed beneath man-made structures such as sheds, houses and roads.

In addition, badgers sometimes sleep above ground, especially in the summer (Fig. 61). For example, I once stumbled across a badger fast asleep, in the middle of the day, in a rudimentary nest that it had made in a field of wheat. There are also anecdotal reports of badgers breeding above ground (e.g. Hancox, 1990), sometimes in man-made structures such as sheds or haystacks but also outside, in patches of scrub. In Serra de Grândola, southern Portugal, badgers sleep above ground on about 40 per cent of days, using a wide diversity of sites within shrubs or hollow trees, beneath rocks or in man-made structures (Loureiro *et al.*, 2007). In the Białowieża Primeval Forest, Poland, they sometimes sleep in the hollow trunks of fallen trees, especially lime trees *Tilia cordata* (Kowalczyk *et al.*, 2004).

FIG 61. Temporary above-ground nests. (left) A badger asleep on the surface. (Dassenwerkgroep Brabant); (below left) Nest in the base of a hollow tree. (M. & K. Blackman)

External appearance of setts

Once you know what you are looking for, it is hard to mistake a badger sett for anything else. From a distance, the most conspicuous external feature is the presence of one or more mounds of soil, or 'spoil heaps', containing excavated earth and stones (see Figs. 56 and 60 above). Where the soil is soft and the sett has been in use for a long time, spoil heaps can contain many cubic metres of material, giving the terrain a lumpy, uneven appearance. The first time I happened on a badger sett, unaware of what it might be, I thought I had stumbled on an old battlefield or the site of a prehistoric mine, so large and ancient were the spoil heaps.

Closer inspection will reveal, adjacent to each spoil heap, a roughly funnel-shaped entrance leading downwards into the earth at an angle of about 45°. Where

FIG 62. Sett entrance with bedding material. (C. Evans)

FIG 63. Part of a well-established main sett. Note the path leading to an entrance, spoil heap and curved furrow caused by removal of excavated soil. (L. & P. Schofield)

the entrance narrows to form a tunnel, it has roughly the shape of a capital 'D' lying on its straight side: that is, the bottom (about 30 cm wide) is more or less flat while the roof (about 20 cm high) is arched (Fig. 62). Badger paths may be seen leading from one entrance to another and, in wet weather, footprints and claw marks may be visible where badgers have clambered out of an entrance. When badgers remove soil that has been excavated from within the tunnel system, they back out of the entrance, scrabbling and kicking the soil backwards until they reach the spoil heap. Sometimes, this produces a conspicuous furrow leading from the entrance to the further edge of the spoil heap (Fig. 63).

Occasionally, large quantities of bedding, consisting of dry grass or other plant material, can be seen lying on a spoil heap. This is bedding that has been

FIG 64. Scratching trees at a sett in the Netherlands. (Dassenwerkgroep Brabant)

taken out of the sett and spread around on the surface, where it is left for a day or two before being taken back underground. This 'airing' occurs most often on sunny days and presumably serves to dry the bedding out or to kill off ectoparasites by exposing them to sunlight. Bedding that has been permanently discarded can also sometimes be seen on spoil heaps, usually mixed up with excavated soil.

Some main setts have latrines close by, but others, for reasons that are unclear, do not. Some setts also have 'scratching trees' displaying vertically oriented claw marks up to a height of about 1 m (Fig. 64). These marks are caused by badgers rearing up against the tree on their hind legs, stretching up their fore legs and then scratching downwards with the fore claws, probably in order to deposit scent from glands on the feet. These scent signals could serve to identify the individual badger and to notify its ownership of the sett in question.

Finally, main setts in the summer sometimes include a 'playing area', where the vegetation is denuded by cubs and adults chasing one another about. Often, this is situated around a tree and sometimes around the scratching tree.

Associated flora and fauna

Unless they are in woodland where lack of light prevents ground cover from developing, setts in the UK are often associated with elders (*Sambucus nigra*), stinging nettles (*Urtica dioica*), thistles (*Carduus* sp.), brambles (*Rubus fruticosus*)

FIG **65.** Collecting nest material. (N. Yeo)

and various species of grasses. In Scotland and Scandinavia, raspberries *Rubus idaeus* tend to replace brambles, and hemp nettle *Galeopsis tetrahit* is common on setts in the Netherlands (Neal & Roper, 1991). In Ireland, an association has been claimed between badger setts and the stinkhorn fungus *Phallus impudicus* (Sleeman *et al.*, 1997).

The most likely explanation of this flora is that the plants in question are good at establishing themselves on disturbed ground. However, defecation and urination in the vicinity of the sett may also play a role, both by making the soil richer and, in the case of defecation, by importing seeds that then germinate (Obidzinski & Głogowski, 2005). Badgers eat soft fruits including blackberries, elderberries, raspberries and yew berries (see Chapter 4), and studies have shown that a high proportion of the seeds of these kinds of fruits survive passage through the badger gut (Pigozzi, 1992).

As already noted, badgers sometimes 'air' their bedding on the surface, which could result in seeds being scattered in the vicinity of the sett. This also applies to bedding collection. Badgers collect bedding by scraping together a bundle of suitable material, hugging it between the chest and fore-limbs, and then dragging it to the sett by means of a series of backward shuffles and jumps (Fig. 65). This method of transport, which is characteristic of badgers, sounds (and looks) cumbersome but is in practice surprisingly effective. The species of plants most likely to be spread around sett entrances by the airing or collection of bedding are grasses and cereals. For example, clumps of wheat *Tritium aestivum* can sometimes be found growing on spoil heaps in my Sussex study area, where straw is a common bedding material.

As regards fauna, the species most commonly associated with setts is the rabbit *Oryctolagus cuniculus*. Setts often originate as rabbit warrens, presumably because badgers and rabbits seek the same kind of soil in which to burrow. For example, Jaap Mulder (1996), in a study of the behaviour of badgers that were reintroduced to a northeastern part of the Netherlands, describes how some of the animals provided themselves with homes by digging out rabbit warrens. Conversely, rabbits are quick to take over a sett that falls vacant. And, despite the fact that badgers prey on them, rabbits also sometimes occupy inhabited setts, often using peripheral entrances and constructing side tunnels that are too small for a badger to enter. Wijngaarden & Peppel (1964) report the removal, by ferreting, of over 100 rabbits from a single large badger sett in the Netherlands.

Red foxes are also regular occupants of both used and disused badger setts in the UK and elsewhere (Neal & Roper, 1991). Badgers and foxes are more tolerant of one another than is sometimes assumed, and it is not unusual for a large main sett to contain breeding females of both species (Macdonald *et al.*, 2004c).

Other occasional occupants of badger setts (in most cases, disused) include the brown rat *Rattus norvegicus*, wood mouse *Apodemus sylvaticus*, bank vole *Myodes glareolus*, polecat *Putorius putorius*, pine marten *Martes martes*, feral cat *Felix silvestris catus*, wild cat *F. silvestris*, golden jackal *Canis aureus*, timber wolf *C. lupus*, Himalayan porcupine *Hystrix hodgsoni*, crested porcupine *H. cristata*, Indian porcupine *H. indica*, Egyptian mongoose *Herpestes ichneumon* and raccoon dog *Nyctereutes procyonoides* (for references, see Neal & Roper, 1991). The invertebrate fauna of badger setts has not been much investigated but is probably extensive (Hancox, 1988a; Sleeman *et al.*, 2003).

SETT ARCHITECTURE AND INTERNAL ENVIRONMENT

Architecture

Thirty years ago, little was known about what setts, especially main setts, were like underground. Badger-diggers and gamekeepers told stories about digging deep down through several 'storeys' of tunnels in order to reach their quarry, or about terriers disappearing into setts and then reappearing at entrances so far away that it was assumed they belonged to a completely different burrow (e.g. Neal, 1977). In addition, the size and number of the spoil heaps at some setts suggest prodigious underground tunnel systems. However, prior to the 1970s,

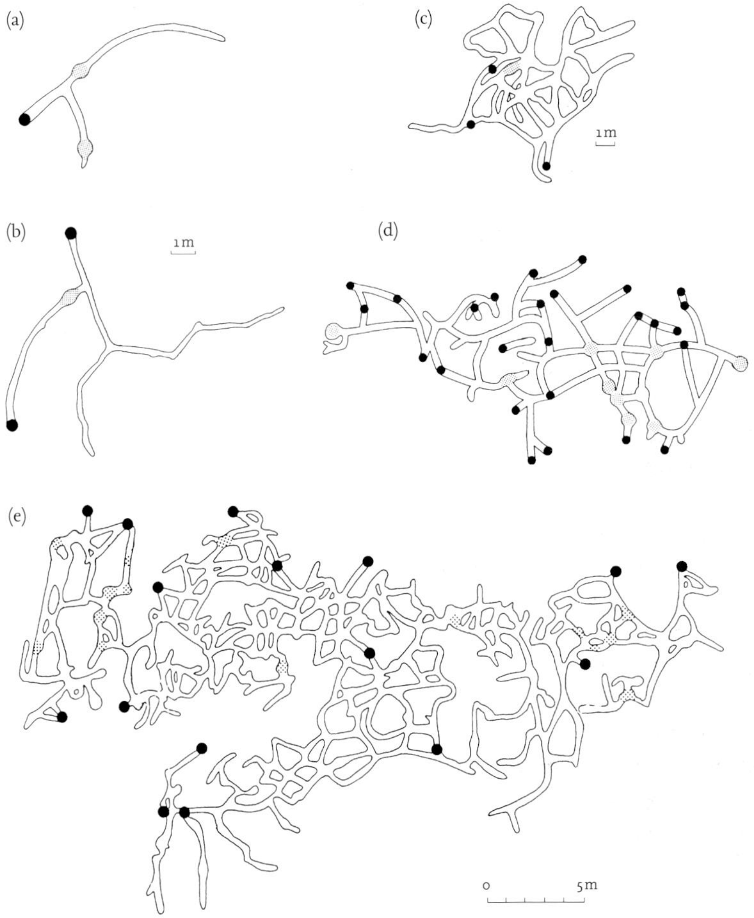

FIG 66. Five setts of different sizes and types. Setts (a) and (b) are outliers; sett (d) is a large subsidiary sett; setts (c) and (e) are main setts. Filled circles: entrances. Stippled areas: chambers containing bedding material. (From Roper, 1992)

very few main setts had been mapped in detail, and we now know that these were relatively small ones. One particular example, described in a classic study of Russian badgers by Likhachev (1956), is illustrated in Figure 66c. In addition, a few outliers had been excavated and mapped, but they proved to be no more complex or extensive than many other animal burrows (see Fig. 66a and b).

The first real indication of what badgers are capable of when it comes to burrowing was provided in 1977 by two UK government scientists, R. C. Leeson and B. M. C. Mills. At that time, the UK Ministry of Agriculture, Fisheries and Food (MAFF) was culling badgers by gassing setts with cyanide, in order to control the disease of bovine tuberculosis in cattle. When doubts were raised as to whether the gas would penetrate to the furthermost reaches of a complex burrow system, MAFF decided that more information was needed about what badger setts were like underground. Accordingly, Leeson and Mills were charged with excavating two main setts in the county of Avon. The setts in question were chosen because they appeared, externally, to be 'typical' main setts.

A seven-man team was dispatched to survey and excavate the first sett in November 1976, in the expectation that the work would be completed in two days. It quickly became apparent that the underground tunnel system was far more complex than had been expected and, at the end of day two, it was decided that another three days of work would be necessary. Additional personnel were drafted in to help with the digging at the end of day three and the operation was finally completed on day eight. The 'typical' sett proved to have contained 16 entrances, 57 chambers and a tunnel network totalling 310 m in length. In plan view, it occupied an overall area of 525 m^2 and its internal volume was calculated to be about 15 m^3, equivalent to 25 tonnes of soil.

The second sett, excavated by the same team over a period of nine days, was even larger, with 38 entrances, 78 chambers and 360 m of tunnels. It occupied an area of 740 m^2 and had an internal volume of 25 m^3 (Leeson & Mills, 1977; see Fig. 66e). Even this sett, however, was eclipsed by one partially excavated by my own research group in 1990. Extrapolating from the excavated part, we estimated that this latter sett possessed 178 entrances, about 50 chambers and 879 m of tunnels. Its total volume was calculated as 39 m^3, equivalent to 62 tonnes of soil (Roper *et al.*, 1991).

Published information about excavated setts reveals an enormous amount of variation in sett size and complexity (Roper, 1992). This is probably a consequence of three factors: the type of sett, the diggability of the soil in which it is located and its age. Main setts tend to be larger than annexes and subsidiary setts, which in turn tend to be larger than outliers. In addition, larger setts are found in more easily worked soil and, since badgers go on extending a sett for as long as it is in use, they get progressively bigger with age. Repeat surveying of the same setts over a period of time suggests that they grow at the rate of one new entrance every two years, though this probably varies according to the nature of the soil (Ostler & Roper, 1998). One point on which all agree is that the number of entrances bears no relation to the current number of occupants.

FIG 67. Part of an excavated sett showing the remains of a nest chamber with two tunnels leading into it. (T. Roper)

Despite this variation in size and complexity, all setts seem to be composed of relatively standardised architectural components. Tunnels are uniformly the shape of a squashed ellipse, being wider than they are high and with a roof that is more curved than the floor (Fig. 67). Their width varies from 25 to 35 cm and their height from 17 to 25 cm, which seems only large enough to allow the passage of a single adult; but tunnel intersections offer plenty of places where badgers can pass by one another. Often, tunnels intersect at, or turn through, more or less perfect right-angles; where three tunnels meet at the same point, they often do so at angles of 120°. This would make structural sense, because the smaller the angle between two tunnels the greater the chance that the soil in between would collapse. However, ability to construct such precise angles implies a remarkable degree of engineering skill on the part of badgers, plus the ability to orient themselves underground in conditions of complete darkness.

When, as is usual, a set is dug into a slope, the entrances tend to occur in a horizontal line across the slope. This, plus the fact that tunnels rarely penetrate more than a metre below the surface and usually run horizontally, means that the tunnel network is essentially two-dimensional. However, one large sett that my research group excavated contained two distinct tunnel 'storeys' running at depths of 50 cm and 110 cm, respectively (Roper, 1992). Badger-diggers and other 'sportsmen' have provided anecdotal accounts of setts containing as many as four different levels of tunnels extending up to 4 m below the surface (e.g. Blakeborough & Pease, 1914), but these have yet to be confirmed by more recent and systematic excavations.

Chambers are typically the shape of a squashed sphere, being roughly circular in horizontal section and wider than they are high, with an arched roof, bowl-shaped floor and smooth walls. Average dimensions are 57 cm wide by 42 cm high. This seems only large enough to accommodate a single badger, especially since a substantial part of the available volume can be occupied by nest material (see below). However, larger chambers must exist in at least some setts, since, as we shall see, radio-tracking evidence shows that two or more badgers do sometimes occupy a single chamber. The siting of chambers is rather variable: they can occur deep inside the tunnel network or within as little as a metre from an entrance; they can be situated within a few centimetres of the surface or over a metre underground; and some occur at the end of a blind tunnel, while others are situated in the middle of a tunnel or at the junction of two or more tunnels (for examples, see Fig. 66d and e).

Given that setts vary so much in size and in the manner in which they are used (see below), it is interesting to ask whether they are all constructed according to the same set of architectural principles. The answer would seem to be that they are, since the number of tunnels, chambers, nests and entrances per unit area is similar for setts of different sizes and types. In addition, tunnel systems run at approximately the same depth below ground in all setts, at least when these setts are all dug in the same type of soil (Roper, 1992). It seems, therefore, that badgers dig according to a single set of rules, irrespective of the size or type of sett that is under construction. Exactly what these rules are, however, remains to be determined.

Internal environment

Temperature and humidity

The most important single benefit of burrowing to mammals is that it provides protection against climatic extremes. In the case of badgers, this usually means protection against cold, though in some of the more southerly parts of the species' range, protection against heat may be more of a consideration. Either way, setts need to provide insulation against external temperature changes, and we can ask how effective they are in this respect.

Jude Moore, working in my research group in Sussex, recorded humidity and temperature in five main setts and seven outliers over the course of two years (Moore & Roper, 2003). Humidity, as would be expected, was 100 per cent in all

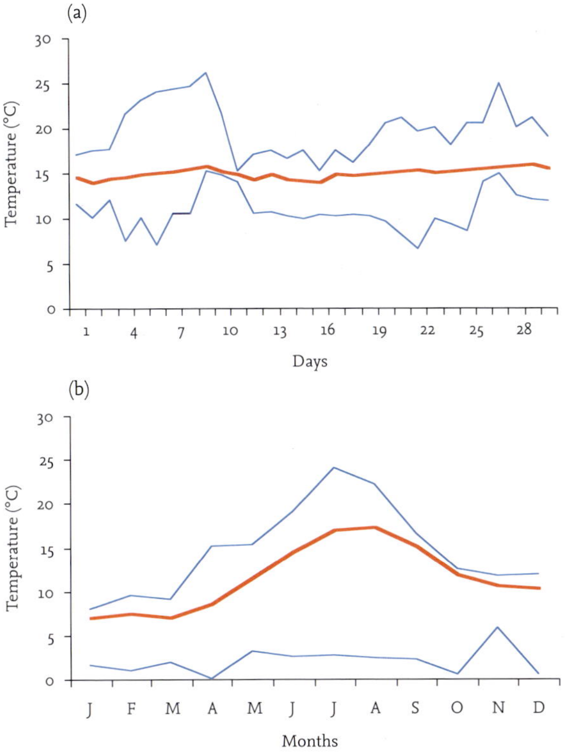

FIG 68. Temperature fluctuations within a typical main sett in southern England in (a) a single month (July 1996) and (b) a single year (1996). Red lines show the average within-sett temperature; blue lines show the maximum and minimum external air temperature. (From Moore & Roper, 2003)

setts at all times of year. Temperature was virtually constant during the course of any one day, varied by a degree or two during the course of a month and by, on average, about 11°C over the course of a year (Fig. 68). Over the same recording periods, ambient temperature varied to a considerably greater extent and, in particular, sett temperature never fell below 7°C, although external temperature occasionally dipped below 0°C. Thus, the interior of a sett is buffered against external temperature changes, but not perfectly so. Temperature within a single large sett could vary by as much as 2.5°C from place to place at any one time, depending on how deep the relevant parts of the sett were below ground.

Unfortunately, little information is available about sett microclimate in more extreme conditions. Nor is there much information about the extent to which a stable internal temperature, at any point within a sett, depends on the vertical depth of that point below ground as opposed to its horizontal distance from the nearest entrance. In a study area about 200 km south of Moscow, Likhachev (1956) found that the ground usually froze to a depth of 10–30 cm in winter and never to a depth of more than 1 m, while nest chambers typically occurred at a depth of about 1.5 m. Thus, a sett does not have to be very deep below ground to avoid freezing, even in a fairly severe climate. Working in a somewhat less climatically extreme alpine region, in southern Germany, Bock (1988a, 1988b) found that parts of a sett that were more than 7 m from an entrance had a constant internal temperature equal to the average outside temperature of 7°C. This appears to contradict our results, insofar as our recordings showed some variation in within-sett temperature during the course of a month or a year. However, the discrepancy can probably be explained by the fact that all of our recordings were within 6 m of an entrance. In short, the available evidence suggests that provided setts are sufficiently deep (both in the sense of penetrating far enough vertically below ground and far enough horizontally from the nearest entrance), they can provide their occupants with conditions of constant temperature and humidity.

Ventilation

While a burrowing lifestyle undoubtedly offers protection against climatic extremes, its main disadvantage is that carbon dioxide is likely to accumulate, and oxygen be depleted, within the confines of the burrow. Ildiko Kemenes and I found that although this does occur in occupied badger setts, the effect is relatively slight: CO_2 concentration increased from its normal ambient level of about 370 ppm to about 450 ppm within setts, while O_2 decreased from about 20.22 per cent to about 20.20 per cent (Roper & Kemenes, 1997). Thus, badgers do not encounter anything like the sort of extreme respiratory conditions that are

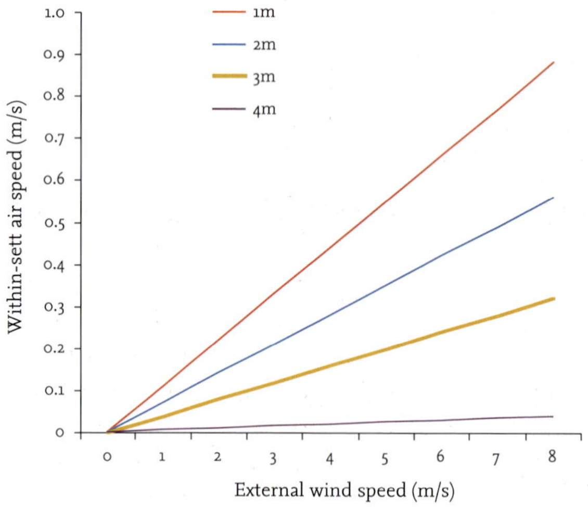

FIG **69.** Relationship between external wind speed and speed of air movements recorded within a sett at distances of 1, 2, 3 or 4 m from the nearest entrance. (Based on Roper & Moore, 2003)

endured by some burrowing mammals, such as hibernating ground squirrels (Reichman & Smith, 1990). However, the story might be different in harsher climates, where snow can block sett entrances and badgers may be confined underground for weeks or months at a time (see Chapter 2).

If the respiratory environment within a badger sett is more or less normal, setts must be well ventilated. Air currents are detectable within setts; and, since the strength of these currents varies in relation to external wind speed and direction, they presumably result from wind blowing into sett entrances. However, these currents are at best weak and they disappear altogether at distances exceeding 4 m from the nearest entrance, so it is unlikely that they contribute significantly to within-sett ventilation (Fig. 69). Some setts contain one or more small (5–10 cm diameter) openings to the surface, where badgers have apparently burrowed vertically upwards from a tunnel below (Fig. 70). These are assumed to be ventilation holes, though they could, in at least some cases, be inadvertent collapses caused, for example, by livestock walking around on the surface of the sett.

However, it seems likely that the main source of ventilation within occupied setts is the 'piston effect', whereby movements of the badgers themselves push air into and out of tunnels and entrances (Roper & Moore, 2003). No one has yet measured the strength of the piston effect, but Jude Moore and I undoubtedly experienced it on one occasion when we were recording air movements within a sett. We had inserted our recording equipment into a tunnel where there was little or no air movement when, suddenly, we heard the patter of feet underground.

FIG 70. Ventilation hole in a sett in the Netherlands. Note frost around the edge of the hole, caused by warm, moist air rising from within the sett. (Dassenwerkgroep Brabant)

A badger, presumably disturbed by us, ran through the sett, though not, as it happens, through the part of the sett in which we were recording. Nevertheless, the monitoring equipment registered a distinct jump in air speed as the draught generated by the badger passed by the sensor.

Sett contents

All but the smallest setts usually contain at least some bedding material and in some setts this is present in considerable quantities. One sett that was excavated by my research group contained many kilograms of dry grass crammed so tightly into blind-ending tunnels that it would have been impossible for a badger to make a nest in it (Roper *et al.*, 1992). Presumably, this material was being stored for future use. Typically, however, bedding material is restricted to sleeping chambers, any one of which might contain up to 15 kg of material. A large main sett can contain more than 20 such nests, but most small outliers contain only one.

Bedding usually consists of dry plant material such as hay, straw, bracken, moss and dead leaves, but sometimes badgers gather greenery such as, in the UK, bluebells (*Scylla non-scripta*) or dog's mercury (*Mercurialis perennis*) (Fig. 71). Nests recovered from excavated setts reveal that the plant material in question has often been shredded into small pieces and its condition can vary from fresh and sweet-smelling to damp and mouldy. Shredded paper has also been found in some nests. In three large setts that were excavated in East Sussex, some chambers had been lined with plastic bags and sacks, on top of which the badgers had made conventional nests of dry grass; while in another sett, a nest of

FIG 71. Large quantities of bedding (cut hay) lying on the surface close to a sett entrance. (Dassenwerkgroep Brabant)

dry grass had been built on top of a mattress of sticks (for references, see Neal & Roper, 1991; Roper, 1992). Presumably, the function of these arrangements was to provide a sort of damp-proof course beneath the nest proper.

The main purpose of bedding is no doubt to insulate a sleeping badger's body from the cold earthen floor and walls of the sett. However, there may be a bit more to it than this. There is good evidence that some species of birds that also incorporate green material into their nests choose plants that have insecticidal properties, presumably in order to combat ectoparasites (for references, see Roper, 1999). As we have seen in Chapter 2, badgers also suffer from a variety of ectoparasites, so it is possible that they sometimes use green nesting material for the same reason.

An even more remarkable suggestion has been made by Wölfel & Schneider (1988), who describe in detail how two captive badgers, kept in an artificial concrete 'sett', chopped up large quantities of straw and hay into pieces about 5–10 cm long and built them into a complex multi-layered pile. This pile then began to ferment, reaching an internal temperature of 38°C. The badgers did not sleep in or on the fermenting material but built themselves a conventional nest that they moved closer to the heat source or further away from it, depending on external conditions. Such ingenuity seems scarcely credible but was not a chance occurrence, since it was repeated on several occasions in two successive winters. Whether similar behaviour occurs in the wild is not known but, as already noted, nests do sometimes contain decomposing material, badgers do sometimes collect damp or green vegetation that could potentially ferment, and nest material recovered from excavated setts often turns out to have been shredded into small pieces.

Apart from bedding material, all of the main setts for which data are available have contained at least one latrine, usually situated in an otherwise empty chamber. Latrines have also been reported in one outlier and one subsidiary sett (Roper, 1992). However, it was clear from the quantity and age of the relevant faeces deposits that the latrines in these cases were only sporadically used and that defecation must have occurred, for the most part, outside the sett. It is likely, therefore, that defecation only occurs within a sett in special circumstances, such as when a female is lactating or when badgers are confined underground in winter.

Badgers have been observed to carry or drag large prey items, such as rabbits, pigeons, pheasants and chickens, into their setts. There have even been reports of the carcasses of a newborn calf and a small deer being found jammed into sett entrances, though the culprits in these cases could perhaps have been foxes. However, very few prey remains have been found in excavated setts, suggesting either that such behaviour is rare or that badgers clear the sett of debris when they have finished eating. Apart from one case, in which the bones of a badger cub were found in a separate disused burrow close to a subsidiary sett, no badger remains have been found in any of the setts that have been excavated. This casts doubt on the old idea that badgers bury their dead companions in disused parts of the sett (Roper, 1994b). On the other hand, badger bones do appear from time to time on spoil heaps.

One sett that we excavated contained a football and a number of tennis balls, which must have been carried in by badgers, since the sett in question was situated beneath dense cover. In general, however, the interior of an inhabited badger sett is surprisingly empty, clean and orderly. Walls and floors of tunnels and chambers are smoothed and polished by the passage of badgers, and are usually free of debris. Nest material is restricted to chambers, and faeces to dedicated latrine areas.

Remote mapping of badger setts

The main reason why we still know relatively little about the internal structure of setts is that, hitherto, the only way of mapping a sett has been to excavate it. Not only is this extremely laborious but, since setts are legally protected and no badger lover would want to destroy one without good reason, excavations can only be carried out if the sett in question has already been condemned for other reasons – for example, because it is in the way of a housing or road development, or is causing a serious nuisance. This has greatly reduced the availability of setts for mapping.

In an attempt to overcome this constraint, efforts have been made to map setts non-destructively, using archeological survey techniques developed to detect underground structures such as the remains of buildings. An early attempt to map badger setts in this way, using a relatively crude form of soil resistivity measurement, succeeded in determining the general extent of the setts in question but not in mapping individual tunnels and chambers (Butler *et al.*, 1994). Since then, other geophysical survey techniques have been developed, the most promising of which are ground-penetrating radar and electromagnetic conductivity mapping. Ground-penetrating radar works by transmitting pulses of radio energy into the ground and recording their reflections from the boundaries between one kind of material and another. Electromagnetic conductivity mapping induces currents in the soil and records the resultant secondary electromagnetic field. Both methods should be able to detect the tunnels and chambers of a badger sett, because, being filled with air, these will have different reflective and conductive properties from the surrounding soil.

Ground-penetrating radar and electromagnetic conductivity mapping have both proved capable of detecting individual tunnels and chambers and of

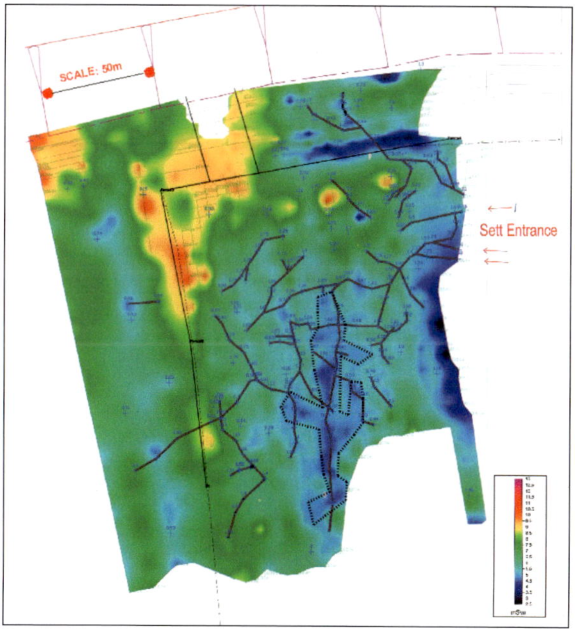

FIG 72. Map of part of a sett surveyed using ground-penetrating radar. (Atkins/Apex Geoservices Ltd)

producing what look like plausible maps of badger setts (Nichol *et al.*, 2003; O'Donoghue *et al.*, 2008: see Fig. 72). However, the question arises as to how accurate these maps are. Recently, I took part in a project intended to answer this question by surveying a sample of setts non-destructively and then excavating them in order to verify their architectural structure. (The setts in question had to be destroyed for other reasons.) We found that ground-penetrating radar and electromagnetic conductivity mapping were able to locate some tunnels and chambers quite accurately; but neither technique could provide an accurate map of parts of the sett where the tunnel network was dense or where tunnels crossed one another in the vertical dimension (Roper & Carpenter, unpublished results).

At present, therefore, it seems that careful excavation is still the best way of obtaining detailed, three-dimensional information about sett architecture. In addition, remote survey techniques are not without their drawbacks: they are costly to implement and can only be used on setts that are on relatively open, level ground, whereas, as we have seen, most setts are located beneath cover and on sloping ground. However, the technology is developing rapidly and it may not be too long before we have ways of investigating the detailed architecture of setts on a large scale, without destroying them in the process.

HOW SETTS ARE USED

As we have seen, badgers sometimes provide themselves with what seems like an inordinate amount of living space, in the form either of an extensive main sett or numerous outliers. This raises questions as to how badgers occupy the variety of homes available to them and whether the benefits of a sett increase in relation to its size.

Use of space within the main sett

Two groups of researchers have investigated how badgers use the space that is available within a single main sett: my own research group working in the chalk downland of southern England (Butler & Roper, 1996; Roper *et al.*, 2001) and Rafał Kowalczyk and his colleagues working in the Białowieża Primeval Forest in Poland (Kowalczyk *et al.*, 2004). Both projects involved trapping and radio-collaring badgers from several social groups, then recording their daytime sleeping locations – not just which sett they were sleeping in, but their precise underground location within that sett. Since the two studies produced strikingly similar results, what follows is a summary of the chief findings of both of them.

In principle, individual badgers could use a main sett in either of two ways: they could share the whole of the space or they could divide it up between them, each member of a group claiming ownership of a particular part of the sett. In fact, the underground 'home ranges' of different members of a group overlap almost completely, showing that the space within a sett is shared (Fig. 73). The Polish study shows, in addition, that males use more underground space, on average, than females.

At a slightly finer level of analysis, both studies show that the underground 'home ranges' of badgers vary in size from season to season, being largest in summer and smallest in winter (Fig. 74). In winter, all members of the group retreat into a relatively confined part of the sett, whereas in summer they occupy a wider variety of sleeping places scattered over a larger proportion of the sett interior.

At a finer level of analysis still, individual badgers move from one chamber to another every day or two. In the Polish study, for example, badgers used an average of 25 different chambers in the course of a year, spending only 2.8 consecutive days, on average, in each one. Thus, the occupancy of chambers within a sett is in a continuous state of flux, with different badgers occupying different chambers on different days. The most common situation is for badgers to sleep singly or in pairs on any one day, but up to five badgers have been found

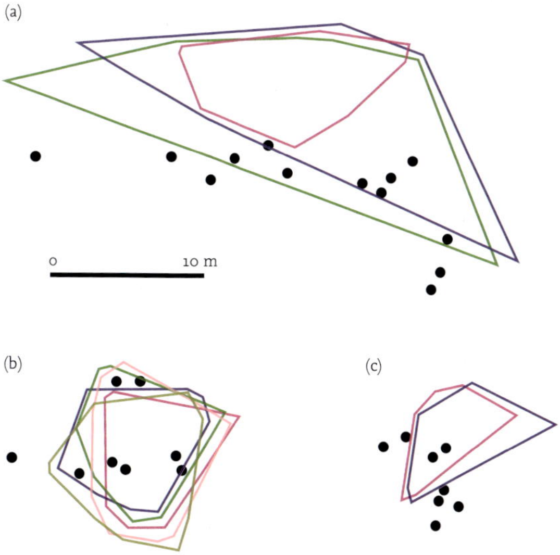

FIG 73. Underground ranges of individual badgers in three different main setts. The ranges of different individuals in any one sett overlap to a considerable extent, showing that the space within the sett is shared. Filled circles: sett entrances. (From Roper *et al.*, 2001)

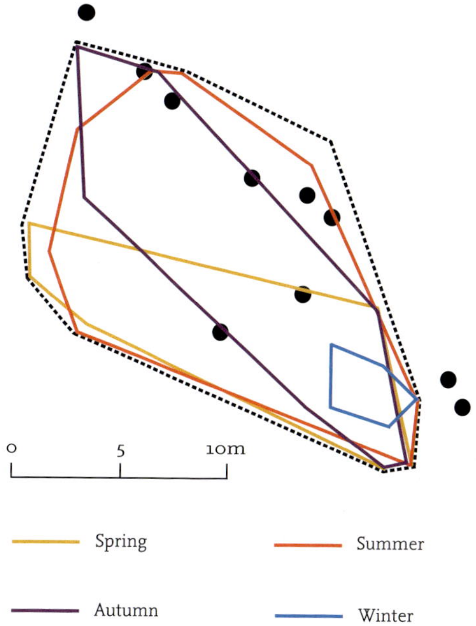

FIG 74. Seasonal changes in the use of within-sett space by badgers. The dashed black line shows the overall within-sett range. Coloured lines show, respectively, within-sett ranges in spring, summer, autumn and winter. (Based on data in Kowalczyk *et al.*, 2004)

to sleep in the same chamber simultaneously. The tendency for badgers to co-occupy a single chamber is highest in winter, presumably reflecting the advantage of huddling together to keep warm.

Clearly, then, the pattern of use of space within a main sett is complex. Before addressing the causes of this complexity, however, it is useful first to consider how badgers use the space offered by the different setts that may be available within a single territory.

Movements between different setts

Anecdotal observations by naturalists and gamekeepers suggest that while badgers remain resident in the main sett during winter, they sometimes sleep in outliers in the summer. Indeed, in the Netherlands, outliers are colloquially known as 'summer setts' (Wijngaarden & Peppel, 1964). This seasonal pattern of outlier use has been confirmed by several more recent studies, including those by my research group in the UK and Kowalczyk's group in Poland (Fig. 75). In both of the latter studies, about half of the individual badgers that were monitored turned out to use outliers or subsidiary setts as daytime sleeping places in the summer. Indeed, some of these individuals hardly used the main sett at all except in winter. The Polish study showed, in addition, that males use outliers more than females, and juveniles more than adults. In both studies, individual badgers switched frequently from one sett to another during the summer, often only spending one day at a time in any one outlier or subsidiary.

As already noted, badgers in Norway and southern Spain occupy large territories in which there are numerous small setts. In these populations, individual badgers use so many different setts, and switch from one to another

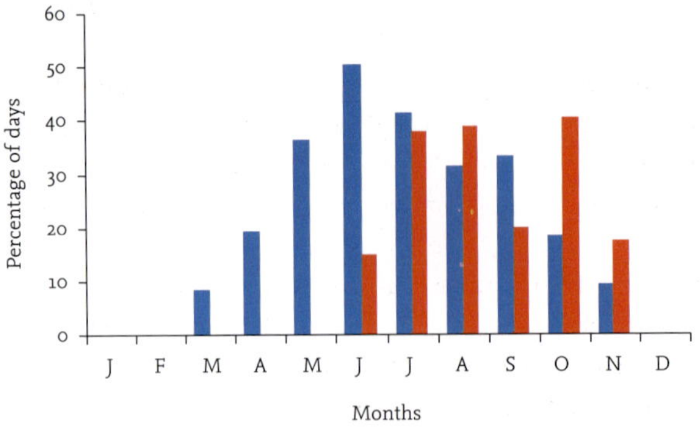

FIG 75. Percentage of days that adults (blue) and juveniles (red) spent sleeping in outliers in different months of the year. (Based on data in Kowalczyk *et al.*, 2004)

so frequently, that there is no identifiable 'main sett'. A similar situation has been reported, though on the basis of less systematic evidence, in other regions where badger population density is low, for example in northern Scotland and parts of Italy (Kruuk, 1989).

Advantages of having multiple nest sites

Three different hypotheses have been proposed to explain why badgers use multiple sleeping sites: the 'anti-parasite hypothesis', the 'social hypothesis' and the 'economic hypothesis'. The anti-parasite hypothesis, put forward by my research group, suggests that badgers move frequently from one sleeping place to another in order to prevent fleas from accumulating in their bedding (Butler & Roper, 1996; Roper *et al.*, 2001). The social hypothesis, espoused by Ernest Neal and Hans Kruuk, suggests that having access to multiple sleeping sites enables different members of a social group, who may be in competition with one another, to gain some degree of physical separation, thus avoiding within-group aggression (Roper, 1992). The 'economic' hypothesis, also suggested by Hans Kruuk, proposes that badgers sleep in outliers after foraging in distant parts of the territory, so as to avoid having to make a long trip back to the main sett (Kruuk, 1978a, 1989).

Evidence supporting the anti-parasite hypothesis is twofold. First, as we saw in Chapter 2, badgers do suffer from high ectoparasite loads, being infested especially with fleas, ticks and lice. Second, and more importantly, an experimental study by Jay Butler has shown that if ectoparasite infestation is reduced, the rate at which badgers switch from one sleeping place to another within a main sett also goes down. Using radio telemetry, she found that normal badgers spent, on average, only 2.5 days in a given nest chamber before moving to a different one, whereas badgers that had been treated with a veterinary insecticidal spray only moved every four days. In addition, there was evidence that when badgers switched from one sleeping place to another, they tended to avoid locations that had been used by other members of the social group on the previous day, as would be expected if they were trying to avoid nests that had become infested as a result of recent occupation (Butler & Roper, 1996). Finally, a later study showed that the badgers that slept in outliers most frequently in the summer were those that had the highest ectoparasite loads, suggesting that the ectoparasite hypothesis may account for the use of outlier setts as well as the use of multiple sleeping locations within a single main sett (Roper *et al.*, 2001).

Although this research undoubtedly suggests a link between ectoparasite infestation and the use of multiple sleeping sites, it is less clear how switching from one nest site to another would, in practice, help to reduce the parasite burden. Ticks and lice remain permanently attached to the host's body, so a badger cannot escape them by changing its nest site. Fleas, however, do infest nests in large numbers, as I have found to my cost when examining the contents of nests taken from excavated setts. It is therefore possible that by vacating a nest, a badger would interrupt the development of flea larvae and pupae, which is known to be temperature-dependent. However, confirmation of this idea is still needed.

As regards the social hypothesis, there is little evidence that social dominance, in the usual sense, operates within badger groups (Macdonald *et al.*, 2002; see also Chapter 7). However, it does seem that the female members of a social group are sometimes in competition with one another with respect to breeding (Kruuk, 1989; see also Chapter 5); and anecdotal evidence suggests that, sometimes, a young female is able to breed by taking up residence in a subsidiary sett or outlier, thereby avoiding interference from older competitor females. For example, in our study area in East Sussex, one young female bred for two successive years in a subsidiary sett and then moved into the main sett when an older female, which had been breeding in the main sett, died. By analogy, it seems not unlikely that a subordinate female could breed in a remote corner of an extensive main sett. Furthermore, there is a tendency for young badgers to use outliers and subsidiaries more than mature individuals, which is consistent with the social hypothesis. However, a large-scale study of badgers in Woodchester Park, by Chris Cheeseman and his associates, extending over many years, failed to find any correlation between the number of occupied setts in a territory and the number of breeding females (Rogers *et al.*, 2003). In addition, the social hypothesis cannot explain why individual badgers switch so often from one sleeping place to another. Nor can it explain why the whole of the space within a main sett is shared by the members of a social group, since, if the intention were to obtain privacy, it would surely be better for each individual to occupy and defend its own, exclusive part of the sett.

Moving on to the economic hypothesis, the most direct evidence again comes from the study by Kowalczyk *et al.* (2004) in Poland, where badgers have home ranges of up to 25 km^2 in size and can travel several kilometres a night in search of food. Here, radio-collared badgers, when they had finished foraging for the night, usually went to the nearest outlier in order to sleep, exactly as predicted by the hypothesis. The economic hypothesis can also potentially explain the seasonal pattern of outlier use, because badgers tend to range further in pursuit of food during the summer than at other times of year. On the other hand, we have observed the same seasonal pattern of outlier use in our study area in East Sussex, where outliers are so close to the main sett (often within 50 m of it) that returning to the main sett would involve essentially no extra cost in terms of energy expenditure. In addition, the economic hypothesis cannot explain why badgers switch from one sleeping site to another within a single main sett.

To summarise, we still lack a convincing explanation of the complex patterns of sett use that badgers exhibit. The anti-parasite hypothesis has experimental evidence in its favour and is the only hypothesis that can explain both why badgers switch so frequently between sleeping sites within a main sett and why they move into outliers in the summer. The economic hypothesis also has direct (albeit anecdotal) evidence in its favour but only makes sense as an explanation of outlier use when territory size is large; and it cannot explain the pattern of space use within a main sett. The social hypothesis is the least well supported of the three but may be relevant in individual cases. However, these hypotheses are not mutually exclusive and it seems likely that all have some validity. Given the obvious importance of setts to badgers, the issue of how they are used and why is ripe for further investigation and experimentation.

One large sett or many small setts?

An additional question that needs to be answered in order to explain the use of underground space by badgers is whether main setts and secondary setts fulfil the same or different functions. In other words, is a given amount of underground space equally valuable regardless of whether it is provided by a single large sett or by several smaller setts?

Several lines of evidence suggest that having one large sett or several small ones may be equivalent ways of achieving the same thing. First, there are similarities in the pattern of use of main setts and outliers. For example, both the use of different sleeping sites within a single main sett and the use of outlier setts follow the same seasonal pattern, increasing in summer and declining in winter; and the sex difference in sett use, whereby males occupy a larger number of sleeping places than females, also applies both to use of space within a main sett and to use of outliers. Second, as we have seen, main setts and outliers are apparently constructed according to the same basic architectural principles, suggesting that they do not fulfil radically different functions. Third, badgers can and do both breed and overwinter in relatively small setts, even in fairly harsh climates (e.g. Brøseth *et al.*, 1997), suggesting that there is no absolute necessity for a large main sett. Finally, if a large main sett can substitute for a plethora of outliers, or vice versa, we might expect an inverse relationship between the size of a main sett and the number of secondary setts associated with it. In fact, just such a correlation emerges when main sett size and total number of setts per social group are compared across different studies (Kowalczyk *et al.*, 2004; see Fig. 76).

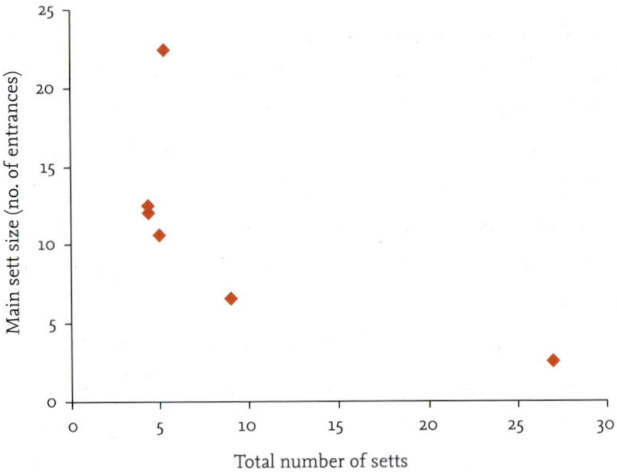

FIG 76. Relationship between main sett size and total number of setts per territory, using data from six different geographically separated studies. (For references and original data, see Kowalczyk *et al.*, 2004)

In order to provide an explanation of why some main setts are so extensive, Eloy Revilla and his colleagues have developed the idea that a large sett offers no particular advantage over a number of smaller ones (Revilla *et al.*, 2001b). They begin by pointing out that sett number and social group size are both related to territory size, such that smaller territories both have fewer setts (Fig. 77) and are home to larger social groups (see Chapter 7). Consequently, in a small territory, a relatively large number of badgers occupy a relatively small number of setts. These setts will tend to become large, Revilla and his colleagues argue, simply because they will be subjected to intensive use by many badgers over sustained periods of time. In other words, large main setts may be an epiphenomenon arising, ultimately, from small territory size and large group size. If this ingenious hypothesis is correct, then it would be a mistake to suppose that large setts offer any benefit purely by virtue of their superior size.

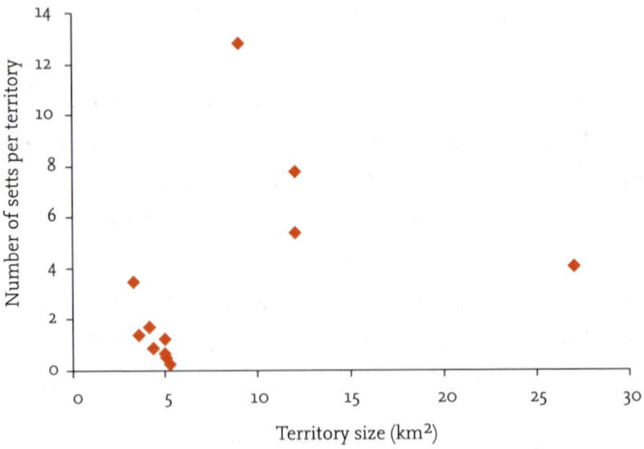

FIG 77. Data from 12 different studies showing that smaller territories tend to have fewer setts. (For references to the original studies, see Kowalczyk *et al.*, 2004)

Other uses of setts

Setts are used for various purposes other than sleeping and breeding. During the course of a nocturnal foraging expedition, badgers will sometimes rest in an outlier for anything from a few minutes to an hour or two (Kruuk, 1989; Kowalczyk *et al.*, 2004). They can also take up residence in outliers or subsidiary setts during the process of dispersing from one social group to another (Roper *et al.*, 2003; see also Chapter 5). And, because setts become impregnated with the scent of their occupants, they may provide information about the occupancy of a territory (Kowalczyk *et al.*, 2004; see also Chapter 6).

In addition, and perhaps most importantly, setts function in the context of defence against predators. Anyone who has radio-tracked badgers will have witnessed how they disappear into a sett when alarmed. However, an ingenious study by Jay Butler took this observation a stage further, by deliberately disturbing foraging badgers and recording which sett they retreated into. She found that when badgers were subjected to low-level disturbance (a human observer walking slowly towards them), they usually ran back to the main sett, even if there was an outlier nearby. With high-level disturbance (a dog running towards them), by contrast, they usually took refuge in the nearest outlier. This suggests that badgers treat the main sett as a more secure refuge but that they will make do with an outlier if threatened by a predator that could outrun them (Butler & Roper, 1994).

The anti-predator function of outliers is likely to be especially relevant in regions where territories are large, such as the Polish area studied by Kowalczyk *et al.* (2004). Indeed, since badgers are most vulnerable when they are on the surface, the reason why Polish badgers tend to retreat into the nearest outlier after a foraging expedition, rather than returning to the main sett, may have as much to do with avoiding predation risk as with saving energy.

WHO DOES THE WORK OF SETT MAINTENANCE?

As we have seen, a sett is a communal resource, available to all the members of a social group. Consequently, we might expect all group members to contribute to sett maintenance. However, a study by Paul Stewart and others, working in Wytham Woods, suggests that this is not the case. By observing individually marked badgers in two social groups, they showed that most of the work of digging and bedding collection was done by a relatively small number of older, larger individuals of both sexes. These individuals usually had breeding status within the group and tended to spend a lot of their time in the sett in question (Stewart *et al.*, 1999).

These results suggest that digging and bedding collection are performed for selfish motives: that is, the individuals who do the most work are those who stand to gain most from it. In the case of both sexes, the benefit in question presumably comes from providing a good environment in which to raise a litter of descendants. However, Stewart *et al.* also speculate that in the case of males, enlarging a sett might increase the individual's reproductive success by providing enough space for more than one female to breed.

URBAN BADGER SETTS

Most of what is known about urban badger setts comes from a recent study conducted by John Davison, Maren Huck and myself at the University of Sussex. We looked at the distribution of setts in four UK towns (Brighton, Hastings, Swindon and Yeovil) for which good data were available, and also carried out a radio-telemetric study of sett use in Brighton (Davison *et al.*, 2008a; Huck *et al.*, 2008).

As regards the distribution of setts, our study did not yield any major surprises. Urban setts, like rural setts, tended to be located on sloping ground and in places where there was some sort of cover. For example, in our Brighton study area, some setts were in odd, inaccessible corners of wasteland, such as a fenced-off area containing an electricity substation, a patch of scrub beside some allotments or an overgrown bank behind a terrace of houses (Fig. 78). Others were in relatively quiet and untended parts of parks and cemeteries, and yet others (though fewer than we

FIG 78. Urban setts (above left) in a back garden (J. Davison); and (above right) on urban wasteland. (Scottish Badgers)

had expected) in private gardens (usually plots that had been neglected for some time) or beneath buildings. Setts tended to be associated with parts of towns where the human population density was neither very high nor very low.

The Brighton badgers also largely resembled rural badgers in their pattern of sett use. Main setts were clearly distinguishable from outlier and subsidiary setts in terms of their size, and they constituted the main place of residence of entire social groups and were used for breeding and overwintering. Main setts did, however, tend to have fewer entrances in urban than in rural areas, perhaps because they were often located in confined spaces; and the number of subsidiary and outlier setts per main sett tended to be lower in urban environments, probably because suitable sett sites were harder to find. Like rural badgers, urban badgers sometimes slept in outlier setts; but they used these at a relatively constant and low level throughout the year, rather than occupying them mainly in summer as do rural badgers.

In other countries, however, the pattern of sett use may be rather different. In Trondheim, Norway, badgers have a relatively large number of setts per territory (8–10) and, except in mid-winter, move between these relatively frequently (Bevanger *et al.*, 1996). Interestingly, this mirrors the way in which rural Norwegian badgers behave (see above and Brøseth *et al.*, 1997). In the suburbs of Yamaguchi City, Japan, territories contain even more setts (20–71), which are used peripatetically throughout the year (Tanaka *et al.*, 2002). It remains to be determined to what extent these variations reflect differences in population density or in habitat factors such as the availability of food or sett sites. In the case of Japanese badgers, the use of large numbers of setts could also have a genetic basis – that is, it could be peculiar to the subspecies *Meles meles anakuma*. But whatever the explanation, it is clear that we cannot yet make safe generalisations about patterns of sett distribution and sett use in urban environments.

CONCLUSIONS

Naturalists have always been fascinated by badger setts and it is easy to see why. Ancient setts, hidden away as they usually are in the depths of woodland and occupied by animals that are rarely seen, seem almost to exhale a sense of mystery. One cannot look at the huge moss-covered spoil heaps of such a sett or peer into its entrance tunnels without wondering how it came to exist, how long it has been there and what lies beneath the surface.

In the last few decades, we have learned a considerable amount about what badger setts are like underground, about their internal environment and also about how they are used – without, I hope, dispelling any of that sense of mystery. Indeed, the sheer scale and complexity of some of the setts that have now been mapped goes way beyond what anyone had previously imagined; and the complicated way in which setts are used, involving an interlocking pattern of daily, seasonal and annual rhythms, was not only unexpected but also remains largely unexplained. Nor do we have any understanding at all of the cognitive skills that badgers must possess in order to be able to construct such elaborate interconnected structures by tunnelling blindly through an opaque medium. When it comes to biology, truth is almost always stranger than fiction, and so it is with badger setts. There is still plenty for the naturalist to wonder at and for the scientist to investigate.

CHAPTER 4

Diet and Foraging Behaviour

THE LITERATURE ON BADGER diet is so voluminous (more so by far than with any other aspect of the species' biology or behaviour) that extracting meaningful principles from it is a major challenge. The original and most straightforward generalisation about the eating habits of badgers, first suggested by Ernest Neal (1948) and subsequently espoused by many others, is that badgers are opportunistic omnivores: that is, they eat whatever happens to be available and edible in a particular locality at a particular time. According to this view, geographic and seasonal variation in badger diet (which, as we shall see, is considerable) reflects geographic and seasonal variation in what is available to eat. However, this seemingly common-sense view was dramatically challenged by Hans Kruuk in a series of papers written in the late 1970s and 1980s, in which he argued that badgers are, in fact, specialist predators of earthworms (see Kruuk, 1989, for references). Kruuk's hypothesis set in motion a debate about the basic nature of badger feeding behaviour that has still to be fully resolved.

I shall begin this chapter by saying something about the methods by which badger diet has been investigated and about the extent to which they provide an accurate indication of what badgers actually eat. I will then review, in purely descriptive terms, what might be called the natural history of badger diet and feeding behaviour: that is, the sorts of foods that badgers consume in different parts of their geographic range, and what foraging methods they use to obtain these foods. Finally, I will discuss the more abstract issue of whether badgers are best characterised as generalist or specialist feeders. I shall not attempt to list all of the different species of animals and plants that fall prey to badgers, since this would almost require a book in itself.

METHODS OF DETERMINING DIET

There are two sources of information about badger diet: namely, stomach contents and faeces. There are also two ways of presenting the data: namely, in terms of frequency of occurrence and in terms of the relative amount consumed. Before we move on to the question of what we know about badger diet, it is worth briefly describing these different approaches and discussing their relative merits. I will start with frequency of occurrence versus relative amount as measures of prey consumption.

Frequency of occurrence means that you simply score the presence or absence of a particular food type in any one stomach or faecal sample, and then calculate the overall percentage of stomachs or faecal samples that contained the food type in question. So, for example, a study might report that vole remains occurred in 33 per cent of faeces samples or that snail shells were found in 15 per cent of stomachs. The calculation of relative amount consumed, by contrast, is considerably more complex, because it involves estimating the relative quantity (either volume or weight) of a particular food type that was eaten by the animal in the first place, before calculating a mean value across all the samples analysed. So, for example, a study of this type might report that voles constituted 7 per cent by volume, or snails 3 per cent by weight, of the total quantity of food ingested by badgers in a particular region over a specified period of time.

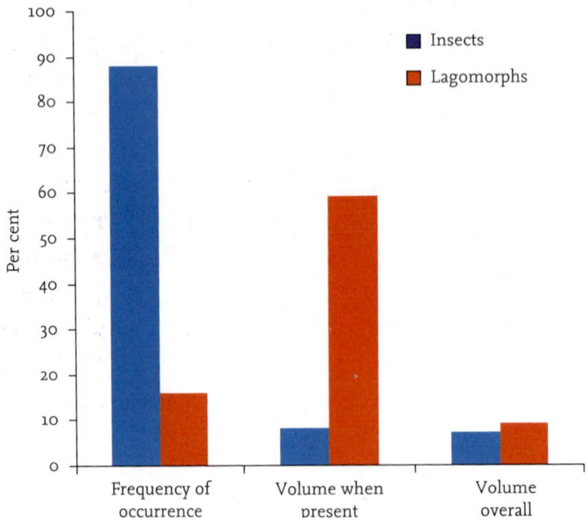

FIG 79. Independence of different measures of food intake. Insects are consumed relatively frequently but only in small amounts; lagomorphs are eaten only rarely but, when eaten, are consumed in large amounts. The net result is that, overall, similar quantities of insects and lagomorphs are eaten. (Based on data in Kruuk & Parish, 1981)

From the animal's point of view, the value of a particular food type is obviously more dependent on the total amount eaten than on the frequency with which it is eaten: and these two measures of diet do not necessarily correlate with one another. For example, in a study of badger diet in Scotland, Hans Kruuk found that almost 90 per cent of faeces samples contained insects – that is, the frequency of occurrence of insects was very high. However, the actual quantities of insects eaten at any one time were never very great, so that the relative volume consumed was, on average, rather low (only about 7 per cent: see Fig. 79). Conversely, although lagomorphs (rabbits and hares) were only eaten infrequently (they occurred in only about 15 per cent of faeces samples), when they were consumed, it was in relatively large amounts. Consequently, they contributed if anything slightly more to the overall diet than did insects (about 9 per cent of the total volume of food consumed). These examples illustrate a general shortcoming of frequency of occurrence as a measure of diet: namely, that it tends to overestimate the importance of small prey and underestimate that of large prey. Studies that report solely the frequency of occurrence of different foods are therefore only useful for compiling a list of the kinds of food that badgers eat; they cannot tell us about the relative importance of these different foods from the consumer's point of view. I shall therefore concentrate in this chapter on studies that provide information about the relative amount of different foods in the diet. Of the more than 200 studies of badger diet of which I am aware, only 39 provide this kind of information and they are listed below in Table 4.

What about the relative merits of stomach contents versus faeces samples as a source of information about diet? In principle, stomach contents are both easier to analyse than faeces and provide a more accurate picture of diet, simply because the material in question has been less subject to the processes of digestion (Fig. 80).

FIG 80. Earthworms recovered from a badger's stomach. (M. Clark)

FIG 81. Typical appearance of faeces from a badger that has been feeding on worms. (L. & P. Schofield)

Consequently, provided the badger in question was recently killed, the contents of the stomach are usually sufficiently intact to enable individual food items to be identified with the naked eye and for their volumes or weights to be measured directly. From a practical point of view, however, analysis of stomach contents has the obvious disadvantage that badger stomachs are hard to obtain. Consequently, studies of diet based on adequate numbers of stomachs are few and far between, and are restricted to countries where badgers are hunted or to occasions when large numbers have been culled for disease-control purposes.

Studies of diet based on analysis of faeces are far more numerous because faeces samples are so much easier to obtain. However, they are significantly less trustworthy. More often than not, badger faeces consist of a homogeneous brown sludge, and it requires a complicated process of sieving, staining and microscopic examination to determine what was originally eaten (Fig. 81). And then, when the remains of a particular food type have been identified (for example, mammals from bones or teeth, beetles from fragments of exoskeleton or fruits from their seeds), it is necessary to estimate the bulk of the corresponding original food items in order to determine their relative contribution to the diet. So, for example, faced with a Petri dish containing multiple fragments of rabbit skeleton, one has first to estimate how many individual rabbits these fragments represent, and their size (Fig. 82). From this information, one can then calculate the volume or weight of that number of intact rabbits.

Estimation of the relative volume eaten is particularly challenging in the case of soft-bodied prey such as earthworms or insect larvae, because these leave almost nothing in the way of visible remains in the faeces. In the 1970s, Hans Kruuk developed what has become the standard way of estimating the percentage volume of earthworms in the diet, which involves counting the

FIG **82.** Shoulder blades of young rabbits recovered from a sample of badger faeces collected in the Doñana reserve, Spain. The aim is to determine how many rabbits were eaten. (E. Revilla)

number of chaetae found in samples of faecal extract (chaetae are the tiny bristles, approximately 1 mm long, that occur on every segment of an earthworm, which it uses to grip the sides of its burrow). In Kruuk's method, a sample of faeces is first washed through a sieve to extract most of the solid matter, after which the filtrate is allowed to settle. Then, a sub-sample of the filtrate is drawn off with a pipette, put into a Petri dish, stained with picric acid and examined under a microscope for the presence of chaetae. Provided that the volumes of the original filtrate and of the sub-sample are known, the number of chaetae in the entire faecal mass can be calculated. This can then be divided by the average number of chaetae per earthworm (1,000 in the case of the most frequently consumed species, *Lumbricus terrestris*) and multiplied by the average weight of an earthworm (4.7 g in the case of *L. terrestris*) to obtain the total weight of earthworms ingested (Kruuk, 1978a; Kruuk & Parish, 1981).

An alternative method is to examine the filtrate for gizzard rings, which are tubes of keratinous material that encircle an earthworm's gizzard. Since each earthworm has only one gizzard ring, the number of rings is equal to the number of worms. In addition, because the size of the gizzard ring varies with the size of the worm, it is possible to measure the diameter of each ring, and then multiply this by an appropriate conversion factor, in order to estimate the weight of the original worm. However, because gizzard rings are relatively fragile and can easily get broken in the process of sieving and extraction, the method of counting chaetae is usually preferred.

Regardless of the precise method used, it is easy to see that there is considerable room for error in this sort of process. Estimating the number of prey by examining their remains in the faeces is difficult enough, while converting prey number into total volume or weight consumed depends on assumptions about the size of the prey that might well not be valid. Consequently, figures for the percentage by volume (or weight) of this or that type of food, when they are derived from the analysis of faeces samples, need to be treated as at best approximate.

Nevertheless, there are two reasons for thinking that we need not despair of reaching any sensible conclusions about badger diet. First, there are a few cases in which both stomach contents and faeces samples have been analysed from the same population of badgers. In these cases, the two techniques have produced broadly similar results, suggesting that the inaccuracies inherent in faeces analysis do not provide a hopelessly misleading picture of diet. Second, most of the studies that have used faeces analysis to estimate the percentage by volume of different food types have employed Kruuk's methodology, which means that the results of these studies can at least be directly compared with one another, even if none of them provides a completely accurate indication of the absolute intake of different kinds of food. The moral, then, is that we should probably not put too much faith in the detailed results of any one study, especially if it is based on faeces analysis. However, enough studies have been carried out, and their results have been sufficiently well validated, to enable us to make, with a fair degree of confidence, broad generalisations about the relative intake of different food categories in different geographical regions and at different times of year.

BADGER DIET IN EUROPE: AN OVERVIEW

As already noted, the literature contains 39 studies providing estimates, based on reasonable sample sizes, of the relative importance (in terms of volume or weight) of different types of food to badgers. These studies cover much of the range of the European badger, including geographical locations ranging from Norway to southern Spain, and from Portugal to Hungary and Poland (Table 4). Here, I shall suggest some broad-scale trends in the pattern of badger diet, based on an analysis of data from these studies. My own analysis largely repeats one previously conducted by Jacek Goszczyński and others (Goszczyński *et al.*, 2000) but with the addition of data published after their study.

The first conclusion from Table 4 is that, as would be expected from their taxonomic status as carnivores, badgers eat more animal material overall than plant material. On average, animal material accounts for about two-thirds of their intake. However, the variation between studies is considerable, ranging from 23 per cent to 99 per cent animal material and, correspondingly, from 77 per cent to 1 per cent plant material. Within the category of animal material,

TABLE 4. Summary of 39 studies of the diet of badgers in Europe, showing percentage occurrence of different categories of food.

LOCATION	Earthworms	Plant material	Vertebrates	Insects	Source
Denmark	56	23	37	11	Andersen (1954)
Italy (Monte Baldo)	21	63	5	15	Kruuk & de Kock (1981)
Scotland	54	25	15	6	Kruuk & Parish (1981)
France (Chizé)	43	38	16	3	Mouchès (1981)
France (Chambord)	52	7	32	9	Henry (1984b)
Italy (Maremma)	1	52	1	46	Ciampalini & Lovari (1985)
Sweden (Grimsö)	58	10	20	11	Hoogeveen (1985)
Switzerland (Bern)	25	43	5	16	Lüps *et al.* (1987)
England (Wytham)	58	31	0	6	Hofer (1988)
England (Essex)	16	49	12	23	Skinner & Skinner (1988)
France (Chambord)	41	43	13	3	Lambert (1990)
England (Sussex)	38	56	0	6	Shepherdson *et al.* (1990)
Spain (Sorbas)	0	77	12	11	Rodriguez & Delibes (1992)
Switzerland (Jura)	50	8	27	15	Weber & Aubry (1994)
Italy (Northern Luino)	0	72	5	23	Biancardi *et al.* (1995)
Spain (Doñana)	0	1	16	79	Martín *et al.* (1995)
Switzerland (Bern)	31	45	11	15	Roper & Lüps (1995)
Norway (Malvik)	65	2	32	5	Brøseth *et al.* (1997)
Spain (Doñana)	0	14	67	19	Fedriani *et al.* (1998)
Poland (Białowieża)	70	7	21	2	Goszczyński *et al.* (2000)
Poland (Rogow)	53	26	16	5	Goszczyński *et al.* (2000)
Italy (Grosseto)	1	77	0	13	Del Bove & Isotti (2001)
Denmark (Jutland)	30	23	30	16	Madsen *et al.* (2002)
Italy (Siena)	3	68	17	12	Melis *et al.* (2002)
Italy (Prealps)	12	54	12	18	Marassi & Biancardi (2002)
Spain (Doñana)	0	22	67	11	Revilla & Palomares (2002)
Spain (Doñana)	0	36	45	20	Revilla & Palomares (2002)
Spain (Biscay)	38	45	3	5	Zabala *et al.* (2002)
Italy (Lago di Piano)	13	56	12	18	Boesi & Biancardi (2002)
Italy (Piedmont)	36	19	19	3	Balastrieri *et al.* (2004)
Hungary (Boronko)	17	13	68	2	Lanski (2004)
Switzerland (Jura/lowland)	10	73	5	4	Fischer *et al.* (2005)
Switzerland (Jura/mid-mtn)	9	59	4	19	Fischer *et al.* (2005)
Switzerland (Jura/mtn)	11	30	17	34	Fischer *et al.* (2005)
Portugal (S. de Grândola)	0	45	10	30	Rosalino *et al.* (2005)
Spain (Madrid)	39	10	6	24	Virgos *et al.* (2004)
Spain (Madrid)	20	9	10	43	Virgos *et al.* (2004)
Spain (Madrid)	13	15	15	38	Virgos *et al.* (2004)
England (Yorkshire)	65	17	5	12	Palphramand *et al.* (2007)
MEAN	**26.9**	**34.3**	**18.2**	**16.7**	

the main categories of food eaten are earthworms (mean = 26.9 per cent), vertebrates (mean = 18.2 per cent) and insects (mean = 16.7 per cent). Again, however, the variation within each of these categories is enormous: earthworm consumption ranges from 0 to 70 per cent between different studies, vertebrates from 0 to 68 per cent and insects from 2 to 79 per cent. On the one hand, then, badger diet can be dominated by a single food type, such as earthworms in the Białowieża Primeval Forest, Poland, vertebrates in the Doñana reserve, Spain, or vegetable material in Grosseto, Italy. On the other hand, the remarkable breadth of the badger's diet is illustrated by the fact that no study records badgers eating material from fewer than three of the four most important food categories (namely, earthworms, plant material, vertebrates and insects), and most record them eating representatives of all four categories. This impression of dietary breadth becomes even more impressive when we consider that three of these four categories are themselves extremely broad: for example, the category 'insects' includes at least hundreds, and possibly thousands, of different species.

Statistical analysis of the same data shows a significant positive correlation between consumption of earthworms and latitude: that is, earthworms dominate the diet to a greater extent in more northerly populations of badgers (Fig. 83a). Conversely, latitude is significantly negatively correlated with consumption of insects (Fig. 83b), though it does not affect consumption of plant material or vertebrates. We can conclude, then, that on a broad geographical scale, badger diet is influenced directly by climatic factors affecting the availability of earthworms and insects. Consumption of plant and vertebrate material, on the other hand, is independent of any major latitudinal trend.

We can also ask whether variation in local habitat, within any one broad geographical region, has any influence on diet. To do this, I first selected, from the studies listed in Table 4, those carried out within the European temperate forest zone. This meant leaving out studies from Italy, Portugal and Spain, where the habitats are so different that meaningful comparison with more northerly regions would have been impossible (cf. Goszczyński *et al.*, 2000). I then classified the 22 European forest zone studies in terms of 3 gross habitat categories: predominately forest, predominately a mixture of forest and farmland, or predominately farmland. The results (Table 5) show that earthworms and vertebrates are eaten most in forest and least in open habitats, while the opposite is true of plant material and insects. However, this difference is statistically significant only in the case of vertebrates and vegetable matter. The take-home message, then, is that it is possible to detect some broad influences of local habitat on diet composition, but these are relatively minor and do not influence intake of the principle food, earthworms.

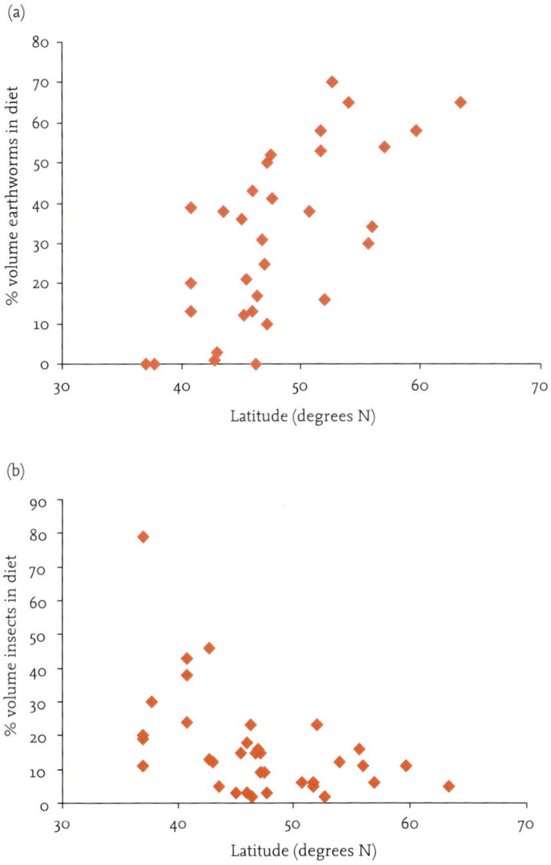

FIG 83. Correlations between latitude and (a) percentage volume of earthworms in the diet, and (b) percentage volume of insects in the diet. (Based on data from the studies listed in Table 4)

TABLE 5. Habitat-related changes in badger diet within the European temperate forest zone. Data show the mean percentage volume for each food category. N = number of study sites in each habitat category.

Habitat type	Earthworms	Plant material	Vertebrates	Insects
Forest (N=5)	47.6	10.4	38	5.8
Forest/farmland mosaic (N=11)	38.6	34.3	13.5	11.8
Open farmland/pasture (N=6)	31.3	43.6	8.8	13.1

What about the diet of Asian badgers? Some years ago, Eduardas Mickevicius and I reviewed 69 studies from the former Soviet Union, but most of these only reported frequency of occurrence of different food types, not relative volumes or weights consumed (Roper & Mickevicius, 1995). Insofar as volumetric data were available, they agreed with western and central European studies in showing that, on average, about two-thirds of the diet consisted of animal material and about one-third of plant material. Within the category of animal material, the Soviet studies suggested that small mammals and insects were more important than earthworms. However, this may be because most of the Soviet studies lacked the facilities for carrying out the sort of microscopic examination that is necessary to detect earthworm remains (Goszczyński *et al.*, 2000).

Little is known about Japanese badgers, but some recent work by Yayoi Kaneko and others, on a population of badgers living in the suburbs of Tokyo, has begun to shed light on their habits. Her data suggest that earthworms are the predominant food, with insects, vertebrates, fruit and scavenged material also being consumed. So far, however, data are only available on the frequency of occurrence of these different food types, not on their relative volumes (Kaneko *et al.*, 2006).

SPECIFIC FOODS EATEN BY BADGERS

No one has compiled a list of all the species of animals and plants consumed by badgers, but if they did, it would be very long. From within the animal kingdom, badgers eat mammals, birds, reptiles, amphibians, fish, annelid worms, molluscs, insects, crustaceans and spiders. From the plant kingdom, they consume the fruits, berries, seeds, roots and tubers of a wide variety of wild plants; mature leaves of grass and other plants; various agricultural and garden crops; and even occasionally bark and wood. They also eat fungi and, in urban and suburban habitats, a wide variety of scavenged foods of human origin.

Animal foods

Earthworms

In western and central Europe, earthworms account for, on average, about a quarter of all food eaten by badgers (Table 4). Several early studies commented on the apparent importance of earthworms to badgers (see, for example, Neal, 1948), but their full significance only became apparent with the work of Hans Kruuk in the 1980s. As already noted, Kruuk developed what has become the standard laboratory procedure for estimating the percentage by volume of earthworms in the diet of badgers, based on counting the number of chaetae found in samples of faecal extract. Using this method, he showed that earthworms constituted, on average, over 50 per cent of the diet of badgers in various parts of Scotland (for references, see Kruuk, 1989). Subsequent studies have shown significant consumption of earthworms in all European countries other than Italy, Spain and Portugal, where conditions are presumably too arid for earthworms to be available on or close to the soil surface. At the other extreme, earthworms account for 65–70 per cent of all food eaten by badgers in Norway, Poland and the north of England (see Table 4).

Very few studies identify the species of worms consumed, but it is clear that by far the most important single species is the common earthworm *Lumbricus terrestris*, also known as the night crawler or lobworm. No doubt one reason why this species is so attractive to badgers is that individuals are comparatively large (up to 20 cm long when extended and weighing up to 10 g), which means that an average-sized badger needs to consume only about 175 worms per night in order to meet its entire energy needs (Kruuk, 1978a). More importantly, however, *L. terrestris* periodically emerges onto the surface, either to feed or to mate, making it readily accessible to badgers (Fig. 84). When climatic conditions are favourable for earthworm emergence (i.e. on warm, still, humid nights), badgers can consume as much as half a kilo of *L. terrestris* in a few hours (e.g. Roper & Lüps, 1995). Much less is known about the importance of other earthworm species, but

FIG **84.** An earthworm *Lumbricus terrestris* on the surface of the ground. (E. Do Linh San)

Kruuk reports that on the west coast of Scotland, where *L. terrestris* is absent, *L. rubellus* is eaten instead. Kruuk also reports badgers turning over cow dung in order to eat what he describes as very small worms (probably *Eisenia foetida*) (Kruuk, 1989).

Insects

Insects are an important food of badgers in most areas and are eaten as adults, pupae and larvae. Judging from individual studies, the variety of insect species taken by badgers across the whole of their geographic range must be enormous, since, for example, Andersen (1954) lists insects from no fewer than 121 different genera in a single study of the diet of Danish badgers. Classes of insects eaten by badgers include beetles, wasps, locusts, grasshoppers, cicadas, ants, bees, bugs, moths, butterflies and flies.

Beetles (Coleoptera) are the most frequently reported class of insects, including in particular large dung beetles (families Geotrupidae and Scarabaeidae) and ground beetles (Carabidae). In Mediterranean countries such as Italy, Spain and Portugal, these sorts of beetles can constitute as much as two-thirds of the total amount eaten at some times of year. They can also be eaten in considerable quantities: the Spanish naturalist Félix Rodriguez de la Fuente mentions a badger stomach containing the remains of 600 beetles. The larvae of these beetles live in the soil and are obtained by digging (Pigozzi, 1989), while adults are gleaned off the surface or acquired by turning over the droppings of cattle, horses and other ungulates.

FIG 85. Remains of a wasp nest dug out by a badger. (E. Do Linh San)

Badgers sometimes eat large quantities of other types of insects, such as locusts, crane flies, wasps or bees. Crane fly larvae (commonly known as 'leatherjackets') feed on the roots of grass and constitute about 10 per cent of the diet of badgers in Ireland (Cleary, 2007). I have also seen badgers snapping at adult crane flies as they emerged, in great swarms, from the soil on a summer evening in Sussex. The nests of bees and wasps are dug out and consumed in their entirety, apparently without much regard for the stings of their defenders (Fig. 85). In Switzerland, single badger stomachs have been found to contain up to 400 ml of wasps (mainly *Paravespula vulgaris*: Schmid & Lüps, 1988). Rat-tailed maggots (the larvae of hoverflies, *Eristalis spp.*) can be obtained in large numbers from dung heaps, and I have watched badgers feeding on them for hours on end, night after night throughout the summer, at a slurry pit in my Sussex study area.

Other invertebrates

The molluscs most commonly eaten by badgers are slugs and snails. The sound of badgers crunching up snails is unforgettable, but I know of no study in which snails or slugs have been found to constitute a significant proportion of the diet. Badgers have also been reported to glean mussels (*Mytilus* spp.) from estuarine riverbanks. Other types of invertebrate prey, taken occasionally, include crustaceans, earwigs, millipedes and spiders.

Mammals

Larger mammals are presumably taken as carrion — for example, rabbit, deer and wild boar (*Sus scrofa*) hairs have been found in badger faeces (Fig. 86). Indeed, in some parts of eastern Europe, badgers feed mainly on wild boar carrion in spring, when the persistence of snow cover makes other food hard to find and when the carcasses of wild boar that have died in the winter are readily available. In addition, badgers are active predators of rabbits, hares, rats, mice, mole rats, hamsters, moles, voles and shrews, mostly taken as young before they leave the nest. For example, in parts of the Doñana reserve young rabbits are a staple food, accounting for up to two-thirds of the total amount eaten year-round (see Fig. 82, above).

FIG **86.** Badger approaching rabbit carrion. (L. & P. Schofield)

Badgers are also significant predators of both adult and young western hedgehogs (*Erinaceus europaeus*). When Patrick Doncaster, then a graduate student at Oxford University, radio-tracked hedgehogs on a farm in East Oxfordshire, he found that 3 individuals from his sample of 12 adult hedgehogs were eaten by badgers within two months of the start of the study. Similarly, when he introduced 30 radio-tagged hedgehogs into Wytham Woods, near Oxford, seven were eaten by badgers (Doncaster, 1992). Subsequent survey work by Doncaster and others, on both local and regional scales, has revealed consistent negative correlations between hedgehog numbers and badger numbers, suggesting that the absence of hedgehogs from rural areas in most of western and central England is a consequence of predation by badgers. Hedgehogs persist to some extent in these regions by occupying suburban habitat, but even there they are unable to survive when badger sett density in surrounding rural areas exceeds about 10 setts per km^2 (Young *et al.*, 2006).

A particular controversy surrounds the killing of lambs by badgers. Many sheep farmers are convinced that this occurs, and Hans Kruuk has published, somewhat provocatively, a photograph of a lamb supposedly killed by a badger (see Kruuk, 1989, Plate 11). However, such incidents are difficult to verify. It would not be surprising if badgers were to eat, as carrion, lambs that were already dead, but the paucity of reports of lamb remains being found in faeces or stomach contents suggests that even this behaviour is rare (see Chapter 9).

Birds

A recent review of 110 published studies of badger diet found that bird remains were present in a majority of cases but usually only at low frequencies of occurrence (about 6 per cent overall: Hounsome & Delahay, 2005). Although no fewer than 45 bird species are known to have been eaten by badgers in one place or another, most reports involve ground-nesting game birds and involve the predation of eggs or chicks rather than adults (which, if eaten, are presumably mainly taken as carrion). However, Hounsome & Delahay also report instances of predation on the nests of genuinely wild birds, including Audouin's gull (*Larus audouinii*), Mediterranean gulls (*L. melanocephalus*), avocets (*Recurvirostra avosetta*) and even kingfishers (*Alcedo atthis*). In cases like these, badger predation could be locally significant. However, a recent report by the Royal Society for the Protection of Birds concludes that badgers do not constitute a threat to any bird species at a national or international level and are not economically significant predators of game birds (Gibbons *et al.*, 2007).

Farmers sometimes accuse badgers of killing chickens and there is no doubt that this does occasionally occur (Neal & Cheeseman, 1996). Indeed, I once saw a badger trying to raid a chicken house in my own study area in East Sussex. However, such observations are comparatively rare, probably because chickens have to be securely shut up for the night in order to avoid the much more likely threat of predation by foxes.

Other vertebrates

Consumption of reptiles includes the eggs of snakes, lizards and tortoises and the adults of snakes, lizards and blindworms. In one study in Kazakhstan, badgers were found to have eaten every species of snake known to exist in the area (Roper & Mickevicius, 1995). The snakes in question were swallowed whole and, since remains of toads, rodents and lizards were found in their stomachs, they were probably captured by badgers when they had recently swallowed prey themselves and so were relatively immobile.

The most common amphibians eaten by badgers are frogs and toads, which are sometimes consumed in considerable quantities. For example, in the 1980s, common toads (*Bufo bufo*) constituted 30 per cent by weight of the food intake of badgers in the forest of Chambord, France, where an estimated average of 1,360 toads, equivalent to 56 kg in weight, was consumed per badger per year (Henry, 1984b). Similarly, amphibian remains were found in 98 per cent of faeces samples in one study conducted in Uzbekistan (Roper & Mickevicius, 1995). Fish have only occasionally been reported and are presumably taken as carrion, perhaps when streams or lakes have dried up.

Plant foods

Fruits

Fruits are the most commonly reported type of plant food and, when they do occur in the diet, are usually the most voluminous. For example, of 11 studies of badger diet that I reviewed some years ago, fruit was reported in 10 and contributed, on average, 21 per cent of the total volume of food consumed (Roper, 1994). Uncultivated fruits usually consist of berries of one kind or another: for example,

FIG 87. Fruit in the diet of badgers: (above left) badger eating a windfall plum (L. & P. Schofield); (above right) cherries from the stomach of a badger. (P. Lüps)

yew, rowan, elder, blackberries, bilberries, wild strawberries, raspberries, dewberries, cloudberries, mulberries, juniper berries, cranberries, wood berries and fruits of the strawberry tree have all been reported. Wild plums, crab apples, medlars and wild figs are also eaten, as are acorns, chestnuts, walnuts, beech mast and hazelnuts. Cultivated fruits include apples, pears, plums, cherries, figs, strawberries, raspberries, grapes and olives (Fig. 87).

When particular fruits are available, they are often eaten in large quantities – for example, plums or cherries in Switzerland (Roper & Lüps, 1995) or strawberry-tree fruits in Italy (Pigozzi, 1991). Olives are especially nutritious owing to their high oil content and in some Mediterranean regions they constitute, year-round, over 50 per cent of the diet of badgers (e.g. Kruuk & De Kock, 1981).

Cereals

The most important cereals from the badger's point of view are maize, oats, wheat, barley and rye. Anecdotal evidence suggests that of these, maize is the most preferred (Fig. 88). For example, in a study by my research group in the

FIG **88.** Consumption of maize by badgers: (above left) damage to standing maize (T. Roper); (left) maize cob eaten by a badger. (E. Do Linh San)

south of England in the late 1980s, badgers ate large amounts of wheat during the summer and autumn (Shepherdson *et al.*, 1990). However, when maize started to become a fashionable crop in the early 1990s, it rapidly became the preferred resource. Badgers will also seek out small plots of maize that have been planted for domestic use or as cover for game birds; and, in the Netherlands, maize is planted specifically as food for badgers in order to encourage an increase in the population. Studies of the amount of damage caused by badgers to different kinds of cereal crops show that wheat and oats are definitely preferred to barley, probably because the long spines that surround the ears of barley act as a deterrent (Kruuk & Parish, 1985; Roper *et al.*, 1995; see also Chapter 9).

Consumption of cereals can be considerable: for example, wheat accounted for over 50 per cent of the diet year-round in one UK study (Skinner & Skinner, 1988), while Andersen (1954) describes single badger stomachs containing as much as 500 ml of oats. This fits with observations made by members of my research group, showing that badgers can feed on standing wheat for up to four hours at a time (Roper *et al.*, 1995). I remember spending many hours during the course of that study sitting in wheat fields, watching the stars and listening to the rustle of the stalks as badgers fed nearby. Pleasant though this could be, I often found myself wishing that they would get on and do something more interesting.

Other plant foods

Rather little has been written about plant foods other than fruits and cereals, and in most studies they only account for a small percentage of total intake. An exception is Kruuk's study of the diet of badgers in Scotland, where 'pignuts' (the pea-sized tubers of *Conopodium majus*) constituted about 5 per cent of the diet overall (Fig. 89). Some studies from the former Soviet Union report the consumption of lily and tulip bulbs (Roper & Mickevicius, 1995), but badgers may well eat a wider variety of plant storage organs than these, and do so more frequently. In a less natural context, peanuts are irresistible to badgers and are commonly used as bait for trapping purposes or to lure badgers into places where they can be seen or photographed.

FIG **89.** Tubers of *Conopodium majus*, a favourite food of badgers in some parts of Scotland. (T. Roper)

Almost all studies of badger diet also report the consumption of material such as grass, leaves and fragments of dead wood, sometimes in surprisingly large amounts. In one study of badger stomach contents in Ireland, carried out by Grainne Cleary (2007), such material constituted a surprising 63 per cent of the total ingested bulk. It is generally assumed that material of this kind is consumed 'by accident' when badgers are rooting around for worms and insects, since a carnivore such as the badger could not digest material with a high cellulose or lignin content. However, Cleary suggests that such material might be deliberately ingested so as to slow the passage of food through the gut, enabling 'real' prey, such as earthworms and insects, to be digested more completely. This intriguing idea deserves further investigation.

Fungi

Fungi are reported in many studies of badger diet but only in small amounts. This is surprising, since badgers are essentially forest-dwelling animals and one would expect fungi to be readily available in this type of habitat in many parts of the species' range. Skoog (1970) suggests that the consumption of fungi has been underestimated because fungal material is too completely digested to be detectable in faeces samples. However, this argument should not apply to stomach contents, which have also been found, in most studies, to contain few or no traces of fungi. The relative absence of fungi from badger diet remains, therefore, something of a mystery.

SEASONAL AND INTER-ANNUAL VARIATION IN DIET

It is generally acknowledged that badgers eat most in the autumn, when they are laying down subcutaneous fat, and least in the winter, when they become relatively inactive. Data from studies of stomach contents confirm this, showing that average total intake varies from about 100 ml per night in winter to about 250 ml per night in autumn (Fig. 90). In parts of their range where winters are severe, causing badgers to remain underground for months at a time (see Chapter 2), winter food intake is presumably negligible.

With respect to specific foods, the categories most susceptible to seasonal variation in consumption are insects and plant material (especially fruits and cereals). This should not surprise us, because these are the types of foods that are most subject to seasonal changes in availability. A striking example is provided by a study carried out in the Maremma Natural Park, Tuscany, by Georgio Pigozzi (1991). Here, badger diet was dominated by insects from April to July and by fruits

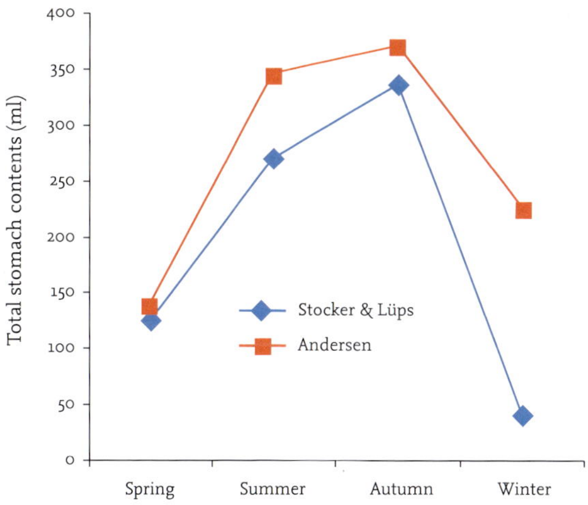

FIG 90. Total amount of food eaten by badgers at different times of year. (Based on data in Andersen, 1954, and Stocker & Lüps, 1984)

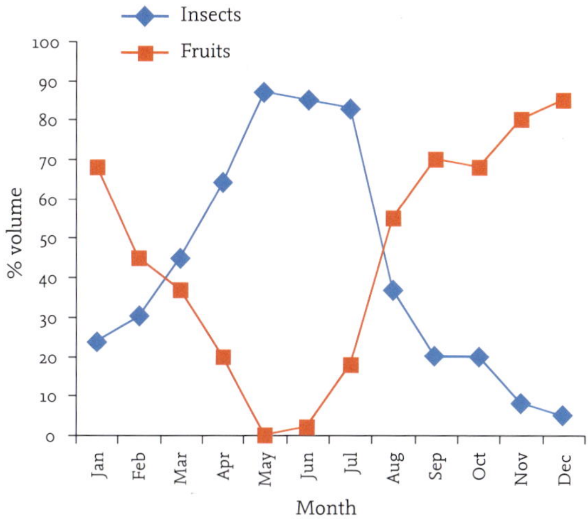

FIG 91. Seasonal changes in the consumption of insects and fruit by badgers in Maremma Natural Park, Italy. (From Pigozzi, 1991)

from September to January (see Fig. 91). Furthermore, more detailed analysis showed that these gross seasonal trends resulted from a finer-scale sequence of temporal changes in diet involving, for example, the consumption of beetle larvae in March and April, cicada larvae and lepidopteran caterpillars in May, adult beetles in June and July, blackberries in August and September, and juniper berries in October. Pigozzi did not measure the availability of any of these prey types, but the link between availability and consumption is so obvious that it hardly needs substantiating.

In a similar vein, when badgers eat cereals they do so mainly in the summer and early autumn, simply because this constitutes the growing season for these types of crop. However, badgers are sometimes sufficiently ingenious to obtain cereals all year round. In our study area in southern England, badgers not only consumed standing wheat during the summer, they also gleaned spilled grain from the fields after the crop had been harvested and raided it from cattle-feed stores or granaries throughout the winter and spring (Shepherdson *et al.*, 1990). In continental Europe, grain (usually maize) put out for game animals provides a similar year-round resource. As regards fruit, olives are unusual, in that the fallen fruit are so slow to decompose that they are available to badgers in every month of the year (Kruuk & De Kock, 1981).

In the Doñana reserve rabbits breed, and their young are eaten by badgers, year-round. In more northerly latitudes, however, consumption of mammalian and avian prey tends to coincide with the breeding season of the species in question, because it is largely young or eggs that are eaten. Consumption of amphibian prey is also highly seasonal. For example, Henry (1984b) found that toads were eaten by badgers mainly in March and September, when they congregated in large numbers after emerging from, or prior to entering, hibernation. During the late spring and early summer, by contrast, when toads dispersed into the forest and were harder for badgers to find, they figured much less prominently in the diet.

Less consideration has been given to inter-annual variation in diet, but three studies demonstrate how badgers react to medium-term changes in the availability of a major food type. In one of these, Weber & Aubry (1994) followed changes in badger diet during and after a natural peak in the abundance of water voles *Arvicola amphibius/A. scherman* in Switzerland. Over a five-year period, the population density of voles declined from about 600 to fewer than 10 individuals/ha, producing a corresponding decline in the percentage by volume of voles in the diet of badgers, from 56 per cent to 2 per cent. The badgers compensated for the lack of voles mainly by eating more earthworms, which increased from less than 1 per cent to more than 70 per cent of total intake (Fig. 92). In an earlier study, Hans Kruuk found that when earthworm availability declined in one of his Scottish study areas, badgers compensated by eating more cereals (Kruuk & Parish, 1985). Similarly, Fedriani *et al.* (1998) showed that when rabbit abundance in the Doñana reserve was reduced by an outbreak of rabbit haemorrhagic disease, a consequent reduction in consumption of rabbits was accompanied by an increase in the consumption of fruits, insects and birds.

To conclude, these studies of seasonal and inter-annual variation in diet show two things. First, they provide compelling evidence of the degree to which

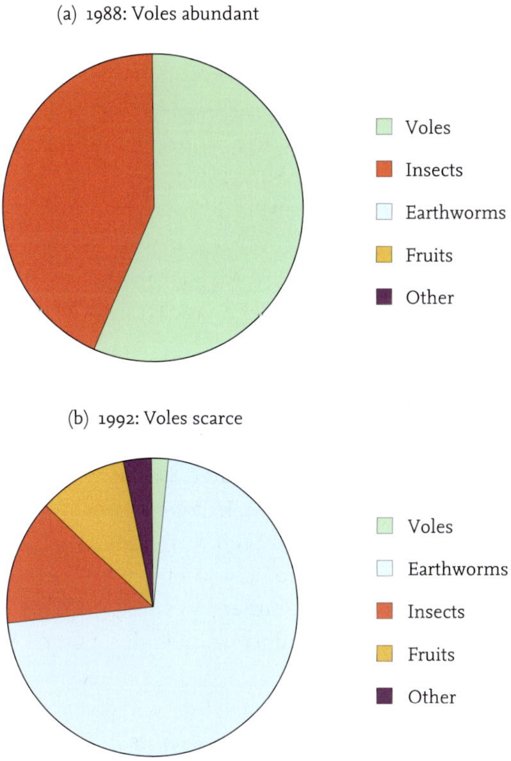

FIG 92. Consumption of different foods by badgers in years when voles were (a) abundant and (b) scarce. (Based on data in Weber & Aubry, 1994)

the consumption of individual foods is linked, both in the short and in the longer term, to changes in the availability of these foods. Second, and perhaps more importantly, they demonstrate the ability of badgers to compensate for changes in the pattern of food availability by making appropriate changes to their pattern of food intake.

FORAGING BEHAVIOUR

As the contents of their diet amply demonstrate, badgers are gleaners or harvesters of small, relatively immobile prey items, not active predators of large, fast-moving ones. Their basic foraging strategy is to meander slowly along, nose to the ground, poised to deal with whatever they find that is edible. This is not to say, however, that they forage at random or that they lack specialised tactics for dealing with particular prey types.

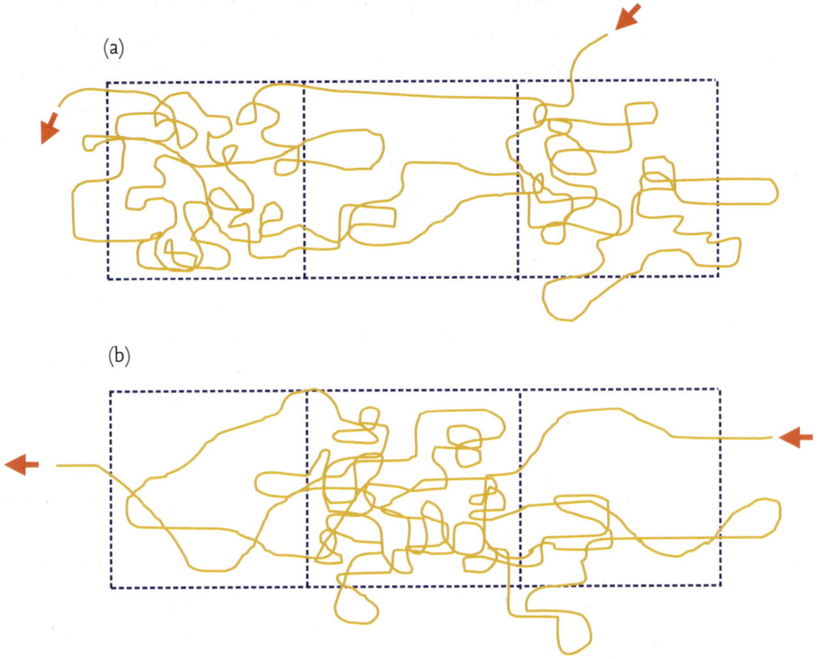

FIG 93. Movements of single badgers in three adjacent artificial food 'patches' (designated by blue lines). (a) Food was scattered over the left and right patches but the centre patch was empty. (b) Food was scattered over the centre patch but the left and right patches were empty. In each case, the badger confined its movements largely to the baited patch(es), even though it had never encountered the patches in question before. (Based on Mellgren & Roper, 1986)

There is no doubt that badgers learn what foods are likely to be found where, enabling them to return repeatedly to good foraging places. Many observers have commented on the way in which badgers, when they leave a sett in the evening, move rapidly and purposefully off, travelling more or less directly to some particular part of the territory where they then settle down to feed. This process of rapid, directional movement to a specific foraging area, followed by a prolonged period of settled feeding, can be repeated several times during the course of a night.

In some experiments devised to investigate badgers' ability to exploit profitable foraging places, Roger Mellgren and I showed that they could remember the location of an artificial food patch after encountering it only once before, on the previous night (Mellgren & Roper, 1986). We also showed that badgers could track the edge of an artificial food patch, even when the patch in question was completely novel to them. They seemed to achieve this by following two simple rules, namely: (1) if a prey item is found, continue to search intensively for other prey in the immediate vicinity; and (2) if, after travelling for some distance, no prey is encountered, double back to where prey were last found. Taken together, these two rules enable badgers to exploit the interior of a patch efficiently and to avoid wandering too far beyond its boundaries (Fig. 93).

Most prey are either gleaned directly off the surface or are dug out of the upper few centimetres of the soil. For example, David Macdonald (1980) has graphically described how badgers use both of these methods to capture earthworms. In the gleaning method, the badger paces slowly about with its nose to the ground, seeking earthworms that have emerged from their burrows onto the surface (Fig. 94). Immediately prior to capture, the badger pauses,

FIG 94. 'Worming' behaviour: (left) badger 'worming' in an apple orchard (M. Clark); (below left) the consequences of worming – a wet coat and a muddy nose. (M. & K. Blackman)

FIG 95. 'Snuffle holes' made by grubbing with the snout and (below left) also by digging with the forepaws. (Dassenwerkgroep Brabant)

moves its head slightly back and then plunges its snout into the grass so as to seize the worm with its incisors. It pulls the worm free with a pronounced upward flick of the head and swallows it down, sometimes snapping at it once or twice in the process. In the digging method, the badger paces slowly forward, nose to the ground, snuffling in the grass. It then suddenly halts, thrusts its nose into the surface and begins simultaneously grubbing with its snout and digging with both forepaws. Grubbing with the snout, with or without digging, produces various forms of what are called 'snuffle holes' (Fig. 95). If the substrate is grassland, sizeable chunks of turf can be torn up by the forepaws, leaving a ragged hole perhaps 5–10 cm deep and up to 20 cm in diameter.

A similarly untidy, but somewhat less frenetic, form of digging is used to forage for soil-dwelling insect larvae, such as leatherjackets and beetle larvae, to excavate bee and wasp nests, and to extract roots and tubers. Giorgio Pigozzi (1989) provides a detailed description of this kind of digging: the badger starts with one paw and then uses both together, while rotating its whole body around the hole that it is in the process of excavating. Digging is also required for the capture of young rabbits, which are consumed while they are still in the nest. In some parts of the Doñana reserve where young rabbits constitute more than 50 per cent of the diet, up to 60 per cent of breeding burrows can be excavated by badgers (Revilla & Palomares, 2002b).

FIG 96. Empty skin of a hedgehog that has been eaten by a badger. (Scottish Badgers)

FIG 97. Remains of a rabbit eaten by a badger. Note that the skin and caecum have been left. (M. Clark)

Toads and hedgehogs are relatively common prey of badgers but require special handling owing to their defence mechanisms: namely, poison skin glands in the case of toads and spines in the case of hedgehogs. In both cases, the badger turns the prey onto its back, holds it down with one paw, slashes open the skin of the belly and chest with the other paw, and eats out the body contents while leaving the skin intact (Fig. 96). Sometimes, hairs caught on the prickles of a hedgehog skin confirm that a badger was indeed the culprit (Doncaster, 1992). In the case of toads, Claude Henry (1984a) reports that badgers always leave the most poisonous glands, the paratoid glands, intact along with the skin. When rabbits are eaten, the caecum is often left, in addition to the skin (Fig. 97).

Most fruits are probably picked up from the ground, but badgers are more agile than they look and I have

FIG **98.** Badger climbing into an experimental cattle trough set at a height of 115 cm. The animal has just hooked its forepaw over the rim of the trough at the right-hand end and is about to haul itself into the trough. (From Garnett *et al.*, 2003)

seen one climbing up a wire fence in order to harvest blackberries. Neal & Cheeseman (1996) report badgers climbing wall-trained plum trees and they can also climb into cattle feeding troughs. In order to determine how high a cattle trough would need to be to deter badgers, one of my students, Ben Garnett, mounted a trough on telescopic steel legs and placed it by a badger sett. One badger managed to climb as high as 115 cm in order to get into the trough, which it achieved by clasping one of the legs between its paws and shinning up it, then hooking a forepaw over the edge of the trough and hauling itself up (Garnett *et al.*, 2003: Fig. 98).

Cereals such as oats, wheat and maize also grow out of a badger's reach, so the stalks need to be pulled down before the seeds can be eaten. I have seen badgers jumping off the ground in order to seize ears of wheat in their jaws, but a more usual technique is to knock the stalks down with one forelimb and then stand on them while consuming the ears (Shepherdson *et al.*, 1990). This results in a characteristic pattern of crop damage in which the stalks are trampled to the ground in a random, crisscross pattern. In the case of maize, many cobs are left partly intact and, with all of these sorts of crops, more is damaged than is actually eaten (see Fig. 88, above). However, because badgers tend to return to the same place to feed on successive nights, any one field of crops usually contains only a single damaged area (see also Chapter 9).

Direct observation is not the only way of obtaining information about the feeding strategies of badgers: we can also make deductions from the examination of stomach contents, provided that the time of death of the donor animal is known. Using this method, Peter Lüps and I found that the stomachs of Swiss badgers killed early in the night showed no bias towards any particular type of food, suggesting that badgers do not search for different food types in any particular order (Roper & Lüps, 1995). Perhaps more surprisingly, there was also no significant correlation between the diversity of the contents of each stomach and the total amount of food present (Fig. 99). Assuming that the total amount of food reflects the length of time for which an animal had been foraging, this

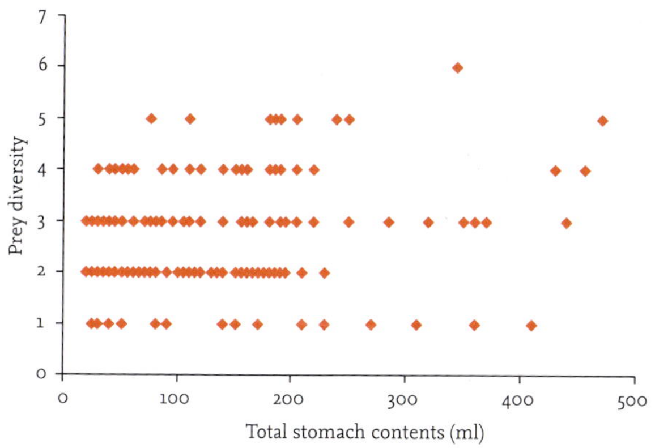

FIG 99. Relationship between total volume of stomach contents and the diversity of prey (number of main prey categories) that the stomachs in question contained. Note that fuller stomachs do not contain a greater diversity of prey. (From Roper & Lüps, 1995)

result suggests that badgers do not generally concentrate first on one type of prey, then on another, and so on throughout the night. Rather, they feed on a mixture of things right from the start of a foraging period. The same study also showed that diet did not differ between male and female badgers, or between juveniles and adults, leading us to conclude that different age and sex classes of badgers do not pursue different foraging strategies.

BADGERS: SPECIALISTS OR GENERALISTS?

It is clear from the above survey that badgers as a species, or even badgers in a single geographical location, can and do eat a wide variety of foods of both animal and plant origin. For example, one Italian study identifies over 30 different families of fruits, insects and mammals consumed by badgers, while another lists almost 100 different species of plants, arthropods, worms, molluscs, birds and mammals (Del Bove & Isotti, 2001; Biancardi *et al.*, 1995). An impressive variety of prey types is even found in single badger stomachs, showing that dietary breadth is a characteristic not just of badger populations but also of the foraging behaviour of individual badgers in any one night. For example, the literature contains descriptions of one badger stomach containing insects belonging to 35 different genera plus earthworms, toads and frogs; another containing voles, insects, earthworms and cherries; and a third containing four adult hedgehogs, four young rabbits, four young moles and the contents of a bee nest (for references, see Roper, 1994). In the face of such evidence, it seems hard to argue with Ernest Neal's statement that 'there are not many omnivorous

FIG 100. Badger sett in the Serra de Grândola, Portugal. Olives are an important food of badgers in this area. (L. Rosalino)

animals, but the badger is certainly one of them' (Neal, 1948, p. 45). Nevertheless, Hans Kruuk has persistently described badgers as dietary 'specialists', and this view continues to be defended in some quarters.

Dietary specialisation is usually defined as the exploitation of a narrow range of food types. When Kruuk first developed his 'earthworm specialist' hypothesis in the early 1980s, not many studies of badger diet had been published and those that were available (including his own) did seem to demonstrate a general preponderance of earthworms in the diet. Considering the evidence available at the time, therefore, the 'earthworm specialist' idea was not so outlandish. However, as we have seen, subsequent studies have revealed that badgers eat few or no earthworms in some parts of their range, making Kruuk's hypothesis, as a generalisation about the entire species *Meles meles*, untenable.

In the face of this difficulty, attempts have been made to rescue the 'specialist' hypothesis by claiming that although badgers as a species do not always specialise on earthworms, individual populations of badgers do often specialise on one food in particular – for example, rabbits in Doñana or olives in Portugal and Italy (Fig. 100). Hence, it has been argued, badgers can be characterised as 'regional food specialists'. Others, following the same kind of logic, have suggested that because diet is often dominated by one prey type in any one season, badgers can be characterised as 'seasonal specialists'. But even these watered-down versions of the specialist hypothesis fall foul of many other studies in which it is impossible to identify a single dominant food category, even in a single study area or a single season (Roper, 1994). An even more suspect idea is that badgers should be described as 'facultative specialists', which merely amounts to saying that they sometimes specialise and sometimes do not, depending on (unspecified) circumstances.

The problem with all of these suggestions is that badger diet is simply too complex and varied to be so easily pigeon-holed. To say that badgers *in general* concentrate on a single type of food is simply untrue, either when referring to badgers as a species, or when referring to particular populations, or when referring to the foraging of individual badgers during the course of a year, a season or even a single night. It is true that sometimes, when a particular food is super-abundant, a badger will eat that and little or nothing else. However, a propensity to capitalise on occasional windfalls does not make the animal a specialist: if it did, then all predators would be specialists. The fact is that most of the time, most badgers eat a variety of things.

However, Kruuk has also used the term 'specialisation' in a different sense, to mean the exploitation of a particular food type independent of its availability (Kruuk, 1989). The crucial piece of evidence here was his finding that in Scotland, the diet of badgers contained a relatively constant proportion (about 50 per cent by volume) of earthworms year-round, despite the fact that earthworm availability varied from season to season and from place to place. In using the term 'earthworm specialist' in this sense, Kruuk was not saying that badgers eat only earthworms, or even necessarily that they eat mainly earthworms. Rather, he was saying that earthworms are unique among the foods of badgers insofar as their consumption is not driven solely by availability. In other words, this particular variant of the 'earthworm specialist' hypothesis holds that when earthworms are in short supply, badgers exert extra effort to maintain their level of consumption of this dietary staple.

The trouble with this idea is that it makes no functional sense. In the event that earthworms are hard to find, why should a badger waste time continuing to look for them rather than switching to another type of food that is more profitable? The only reason could be that earthworms provide some kind of unique nutritional benefit, but there is no evidence that this is so. Indeed, in some places, badgers survive perfectly well without eating earthworms at all. Conversely, suppose earthworms are available in super-abundance (as, according

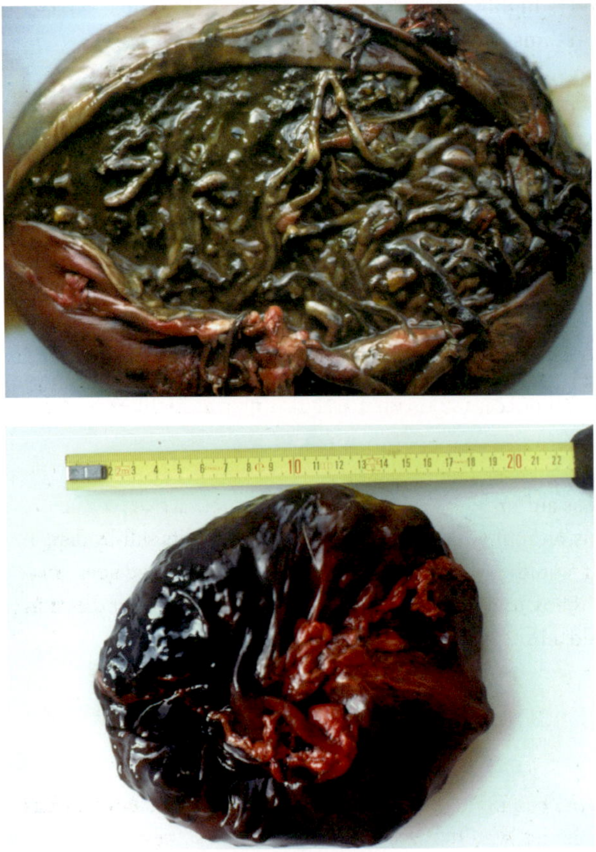

FIG 101. Badger stomachs containing large quantities of (left) earthworms and (below left) cherries – evidence that when a particular food is freely available, badgers will eat a lot of it. (P. Lüps)

to Kruuk, they quite often are). Should badgers then curtail their intake of earthworms so as not to exceed a 50 per cent proportion in their diet? On the contrary, common sense suggests that if a valuable food is readily available, the animal should exploit it to the fullest possible extent, which is why badger stomachs have sometimes been found to contain nothing but large amounts of earthworms.

This variant of the 'earthworm specialist' hypothesis can also be questioned on empirical grounds, since subsequent studies have not revealed the same absence of seasonal or inter-annual variation in earthworm intake as Kruuk reported in Scotland (see Roper, 1994, for references). In short, there is little reason to believe that earthworm consumption is not, like consumption of everything else that badgers eat, driven primarily by cost–benefit considerations.

If a particular type of food is highly profitable (i.e. readily available and nutritionally valuable), as seems to be the case for earthworms in Scotland, badgers, like any other sensible predator, will eat a lot of it (Fig. 101); but this does not make them 'food specialists' in any meaningful sense.

These criticisms of Kruuk's hypothesis are not intended to deny that earthworms occupy a somewhat special position in the diet of badgers. They do, after all, turn up more consistently and in larger amounts than any other single food type. It would be justifiable, therefore, to refer to them as a 'staple' food of badgers, so long as we remember that there are substantial parts of the species' range in which they are more or less absent from the diet. I maintain, however, that referring to badgers as dietary 'specialists' is not only confusing, because of the multiplicity of ways in which the term has been used, but also downright misleading, given the wealth of contrary evidence that is now available (see also Roper, 1994a).

Scientific ideas often linger on despite adverse evidence, especially when they have been put forward by as authoritative a figure as Hans Kruuk. However, the 'food specialist' hypothesis, as applied to badgers, is now well past its sell-by date. I doubt that Kruuk himself would ever have characterised badgers as food specialists had he had access, in the 1980s, to the wealth of information about badger diet that is available now. We should admit that he was wrong, and move on.

DRINKING

Very few observations have been made of badgers drinking and little thought has been given to the influence that water availability might have on their distribution and habits. This is perhaps surprising, since badgers occupy some very dry habitats towards the southern edge of their range.

The general view seems to be that because most of the foods that badgers eat have a high water content, they probably do not need to drink much free water. Consequently, small ephemeral sources of water, such as puddles, may be sufficient to meet their needs. This may be why a study of badgers in southern Portugal, where water is scarce, found, contrary to expectation, no correlation between the presence or absence of setts and the availability of water. Rather, sett locations were determined almost entirely by the availability of soil suitable for digging (Rosalino *et al.*, 2005b).

In my study area in the South Downs, natural sources of free water are almost non-existent, yet the area supports a high population density of badgers. In dry summers, however, the badgers get noticeably thin and can even starve, because lack of water prevents them from digesting the cereals that are their staple food. In such circumstances, I have seen them drinking from cattle troughs and even licking up droplets of dew from the grass.

CONCLUSIONS

Quantifying the diet of badgers is fraught with difficulties, especially when the analysis is based on faeces samples rather than stomach contents. However, a few generalisations can be made with a reasonable degree of confidence. Badgers generally eat more animal than plant material and, in particular, they often consume large quantities of earthworms, especially in more northern parts of their range. In more southerly regions, by contrast, the diet tends to be dominated by insects or vertebrate prey. As regards plant material, cereals and fruits are of primary importance. However, badgers feed on many different types of prey, not only overall but also within a single locality and season; and their diet is also subject to substantial amounts of regional, seasonal and inter-annual variation. Consequently, badgers are best regarded as opportunistic omnivores in which prey consumption, including the consumption of earthworms, is determined primarily by the pattern of prey availability. Very little is known about the drinking habits of badgers, but there is no evidence that availability of water limits their distribution, even in southern parts of their range.

CHAPTER 5

Reproduction and Development

THE REPRODUCTIVE BIOLOGY OF badgers is complex, puzzling and, in some respects, still poorly understood. In addition, reproductive biology is at the best of times a highly technical area involving a welter of abstruse anatomical and physiological terminology. Consequently, lay readers may find this chapter hard going, though I will do my best to explain things clearly and with a minimum of jargon. With this in mind, it will be as well to summarise the basic form of the badger's reproductive cycle before embarking on a detailed account of its various component stages (see Table 6, overleaf).

Pregnancy is strictly seasonal in badgers, beginning in mid-winter and terminating with the birth of cubs about seven weeks later (i.e. in early spring). Most mating occurs in the spring, relatively soon after cubs are born and well before they are weaned (so-called 'postpartum mating'). However, mating can continue, albeit at a lower level, throughout the rest of the year, ending only with the onset of pregnancy the following winter. This temporal dissociation between mating and pregnancy is possible owing to delayed implantation – a process in which the embryo (at this stage, a small ball of cells called the blastocyst), instead of implanting immediately into the wall of the uterus, floats freely in a kind of suspended animation. Only when the blastocyst finally implants into the uterus wall in winter, enabling the placenta to become established, does true pregnancy begin.

From implantation onwards, the sequence of events is more straightforward. Litters, as has already been noted, are born in early spring. Litter size varies from one to five, with two or three cubs being the norm. Cubs are born helpless and first emerge from the sett at about eight weeks old. Weaning starts at about 12 weeks and most individuals of both sexes become sexually mature at age 12–15 months (i.e. in the spring of their second year).

TABLE 6. Summary of the reproductive cycle, showing the month(s) in which different reproductive events are most likely to occur and the range of months during which they can occur, in badgers in the south of England.

Activity	Most likely	Possible	Year
Mating	Feb	Jan to Dec	0
Delayed implantation	Feb to Dec	Jan to Dec	0
Implantation	Dec	Nov to Jan	1
Pregnancy	Dec to Feb	Nov to Mar	1
Birth	Feb	Jan to Mar	1
First emergence	Apr	Mar to July	1
Weaning	May to June	Apr to July	1
Sexual maturity	Mar to Apr	Mar to Nov	2

As far as we know, the basic form of this cycle of reproduction and development is the same across the badger's geographical range. However, there is regional variation in the precise timing of the various stages of the cycle, such as mating, implantation, birth and age at sexual maturity, and also in such aspects as the percentage of females that breed, the percentage of litters that survive and the percentage of offspring that disperse. Where evidence of this kind of geographically based variation is available, I will give it due attention. However, the fact is that the literature on badger reproduction is very heavily biased towards studies carried out in the south of England — in particular, at Woodchester Park, Gloucestershire (Fig. 102), and Wytham Woods, near Oxford. Inevitably, therefore, most of what I shall say in this chapter refers to

FIG 102. Aerial view of Woodchester Park, Gloucestershire, scene of a long-running study of badger population biology. Setts are located mainly in the central wooded valley but badgers frequently emerge from the woodland to forage on surrounding farmland. (Food and Environment Research Agency)

reproduction in badgers from this particular region. It is also worth noting that Woodchester Park and Wytham Woods probably contain the highest-density rural populations of badgers anywhere in the world. Consequently, the literature is not only biased towards studies from a particular geographical region but also towards studies from areas where badgers are exceptionally numerous.

COURTSHIP AND MATING

Courtship and mating almost always occur at the main sett. The first sign of arousal on the part of a boar is that he raises his tail in a display called 'bottle-brushing' and starts to emit a deep, throaty, vibrant purring sound called 'churring', which continues throughout the whole process of solicitation and mating, increasing in intensity and pitch as the boar's level of excitement rises (see also Chapter 6 for further details). In addition, the boar adopts a stiff-legged, strutting kind of posture and gait. If the sow in which he is interested is still inside the sett, the boar will strut from entrance to entrance, churring constantly in what looks like an attempt to entice the sow out. He may also squat-mark on a spoil heap, dig the marked soil up with his forepaws, and then rake it into the sett entrance with his hind legs, presumably in order to send some kind of olfactory message to the sow in question. In addition, courtship is often accompanied by emission of the unmistakable musky scent of anal secretion (see also Chapter 6), sometimes to such an extent that it is still evident to the human nose several hours later.

If and when the sow emerges, mounting may occur without much further ado or it may be preceded by a lengthy period of solicitation on the part of the male and, sometimes, of coyness on the part of the female. For example, the male may scratch at the ground and both partners may engage in mutual grooming and scent-marking. If the sow is reluctant to mate, she may try to avoid the boar's attentions, in which case a chase can ensue in which the sow may or may not periodically turn and lunge at the boar in what looks like a burst of aggression.

Once both partners are ready to copulate, the act itself is straightforward: the boar mounts the sow from behind, holding her around her waist with his forelimbs and keeping her immobile by grabbing hold of the scruff of her neck, or sometimes an ear, with his teeth. However, copulation is very variable in duration. At one extreme ('short-duration' copulation), a boar can mount a sow for less than a minute, sometimes without even achieving intromission. At the other extreme, 'long-duration' copulation can last for as long as 90 minutes. Lengthy matings are most frequent between February and May and their extreme duration suggests that badgers may be induced ovulators – that is, the physical stimulus of copulation may be required in order to trigger release of eggs from the ovary (Neal & Harrison, 1958). However, this hypothesis remains, at present, unconfirmed and there are alternative possible explanations of prolonged copulation, such as that it prevents other males from copulating with the same female immediately afterwards.

Copulation is usually terminated by the sow, who may twist around so as to dislodge the boar, crawl away from him or even crawl under a fence so as to push him off. The sow then often runs back into the sett, but she may emerge later the same evening to mate again with the same or another boar. More detailed, eye-witness accounts of mating are provided by Paget & Middleton (1974) and Christian (1993).

The oestrus cycle

Field observations suggest that oestrus lasts for between four and six days, during which a sow can mate repeatedly with one or more males, including males from neighbouring social groups. Indeed, recent genetic evidence has confirmed that the cubs in a single litter can be the progeny of more than one father, a phenomenon known as 'superfecundation' (Dugdale *et al.*, 2007). However, it is less clear what triggers oestrus. When a sow comes into oestrus shortly after giving birth ('postpartum oestrus'), the cycle is presumably triggered by the hormonal events associated with birth and lactation. In sows that have not just produced a litter, however, behavioural and hormonal evidence suggests that oestrus occurs spontaneously about every 28 days, until the sow in question conceives. One study suggests that copulation is most frequent at about the time of the new moon, suggesting that the timing and duration of the oestrus cycle are regulated at least in part by the lunar cycle (Dixon *et al.*, 2006).

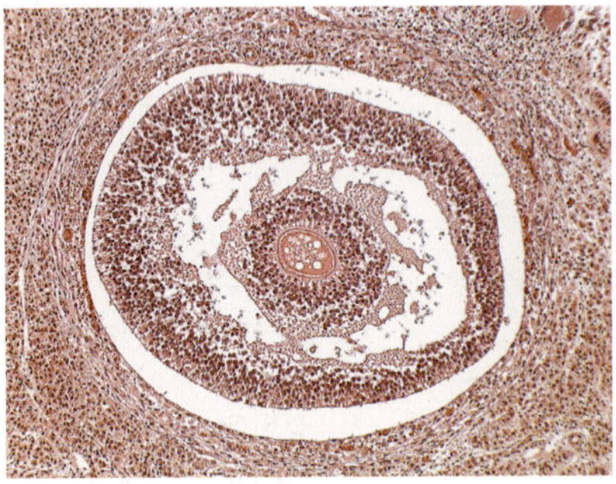

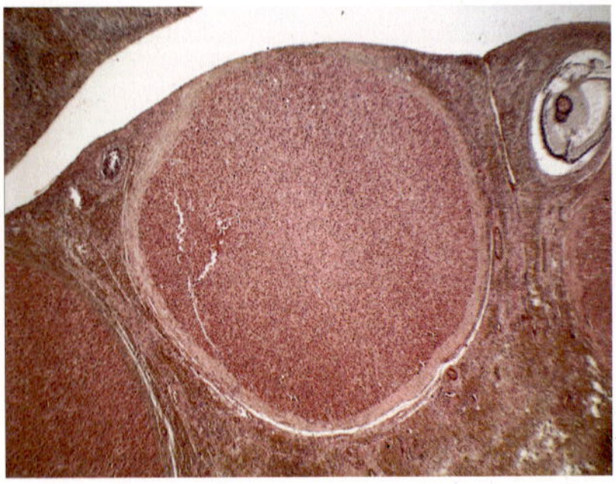

FIG 103. Pre-ovulatory follicle (above left), magnified × 100. The developing egg is seen at the centre. Follicles of this type indicate that the animal is about to ovulate. Corpus luteum (above right), magnified × 200. The presence of corpora lutea indicates pregnancy. (L. Stuart)

TABLE 7. Postmortem studies of badger reproduction, showing sample sizes and locations.

Location	male	*Sample size*	females	Reference
SW England	14		70	Neal & Harrison (1958)
SW France	0		700	Canivenc (1966)
Sweden	542		543	Ahnlund (1980)
Switzerland	0		230	Wandeler & Graf (1982)
SW England	298		352	Cresswell *et al.* (1992)
Ireland	0		548	Whelan & Hayden (1993)
SW England	822		1053	Page *et al.* (1994)

Field observations also confirm that, at least in the UK, mating can occur in any month of the year, though observers generally agree that there is a peak of mating activity in early spring. However, because of the potential bias in observational data (badger-watchers are more likely to be active in spring, say, than in the middle of winter), the best source of data on the timing of fertile periods comes from histological examination of the reproductive tracts of dead badgers (Fig. 103). Several studies of this type have been undertaken, using the carcasses of badgers killed by cars, shot by hunters or culled for reasons of pest control (Table 7).

In the case of badgers in southern England, the relevant evidence suggests that adult females can ovulate in any month of the year except December but that they do so most frequently in early spring (January to March) and late summer/early autumn (July to September) (Fig. 104). Additional histological evidence, in the form of the presence of active corpora lutea (specialised

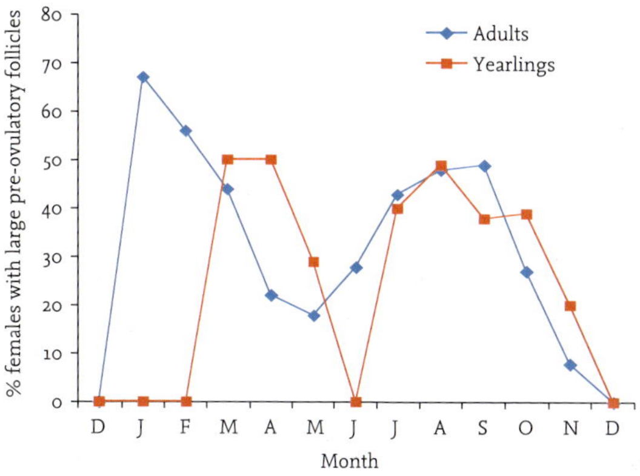

FIG 104. Seasonal changes in the percentage of adult and yearling females with large pre-ovulatory follicles, indicating incipient ovulation. (From Cresswell *et al.*, 1992)

glandular cells in the ovary), suggests that almost all adult females have ovulated by the end of April. In yearlings, however, the spring peak in ovulation (i.e. the first time these females come into oestrus) occurs about two months later, in March to April. Studies in other countries show the same general pattern, except that ovulation commences about a month later in Sweden than in the UK, and later still in some parts of the former Soviet Union (Danilov & Tumanov, 1975).

Fertility in males

As regards males, postmortem studies carried out in Scandinavia and France show that testis size reaches a maximum in February to March, coinciding with the peak mating season (Ahnlund, 1980; Maurel *et al.*, 1984). Thereafter, testis size gradually declines, reaching a minimum in November (see Fig. 105a). Blood testosterone levels are more variable but generally remain high during a longer period (February to July: see Fig. 105b); and a Swiss study reveals the presence of spermatozoa in the epididymides (tubes, connected to the testes, in which sperm are stored) throughout the year (Graf & Wandeler, 1982). This has led to the suggestion that boars probably

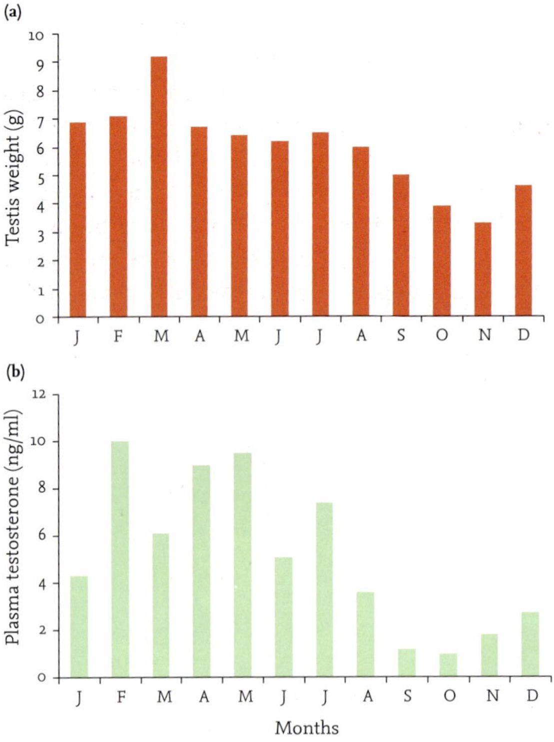

FIG 105. Seasonal changes in (a) testis weight and (b) circulating level of testosterone in male badgers. (Based on data in Maurel *et al.*, 1984)

retain some degree of year-round fertility, at least in western European populations. Very recent evidence, however, suggests that these average data on seasonal changes in testosterone levels and sperm production may mask the existence of two distinct classes of males: those that cease to be reproductively active after the spring mating season and those that maintain high testosterone levels throughout the summer (Buesching *et al.*, 2009; Stuart, 2009). In harsher climates, on the other hand, all males become infertile in winter owing to the complete cessation of sperm production (Ahnlund, 1980; Danilov & Tumanov, 1972).

Not much is known about the hormonal basis of seasonal changes in male fertility, except that these probably involve the hormones prolactin and luteinising hormone, and are ultimately controlled by changes in daylength (Maurel *et al.*, 1984).

DELAYED IMPLANTATION

Following a successful copulation, the fertilised egg starts to divide to form a hollow ball of cells called the blastocyst. In most mammals, this immediately attaches itself to the uterine wall and begins to grow, drawing its nourishment through the placenta. As we have seen, however, badgers are capable of a prolonged period of delayed implantation (sometimes called 'embryonic diapause'), in which the blastocyst remains floating freely in the uterus (Fig. 106). During this period, the blastocyst grows slowly, though it is still only about 3 mm in diameter by the end of the period of delayed implantation. Since the timing of implantation is relatively fixed, it follows that the duration of delayed implantation depends on the time at which mating occurs. If mating takes place immediately after giving birth,

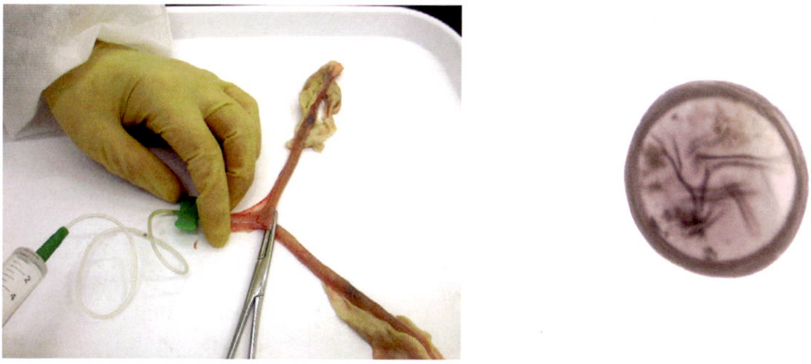

FIG 106. Flushing out the reproductive tract of a female badger (above left) in order to collect blastocysts; (above right) a blastocyst measuring about 1.6 mm in diameter. (L. Stuart)

in February, then the period of delayed implantation can be as long as ten months. Conversely, if mating occurs in December, implantation can be immediate.

Delayed implantation probably evolved fairly early on in the history of the mustelids, since it seems to be present in most members of the family. Physiologically, it is probably caused by reduced secretion of prolactin and luteinising hormone by the pituitary gland, which in turn results in low levels of the hormone progesterone (see Yamaguchi *et al.*, 2006).

Mating during delayed implantation

The fact that mating can occur throughout the summer and autumn raises the question as to when most eggs are fertilised. Data on the percentage of adult females carrying blastocysts (Fig. 107) reveal a steep rise during the early months of the year, showing that about 40 per cent of adult females have mated successfully by the end of March and 80–90 per cent by the end of April. In yearling females, the curve is similar in shape but slightly delayed, such that about 30 per cent have been successfully mated by the end of April and about 70 per cent by the end of July. The average number of blastocysts carried per female at this stage of the cycle is about three.

During the remainder of the delayed implantation period, from April to December, the percentage of adult females carrying blastocysts first declines slightly, from May to June, and then increases again from July to October. Similarly, the number of yearlings carrying blastocysts shows a temporary reduction following the June/July peak but recovers again in the autumn. These findings suggest that some females, having mated successfully in the spring, lose

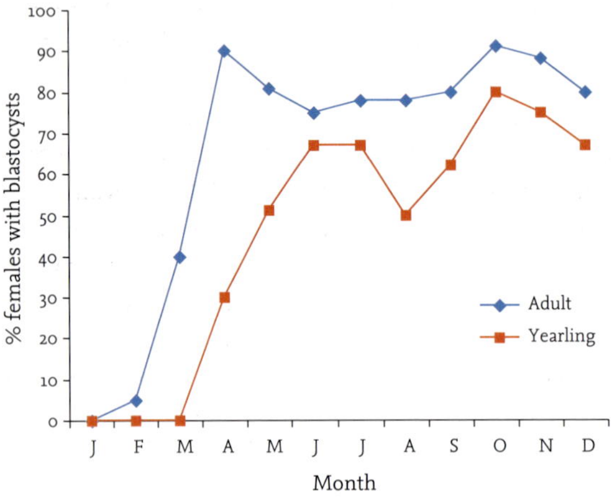

FIG 107. Seasonal change in percentage of adult and yearling females with blastocysts. (From Cresswell *et al.*, 1992)

their entire complement of blastocysts during the summer. However, they then mate again in the late summer and autumn, bringing the number of pregnant females back up to its previous level. In the case of yearlings, some females must mate for the first time in the autumn, because the percentage of females carrying blastocysts in October exceeds the previous peak in June and July.

In addition, the uteruses of some females autopsied late in the year have been found to contain two distinct size classes of blastocysts – large ones and small ones (Cresswell *et al.*, 1992). Since blastocysts grow at a more or less constant rate during the period of delayed implantation, the size of a blastocyst can be taken as an indication of its age. Accordingly, it has been inferred that in the females in question, large blastocysts must have resulted from spring mating and small ones from autumn mating. This suggests that badgers are capable of what is called 'superfetation' – that is, a female who has already conceived may be able to 'top up' her supply of blastocysts by additional oestrus and mating episodes during the period of delayed implantation. Superfetation is also suggested by hormonal studies showing periodic, repeated peaks in the level of estradiol (a hormone associated with oestrus) throughout the summer and early autumn, though whether these hormonal changes are associated with actual ovulation and mating remains unproven.

Until recently, the existence of superfetation has been controversial owing to various technical limitations on the available evidence (see Yamaguchi *et al.*, 2006, for a discussion). However, very recent work by Lynsey Stuart (2009), at Trinity College, Dublin, seems finally to have settled the matter. Unlike previous investigators, Stuart not only examined the reproductive tracts of sows for the presence of blastocysts but also looked for other evidence of oestrus in the same animals – in particular, she examined the lining of the vagina to detect histological changes (so-called 'vaginal cornification') associated with oestrus. A small number of sows did indeed display both vaginal cornification and the presence of blastocysts in the uterus, confirming that oestrus can occur during delayed implantation. In short, there is now very good evidence that superfetation occurs in badgers, albeit only in a minority of sows. Given that superfetation is an extremely rare phenomenon among mammals in general and is not usually associated with delayed implantation, its existence in badgers is doubly surprising.

To summarise, most adult sows conceive in spring or early summer and most blastocysts survive the period of delayed implantation. However, mating can undoubtedly occur later in the year. Later mating is mainly confined to females who have not already conceived or who have conceived but have subsequently lost their entire litters; but it also occasionally occurs in females who are already carrying unimplanted blastocysts.

Failure to conceive

By the time of implantation in December, a large majority of females (80–100 per cent, depending on the study) are carrying blastocysts. Of the remainder, postmortem evidence suggests that most have ovulated but have failed to conceive. These infertile females are characterised by low body weight, low body fat deposits, larger adrenal glands, poorer health and higher bite-wound scores: that is, they are in generally poor condition and may have suffered harassment from other members of their social group (Cresswell *et al.*, 1992). Whether their infertility results from failure to conceive per se, or failure to mate, is unknown.

Functional basis of delayed implantation

It is reasonable to ask why badgers have delayed implantation at all. In general terms, delayed implantation enables mating and pregnancy to be decoupled, so that neither has to occur at a time of year dictated by the other. In the case of badgers, it is advantageous for cubs to be born as early as possible in the year so that they have maximum opportunity to put on enough weight to survive their first winter. Therefore, it is argued, birth has to occur as early as February or March. In this case, given that pregnancy lasts about 50 days, conventional reproduction would require mating to occur in December or January, which would be impossible, because badgers have then entered their period of winter dormancy and, in many parts of their range, are unable to leave the sett. By having delayed implantation, therefore, badgers are able to mate at a time of year when they are fully active while still being able to give birth in early spring.

This argument seems plausible but does not explain why the period of implantation is so long. In other words, why does most mating occur in the early spring, when both sexes are at a low point as regards energy reserves and when at least some females are occupied with lactation? Would it not be more sensible for mating to be postponed until autumn, when food is plentiful? The probable reason is that precisely because food availability peaks in autumn, badgers have something more important to do at that time of year: namely, put on as much weight as they can prior to the onset of winter. Spring, by contrast, may provide a good window of opportunity for mating, because the absence of readily available food at that time of year means that there are few conflicting demands on the animals' time.

Be that as it may, the badger's unusual reproductive timetable means that the most energy-intensive parts of the cycle (mating, pregnancy and lactation) are fuelled by fat reserves laid down during the previous summer and autumn. Consequently, ability to store fat for the winter is crucial not just to survival (see

Chapter 2) but also to successful reproduction. Indeed, as we shall see later, poor body condition, in the form of insufficient body fat, is an important cause of post-conception reproductive losses.

IMPLANTATION

Although a large majority (80–100 per cent: see above) of females are carrying blastocysts by the time of implantation, by no means all of them succeed in producing viable litters. As will become evident later, substantial loss of foetuses or cubs occurs at various stages of pregnancy and lactation, and also later on in the first year of life (see Table 8, below, for a summary). However, the largest single cause of reproductive loss is failure to implant. Postmortem studies carried out in southern England and Ireland suggest that up to 60 per cent of sows that are carrying blastocysts by the start of the winter fail to implant them, with losses being especially marked in yearlings. Losses seem to be all-or-none: that is, females either implant all of their blastocysts successfully or none at all.

Implantation occurs from about the middle of December to the middle of January (somewhat earlier in southwest France and somewhat later in Sweden). A French study has shown that a reduction in the daylength experienced by captive sows can advance the date of implantation by as much as six months, suggesting that the timing of implantation is influenced by photoperiod (Canivenc & Bonnin-Laffargue, 1981). Neal & Cheeseman (1996) have questioned the relevance of this finding on the grounds that wild badgers, over much of their geographical range, are permanently immured in their setts in the middle of winter and so would be unaware of changes in daylength. However, this argument does not carry much weight, because the internal 'clock' that triggers implantation could be set by daylength changes occurring earlier in the year, when badgers are still active.

From a physiological point of view, the probable sequence of events is that changes in daylength cause increased activity of the pituitary gland, hormones from which in turn cause development of the corpora lutea or 'yellow bodies' (specialised glandular cells in the ovary). The corpora lutea then secrete increased amounts of the hormone progesterone, which is thought to be the immediate trigger for implantation. The main evidence for this hypothesis is that progesterone levels rise rapidly immediately prior to implantation. However, some caution is warranted, because attempts to stimulate implantation artificially, by administering progesterone, have so far failed (for references, see Yamaguchi *et al.*, 2006).

Even within a single population, however, there is considerable individual variation in the timing of implantation. At least some of this variation is caused by differences in body condition, such that females in better condition implant earlier (Dugdale *et al.*, 2003). The same factor might also explain fine-scale regional variation in the timing of implantation. For example, badgers living in high alpine valleys in Switzerland implant later than those living at lower altitudes, and this may be because food is more plentiful in the lowlands (Wandeler & Graf, 1982). However, the correlation between body condition and implantation date is not very strong, suggesting that other factors are also involved.

PREGNANCY

The gestation period lasts about 50 days, but it is clear that not all pregnancies proceed to completion. Two studies carried out in southern England suggest that about 20–30 per cent of pregnant females lose all of their embryos, while an additional 10 per cent suffer partial loss. Taken together, these studies suggest that somewhat more than a third of all implanted embryos are aborted or reabsorbed. We will come back later to consider the causes of these losses but body condition is once again a probable contributor, with females in poorer condition being more likely to lose their litters (Woodroffe, 1995).

BIRTH DATES AND LITTER SIZES

Birth dates are hard to determine, because, of course, birth usually takes place underground in the sett. However, data are available from captive badgers; there are anecdotal accounts of newborn cubs being dug out of setts on known dates; and birth dates can be estimated prospectively from data on the sizes of foetuses recorded in postmortem studies of females that were killed in the late stages of pregnancy (Fig. 108). Taking information from all such sources, Neal & Cheeseman (1996) estimate that in southern England, 76 per cent of births occur between mid-January and mid-March, with a clear peak in the first half of February (Fig. 109). However, the peak period of births can vary by as much as four weeks between one year and the next (Whelan & Hayden, 1993). On a larger geographical scale, the timing of birth is correlated with the severity of winter climate, with peak birth times varying from the first week of January in southern Spain, through the end of January in southwest France and the first half of March in Sweden, to late March or April in parts of the former Soviet Union (for references, see Revilla *et al.*, 1999; Neal & Cheeseman, 1996).

FIG 108. Near-term badger foetuses. (M. Clark)

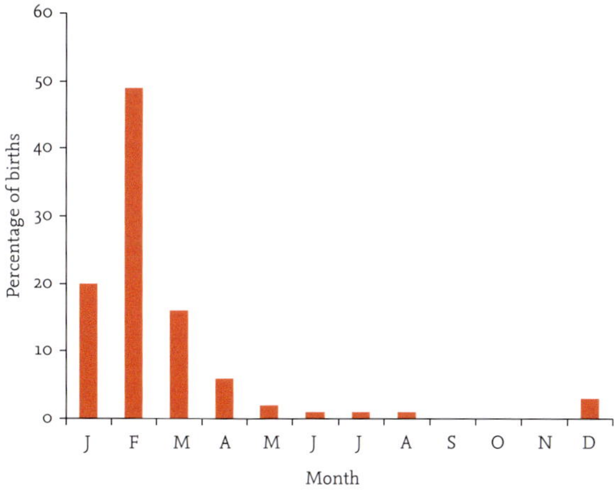

FIG 109. Percentage of births occurring in different months of the year, in the south of England. (Based on data in Neal & Cheeseman, 1996)

Litter size varies from one to five cubs, but more precise information is hard to obtain because newborn litters can rarely be observed in the wild. Consequently, most of the evidence relating to litter sizes at the time of birth comes from captive animals or from postmortem examination. For example, litter size can be inferred from the number of foetuses present in females killed late in pregnancy, or from the number of recent placental scars (scars left on the uterus wall when the placentas detach themselves) in females killed after giving birth. Pooling all of the available evidence from southern England, Neal & Cheeseman (1996) report an average litter size of 2.9 (Fig. 110), while an earlier study by Anderson & Trewhella (1985), using a geographically more varied but possibly less reliable sample of data, arrived at a very similar estimate of 2.7. Overall, equal

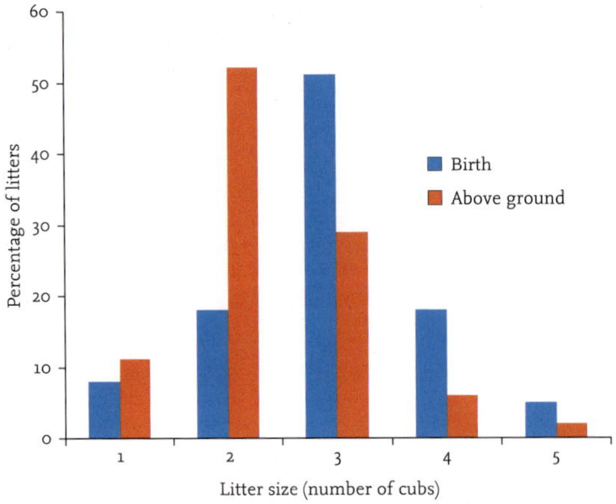

FIG 110. Frequency distribution of litter sizes at birth and when cubs first appear above ground. (Based on data in Neal & Cheeseman, 1996)

numbers of male and female cubs are born, but there is a suspicion that females in better body condition may produce litters with a slight bias towards more male offspring (Dugdale *et al.*, 2003).

By comparison, data on the numbers of cubs appearing above ground should be accurate because they derive from direct observations. Pooling data from various sources, Neal (1977) found that the mean litter size at this stage of development for badgers in southern England was 2.4, with the most frequent number of cubs being two (Fig. 110). A similar average figure of 2.5 is reported for Switzerland (Do Linh San *et al.*, 2003). Thus, litter sizes at emergence are significantly reduced by comparison with those at birth, implying that about 20 per cent of cubs die during their first two months of life. Even higher rates of early cub mortality have been estimated on the basis of capture–recapture data (38 per cent: Cheeseman *et al.*, 1987) and postmortem data (35 per cent: Cresswell *et al.*, 1992). It seems that this reduction in average litter sizes between birth and emergence results mainly from females losing their entire litters. We shall return later to the issue of what causes these losses.

DEVELOPMENT OF CUBS

Newborn cubs are about 120 mm long, excluding the tail, and their average weight is about 90 g (range 75–132 g). They are blind and helpless, and have pink skin thinly covered with sparse, greyish-white, glossy, silky fur in which the dark stripes of the facial mask may be just visible (Fig. 111a). The nose is also pink. By age 4 weeks, the nose has darkened in colour and the pelage has become

FIG 111. Badger cub aged: (a) 3 weeks; (b) 4 weeks; (c) 5 weeks; and (d) 11 weeks. (M. Edwards)

differentiated into the white, black and grey zones characteristic of adults (Fig. 111b). Newborn cubs are probably unable to thermoregulate effectively, since they require a temperature of about 20°C to survive in captivity. In the wild, of course, the body of the sow acts as a heat source and a generous cocoon of bedding material provides insulation (Neal & Cheeseman, 1996).

The milk teeth begin to erupt at about four weeks and the eyes open at about five weeks (Fig. 111c). Cubs start to become mobile within the sett at about six to seven weeks old and they first appear above ground at about eight weeks (Fig. 112). Early emergences usually take place late at night when most adult members of the group have already left the vicinity of the sett, but during subsequent weeks, this gets gradually earlier until, by about age 12 weeks, the cubs are emerging at dusk, at the same time as the rest of the social group (Fig. 113). Over the same period, appearances above ground also become more frequent and more prolonged, and the cubs become more exploratory. Self-grooming starts at about 11 weeks and increases in frequency thereafter, while bedding collection is first seen in about

FIG 112. Newly emerged cubs at a sett entrance. (Dassenwerkgroep Brabant)

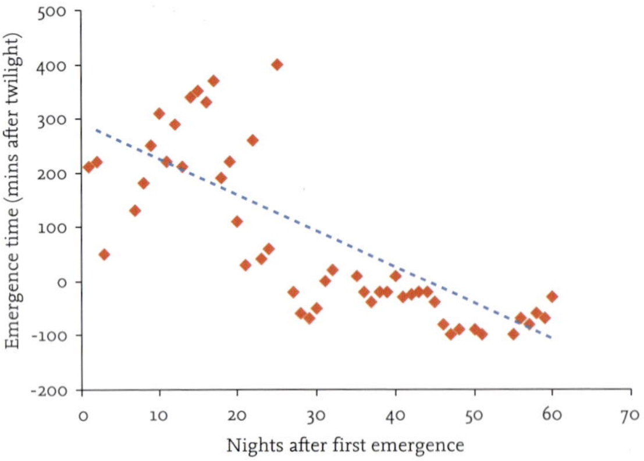

FIG 113. Emergence time of cubs relative to their age. Emergence time is measured relative to twilight; age is measured in days following the date of first emergence from the sett. (From Fell *et al.*, 2006)

week 11 and occurs regularly by week 14 (Fig. 111d). Other activities, such as snuffling and digging in the soil for prey, and scent-marking, appear at about 9–12 weeks, and by 16 weeks the cubs show the full range of adult behaviours.

Detailed observations by Rebecca Fell and others of the badgers of Wytham Woods, Oxfordshire, have shed interesting light on how cubs become integrated into their social group. Initially, cubs spend very little time above ground, remain close to a sett entrance and are usually either left completely alone or are accompanied only by their mother. As they mature, they spend progressively less

FIG 114. Cubs playing at the sett. (Dassenwerkgroep Brabant)

FIG 115. 'Playing tree' at a sett in the Netherlands. (Dassenwerkgroep Brabant)

time with their mother and more with other adults and sub-adults until, by about week 16, they are interacting regularly with all or most members of their social group. Play-fighting (Fig. 114) also increases in frequency and duration as the cubs get older, and it becomes more likely to involve members of the social group other than the cub's own mother or siblings. The members of a social group often have a favourite place for playing, which becomes denuded of vegetation as a result. Sometimes it is also possible to identify a 'playing tree', around which the cubs chase one another and on which they may climb (Fig. 115).

FIG **116.** A mother and her cub foraging together in late summer. (L. & P. Schofield)

Overall, then, the picture that emerges is that cubs undergo a gradual process of social integration in which they themselves, rather than adult members of the group, take the initiative. A particularly compelling example of this is what Fell and her collaborators call 'scent-theft' – a behaviour in which the cub pushes itself beneath the belly of an adult and then crawls out between the adult's hind legs, brushing its back against the adult's anal region. Presumably, this serves to impregnate the cub with the mixture of adult odours that is thought to constitute a signal of group membership (Fell *et al.*, 2006; see also Chapter 6). The point to be emphasised here, though, is that it is the cub, not the adult, that initiates this sharing of scent.

Weaning begins at the age of about 12 weeks, but some suckling may continue well into the summer and cubs continue to accompany their mother on foraging trips for several months and even, sometimes, into their second year (Fig. 116). They will also travel with her if she disperses (see below) or moves into another sett in the same territory. Growth starts slowly but speeds up during the summer and autumn, such that adult body and skull length are achieved by about the age of six months. Weight continues to increase for longer, enabling cubs, at least in good years, to reach something approaching adult body weight by the beginning of their first winter (Lüps, 1983b: see Fig. 117).

Nevertheless, capture–recapture data from the Woodchester Park population suggest that 56 per cent of cubs that survive to emergence do not make it

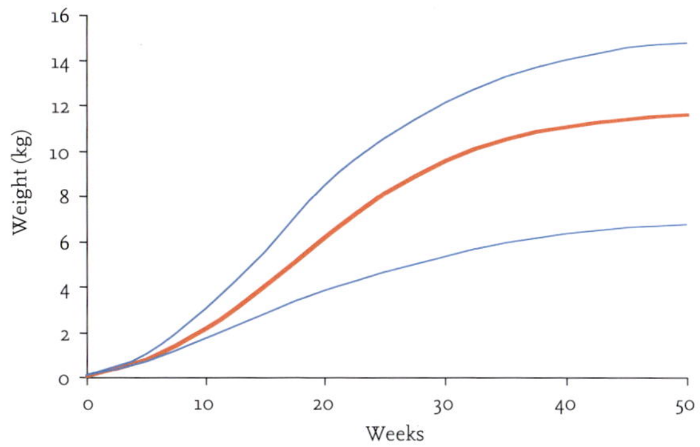

FIG 117. Growth of cubs during the first year of life. Red line: median value. Blue lines: range. (Based on data taken from Dumartin *et al.*, 1989, and from studies cited by Lüps, 1983b)

through to the following spring (Cheeseman *et al.*, 1987). Most of these post-emergence losses probably result from cubs not putting on enough weight in their first summer and autumn to enable them to survive the winter. However, cubs have been known to die of starvation or dehydration during exceptionally dry summers in my study area in Sussex, and some cubs no doubt succumb to disease or are killed by humans or predators.

SEXUAL MATURITY

Age of sexual maturity is very variable. In countries with relatively mild climates, such as the UK, a few females mature at the age of about 9 months (i.e. in the autumn of their first year) but they seldom, if ever, breed successfully. Most individuals of both sexes probably become sexually mature at age 12–15 months (i.e. in the spring of their second year) but some not until age 16–19 months (i.e. in late summer/early autumn of their second year). Reproductive maturity may be delayed until the third year in countries with harsh winters, such as Sweden and parts of the former Soviet Union, perhaps because it takes longer for young animals to reach adult body size and weight (Ahnlund, 1980; Danilov & Tumanov, 1972, 1975).

ALLO-PARENTAL BEHAVIOUR

Allo-parental behaviour is when animals care for offspring that are not their own. Since allo-parental behaviour is fairly common in other social carnivores, there has been some interest in the question of whether it occurs in badgers.

Rosie Woodroffe (1993), citing anecdotal evidence based on observations of a single social group of badgers at Wytham Woods, has suggested that non-breeding females may help a breeding female to look after her cubs by grooming them and 'babysitting' while the mother is away from the sett. Most of the time, the evidence of 'babysitting' was not very convincing: it merely amounted to a non-breeding female being present at the sett while cubs were above ground and their mother was away. In such cases, therefore, it could just have been coincidence that the cubs and a non-breeding female were at the sett at the same time. On several occasions, however, a non-breeding female 'babysitter' seemed actively to protect cubs from danger, for example by seeing off an aggressive male or by chasing cubs back to the sett when they had wandered too far away. These observations, although anecdotal and few in number, provide stronger evidence that non-breeding females are actively involved in caring for cubs.

Subsequent data, however, from the same badger population, show that the presence of non-breeding females in a social group has no effect on cub production and negative effects on the physical condition of the breeding female herself (Woodroffe & Macdonald, 2000). Thus, it does not seem that the intervention of non-breeding females, if it occurs at all, improves the survival of cubs or alleviates the load on their mother. Altogether, then, the evidence for allo-parental behaviour in badgers is weak. Indeed, anyone who has watched setts regularly during the breeding season will have been struck by how casually cubs are sometimes treated, not only by other members of the group but also by their mother. For example, it is not unusual for cubs to be left completely alone outside a sett at an age when they would seem, from their relative immobility and imperviousness to danger, to be highly vulnerable.

DISPERSAL

Dispersal occurs when an individual leaves the group in which it was born and takes up residence elsewhere, either permanently or semi-permanently. In most mammals, males disperse as a matter of course at about the time of sexual maturity. However, in the sorts of high-density badger populations that exist in the south of England, dispersal is infrequent and unpredictable, both with respect to its timing and with respect to the sex of the dispersing individuals.

Dispersal has been studied in three populations in the south of England: Woodchester Park; Wytham Woods; and South Downs, East Sussex (for references, see Macdonald *et al.*, 2008). These studies suggest that, overall, the

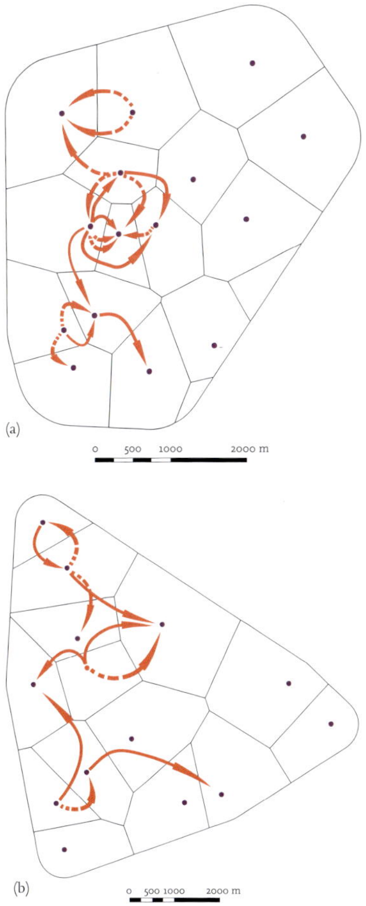

FIG **118.** Dispersal events (solid arrows) and temporary movements (broken arrows) between social groups in badger populations in (a) Luxembourg and (b) Belgium. Note that both dispersal movements and temporary visits are usually to a neighbouring group. (From Scheppers, 2009)

chance of any one badger dispersing in any one year is small. Consequently, many badgers, perhaps even a majority, never disperse at all, instead remaining in their natal group for the whole of their lives. Those that do disperse can be of either sex and of almost any age – in one or two cases, quite young cubs have been known to disperse in the company of their mothers. However, the majority of dispersal events involve sexually mature animals. Whether or not there is a sex bias in dispersal remains unclear: several studies have reported more frequent dispersal in males than in females and one has reported the reverse. However, a recent capture–recapture study based on a large sample size suggests no difference in dispersal rate between males and females (Macdonald *et al.*, 2008).

Dispersal 'coalitions'

Usually, individuals disperse singly, but sometimes they do so in 'coalitions': that is, two or three members of the same social group disperse at the same time and to the same destination (e.g. Woodroffe *et al.*, 1993; Macdonald *et al.*, 2008). The reason for this is unclear. One possibility is that all of the individuals involved in a coalition have decided independently to disperse to the same place at the same time, in which case the term 'coalition' would be a misnomer,

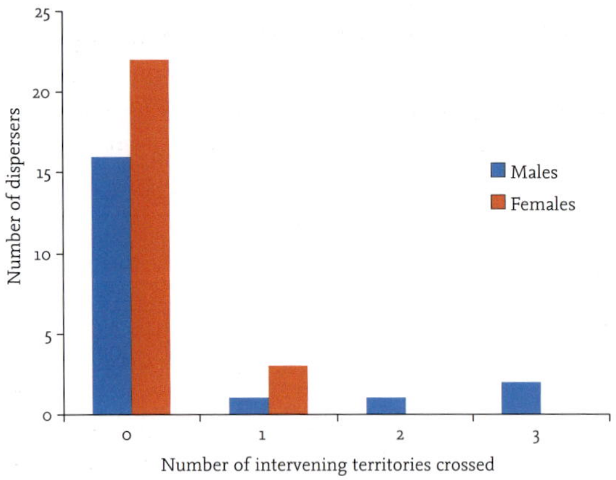

FIG 119. Distances travelled by dispersing badgers during a 17-year study at Wytham Woods, near Oxford. Most animals of both sexes dispersed to a neighbouring territory (i.e. they crossed no intervening territories) but a few crossed from one to three intervening territories. (From Macdonald *et al.*, 2008)

because it implies active cooperation between the individuals in question. Alternatively, it may be that dispersing in the company of others does confer some sort of advantage, for example by facilitating integration into the new group.

Dispersal distance

Dispersal is generally to a neighbouring social group but occasional relatively long-distance dispersal events, in which an individual crosses several intervening territories before reaching its destination, have been documented by radio-tracking and capture–recapture studies (e.g. Rogers *et al.*, 1998; Macdonald *et al.*, 2008; Scheppers, 2009: see Figs. 118 and 119). In one exceptional case, a radio-collared female badger that was released in the Netherlands after a period in captivity travelled a linear distance of 115 km during a two-week period (Mulder, 1996). Of course, the movements that this animal made following re-release in a strange location are not necessarily indicative of what happens in normal, unforced dispersal, but this example does show that badgers are capable of travelling long distances in search of a new home.

Data from radio-tracking and capture–recapture studies probably underestimate the frequency of long-distance dispersal, because when a marked animal 'disappears' from the study area, its fate usually remains unknown – it might have dispersed too far away to be detectable, but it could equally well have died. That long-distance dispersal may in fact be quite common is suggested by a recent population genetics study by Lisa Pope and others. This shows, first, that badgers exhibit an overall level of genetic diversity similar to that of most other vertebrates (i.e. they are not especially inbred by vertebrate standards) and, second, that they lack the sort of local genetic structure that would be expected if mating contacts were limited to the immediate vicinity of any one social group (i.e. the badger population is, genetically speaking, relatively homogeneous) (Pope *et al.*, 2006). Together, then, the genetic evidence suggests a significant amount of genetic mixing within badger populations, and dispersal is the most likely cause of this. In addition, the same study suggests a tendency for short-distance dispersal (up to 2 km) to be more common in females and long-distance dispersal (at least 5 km) in males (Pope *et al.*, 2006).

The process of dispersal

Work by my own research group in Sussex, using radio-tracking to monitor the movements of individual badgers, shows that dispersal can be a surprisingly protracted and complex process. The first sign that an animal might be about to disperse is when it begins to make nocturnal forays into a neighbouring territory, albeit returning to its own territory to sleep. After some weeks of this, the disperser begins to spend occasional days sleeping in the new territory, often in the main sett but sometimes using an outlier as a kind of temporary staging post before transferring to the main sett. The amount of time spent in the new main sett then gradually increases until transfer to the new social group is complete (see Fig. 120). Altogether, the process of dispersal can take as long as nine months.

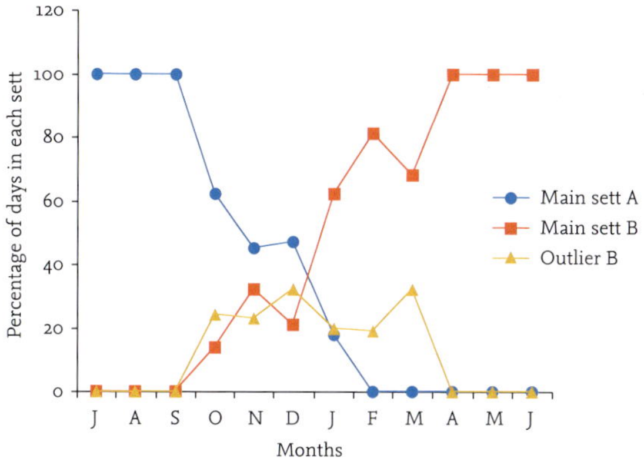

FIG 120. Sett use by a single male badger during dispersal from one territory (A) to another (B). The dispersal process lasted from September to April, during which time the male spent progressively less time in his original main sett and more time in the new main sett. He also used an outlier in the new territory. (Based on data in Roper *et al.*, 2003)

These observations suggest that a dispersing badger needs to infiltrate its way gradually into a new group. One possible reason for this is to minimise aggression from the existing members of the new group, although intensive observational studies have not reported the occurrence of especially high levels of fighting during dispersal events, despite the fact that fighting among badgers is a noisy business and is unlikely to go undetected. On the other hand, a long-term capture–recapture study has revealed that animals with a history of moving from one social group to another tend to have more scars, so fighting associated with dispersal may be a factor (Macdonald *et al.*, 2008). An alternative explanation is that dispersal proceeds gradually so as to enable the disperser to retain the option of returning to its original group, should the new one prove unsatisfactory or inhospitable (Roper *et al.*, 2003).

What triggers dispersal?

It remains to be determined what triggers dispersal by a particular individual at a particular time. Folk wisdom has it that dispersers are actively expelled by other members of their social group, but there is no evidence that this happens in badgers.

Instead, it seems more likely that individuals disperse because it is in their own interests to do so; in which case, the most obvious hypothesis is that they are seeking to increase their chance of being able to reproduce. As we shall see, in high-density populations, reproduction is usually monopolised in any one year by one or two individuals of each sex; and these individuals tend to be older members of the social group. Thus, younger members of a social group can be considered to be queuing up for the chance to breed. One option for a young animal is to stay in its natal group and hope to survive long enough to reach the front of this 'breeding queue'; and some individuals do seem to adopt this strategy, insofar as they remain in their natal group throughout their lives. An alternative strategy, however, would be for an individual to disperse if, by doing so, it would find itself higher up the breeding queue in the new group.

A variety of evidence is consistent with this 'queue-jumping' hypothesis. For example, individuals could monitor the membership of adjacent social groups, and thus obtain information about the occurrence of breeding vacancies, via the latrine system (see Chapter 6), which could explain why dispersal is almost always to an immediately adjacent territory. If dispersal is triggered by the chance occurrence of a nearby breeding vacancy, this could explain why it is not restricted to either sex or to any particular time of year, and why it usually involves animals that are already sexually mature. In addition, dispersing females have sometimes been observed to breed soon after joining a new group

(Woodroffe *et al.*, 1993; Christian, 1994). And, finally, there is a tendency for males to disperse to groups containing large numbers of females and for females to disperse to groups containing fewer females (Macdonald *et al.*, 2008).

On the other hand, there are cases of females dispersing when they have already bred successfully in their original group, and these are hard to explain in terms of increased opportunity to breed. Conversely, dispersal does not affect the subsequent likelihood that a female will reproduce (Macdonald *et al.*, 2008). Also, it is hard to see why dispersal seems not to be met by more resistance on the part of existing members of the new group, who would be pushed further down the breeding queue by the arrival of an older newcomer. Finally, the 'breeding opportunity' hypothesis cannot explain why individuals sometimes disperse in coalitions if the purpose of dispersal is to fill a single breeding vacancy. To summarise, the 'breeding opportunities' hypothesis is plausible in principle but lacks direct evidence in its favour. At best, it is unlikely to constitute a complete explanation of dispersal.

Dispersal in low-density populations

Everything that I have said so far about dispersal is based on studies of relatively high-density populations in the south of England, where badgers form stable social groups containing more than one sexually mature individual of each sex. In some parts of the species' range, however, badgers live in pairs or solitarily (see Chapter 7), and for this to happen, all surviving offspring, of both sexes, must presumably disperse at a relatively young age. Unfortunately, nothing is known directly about dispersal in such populations. However, culling of badgers (which necessarily reduces population density) results in an increase in dispersal movements (Tuyttens *et al.*, 2000). In addition, in cases where culling eliminates an entire social group, the vacated main sett is usually reoccupied quite quickly by immigrants from surrounding groups (Cheeseman *et al.*, 1993). By analogy, therefore, it seems likely that in naturally low-density populations (which are presumably low in density because of a naturally high mortality rate), breeding vacancies arise more frequently and dispersal at an early age becomes the norm for both sexes.

MATING SYSTEM

The mating system of a species is a description of who mates with whom. As a result of Hans Kruuk's pioneering work on badgers in the 1970s and 1980s, a picture emerged of badgers as highly territorial animals in which contact between the members of different social groups was minimal and, when it did

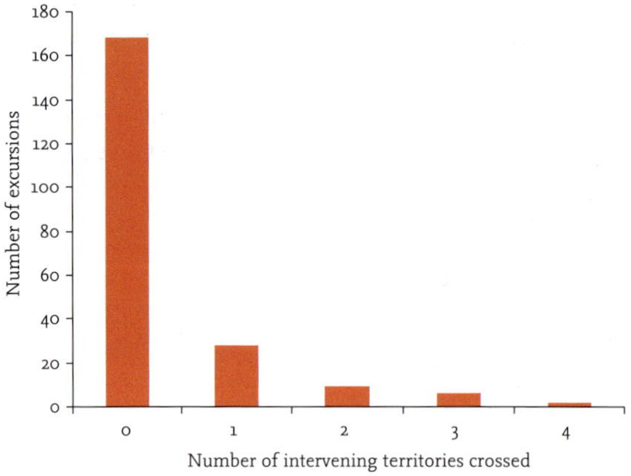

FIG 121. Distances travelled by badgers making temporary excursions into surrounding territories during a 17-year study at Wytham Woods, near Oxford. Most visits were to a neighbouring territory but a few involved crossing from one to four intervening territories. (Based on data in Macdonald *et al.*, 2008)

occur, hostile (see also Chapter 7). It was therefore assumed that most mating must occur within a social group and that, as a consequence, badgers were probably rather inbred. Subsequently, however, observational evidence emerged of badgers of both sexes making temporary visits to other social groups for mating purposes (e.g. Christian, 1994; Macdonald *et al.*, 2008; Scheppers, 2009: see Figs. 118 and 121). In addition, an early study of parentage, using a form of DNA 'fingerprinting', suggested that badgers were less inbred than had been assumed and that a significant proportion of cubs were fathered by males from outside the mother's social group (Evans *et al.*, 1989). Thus, the mating system of badgers began to appear more complex, and individual badgers more promiscuous, than the simple territorial model had suggested.

Spectacular confirmation of this has come from two recent studies of badger genetics, one involving the Woodchester Park population (Carpenter *et al.*, 2005) and the other the Wytham Woods population (Dugdale *et al.*, 2007, 2008). Both studies show that only about 30 per cent of adult males, and the same proportion of adult females, produce cubs in any one year. In the case of females, this means that the norm is for only one female to breed in any one social group in any one year. Evidently, therefore, there is often strong competition, in both sexes, for breeding status. In both males and females, the most successful competitors turn out to be animals in the age range four to six years, with younger and older individuals being less likely to achieve parentage (Fig. 122). The source of this competition for the opportunity to breed is probably limited food resources in the case of females, while in males it presumably arises from the drive to fertilise as many females as possible.

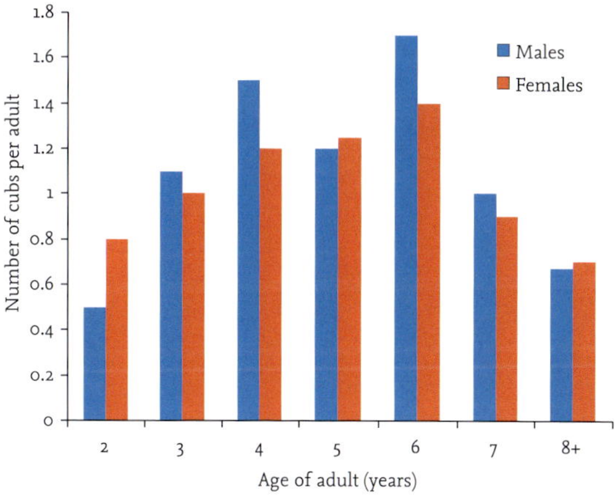

FIG 122. Number of cubs produced per male or female of a given age. (Based on data in Carpenter *et al.*, 2005)

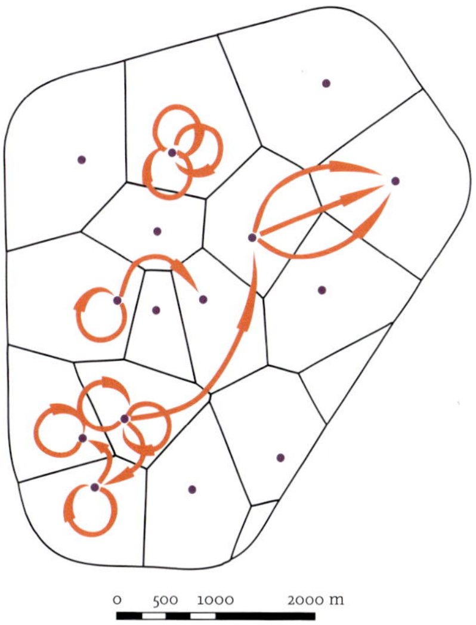

FIG 123. Paternity of cubs in a population of badgers in Luxembourg. In eight cases where paternity could be determined, cubs were sired by males from their own social group (circular arrows); in seven cases, they were sired by a male from a different social group (curved arrows). (From Scheppers, 2009)

Genetic studies have also shed important new light on issues relating to paternity. First, about 50 per cent of cubs in any one social group are sired by males from a different group — usually, one that is immediately adjacent to the mother's group (see Fig. 123). Indeed, a single litter can contain cubs sired by males from different social groups. This fits with observations that females can mate with more than one male during a single oestrus and that both males and females make temporary visits to other social groups, apparently for purposes of mating (see above). Second, in cases where the father and mother are both residents of the same social group, they rarely turn out both to have been born in that group – rather, one or other, or both, have usually immigrated from another group at some previous time. This suggests that some kind of incest avoidance mechanism operates within social groups.

Altogether, then, three mechanisms seem to combine to reduce the degree of inbreeding. These are, first, the occurrence of extra-group mating; second, the incidence of dispersal; and, third, the avoidance of incest. As a result, relatedness within social groups is not nearly as high as it would be if they consisted solely of close kin and if mating always occurred within the group (Pope *et al.*, 2006). What is unusual about badgers, however, is that they achieve outbreeding not primarily by means of dispersal, but by adults of both sexes making temporary visits to neighbouring social groups purely for mating purposes. At least, this seems to be true of high-density populations, in which, as we have seen, dispersal is rare.

To summarise, badgers have what is termed a 'polygynandrous' mating system: namely, a system in which females can mate with multiple males and males with multiple females. The system can also be described as 'promiscuous', in the sense that a single female can mate outside, as well as within, the social group. This may sound more like a television soap opera than the comfortable world of a children's book, but we have to remember that the actions of animals are shaped by the inexorable logic of natural selection, not by moral codes.

FEMALE REPRODUCTIVE TACTICS IN RELATION TO REPRODUCTIVE LOSSES

As we have seen in previous sections, a large majority of female badgers mate and conceive in the spring of every year, yet relatively few succeed in rearing offspring. So dramatic are the reproductive losses that of every 100 blastocysts that are carried by sows prior to implantation, only 5 eventually turn into cubs that survive to the time of emergence (Table 8). This seems an astonishingly high rate of attrition, leading one to wonder why reproduction is so wasteful and inefficient. What we now know about the mating system of badgers may shed light on this issue.

The ability of a female to raise cubs seems to depend on two factors: her age relative to other female members of the same social group and her body condition. At the time of mating, in the spring, an individual female can predict neither of these with any degree of certainty; they depend on the survival of other females within the group, the availability of breeding opportunities in neighbouring groups and the availability of food during the rest of the year. On the other hand, neither the act of mating itself nor the support of a few blastocysts is very costly. Therefore, it is argued, a female might as well mate in the spring, even if she is relatively young and not in very good condition, because the prospects of her reproducing successfully might have improved by the autumn.

TABLE 8. Percentage of surviving offspring lost at each stage of the life cycle, and percentage of original offspring that survive to the end of each stage. For example, of foetuses that survive to the end of implantation, 35% are lost during pregnancy; and of every 100 foetuses conceived, 14 survive to the end of pregnancy (for references see text).

	% surviving foetuses or cubs lost at each stage	% original foetuses that survive to the end of each stage
Pre-implantation	0	100
Implantation	60	40
Pregnancy	35	14
Birth to emergence	37	5
Emergence to end of first year of life	56	3

By the time of implantation, however, a female will be in a much better position to predict her ability to carry a pregnancy through to completion. Furthermore, this is the point at which she will begin to incur serious energetic costs as the foetuses that she is carrying grow in size. Therefore, it would make sense for a sow to terminate her attempt to reproduce at this stage if the probability of eventual success seemed low. This, I would argue, is why implantation constitutes a crux point in the reproductive cycle, in the sense that so many females lose their complete litters at this stage. Of course, I am not proposing that female badgers make a conscious decision as to whether or not to implant. Rather, evolution has endowed them with a mechanism linking implantation to factors associated with reproductive success. Reabsorption or miscarriage of foetuses during pregnancy are probably a product of the same process: namely, females cutting their losses if their chance of being able to rear cubs successfully diminishes. This is suggested by the fact that sows that reabsorb their foetuses tend to be in poor physical condition (Woodroffe & Macdonald, 1995).

However, there is also evidence implicating another, and somewhat uglier, cause of reproductive losses at the time of implantation and during early pregnancy: namely, interference from other sows. Each sow should seek to optimise the future prospects of her own offspring and one way of doing this is to eliminate potential competitors. Therefore, stronger sows may try to harass other, weaker female members of the same social group to such an extent that they fail to implant or, if they have implanted, abort. The main evidence implicating this type of reproductive competition is that females show high levels of bite-wounding during November and December: that is, at about the time of implantation (Fig. 124).

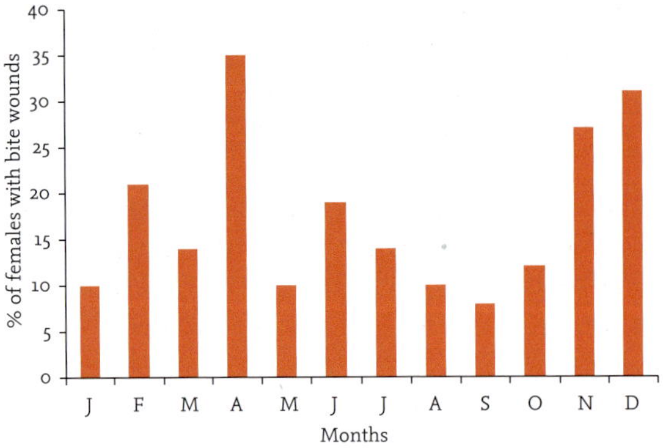

FIG 124. Seasonal changes in the frequency of bite-wounding in adult sows. (Based on data in Cresswell *et al.*, 1992)

When it comes to cub losses during lactation, interference from other sows may be the dominant factor. One piece of evidence favouring this hypothesis is that data on bite-wounding in sows show a peak in April in addition to the peak, already mentioned, in November/December. Another is that dead suckling cubs are sometimes found on the surface, with bite wounds suggestive of infanticide (Fig. 125). In addition, one case has been recorded of the remains of a badger cub being found in the stomach of a female who had herself recently bred, though it is not known whether this was the cub of another female or whether the sow that ate the cub was also responsible for killing it (Lüps & Roper, 1990).

Somewhat more substantively, Hans Kruuk (1979) describes how, in a captive colony of badgers, the dominant female (a sow called 'One-Lug') certainly killed her sister's newborn litter on one occasion shortly after she had herself given

FIG 125. Dead cub found at a sett on 16 March 2009. Note the bite wounds, suggesting that the cub was a victim of infanticide. (Stuart Robinson, University of Sussex)

birth, and probably did so on another occasion in similar circumstances. In subsequent years, One-Lug also became highly aggressive towards other non-breeding adult females, including her own daughters, whenever she was lactating. However, the behaviour of captive animals may not be indicative of what happens in the wild.

To summarise, various lines of evidence all seem to point in the direction of harassment and infanticide by dominant females but none of them, in and of itself, is very convincing. Consequently, it is difficult to know what to conclude. My own feeling is that infanticide is probably a significant cause of pre-emergence cub losses, not least because it has been amply demonstrated in field studies of other species, including other social carnivores, in which females compete for the opportunity to breed. However, as far as badgers are concerned, the case is by no means proven.

CONCLUSIONS

In recent years, our knowledge of reproduction in badgers has advanced in leaps and bounds. While we have known about the basic reproductive timetable for some time, we now understand much more than we did, even a few years ago, about dispersal, the mating system and cub development. In particular, recent molecular genetics studies have provided us with a functional perspective on reproduction that was previously completely lacking.

However, four sets of problems remain. The first of these is that various technical questions about the details of the reproductive cycle still await resolution. For example, we do not know whether badgers are induced ovulators, or whether this is why copulation is sometimes so prolonged; we do not have a satisfactory explanation as to why certain individuals disperse when they do; we do not know why some males maintain high testosterone levels throughout the summer whereas others do not; we do not understand the hormonal basis or functional advantage of superfetation; and we do not know for sure whether some reproductive losses are a consequence of active competition between sows.

The second set of problems arises from the fact that, as I have repeatedly emphasised, information about all aspects of reproduction in badgers is heavily biased towards studies of high-density populations in the south of England, where badgers live in social groups containing more than one mature individual of each sex. Such groups obviously offer abundant potential for competition over the opportunity to breed. Over much of the species' range, however, badgers live in groups containing only one adult of each sex (see Chapter 7), in which case the pressures of competition are likely to be less. This has implications for the mating strategies of both sexes, as follows.

From the male's point of view, it is much easier to defend a single female against the attentions of other males than it is to defend several females. In addition, in low-density populations, territories tend to be large and the use of latrines for communication is less obvious (see Chapters 6 and 7), so it may not be so easy for males to keep tabs on the oestrus cycles of neighbouring females, or for either sex to make short-term visits to neighbouring territories for mating purposes. Consequently, it seems unlikely that there is so much sharing of paternity in low-density populations. However, we lack the genetic evidence needed to test this prediction.

From the point of view of females, absence of competition from other mature sows within the same social group is likely to result in a reduction in reproductive losses, especially those occurring after implantation. Therefore, we would predict successful breeding in a higher percentage of females in low-density populations. One piece of evidence supports this prediction: namely, that 65 per cent of adult females breed in any one year in the very low-density Doñana reserve population in southern Spain (Revilla *et al.*, 1999), compared with only 20–40 per cent in southern England. However, comparable data from other low-density populations are badly needed.

The third set of problems also stems from the geographical bias inherent in the literature but it concerns dispersal rather than reproduction per se. As we have seen, dispersal is surprisingly infrequent in high-density badger populations: instead, adults of both sexes make temporary forays into neighbouring territories for mating purposes. This is a highly unusual way of achieving outbreeding. Consequently, it would be interesting to know whether it is characteristic of all badger populations or occurs only in those in which high population density limits the opportunities for dispersal.

The fourth and final set of problems concerns the fact that all of the relevant studies indicate a striking amount of individual and inter-annual variation in the precise timing of major reproductive events. Whatever the cause of this variation, it suggests a considerable degree of flexibility in the timing of the reproductive cycle. The likelihood is that individual factors such as age, body condition and previous reproductive history, plus environmental factors such as climate, are involved; but confirmation of this is a matter for future research.

CHAPTER 6

Communication

THERE IS NO DOUBT that badgers have an acute sense of smell (see Chapter 2). They also, as we shall see in this chapter, possess an impressive variety of scent-producing organs and scent-marking behaviours. We can therefore safely deduce that they are able to communicate by means of odour signals. When it comes to vocal and visual signals, however, the general opinion is that badgers are poorly endowed, at least by the standards of most social carnivores. Hans Kruuk, for example, describes badgers as 'inarticulate', pointing out that few naturalists, let alone ordinary people, are familiar with the sounds that they make (Kruuk, 1989, p. 146). Similarly, he comments on the dearth of visual displays in badgers and describes only a few postures or movements that he thinks might have a signalling function. Although we should not be surprised to find that a nocturnal species like the badger lacks a rich repertoire of visual signals, a paucity of vocal signals would be more puzzling.

Is this characterisation of badgers, as relatively uncommunicative animals in the vocal and visual modalities, justified, or does it reflect a lack of research into this aspect of their lives? The fact is that it takes a prolonged period of careful, informed observation and experimentation to understand the signalling code of any species, and in the case of badgers this is made more difficult by the necessity of gathering the requisite data at night. It is perhaps not surprising, then, that of the hundreds of scientific studies of badgers that have been published, few have been explicitly concerned with communication and almost none with vocal or visual signals.

Two unusually detailed and relatively recent studies, one by Séan Christian at the University of Sussex and the other by Josephine Wong *et al.* of the University of Oxford, have begun to redress this imbalance and to question whether badgers really are as undemonstrative and inarticulate as has generally been supposed. Here, I shall draw on these and other studies to review what is now known about communication in badgers, concentrating mainly on signals that they use when interacting with other members of their own species.

VISUAL SIGNALS

Hans Kruuk (1989) describes four visual signals in badgers, which he terms 'upright', 'forward', 'curl-up' and 'pilo-erection'. In addition, he observed badgers making a scraping movement with their hind legs prior to launching an attack (in this case, an attack on Kruuk himself). To these, Séan Christian (1993) has added several others, suggesting that badgers employ at least a dozen distinct postures or movements as visual signals. These signals are used mainly in the context of agonistic behaviour (i.e. aggression and defence) and also, to some extent, during mating.

Aggression

Upright is generally agreed to be a threat posture. The animal stands erect, with its head held up but its nose pointing downwards so as to display the facial mask to full advantage. The hairs on the cheeks may also be raised so as to exaggerate the breadth of the head. 'Upright' has so far only been reported in males, when threatening either another male or a human observer. Its function is almost certainly to make the signaller look as large as possible, thereby dissuading its opponent from launching an attack.

Body-ripple consists of a badger shaking its body in a ripple that progresses from head to tail, like a dog shaking off water. It is sometimes accompanied by 'bottlebrushing' (see below) and seems to be another type of threat display.

Forward is an elongated posture in which the signaller stands relatively low to the ground with its whole body, including the head and neck, stretched out towards the receiver. Unlike 'upright', 'forward' has been observed in both sexes. It may occur in response to 'upright' threat by an aggressor, or two badgers may both adopt the 'forward' posture before or during the course of a fight (Fig. 126). Kruuk interprets 'forward' as a defensive posture, and sometimes the context in which it occurs suggests wariness on the part of the signaller. However, its physical form is suggestive of an intention movement prior to launching an attack, and this is indeed the context in which it most often occurs. It seems more likely, therefore, that it is a more intense threat signal than either 'upright' or 'body-ripple', communicating a willingness to attack immediately if the opponent does not back down.

FIG 126. Two badgers facing one another in the 'forward' posture. (From Christian, 1993)

Hind-leg raking is a curious movement in which the badger scrapes the ground alternately with its hind legs, sometimes also flicking its tail. Like 'forward', it seems to be a signal of extreme aggressive intent and usually occurs just before launching an attack.

Pilo-erection, or the raising of hair all over the body, can be associated with either attack or defence. For example, Christian reports its occurrence when a badger was startled by a human observer; when a cub was threatened by an adult; and immediately prior to one adult attacking another. In cubs, pilo-erection also occurs when the animal is suddenly frightened (for example, by a human observer: Fig. 127). In all these contexts, the most likely primary function is to make the displaying individual look as large, and therefore as threatening, as possible.

Bottlebrushing is a particular form of pilo-erection in which the hairs on the tail are fluffed out and the tail itself is raised vertically. The tail may also be waved from side to side. Like pilo-erection, bottlebrushing has been observed in both defensive and offensive contexts; and it also occurs in males during courtship and mating (see below and Chapter 5).

FIG 127. Pilo-erection: a frightened cub with fluffed-up pelage. (G. Shepherd)

FIG 128. Partial pilo-erection: the hair on the rump has been raised to produce a white patch on either side of the tail. Note also that the tail itself is fluffed up. This badger was disturbed by the sound of a camera shutter. (M. Clark)

Since bottlebrushing exposes the white underside of the tail in a flag-like manner, it has generally been assumed to be a visual signal. However, the pelage of the underside of the tail is contaminated with secretions from the anal and caudal glands (see below), suggesting that an important function of bottlebrushing is to release scent into the atmosphere. The same may also apply to whole-body pilo-erection and body-ripple. Indeed, Christian comments that all three of these displays are often accompanied by a smell of musk that is sufficiently strong to be discernible to the human nose.

A final form of pilo-erection is *rump pilo-erection*, in which a startled badger erects the pelage on either side of its tail, so as to reveal patches of pale under fur (Fig. 128). I have listed this display here because of its physical similarity to other forms of pilo-erection. However, its function is unknown and it may be a signal of defence rather than of aggression. The fact that the signal is directed backwards may also mean that it is oriented towards a potential threat, such as a predator, rather than to other members of the same species.

Defence

Facing away, backing off, crouching and *curl-up* are all used in a defensive context and seem to signal progressively increasing degrees of submissiveness. In 'facing away', an animal that is being threatened turns its head to the side and downwards, so as to present its neck and shoulder to its opponent (see Chapter 7, Fig. 166); in 'backing off', it retreats from the aggressor with its head lowered and its rump lifted; in 'crouching', it crouches down onto the ground; and in 'curl-up', it curls up into a ball, tucking its nose beneath its body and covering its head with its forelegs. All of these postures have been observed in response to threat or attack by another badger, but 'curl-up' also often occurs when a badger is caught in a trap: it seems to signal extreme fear and defencelessness (Fig. 129).

FIG 129. Badger cub in curled-up 'defensive' position, drawn from life. (Copyright © Michael Clark. Reproduced by permission of the artist)

As Hans Kruuk has pointed out, these defensive displays are in various respects the physical opposites of the offensive 'upright' and 'forward' postures. That is, whereas offensive postures emphasise body size and the facial mask, and involve a badger facing directly towards its opponent, defensive postures involve it turning away from its opponent, hiding its facial mask and trying to make itself literally 'look small'. This kind of antithesis, in which signals that have opposite meanings take on opposite forms, is a common feature of animal communication.

Mating

Stiff-legged walking is a particular kind of gait in which the animal struts around in an exaggerated manner. It has been observed during visits to latrines but is especially associated with pre-mating behaviour on the part of males (see Chapter 5). It is often accompanied by pilo-erection and bottlebrushing.

Hind-leg raking appears to be primarily an aggressive signal (see above), but males have been seen to do it during mating (Stewart *et al.*, 2002).

Play

Séan Christian has observed that cubs often keep their mouths half-open during play, which he likens to the 'open-mouthed playface' signal used by some primates to indicate playful intentions. He also notes that badger cubs adopt a particular kind of 'bouncing, bounding' gait while playing (Christian, 1993, p. 209). Christian speculates that this facial expression and gait may tell the playmate that the signaller's behaviour is indeed playful, as opposed to representing serious threat, aggression or submission.

VOCAL SIGNALS

A number of amateur naturalists and professional biologists have described what they consider to be distinct badger vocalisations (e.g. Simms, 1957; Neal, 1986; Christian, 1993). However, describing a sound in words is almost impossible, so it is often difficult for a reader to determine whether, say, what one observer calls 'keckering' is the same as what another calls 'whickering', or whether what one calls a 'cough' is different from what another calls a 'bark'.

More recently, however, Josephine Wong and her colleagues have brought a new level of sophistication to the study of badger vocalisations by applying sound spectrographic analysis (Wong *et al.*, 1999). This not only enables the sounds made by badgers to be visualised but also makes it possible to measure acoustic characteristics such as duration, bandwidth, fundamental frequency and number of repetitions, and to apply statistical analysis to these measurements in order to objectively distinguish different vocalisations. A further strength of the same study is that the animals were simultaneously video-recorded, enabling the behavioural context of the various vocalisations to be determined. Some of Wong's audio recordings have been made publicly available, enabling the rest of us to match her terminology with the vocalisations in question (see www.wildcru.org/research/research-detail/?project_id=58).

Wong and her collaborators have distinguished 16 discrete vocalisations, some specific to adults, some specific to cubs and some employed by both. Reassuringly, many of these correspond to vocalisations identified and described verbally by previous authors. What follows, therefore, is based largely on Wong *et al.*'s study, though I will incorporate additional information, where relevant, from the observations of others, including my own. The vocalisations described by Wong *et al.* were used in five main contexts: affiliation, aggression, surprise or fear, mating and play. I shall discuss each of these in turn and then comment on the curious lack of a social alarm signal in badgers.

Affiliation

Chirp, cluck, coo, grunt and *purr* seem to function as contact or reassurance calls. Chirps are moderate-pitched, soft, bird-like sounds; clucks are like the soft quacking of a duck; coos are soft, gentle, dove-like sounds; grunts are short, low-pitched, blunt sounds of the noisy type (that is, they consist of a wide range of frequencies of approximately equal intensity, and therefore lack any discernible pitch); and purring is a more prolonged, soft, vibrant vocalisation reminiscent of the purring of a cat. In purring, each individual purr in a sequence corresponds with a single exhalation and sometimes terminates in a click-like sound, suggesting that purring may encompass two different vocalisations (termed 'purr' and 'purr-click'), conveying different messages. All of these affiliation signals are low in volume and can only be heard within a distance of a few metres.

Grunts are emitted by both adults and cubs; chirps, clucks and coos only by cubs; and purring only by mothers with cubs. Grunts, chirps, clucks and coos are used during greeting, grooming, foraging and play – that is, situations in which members of the same social group are close to one another and are in a friendly mood. Purring is a more specific vocalisation used by a mother to call her cubs out of the sett, to encourage them to follow her or, sometimes, seemingly just to reassure them that she is present.

Aggression

Bark, hiss, growl, snarl and *kecker* are associated primarily with aggression, though 'bark' may also indicate surprise or fear (see below). The bark is an abrupt expiratory sound of the noisy type, usually emitted as a series. Hisses, by contrast, are unvoiced expiratory sounds, usually emitted singly, and have been likened to the hiss of a cat. Growls and snarls are both relatively lengthy vocalisations but snarls have a higher-pitched, sibilant quality, while growls consist of a coarse, low-pitched rumble (fundamental frequency 32 Hz). Snarls are also more complex than growls, consisting of a harmonic phase sandwiched between two noisy phases. The kecker is a rapid series of staccato sounds of variable pitch, difficult to describe but easy to recognise when you hear it, and resembling no other animal vocalisation of which I am aware.

Barks, hisses and growls seem to be relatively low-intensity threat signals, used for example to warn another group member away from food, or directed towards a member of another group that has entered the signaller's territory. All three signals often cause the receiver to retreat. The snarl is a higher-intensity threat signal, often accompanied by the 'upright' or 'forward' posture, apparently indicating intention to attack if the receiver does not give way. Keckering is also associated with the 'forward' posture but is most conspicuous during actual fighting, becoming louder and more insistent as the conflict escalates in intensity.

Startle, surprise, fear and pain

Snort, yelp, squeak and *wail* are associated with frustration, surprise, fear or pain, though snorts may also function as threat signals. Like the bark, the snort is an abrupt, noisy expiratory sound, but it is longer in duration than the bark and is emitted through the nose rather than the mouth. It usually occurs singly. The yelp is a short, abrupt, high-pitched sound, usually emitted in series. Squeaks are very high-pitched (fundamental frequency 576 Hz), very short, harmonic sounds that are only emitted by cubs, usually in series. Wails are equally shrill but more intense and protracted.

Snorting is usually elicited when a badger is surprised by something potentially threatening, such as the appearance, at close range, of another badger, a potential predator or a human being (see below). It is sometimes accompanied by the 'upright' posture. There has been some debate as to whether snorting is more indicative of surprise or of threat, but these two contexts are often difficult to distinguish. Indeed, they may be inseparable in principle, since an animal that is suddenly confronted by a strange badger or a potential predator is likely to be both surprised and on its guard. I can only say that on the few occasions when I have found myself face to face with a snorting badger, I have found the experience pretty intimidating.

The yelp indicates fear or actual pain: for example, when an animal is being bitten. Cubs sometimes yelp when play-fighting, perhaps to indicate when a game is becoming too rough; and females may yelp when a male bites them during mating. Squeaking and wailing are both signs of distress in cubs: for example, when they are separated from their mother. Both signals are easy to locate and seem to serve to attract the mother's attention. Possibly, therefore, they convey a similar message but with different intensity.

Neal & Cheeseman (1996) describe several accounts of badgers *screaming*. This is a very loud, almost human-like vocalisation that is truly frightening when experienced at close quarters. Observers have used words such as 'fiendish', 'heartrending' and 'awful' to describe it, and I can personally attest to this. One night, while radio-tracking badgers, I was walking along a fence line when a terrible noise, part scream and part growl, suddenly erupted at my feet, almost giving me a heart attack. When I had calmed down sufficiently to get out my torch and shine it downwards, I was confronted by a tiny cub, completely fluffed up and obviously very frightened, cowering against the fence. It was hard to believe that such a small animal had produced this blood-curdling sound.

Most accounts of screaming, like mine, involve cubs reacting to danger, either in the form of a human or an aggressive adult badger. However, it seems that screaming can also occur when adults fight, probably when one animal is getting much the worst of the encounter. It seems, therefore, to be an expression of extreme fear or distress, directed primarily towards the cause of the threat. However, it may also sometimes serve as a cry for help. Chris Cheeseman tells of a young badger screaming when he approached it, whereupon an adult (presumably a parent) shot out of the sett and attacked him.

Mating

The vocalisation most characteristic of mating is the *churr*, a sort of purring sound but deeper in pitch and more insistent than a normal purr. Christian (1993, p. 194) describes it as 'deep', 'throaty' and 'vibrant', with an 'oily, bubbling' quality. It is emitted only by males and is mainly used to call an oestrus female out of the sett or to induce her to mate (see Chapter 5). However, Paul Stewart reports male badgers churring while visiting latrines during the mating season, despite there being no other badger in the vicinity at the time (Stewart *et al.*, 2002). Churring may, therefore, be a general signal of male sexual excitement.

Chittering is a short, high-pitched, chattering sound, harmonic in character and usually given in series. It is heard most commonly when a female is being harassed by a male and may accompany the 'forward' threat posture, suggesting that it is a signal to the male to back off. It can also occur when the male has mounted the female and is biting her neck, in which case it may, like yelping, indicate pain.

Play

Of the vocalisations identified above, bark, yelp, chitter, squeak, chirp, cluck and growl have all been recorded during play, when they often follow one another in rapid sequences. Sometimes, indeed, these sequences are so rapid that the separate vocalisations are difficult to distinguish, even with the help of spectrographic analysis. On other occasions, what are supposedly discrete vocalisations really do merge physically into one another with no discernible break, such as chitters into yelps and growls into keckers. Judging from the context in which they are given, these signals seem to have much the same function in play as they do in adult life.

Alarm signalling

An alarm signal is a signal (usually either visual or vocal) given by one member of a group of animals in order to warn others of the approach of a predator. Alarm signalling occurs in a wide range of group-living species and the communal protection that it provides is thought to be one of the most basic advantages of group living. Consequently, we would expect it to occur in badgers.

There seems little doubt, however, that badgers have no system for warning one another of danger. While radio-tracking badgers, I have sometimes observed two or more members of the same social group foraging within a few metres of one another, only to see one of them take fright and dash noisily off while the others continued to forage as if nothing had happened. One of my students, Jay Butler, investigated this phenomenon more systematically by creeping up on badgers that were foraging in pairs and then deliberately disturbing one of them. She observed exactly the same thing. Even when the disturbed individual snorted at Jay, its companion usually took no notice; and on two occasions, a quite young cub took no notice when its mother snorted and ran off. This lack of response on the part of other badgers, plus the fact that they are just as likely to snort at an intruder when foraging on their own as when they are in a group, led us to conclude that the snort is a warning call to a potential predator, not an alarm call directed towards other members of the social group (Butler & Roper, 1995).

Why badgers have failed to evolve this most basic form of social communication remains unclear. One reason may be that they forage solitarily most of the time; another may be that they are not particularly vulnerable to predation when out foraging; yet another may be that group living is a relatively recent, and still relatively unusual, development in the species' history. Whatever the reason, the absence of an alarm signal is consistent with Hans Kruuk's characterisation of badgers as a 'primitively social' species (see Chapter 8).

OLFACTORY SIGNALS

Badgers are generally credited with having a good sense of smell (see Chapter 2) and they also, like many mammals, have a well-developed vomeronasal organ (a special organ for the detection of pheromones). In addition, badgers themselves have an instantly recognisable, species-specific smell, though they are not, as Hans Kruuk has pointed out, especially smelly by the standards of mustelids, or even of wild mammals in general. The odour in question, which is musky, penetrating and clinging, comes from the anal glands, since pure anal gland secretion smells just like a live badger.

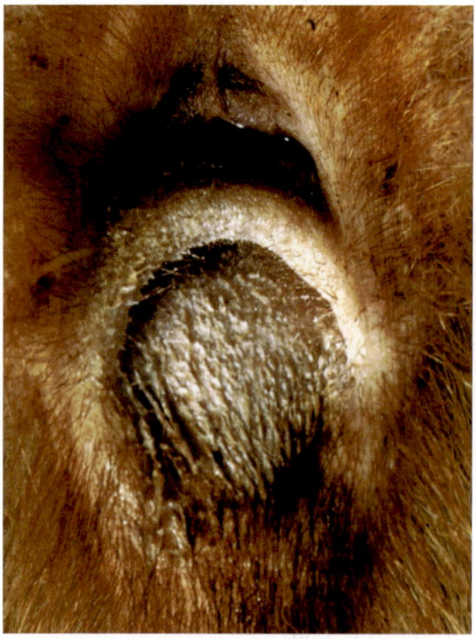

FIG 130. Anal region of the badger showing (above) anus and (below) crescent-shaped opening of the caudal gland. (E. Do Linh San)

Badgers also have a conspicuous caudal gland just beneath the tail (Fig. 130); they have glands within the intestine that may contribute scent to faeces; and it has been suggested that they have scent glands on their feet and elsewhere on their bodies, though this has yet to be confirmed. They defecate, urinate and scent-mark communally at particular places called 'latrines'; they scent-mark the substrate individually, both at the sett and elsewhere; they scratch with their fore claws on trees and logs (Fig. 131); and they scent-mark one another. Altogether, then, badgers

FIG 131. Holly tree that has been extensively scratched by badgers. This may be a form of scent-marking. (H. Clark)

have the potential to distribute olfactory information in a variety of ways, and that information has the potential to serve a variety of functions.

In this section, I shall first describe what are thought to be the four main sources of olfactory information in badgers: namely, anal gland secretion, caudal gland secretion, faeces and urine. I shall then describe two types of scent-marking behaviour: namely, marking of other individuals ('allo-marking') and marking of the substrate. Finally, I shall discuss what scent-marking behaviour tells us about the function of territoriality in badgers.

Anal gland secretion

The anal glands of the badger are paired, sac-like structures lying just internal to the anus on either side. Each opens into the anus via a sphincter. They contain holocrine and apocrine cells that produce a thick, orange, semi-liquid secretion, the odour of which is, as already noted, powerful, musky and redolent of badgers themselves. The muscular walls of the sacs, and the sphincters that close them off from the anus, are under neural control, enabling anal secretion to be discharged at will.

Gas-chromatographic analysis by John Davies has shown that anal secretion contains a complex mix of long-chain fatty acids plus a small amount of protein.

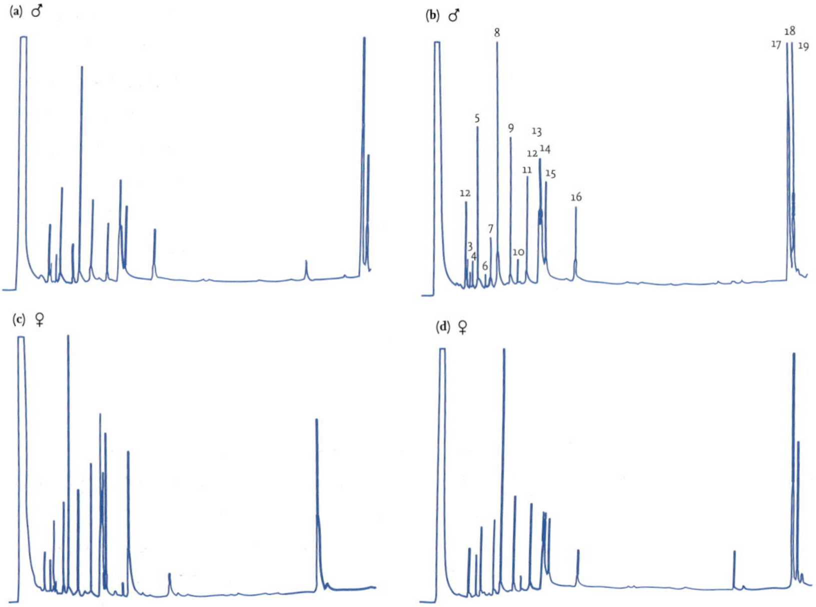

FIG 132. Gas chromatograms of anal secretion sampled from two male and two female badgers. Numbers 1–19 identify individual chemical components that occur in significant amounts in all samples. (From Davies *et al.*, 1988)

Five of these fatty acids (palmitic, stearic, oleic, linoleic and eicosatrienoic) seem particularly important, insofar as they comprise about 45–50 per cent of the total secretion, but at least 19 different chemicals occur reliably and in reasonably large amounts (Davies *et al.*, 1988: see Fig. 132).

The most striking impression when one compares the chromatograms of samples of anal secretion from different individuals is how similar they are, substantiating the fact that, at least to the human nose, all samples (and all badgers) have the same unmistakable 'badgery' smell. One function of the secretion, therefore, may be to communicate species identity. Statistical comparison of chromatograms by Davies *et al.* provided some suggestion of a difference between social groups, suggesting that members of each group may share similar scent profiles. On the other hand, there was no evidence of a difference between sexes, which is surprising, because behavioural evidence suggests that anal secretion communicates information related to mating (see below). Even more mystifyingly, the scent profiles of some individuals were extremely stable over time, while those of others varied. All in all then,

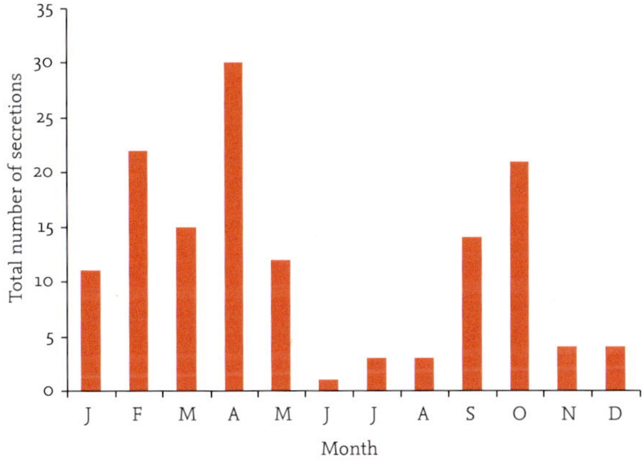

FIG 133. Seasonal changes in the number of deposits of anal secretion in a sample of latrines in the south of England. (From Roper *et al.*, 1986)

chromatographic analysis has so far failed to shed much light on what information anal secretion communicates, though judging from its complexity, it must surely say something more than merely 'I am a badger'.

Anal secretion is used in two different ways, which provide additional clues as to its function. The first of these is that it is deposited together with faeces, or, occasionally, in a pit on its own, at latrines, where it is visible as a small orange blob or smear. Deposition of anal secretion at latrines varies seasonally, with peaks in the spring (February to April) and autumn (September to October) (Roper *et al.*, 1986: Fig. 133). The fact that the timing of these peaks corresponds roughly with peak periods of mating activity suggests that anal secretion serves the purpose of mate defence or mate attraction. That is, male members of a social group could use anal secretion to warn off other males, while oestrus females could use it to advertise their availability (see Chapter 5).

The second way in which anal secretion is used is in the context of short-term signalling. The secretion impregnates the skin and fur surrounding the anal region and on the underside of the tail, where it stains the pelage with a telltale orange colour. It also presumably contaminates the fur over the rest of the body, albeit at a lower concentration, since the whole of a badger has the same characteristic musky smell. As already noted, some of the visual displays associated with aggression, surprise and mating are accompanied by a strong whiff of anal secretion, which probably emanates from the animal's pelage during pilo-erection. Additionally, badgers may be able to squirt out anal secretion when excited, in the same was as skunks do but with somewhat less noisome results. Either way, the fact that the secretion can be smelled at a distance shows that it must contain volatile components in addition to the high molecular weight (and therefore relatively non-volatile) fatty acids identified by Davies and his colleagues.

Caudal gland secretion

While all mustelids possess anal glands, the caudal gland is unique to badgers and has the distinction of being the largest scent gland so far described in any carnivore. It consists of a thick layer of sebaceous tissue plus a thinner outer layer of apocrine cells, both of which secrete material into a large interior pouch formed from an invagination of the skin (Fig. 134). The pouch opens to the outside via a horizontal, crescent-shaped slit, 3–5 cm wide, between the anus and the base of the tail. The whole organ measures about 5 × 6 cm and the inner pouch contains several grams of secretion, which is of a thick paste-like consistency and varies in colour from white to brown. Its scent is surprisingly subtle – a faint musky odour, nothing like as pungent as that of anal gland secretion. The gland is more than twice as large, and contains up to four times as much secretion, in males as in females (Kruuk *et al.*, 1984); and in both sexes, the volume of secretion contained within the gland is greatest in winter and spring, and least in autumn (Buesching *et al.*, 2002a: see Fig. 135).

Quite a lot is known about the chemical composition of caudal gland secretion, thanks to gas-chromatographic analysis undertaken by Martin Gorman and others at the University of Aberdeen and, more recently, by Christina Buesching and others at the University of Oxford (Gorman *et al.*, 1984; Buesching *et al.*, 2002b, 2002c). These studies show that the secretion consists mainly of long-chain carboxylic acids, water and protein. No fewer than 110 different chemical components have been identified, of which 21 have been present in every sample so far analysed. Each individual badger has a characteristic scent profile that remains stable, at least in the short term, while different badgers have markedly different profiles. In addition, members of the

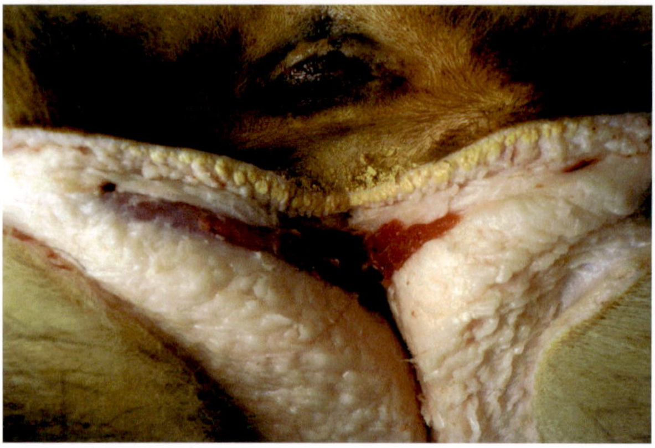

FIG 134. Caudal gland cut open longitudinally. The white areas are apocrine and sebaceous tissue in which the secretion is produced. The red area is muscular tissue. (E. Do Linh San)

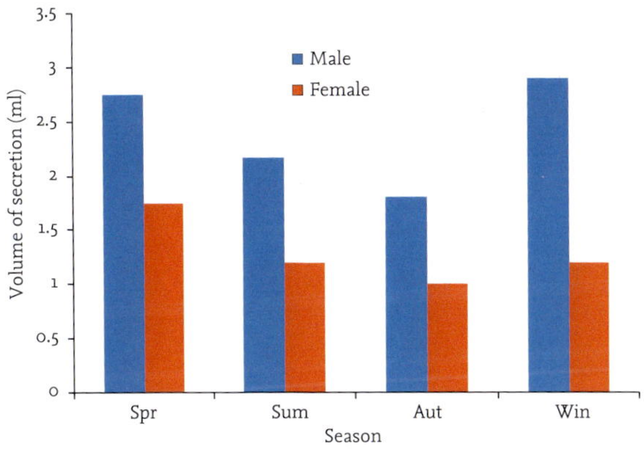

FIG 135. Seasonal and sex differences in the volume of secretion produced by the caudal gland. (Based on data in Buesching *et al.*, 2002a)

same group tend to have more similar scent profiles than members of different groups and there is some evidence that the chemical composition of the secretion varies according to sex, age, body condition and reproductive status. Taken together, these results suggest that caudal secretion almost certainly codes for individual identity and probably for group identity. In addition, the fact that the gland is larger in males, and that the amount of secretion varies seasonally, suggests some function related to mating or territorial activity.

Chromatographic analysis on its own, however, suffers from a major disadvantage: namely, that it does not show what features of the olfactory stimulus are meaningful to real live badgers. A badger may not be able to detect

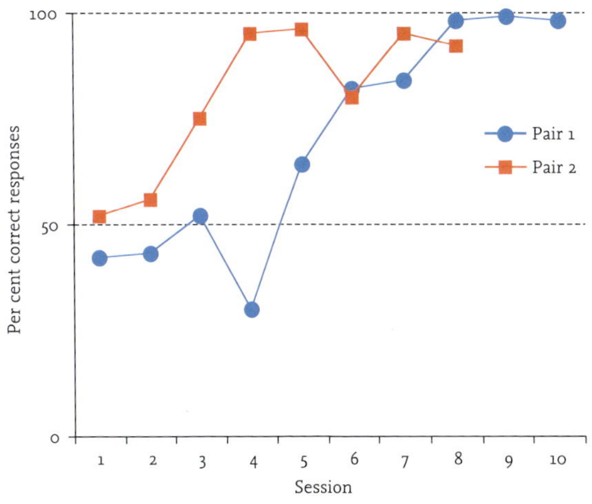

FIG 136. Speed with which a tame badger learned to discriminate between the caudal gland scents of two other badgers. Each curve shows the results for a different pair of donor badgers. The horizontal line indicates chance performance. (From Kruuk *et al.*, 1984)

some of the differences revealed in chromatograms or, conversely, may be able to distinguish scent profiles on the basis of differences that are too subtle to be revealed in chromatograms. In order to be really sure about the function of scent signals, therefore, chromatographic analysis needs to be backed up by behavioural discrimination experiments. In the case of caudal secretion, Kruuk *et al.* (1984) have confirmed that badgers can indeed learn to distinguish the scents of different individuals (Fig. 136). However, more work of this kind is needed in order to determine whether the other types of information that caudal secretion seems to contain are indeed detectable by the animals themselves.

Faeces

Badgers characteristically defecate in small specially dug pits called dung pits, though sometimes they defecate directly onto the surface of the ground. Collections of dung pits, known as latrines, are found around the territory boundary, at the sett and elsewhere, and it is generally assumed that these have territorial significance (see below and Fig. 137). Latrines remain active more or

FIG 137. (above left) Latrine (T. Roper); and (left) close-up of dung pit. (L. & P. Schofield)

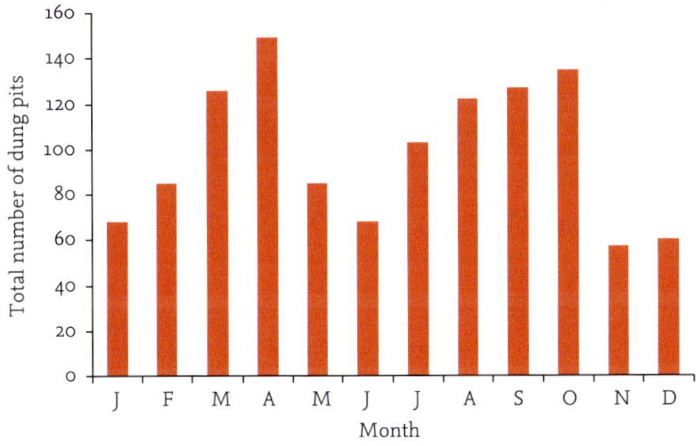

FIG 138. Seasonal changes in the number of used dung pits per month in latrines in the south of England. (From Roper *et al.*, 1986)

less year-round but they contain especially large numbers of pits (and therefore more deposits of fresh faeces) in spring and autumn (Roper *et al.*, 1986: Fig. 138). They are visited by badgers of both sexes and all ages, and are used for purposes of defecation on about 50 per cent of visits (Stewart *et al.*, 2002). (On the other 50 per cent of visits, badgers may just sniff at the contents of the latrine or may deposit urine or scent gland secretions: see below.)

Since badgers also urinate, and deposit anal and caudal secretion, at latrines, the question arises as to what information, if any, faeces communicate. One possibility is that faeces are an 'alerting signal', adding to the olfactory conspicuousness of a latrine but not conveying any specific information. Alternatively, faeces could just function as a vehicle for other secretions, the most likely candidates being secretions from the anal glands or from glands within the intestines (Stubbe, 1971). This hypothesis may seem unlikely at first sight in the case of anal gland secretion, since faeces are often unaccompanied by anal secretion and anal secretion is sometimes deposited independently of faeces. However, it could be that all faeces deposits carry amounts of anal secretion that are perceptible to badgers, even if they are often too small to be visible to us. Finally, it is possible that faeces convey specific information about the animal responsible for the deposit.

If faeces (or associated glandular secretions) do carry specific information, then badgers should be able to discriminate one class of faecal deposits from another. Kate Palphramand and Piran White tested wild badgers to see whether they could discriminate faeces deposits collected from an alien territory (i.e. a territory at least 5 km away) from faeces collected either from their own territory or from a neighbouring territory. The logic behind this experiment was that for a resident badger, the sudden appearance in its territory of completely alien faeces should be more surprising than the appearance of faeces deposited by members

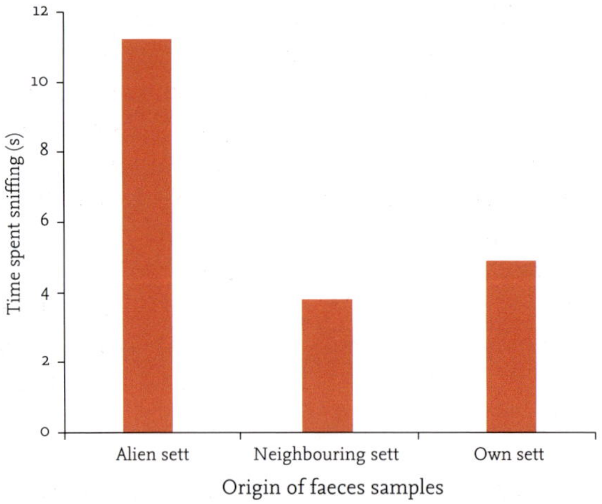

FIG 139. Time that badgers spent sniffing at faeces taken from the main sett of an alien group, from that of a neighbouring group or from their own main sett. (Based on data in Palphramand & White, 2007)

of its own or a neighbouring group, with both of which it should already be familiar. Therefore, alien faeces should elicit more investigation. In the event, badgers did indeed spend longer sniffing at alien deposits, suggesting that faeces (or the glandular secretions that they carry) may contain information about group membership (Palphramand & White, 2007: see Fig. 139).

Urine

Not much is known about urine-marking by badgers but it is clear that they urinate in several different ways and in a variety of contexts. At latrines, badgers usually dig a small pit (separate from the pits used for faeces and anal gland secretion) and urinate into it. Elsewhere, they usually urinate directly onto the ground, either when stationary (in which case, the urine forms a 'patch' about 10 cm in diameter) or while walking along (in which case, it forms a 'trail' up to about 1.5 m long) (Brown *et al.*, 1993). In addition, Hans Kruuk (1978) reports that badgers sometimes urinate at the same time as squat-marking, and Christina Buesching has observed badgers of both sexes urinating against a vertical object by raising one hind leg. Finally, badgers sometimes urinate on top of a sett (Buesching & Macdonald, 2004).

The most detailed information about urination patterns comes from a study by Julian Brown, using the technique of spool-and-line tracking. This involves fitting a collar, to which is attached a long spool of very fine thread, to a captured badger, which is then returned to its sett. The following night, as the badger leaves its sett and moves about its territory, the spool unwinds, leaving a record of where the animal has been. It is then possible to reconstruct the animal's entire night's peregrinations by following the thread. In the case of Brown's study, each badger was also injected, at the time of capture, with a substance called fluorescein, a kind of dye that finds its way into the urine and faeces and makes them fluoresce when illuminated with ultraviolet light. In this way, Brown was able, by shining an ultraviolet light onto the ground as he followed the spool-and-line thread, to detect deposits of urine from the animal in question (Brown *et al.*, 1993; White *et al.*, 1993).

Brown's results show that, overall, about half of all urinations (52 per cent) are at latrines, with this proportion being slightly larger in the spring than in other seasons, and slightly larger in males than in females. Of the urinations not found at latrines, most occur where a badger path crosses some linear feature such as a fence or hedge, or the edge of a wood. These 'crossing point' urinations are mostly in the form of trails (62 per cent) and are more frequent in spring and summer than in autumn or winter (Fig. 140). Since a single animal can urinate several times in one night, it seems likely that badgers do not completely empty their bladders when they urinate but, rather, dribble out small quantities of urine periodically. This, plus the fact that urination usually occurs at conspicuous places such as latrines and crossing points, suggests that it does indeed serve some signalling function.

What information urine serves to communicate is unknown. A chemical analysis using chromatography in conjunction with mass spectrometry identified about 300 different compounds in badger urine, of which about a dozen occurred in a majority of samples (Service *et al.*, 2001). There was some evidence of seasonal changes in the relative concentrations of these compounds, probably related to changes in diet, but not much evidence of differences between males and females. In many other species of mammals, including some

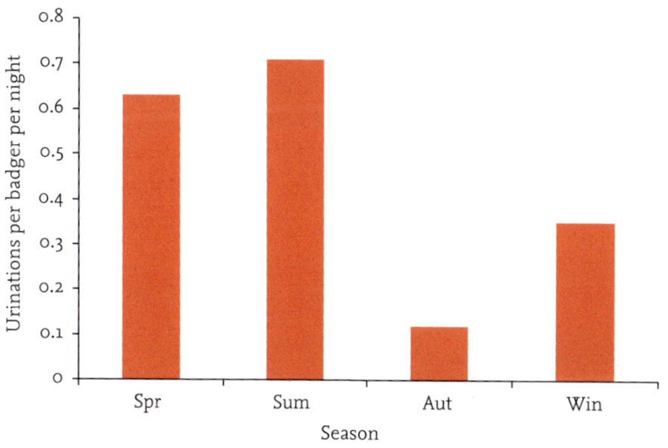

FIG 140. Seasonal variation in the number of 'crossing- point' urinations per badger per night. (Based on data in White *et al.*, 1993)

carnivores, urine contains information about gender and state of sexual readiness, and it would be surprising if it did not do the same in badgers. At present, however, this is purely a matter of speculation.

Allo-marking

Allo-marking, the scent-marking of one animal by another, takes two different forms. In *sequential allo-marking*, one badger backs towards another with its tail raised and plants or smears its anal region onto the recipient – usually onto its rump, but sometimes onto its flank, head or face. The recipient may or may not then perform the same action in return. Males sometimes sequentially mark females during mating, and cubs sometimes actively solicit sequential allo-marking by crawling beneath the legs of an adult (a behaviour called 'scent theft': see Chapter 5). In *mutual allo-marking*, two badgers back up simultaneously towards one another, lift their tails and press or rub their sub-caudal regions together, sometimes so vigorously as to lift one another's hindquarters off the ground (Christian, 1993: see Fig. 141). Allo-marking has been discussed primarily in the context of sub-caudal gland secretion. However, since the peri-anal region and the underside of the tail of a badger are impregnated with anal gland secretion as well as caudal gland secretion, a cocktail of secretions from both glands is probably transferred.

FIG 141. Sequence of actions involved in mutual allo-marking by badgers. (From Christian, 1993)

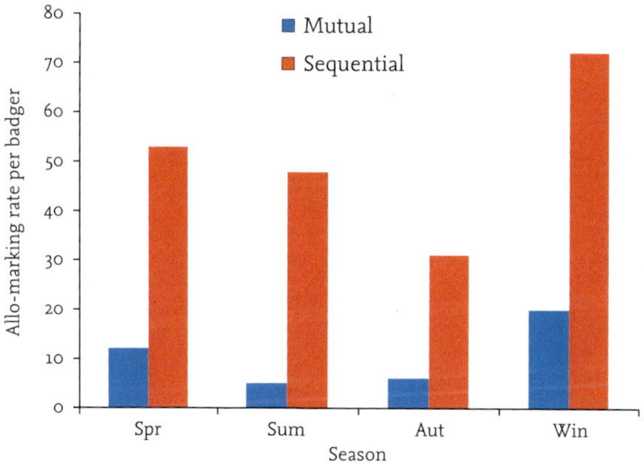

FIG 142. Seasonal changes in rates of mutual and sequential allo-marking. (Based on data in Buesching *et al.*, 2003)

By carefully analysing many hours of video recordings of groups of badgers interacting at their setts, Christina Buesching has shown that both types of allo-marking occur more frequently in males than in females. Both are also more frequent in winter and spring (i.e. in the mating and cub-rearing seasons) than in summer or autumn (Buesching *et al.*, 2003: see Fig. 142). However, there are also differences between sequential and mutual allo-marking. Sequential allo-marking is much more frequent overall than mutual marking; mutual marking only occurs between members of the same social group, whereas sequential marking sometimes involves individuals from different groups; and sequential marking varies between individuals according to characteristics such as age and reproductive status, whereas mutual marking does not.

These observations suggest that mutual and sequential allo-marking probably serve different functions. As regards mutual marking, a variety of evidence suggests that the odours produced by scent gland secretions are usually a consequence of bacterial action on the chemical constituents of the secretion, rather than being a property of the secretion itself. Therefore, individuals whose glands carry the same mix of bacteria will have similar scent profiles. Following this logic, Buesching and her colleagues suggest that mutual scent-marking serves to exchange bacterial fauna between the individual members of a social group, resulting in the formation of a common group odour (see also Gorman *et al.*, 1984; Kruuk *et al.*, 1984). This fits with chromatographic evidence that both anal gland and caudal gland scent profiles do differ more between the members of different social groups than between the members of any one group (see above). In addition, it would explain why mutual marking only occurs within a social group, why all members of a group mutually mark one another and why the rate of mutual marking is generally low. On the other hand, the 'bacterial exchange' hypothesis does not so easily explain why males engage in more mutual marking than females or why there are seasonal differences in marking frequency.

Sequential allo-marking, by contrast, is thought to have two functions: to distribute the common group odour generated by mutual allo-marking and to communicate information such as age and reproductive status. What precise function the latter information serves is unclear, but given the seasonal pattern of allo-marking activity, it could be related to the advertisement of sexual receptivity or the defence of mating rights (Buesching & Macdonald, 2001; Buesching *et al.*, 2003).

Squat-marking

In squat-marking, a badger briefly lifts its tail and dips its rear end down onto the substrate (Fig. 143). Most observers have tended to assume that squat-marking, like allo-marking, serves to deposit caudal gland secretion. However, as has already been noted in the context of allo-marking, the badger's peri-anal region is impregnated with anal as well as caudal gland secretion, so squat-marking probably deposits both. Indeed, when a badger squat-marks on snow, the orange colour of anal gland secretion is plainly visible (Kruuk, 1989).

Badgers squat-mark at latrines, at the sett, on frequently used paths and at foraging places; and they also squat-mark during mating and threat displays. Sometimes the mark is made on a particular feature such as a clump of grass, and Kruuk *et al.* (1984) write of badgers having regular squat-marking 'stations'

FIG 143. Badger squat-marking, showing hunched posture and raised tail. (M. Clark)

such as tussocks or flat stones. More often than not, however, marking occurs directly onto the surface of the ground, wherever the badger happens to be and whatever it happens to be doing, at rates varying from several times per minute to a few times per hour (Kruuk *et al.*, 1984). About a third of squat-marks are over-marked, either by the same or another individual, usually within 24 hours of the first mark being deposited (Buesching & Macdonald, 2004).

Careful observations by Christina Buesching and Paul Stewart indicate that squat-marking has some function related to mating (Buesching & Macdonald, 2001; Stewart *et al.*, 2002). Although all members of a social group engage in squat-marking, oestrus females mark more often than non-oestrus females, and reproductively active males more than immature males. In addition, marking is most frequent in adults of both sexes during the winter breeding season. Finally, the fact that squat-marking is more frequently performed at boundary latrines than at hinterland latrines suggests a role in communication between neighbouring social groups, for example in mate advertisement or mate defence. However, badgers do also squat-mark at their own setts, suggesting an additional role in communication within the group. For example, individuals tend to squat-mark the sett entrances that they themselves prefer to use, perhaps indicating personal ownership. In general, however, it is remarkable how little is known about squat-marking or its function, given the fact that it occurs more often than any other kind of scent-marking behaviour and that the production of large volumes of fat-rich caudal secretion must incur a significant cost in terms of energy.

Latrines and their function

As has already been noted, badgers deposit faeces preferentially at particular sites known as latrines. They also urinate at latrines, deposit secretions from the anal and caudal glands, and scratch around in the soil with their fore and hind claws (Fig. 144). Latrines can contain from as few as one to as many as 50 separate dung pits and in a large latrine these can be spread over an area of tens of square metres. Altogether, then, latrines constitute conspicuous olfactory and visual landmarks and have the potential to convey a wealth of information (Stewart *et al.*, 2002).

Latrines tend to occur in places where a badger path crosses or runs alongside a linear feature such as a hedge, fence or road, or where two badger paths cross one another. However, sometimes a latrine can occur apparently in the middle of nowhere, such as halfway along a badger path that crosses a large field. Several studies suggest a preference for siting latrines in woodland (often on the edge of a wood) and, in particular, at the bases of conifer trees. This may protect the latrine from rain, thus preserving for as long as possible any olfactory information that it contains (Stewart *et al.*, 2002).

FIG 144. Badger digging in a dung pit. (M. Clark)

During the course of his classic studies of the behaviour of badgers in Oxfordshire and Scotland, Hans Kruuk used bait-marking to discover which latrines belonged to which social groups. The principle behind bait-marking is simple: you feed badgers with bait that contains some kind of indigestible and easily recognisable material (the 'markers'), then look for faeces deposits containing this material. In his early studies, Kruuk made markers by cutting up plastic carrier bags of different colours into small pieces and mixing them into bait composed of peanuts and honey. Nowadays, small plastic beads (which are commercially available, are non-toxic and come in a variety of shapes and colours) are used as markers and golden syrup is substituted for honey in the bait mixture, but the principle is the same. Bait containing, say, red markers is put down at one main sett every day for several days, bait containing blue markers at another, and so on, after which the area in question is searched for marked faeces. Because each main sett, and therefore each social group, is associated with a particular colour of marker, bait-marking enables one to determine which social groups use which latrines (see Delahay *et al.*, 2000a, for details).

Bait-marking is extremely satisfying to do, because it is fun and easy and you always get results. After several days of putting bait down at setts, there is an almost magical pleasure in surveying the area for latrines and finding, sure enough, faeces deposits containing coloured bits of plastic. As the data accumulate, a picture gradually emerges of each main sett being surrounded by a scatter of latrines at which the members of that group regularly defecate. At boundaries where two territories meet one another, one typically finds a string of latrines shared by members of both of the relevant social groups. Eventually, a patchwork quilt of badger territories is revealed, with little or no overlap and little or no spare space between them (Fig. 145). Bait-marking also shows that

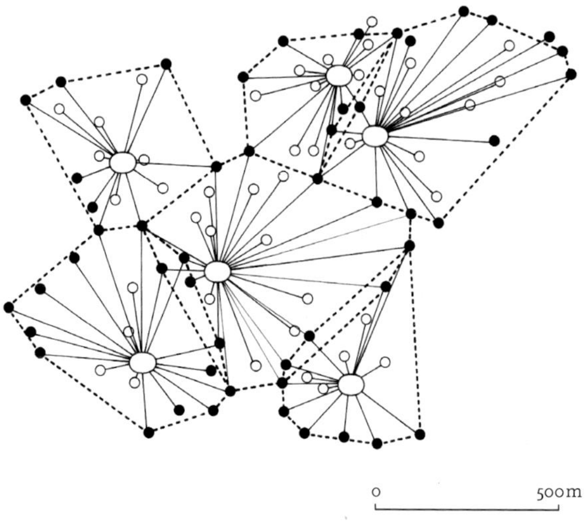

FIG 145. Bait-marking map from part of the author's study area in East Sussex. Large ovals show the position of main setts; filled circles denote boundary latrines; open circles denote hinterland latrines. Continuous lines join a latrine where bait-markers were found to the corresponding main sett. Broken lines denote territory boundaries.

latrines occur throughout the territory of a social group ('hinterland latrines') but are especially frequent around the territory boundary ('boundary latrines'). In addition, most main setts also have at least one latrine at the sett itself.

The most detailed information on how badgers use latrines has been provided by Séan Christian and Paul Stewart, working in East Sussex and in Wytham Woods, near Oxford, respectively (Christian, 1993; Stewart *et al.*, 2002). A latrine visit typically lasts about half a minute, and about half of this time is spent sniffing at the latrine contents. Sometimes a foraging badger will suddenly dash off to a latrine, do whatever it wants to do there, and return to its previous foraging place; on other occasions, it will make a partial or complete circuit of the territory, stopping en route at every latrine that it encounters. Patrolling of the territory boundary in this way is sufficiently frequent that it is possible to see, in areas of high badger population density, a clear path linking each latrine to the next one (Fig. 146).

During the course of a latrine visit, badgers tend to squat-mark on entering and leaving the latrine area. They defecate on about 50 per cent of visits, tending to use a small subset of the available dung pits for a period of several days and then switching to another subset. Because of this behaviour, the same dung pit can be used repeatedly in the course of a few days, resulting in separate faeces deposits piling up on top of one another (a phenomenon called 'over-marking': see Fig. 147). All the members of a social group visit the latrines within their territory but adult males visit boundary latrines more than hinterland latrines,

FIG 146. Badger paths. Paths like these can sometimes be seen linking adjacent boundary latrines. (M. Cowan and H. Clark)

FIG 147. Over-marking with faeces. In this case, two faeces deposits are easily discernible, one containing maize and one containing plum remains. (E. Do Linh San)

whereas the reverse is the case for adult females. In addition, as we have already seen, defecation, deposition of anal secretion and squat-marking at latrines are all most frequent in the breeding season.

From the location of latrines and the manner in which they are used, it seems self-evident that one of their functions is to demarcate territory boundaries. But what information, exactly, is being communicated? The classical view is that boundary marks, not just in badgers but more generally, constitute 'keep out' signals, posted to deter intruders from entering the territory. However, this idea is almost certainly an oversimplification, for a number of reasons. First, it fails to do justice to the wealth of olfactory information that is being deposited or to explain why, if the message is so simple, badgers spend so much time sniffing at the contents of latrines. Second, it fails to explain why badgers do, in fact, invade one another's territories on a regular basis for foraging, mating and scent-marking purposes, often without meeting any resistance on the part of residents (see Chapters 5 and 7). Third, it is hard to see why, in principle, a 'keep out' notice, in and of itself, should act as a deterrent. And finally, the 'keep out' hypothesis fails to acknowledge what is perhaps the most striking feature of boundary latrines: namely, that when neighbouring groups share a common territory boundary, they also share the latrines along that boundary. This suggests that boundary latrines exist for the mutual sharing of information between neighbours, rather than for delivering a one-way threat from a resident group to would-be intruders.

These sorts of considerations have given rise to more sophisticated views as to what latrines communicate. As regards territory defence, an influential theory by Morris Gosling (1982), termed the 'scent matching' hypothesis, suggests that territory marks may enable an intruder to identify the owners of the territory, should it meet them in the course of its incursion. A wealth of data from many different species shows that if it comes to a fight, a territory owner almost always has the advantage over an intruder. Therefore, it would be advantageous to an intruder, on meeting another individual in an occupied territory, to know whether this individual is the territory owner – in which case, the intruder should make itself scarce without further ado – or is another intruder like itself. The territory owner would also benefit by communicating its own identity, because it would avoid a fight in which it might get injured. Gosling's hypothesis is that scent marks provide this information: that is, by depositing a scent mark that smells like itself, the territory owner enables an intruder to recognise it as the owner, should they meet face to face. According to this idea, then, boundary latrines advertise the scent of individual territory occupants.

Almost certainly, however, there is more to latrines than territory defence. The fact that badgers squat-mark, defecate and deposit anal secretion at latrines most frequently in the mating season, plus the fact that squat-marking is more frequent in sexually active individuals, suggests a function related to mating. As we saw in Chapter 5, both males and females make forays into neighbouring territories for mating purposes, males in order to increase their reproductive success and females in order to avoid inbreeding. A territory-holding male would benefit from preventing neighbouring males from coming into the territory for mating purposes, and I have suggested that marking at boundary latrines by males might function as a deterrent in this context – that is, it might function to defend resident females from the attentions of neighbouring males, rather than to defend the territory per se (Roper *et al.*, 1986, 1993; see also Chapter 8). On the other hand, a resident male would also benefit from trying to attract neighbouring females, and it is perfectly possible that boundary scent marks advertise a male's sexual status. Conversely, a resident female would benefit from attracting neighbouring males into her territory, which she could do by advertising her oestrus state at latrines.

Since there is also competition for the opportunity to reproduce within a social group (see Chapter 5), latrines could also function for within-group communication of information related to reproductive status. Put simply, a reproductively dominant boar or sow might proclaim its status by depositing copious scent marks and also by over-marking the signals left by rivals. This kind of function seems especially likely in the case of scent-marking that occurs close to the sett, which is a place where all members of the group congregate and share olfactory information (Buesching & Macdonald, 2001). Alternatively, I have suggested that latrines close to the sett could function to defend the sett itself from intruders that might be tempted to try to usurp it (Roper *et al.*, 1993). Either way, the fact that males mainly visit boundary latrines, whereas females mainly visit hinterland latrines, suggests that these two types of latrines have different functions.

To summarise, it still seems likely that one function of latrines, especially boundary latrines, is to signal that a territory is occupied – though whether this is to defend the territory per se, or resident females, or the main sett, remains unclear. However, even if latrines do serve a defensive function in any or all of these contexts, it seems likely that they do so by communicating information about the characteristics of individual group members rather than serving as simple, anonymous 'keep out' notices. In addition, there is good reason to suppose that latrine use is related to mating activity, and it is easy to see how both sexes could gain by using latrines to signal their reproductive status, both within their own social group and to the members of neighbouring groups. However, although the idea that latrines convey information about individual identity and reproductive status is both attractive and plausible, it remains largely speculative. The fact is that we need more evidence against which to evaluate the various hypotheses.

Scent-marking patterns in areas of low population density

I have commented in previous chapters on the fact that studies of badger biology have been mainly carried out in areas of high badger population density. In the case of communication, this bias is almost total: virtually everything I have said about communication so far is based on studies carried out in the south of England.

My own experience suggests that the use of latrines to demarcate territory boundaries becomes less obvious as population density declines – in areas of low population density, it becomes harder to find latrines or to trace territory boundaries between neighbouring social groups. This probably explains why, although there have been good studies of low-density badger populations in, for example, Poland and Spain (see Chapter 7), these say little or nothing about territory-marking and have not included bait-marking as part of their methodology. Indeed, this is explicitly stated by some of the researchers in question.

A decrease in territory-marking with declining population density would not be surprising, because low population density means larger territories and smaller social groups (see Chapter 7). Hence, fewer badgers are available to maintain latrines, and these latrines have to be spread over a larger area. One strategy used by badgers to overcome this problem may be to rely more on single dung pits, rather than latrines, to communicate information about territory ownership: this would enable a larger number of locations to be scent-marked with a given number of faeces deposits (Hutchings *et al.*, 2002). At very low population density, however, badgers may abandon the marking of territory boundaries altogether and confine scent-marking behaviour to the immediate vicinity of their setts (Kruuk & Parish, 1987; Kowalczyk *et al.*, 2004). In short, the intensive marking of territory boundaries by well-used latrines, which is so apparent in south of England badger populations and which makes the technique of bait-marking possible, probably represents one end of a continuum of scent-marking strategies (see also Chapter 8).

COMPLEX DISPLAYS

So far, I have described the individual signals that badgers use to communicate as if these were separate entities, each with its own discrete function. In the real world, however, displays often involve a combination of signals, both within and between modalities. By way of illustration, the following are descriptions of three incidents involving different combinations of vocal, visual and scent signalling, taken more or less verbatim from the field records of Séan Christian (1993, pp. 198 and 219). The first involves aggression, the second threat and the third mating.

Scene 1: Aggression

Suddenly there is the noise of a fight – a terrible noise incorporating snarls, barks, growls, keckers and crashing about in the nettles. Two badgers are grappling, each has hold of the other's neck and I can hear them panting and gasping, growling every few seconds. Suddenly they separate and stand facing one another in the 'forward' posture. One badger snaps at the other and the keckering starts again, followed by squeals and wails. All the time there is a low vibrating growl. Suddenly the two are fighting again – grunts, snorts, squeals, yelps, growls and barks. The noise has built up to a deafening crescendo and it sounds as if the vocalisations are coming from lots of different badgers: rattling keckers, high-pitched squeals, low growls, sharp barks and yelps. Again the two separate and reach a stand-off, keckering. Both have their hair on end, one is standing head upright and the other standing head lowered, body flattened, looking much smaller. The vanquished badger breaks away down the nearest sett entrance. The other follows and stands growling into the sett.

Scene 2: Threat

A male badger moves towards me. I cough. He reacts by snorting and bottlebrushing, waving his tail around. He growls, squat-marks and stares straight at me, still growling. He does a body-ripple and all his hair stands on end. Still staring (upright posture), he kicks up the turf with first his right then his left hind foot. The smell of musk is overpowering. Eventually, the badger's hair goes down, except for his tail, and he moves away.

Scene 3: Mating

A large boar arrived at the sett. He went from entrance to entrance with his tail bottlebrushed, churring constantly. A female emerged from the sett, approached the male, seized his rump and shook him, then dived back into the sett. The boar returned to churring into the sett entrances and the female emerged again. After a short chase, they mated. For an hour after mating, the boar went from entrance to entrance, still churring loudly, with his tail bottlebrushed, squat-marking on the spoil heaps and then digging up the earth with his fore claws and raking it into the sett entrances with his hind paws. On several occasions, the female growled and snarled at him from underground. Before, during and after copulation, the male kept up a resonant churring and kept his tail bottlebrushed. There was a strong smell of musk that persisted for several hours.

CONCLUSION

I began this chapter by saying that badgers have been characterised as rather uncommunicative animals. Reading the above descriptions, one might doubt the validity of this judgement. On the other hand, anyone who has routinely watched badgers at their setts will have experienced occasions when the members of a social group seemed peculiarly uninterested in one another, almost as if they were reluctant to acknowledge one another's presence. Similarly, when two badgers meet while out foraging, they often pass by without any overt sign of recognition. Of course, it is always possible that in these kinds of situations, the badgers in question are communicating by scent. However, one cannot imagine two dogs, for example, ignoring one another in quite the same way, despite the fact that dogs probably have at least as good a sense of smell as badgers. In addition, there is the genuinely puzzling fact that badgers lack a social alarm signal.

There is, then, some basis for the idea that badgers are a relatively undemonstrative species, at least by carnivore standards. However, we probably underestimate the role that communication, especially in the visual and vocal modalities, plays in their social lives. Techniques such as the use of infrared video surveillance to investigate visual signalling, or of spectrographic analysis to distinguish different types of vocalisation, have scarcely begun to be applied to badgers and have much to offer. In addition, we still have only an inkling of the complexities of olfactory communication: we know relatively little about the information contained in the various scent marks, or putative scent marks, that badgers deposit, and almost nothing about whether badgers can actually use this information and, if so, how they use it. In short, we are still a long way from understanding badger language.

CHAPTER 7

Social Organisation and Use of Space

BADGERS AS SOCIALLY TERRITORIAL ANIMALS

Hans Kruuk and the badgers of Wytham Woods

IT IS HARD TO IMAGINE that not much more than 30 years ago, we knew little about the social organisation of badgers. Ernest Neal's meticulous observations, carried out first in Conigre Wood in the Cotswolds, and then elsewhere, showed that, contrary to what had often been supposed, badgers live in family groups (Neal, 1948, 1977). However, how these groups were organised and how badgers behaved once they were away from the sett were more or less a matter of speculation.

All that changed in 1978 with the publication, by Hans Kruuk, of a landmark study of the badgers of Wytham Woods, near Oxford (Kruuk, 1978a: see Fig. 148). I have read this paper many times and never cease to be impressed by the breadth of topics that Kruuk was able to address, by his methodological inventiveness, by his insightfulness and by the extent to which his findings have been substantiated by later work. Such is the importance of this study that virtually everything that has subsequently been written about the social and territorial organisation of badgers refers back to it, either directly or indirectly.

First, Kruuk distinguished main setts from secondary setts (see Chapter 3) and established that each social group is normally associated with only a single main sett. More important from the present point of view, he also noticed that main setts were rather evenly spaced out in relation to one another, as opposed to being clumped together or randomly located (see Chapter 3, Fig. 59). From this, Kruuk made the important deduction that badgers exhibited some kind of 'social spacing-out mechanism'.

FIG 148. Wytham Woods, near Oxford – the scene of Hans Kruuk's classic study of badgers. (Michele Taylor, Centre for Ecology and Hydrology)

Second, Kruuk used the then rather novel technique of radio-telemetry to show that the home ranges of members of the same social group overlapped to a large extent, so that one could speak of each group having a 'communal home range' that was shared by all of its members. By contrast, the home ranges of different social groups of badgers did not overlap at all (in the jargon, they are said to be 'exclusive'), providing additional evidence of the 'social spacing-out mechanism' referred to above.

Third, Kruuk used bait-marking (see Chapter 6 for an explanation) to show that the boundaries of each group home range were demarcated by lines of latrines, often linked together by well-used paths suggestive of boundary 'patrolling' behaviour. In addition, direct observations revealed that members of a social group rarely ventured beyond their own range boundary and that if two badgers from neighbouring groups happened to meet at a shared boundary, a fierce fight often ensued. These findings suggested that the 'social spacing-out mechanism' that Kruuk had inferred on the basis of other evidence was, in fact, territoriality. That is, each group actively defended its home range against incursion by the members of neighbouring social groups.

FIG 149. A badger family at the sett. (Dassenwerkgroep Brabant)

Finally, Kruuk showed that badger groups in Wytham Woods contained seven members on average but could contain as many as twelve, including reproductively mature individuals of both sexes. In other words, badgers lived in what would now be called 'multi-male multi-female' groups (Fig. 149). He also noted that only one female in any one group bred in any one year, leading him to suggest that there was reproductive competition between the adult female members of a social group (see also Chapter 5).

To summarise, Kruuk showed that the Wytham badgers lived in mixed-sex groups that defended communal territories. We now turn to the question of the extent to which these key findings apply more widely.

Subsequent studies of social and territorial organisation

Since Kruuk's pioneering work, similarly oriented studies have been carried out elsewhere in England and also in Scotland, Finland, Germany, Ireland, Italy, Luxembourg, Norway, Poland, Portugal, Spain and Switzerland (for references, see Table 9, below).

As far as England is concerned, Kruuk's characterisation of badgers has been amply confirmed. Further studies by David Macdonald and others at Wytham Woods have shown that the situation has remained much as Kruuk described it, the only significant change being that group sizes have increased over time, to

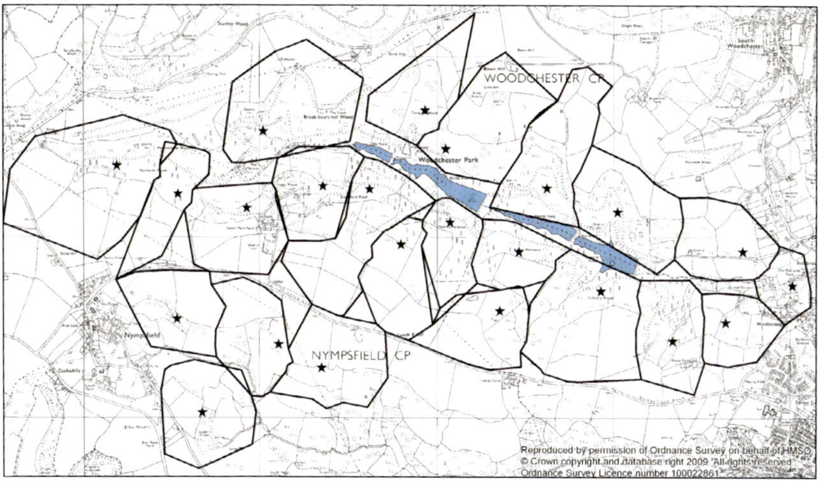

FIG 150. Map of badger territories at Woodchester Park, Gloucestershire. Asterisks show the location of main setts. Note that there is scarcely any overlap between neighbouring territories and little vacant space between them, except where a lake (shaded blue) separates parallel rows of territories in the northeast of the study area. (R. J. Delahay, Food & Environment Research Agency)

such an extent that groups of a dozen or so individuals are now common and groups of 30 or more are not unknown. The same pattern of social territoriality has been shown in a long-running study at Woodchester Park, Gloucestershire (Fig. 150); it has been reported in the north of England by Kate Palphramand and others; we have found it in the South Downs, near Brighton; and it has been reported in two studies of urban badgers (see below).

In Scotland, however, where Kruuk went on to study badgers after leaving Oxford, the situation was somewhat more complex. On the east coast of Scotland, near Aviemore, where the landscape is mainly a mixture of forest and agricultural land, Kruuk found badgers to be socially territorial, though group sizes, at three to five individuals per group, were somewhat smaller than in England and territories larger (a few hundred hectares). In Ardnish, on the west coast, where the landscape is more mountainous and food in shorter supply, social groups were smaller still and range boundaries were less distinct. Moreover, instead of having latrines on the range boundaries, groups used latrines close to their setts, so that the sett locations themselves constituted scent-marking stations. Altogether, then, there was less sign of social cohesion in the west coast badgers and less evidence of territoriality.

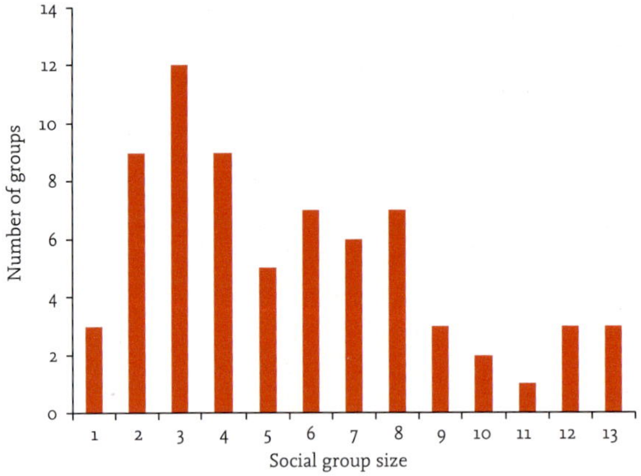

FIG 151. Frequency distribution of social group sizes (number of adults per group) in the UK. (Data combined from Kruuk, 1978; Kruuk & Parish, 1982; Harris & Cresswell, 1987; Rogers *et al.*, 1997; and Palphramand *et al.*, 2007)

Unfortunately, Kruuk had to abandon the Ardnish study site before this unusual badger population could be studied in more detail. Nevertheless, as far as the UK is concerned, we can say with some confidence that badgers live in mixed-sex groups, typically containing four to eight adults (see Fig. 151) and occupying territories in the order of 20–100 ha. However, larger groups and smaller territories than this have occasionally been reported.

Elsewhere in western and central Europe, the 'typical' pattern of mixed-sex communally territorial groups has been reported in Ireland, northern Italy, Norway, Luxembourg and Germany, subject to some degree of geographical variation in group and territory sizes. The Doñana region in southwestern Spain seems to be slightly exceptional, in that group size is rather smaller than in most other western European locations (average 3.2 adults plus offspring) and territory size somewhat larger (400–700 ha). However, the basic pattern of socio-spatial organisation seems to be the same in Doñana as elsewhere, and latrines occur along shared boundaries. A similar situation seems to obtain in the southwest of Portugal.

In the Jura mountains, Switzerland, the trend towards smaller group sizes is taken a step further. Here, the basic social unit consists of a single adult male and a single adult female, plus cubs and juveniles that have not yet reached the age of sexual maturity. These badgers also show reduced evidence of territoriality, in the sense that boundary latrines are infrequent and home ranges of neighbouring groups are not always contiguous: sometimes they are separated by unoccupied space and sometimes they overlap. However, home-range sizes are not especially large (a few hundred hectares).

A similar situation as regards group size seems to occur in the Białowieża Primeval Forest in Poland (Fig. 152), where the basic social unit is again a pair plus their dependent offspring. In addition, latrines are found close to setts

FIG 152. Sett in Białowieża Primeval Forest, Poland. (R. Kowalczyk)

rather than around territory boundaries, as in the Swiss study. However, the Polish groups occupy significantly larger home ranges than have been reported anywhere else (1,000 or more hectares in size) and, unlike those of the Swiss population, these ranges are mainly non-contiguous (i.e. there are unoccupied spaces between them: see Fig. 153).

Finally, one study, carried out in the Maremma Natural Park, central Italy, has reported the existence of solitary territory holders (Pigozzi, 1987). However, there are several reasons for doubting that the badgers in this region are indeed solitary. First, Pigozzi's main evidence for this claim was that he was unable to capture more than one animal at any one sett. However, as I and others can

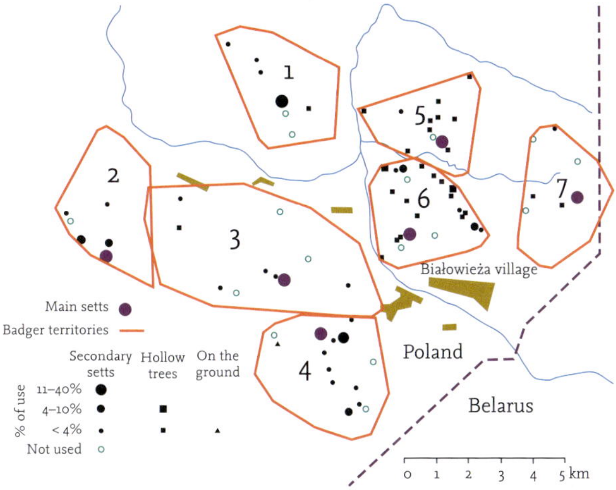

FIG 153. Badger group territories in the Białowieża National Park, Poland. Red lines show group territory boundaries; large purple circles show main setts; smaller black circles show secondary setts of various kinds. (Original from Kowalczyk *et al.*, 2004)

testify, catching multiple members of a social group is far from easy, especially in low-density populations. Second, Pigozzi reports that the badgers he did manage to radio-collar were observed foraging together with other unmarked badgers. This suggests that even if these badgers were denning solitarily, they were not defending individual territories. Third, as Revilla & Palomares (2002b) have pointed out, badgers living elsewhere in similar habitats to that of the Maremma Natural Park, and eating a similar diet, have been found to live in pairs or groups. Altogether, then, the evidence of solitary territoriality in the Maremma badger population is unconvincing.

Other odd reports of territories being occupied by single adults have also cropped up from time to time in some of the studies that I have already cited, though it is clear, in all of these cases, that the majority of territories were held by groups of badgers. Almost certainly, therefore, instances of single territory holders were the result of a larger group being temporarily reduced, by chance processes of mortality or dispersal, to a single individual. There is, however, rather better evidence that Japanese badgers *Meles meles anakuma* live solitarily (see below).

To summarise, the overwhelming majority of evidence suggests that European badgers live in groups containing at least one reproductively mature individual of each sex and that these groups occupy more or less exclusive ranges. However, there is considerable geographical variation in social group size and territory size. In addition, evidence of territoriality, at least in the form of boundary latrines and paths, is less obvious in populations whose range sizes are towards the larger end of the spectrum. We now turn to the possible causes of this variation.

FACTORS UNDERLYING GEOGRAPHICAL VARIATION IN GROUP AND TERRITORY SIZE

Group size, territory size and population density

Unfortunately, most published data on group and territory sizes are probably not very accurate (see the Appendix for a detailed discussion of relevant methodological problems). Nevertheless, it seems worth asking whether the available data provide any clues as to the factors underlying geographical variation in the sizes of social groups and their territories. With this aim in mind, I have compiled and analysed 14 different sets of data on average social group size, territory size and population density (see Table 9). In compiling this dataset, I decided to lump together any studies that were carried out at locations less than 100 km apart, so as to avoid the problem of what statisticians call

TABLE 9. Data on social group size, territory (or home-range) size and population density from studies in different parts of Europe.

Country	Area	Latitude (deg N)	Group size	Territory size (ha)	Popn density (badgers/km^2)	Source
England	Gloucestershire, Oxford	52	5.2	61	14.5	Johnson *et al.* (2002)
England	Yorkshire	54	5.5	53	4.9	Palphramand *et al.*(2007)
Scotland	Ardnish	57	3.3	173	2.03	Johnson *et al.* (2002)
Scotland	Aviemore	57	4	206	2.2	Johnson *et al.* (2002)
Germany	Hakel	53		140	6.5	Hofmann *et al.* (2000)
Ireland	Castleward	55	6.4	50	11.9	Johnson *et al.* (2002)
Italy	River Po Park	45	3.5	380		Remonti *et al.* (2006)
Luxembourg	Eppeldorf	50	5	87	4.7	Scheppers *et al.* (2007)
Norway	Malvik	63	2.5	540		Johnson *et al.* (2002)
Poland	Białowieża	52	2.4	1,280	1.75	Johnson *et al.* (2002)
Poland	Suwalki	54	2.3	1,000	0.59	Johnson *et al.* (2002)
Portugal	Serra de Grândola	38	3.5	530	0.45	Rosalino *et al.* (2004)
Spain	Doñana	37	2	610	0.95	Johnson *et al.* (2002)
Switzerland	Jura	47	2.2	160	2	Do Linh San *et al.* (2007a, b)

'pseudoreplication'. Consequently, data from all studies carried out in Gloucestershire and Oxfordshire have been lumped together, so as to provide average values of group size, territory size and population density for this region. Similarly, I have averaged over five separate studies that were all carried out in the Doñana reserve. Conversely, the table includes separate entries for each of two studies carried out in Scotland and for each of two studies carried out in Poland, because in both cases the study areas in question were more than 100 km apart.

Table 9 includes data on population density, because logic tells us that, other things being equal, population density should be linked to group size and/or territory size. Specifically, small group size should be associated with low population density, whereas small territory size should be associated with high population density. However, we can still ask whether differences in population density arise from differences in group size, territory size, or both. In fact, analysis of the data reveals that population density is indeed linked, in the expected

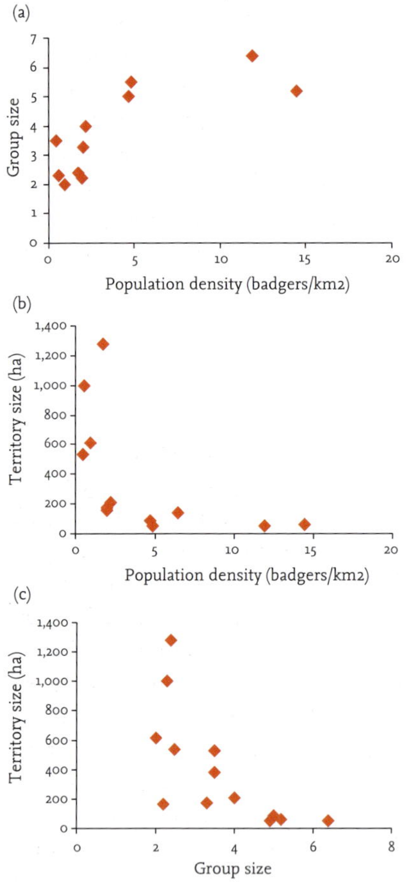

FIG **154.** Relationships between (a) social group size and population density; (b) territory size and population density; and (c) social group size and territory size. (From data shown in Table 9)

manner, to both group size and territory size (see Fig. 154a and b). However, in both cases, the relationship is distinctly non-linear: that is, large increases in territory size, or reductions in group size, are only seen at very low population densities, such as occur, for example, in Spain, Poland and Portugal.

If group size varies directly with population density, while territory size does so inversely, then it follows that group size and territory size should vary inversely with one another. It is reassuring to find that this is indeed the case (Fig. 154c). To summarise, group size, territory size and population density are all linked together, such that systematic variation in one is associated with systematic variation in the other two. Having established this, we can now ask what drives this variation.

Factors underlying variation in group size, territory size and population density

Intuitively, one might expect geographical variation in group size, territory size and population density to be determined at least partly by climate, because climate affects variables such as food availability and winter mortality. However, a study by Johnson *et al.* (2002), using a similar but smaller dataset to the one shown in Table 9, found no evidence that either group size or territory size were correlated with any of a host of climatic variables involving various measures of temperature, rainfall and solar radiation. Population density was weakly related to temperature range (i.e. the difference between maximum and minimum annual temperatures), suggesting that badgers do somewhat better in

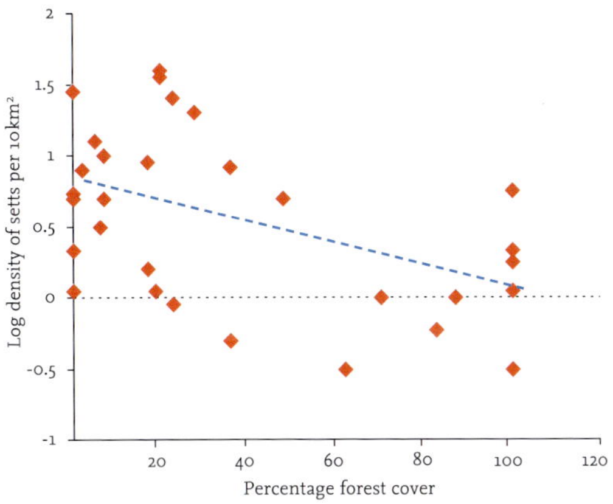

FIG 155. Relationship between density of badger setts and percentage forest cover, using data from 31 different locations in Eurasia. (From Kowalczyk *et al.*, 2000)

more equable climates. However, most of the variation in group size, territory size and population density seems to result from factors other than climatic variation.

A second possible factor is food availability, but this is difficult to measure. Rafał Kowalczyk and others, using data from 31 locations in Eurasia, found a tendency for sett density to decrease as the percentage of forest cover increased (see Fig. 155). Their interpretation was that less forest cover means more open pasture of the kind that badgers favour for foraging on earthworms. However, even if we accept that less forest cover means that more food is available, the correlation shown in Figure. 155 is rather weak. Once again, then, we have to conclude that additional, as yet unidentified, factors are responsible for most of the variation in population density.

In short, it remains unclear what determines large-scale geographic variation in group and territory sizes, just as it remains unclear what determines differences in the average population density of badgers in different countries (see Chapter 1 for a discussion). All we can say for certain is that group sizes tend to be small and territory sizes to be large in places that, for whatever reason, are unable to support large numbers of badgers.

DIFFERENCES IN THE DEGREE OF EXPRESSION OF TERRITORIAL BEHAVIOUR

As already noted, the degree to which territoriality is manifest varies with population density. In high-density populations, such as those in the south of England, territory boundaries are physically discernible as well-trodden paths linking strings of latrines (Fig. 156). In such populations, latrines also occur in the hinterland of the territory and at the main sett. In very low-density

FIG 156. A well-used badger path. In areas of high population density, paths like this demarcate territory boundaries. (Dassenwerkgroep Brabant)

populations, by contrast, such as occur in Poland, boundary paths and latrines are no longer evident and scent-marking occurs only in the vicinity of setts. In populations of intermediate density, for example in Luxembourg, the situation is intermediate: boundary latrines occur sporadically where neighbouring territories meet but most latrines are in the territory hinterland or at setts.

These differences are probably explicable in terms of simple economics. In high-density populations, social groups tend to be large and territories small. Consequently, the cost of scent-marking a territory boundary can be shared between several individuals, and this cost is in any case low because the boundary is small in circumference and is located within easy reach of any part of the territory. In high-density populations, therefore, latrines can be located on territory boundaries. Similarly, visible paths develop in such circumstances because boundaries are small enough to be 'patrolled' and because this patrolling involves several badgers.

Conversely, at low population densities, territory boundaries are too long to be regularly patrolled and too far away to be visited very often; and there are fewer badgers available to share the cost of marking them or to create boundary paths. It therefore makes sense, when population density is low, to place scent marks at locations that are regularly visited for other reasons, the obvious candidates being setts. In medium-density populations, where territories are intermediate in size, it seems to be worthwhile maintaining latrines at boundaries that are shared with an adjacent social group, presumably because these are places where the threat of incursion is greatest. Otherwise, however, it makes economic sense at moderate population density, as it does at low population density, to confine scent-marking to the territory hinterland and, in particular, to the vicinity of setts.

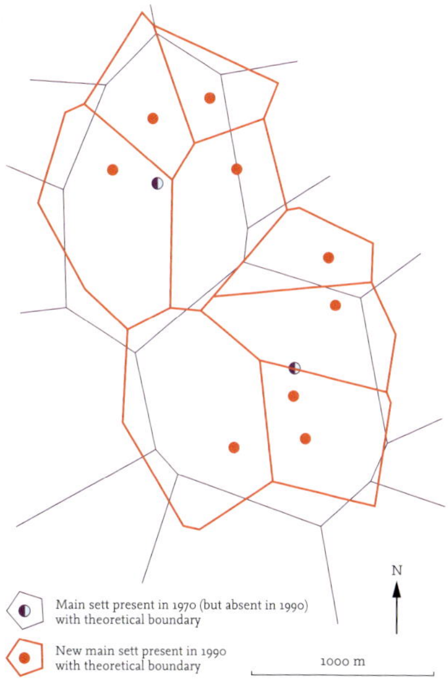

FIG 157. Main sett locations and estimated territory boundaries for the same population of badgers in 1970 and 1990. During this period, the upper large territory became divided into four smaller territories, while the lower large territory became divided into three smaller territories. In each case, the original main sett disappeared and a new main sett appeared within each of the new territories. (Original from Ostler & Roper, 1998)

THE ESTABLISHMENT OF NEW TERRITORIES

In general, territory boundaries are extremely stable over time – at least, this is true of high-density populations. At Woodchester Park, for example, most territory boundaries have remained unchanged for the whole of the 30-odd years during which bait-marking has been carried out. Nevertheless, new social groups do sometimes come into being and establish new territories, and the question arises as to how they do this.

A study by a member of my own research group, Jessica Ostler, sheds some light on this issue. The setts in her Sussex study area had been thoroughly surveyed by a badger enthusiast E. D. Clements in the early 1970s, long before she started working there. Ostler resurveyed the same area in the early 1990s to see to what extent the situation had changed. She also estimated the locations of territory boundaries, for both sets of survey data, using what is called the 'Dirichlet tessellation' method (i.e. she

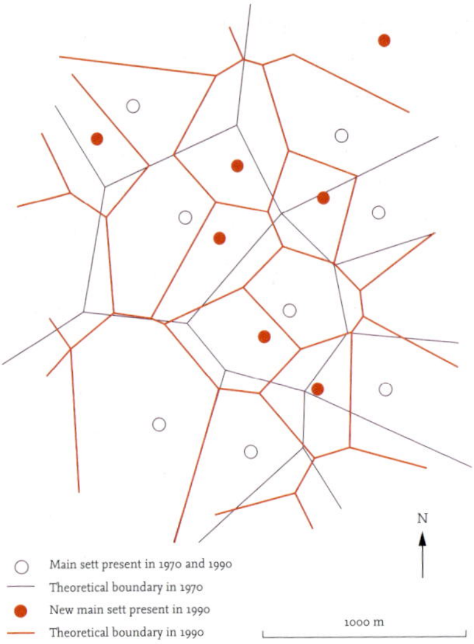

FIG 158. Main sett locations and estimated territory boundaries for the same population of badgers in 1970 and 1990. Two cases are shown in which a main sett that existed in 1970 was still present in 1990, but in which the original territory became smaller owing to the appearance of new main setts and territories. (From Ostler & Roper, 1998)

assumed that territory boundaries were located halfway between neighbouring main setts: see the Appendix for details). She found that the number of main setts more than doubled (from 30 to 70), while territory size more than halved (from 0.7 to 0.3 km^2) during the 20-year period that separated the two surveys. Thus, a considerable number of new social groups had come into existence (Ostler & Roper, 1998).

By looking at the Dirichlet tessellation maps, Ostler was able to detect two kinds of changes to territory boundaries. In one, a single large territory had become subdivided into two or more smaller ones, so that the outer boundaries of the new territories more or less corresponded with the boundary of the original large one (see Fig. 157). In these cases, the original main sett had disappeared and a new main sett had become established in each of the new, smaller territories. In the second kind of development, an original main sett persisted but its territory had become compressed as new main setts and their associated territories became established close to it (see Fig. 158). In this case, the squeezing in of new territories caused wholesale restructuring of the pattern of boundaries in the relevant part of the study area.

As luck would have it, we were able to witness a change of the second type taking place at around the time of Jessica Ostler's survey, though we did not have the sense to realise its significance and so did not pay it a lot of attention. One spring, one of our radio-collared females moved out of the main sett and took up residence in an outlier that was situated close to the point where the territory boundary of her own group intersected with those of two other groups. When the sow in question first moved into the outlier, a latrine appeared immediately outside its entrance; during the course of the next few weeks, more and more deposits of faeces appeared around the sett and along nearby fence lines, until the region surrounding the sett almost became a single huge latrine. Since the female herself cannot possibly have been responsible for all of this defecation, members of neighbouring social groups must have been responding to her presence.

Unfortunately, at that point we took our eye off the situation because we were busy with other things, but when we bait-marked the area a year later we found that the female had established a modest territory for herself and, in doing so, had pushed back the boundaries of two of the surrounding territories (including the boundary of what used to be her own social group). By that time she had also acquired a mate, who might have helped her to enlarge her new territory. There was still a small latrine at the sett itself, but most were now located on the new territory boundary. To my great regret, we do not know what happened to the territory boundaries from then on because we ceased bait-marking that part of the study area. However, the outlier (by then a main sett) did continue to be occupied and we saw cubs at it two years later.

RANGING BEHAVIOUR OF INDIVIDUAL BADGERS

Home-range overlap within and between groups

As we have seen, Hans Kruuk's original Wytham Woods study showed that the home ranges of individual members of the same social group overlapped almost completely, showing that the territory was a communal resource shared by all group members. In addition, he observed that individual badgers rarely ventured outside their own territory, meaning that there was a high degree of correspondence between the size and shape of individual home ranges and the size and shape of the group territory (Kruuk, 1978a). Indeed, he regarded the terms 'home range' and 'territory' as being, as far as badgers were concerned, synonymous (Kruuk, 1989, p. 83). To what extent have these findings been replicated in subsequent studies?

As far as I am aware, every radio-tracking study of badgers that has so far been carried out has confirmed that the home ranges of individual group members overlap to a substantial extent (Fig. 159). In addition, a few studies have reported that male ranges are larger than those of females, though most have found, like Kruuk, no evidence of a sex difference. A more general finding is that home-range sizes vary seasonally, being largest in summer and autumn when badgers roam furthest in search of food, and smallest in winter when they rarely venture far away from the sett (e.g. Palphramand *et al.*, 2007).

It is less clear, however, that badgers are always as strictly territorial as Kruuk

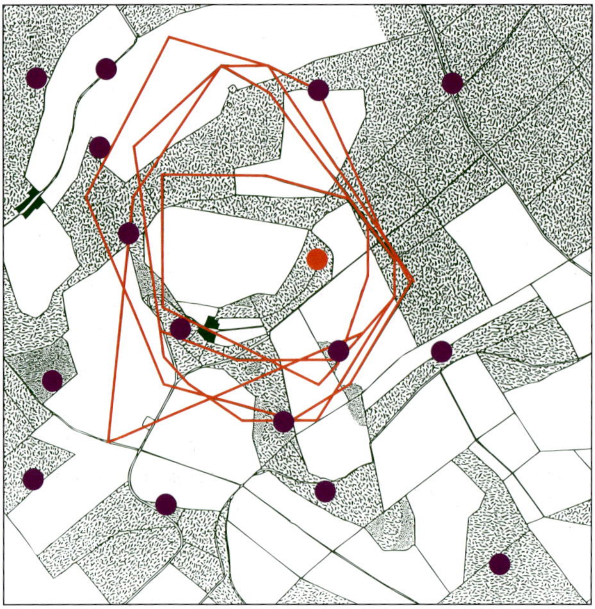

FIG 159. Home ranges of five individual badgers from the same main sett (filled red circle) in East Sussex. Note the extent to which the home ranges overlap with one another. Filled purple circles denote surrounding main setts; shaded areas show pasture fields; unshaded areas show arable fields. (From Christian, 1993)

reported them to be. I first began to doubt this when I started radio-tracking badgers in the Sussex Downs. I can still remember a night, early on in the study, when I arrived at a sett intending to track a particular adult female. I settled down on the hillside above her sett and tuned in my receiver. The signal was weaker than I expected it to be but I was able to determine its direction, so I took out my binoculars to see if I could spot the animal. (It was a summer night and the badgers were active well before dusk.) Eventually, I saw her on the hillside opposite me, way out in the middle of an adjacent territory, foraging peacefully alongside a female member of the neighbouring social group. The two sows remained together, without visibly interacting, for over half an hour, after which the neighbouring sow departed. Some time later, the sow that I was tracking returned, at a leisurely pace, to her own territory.

I was intrigued, to say the least, by this observation: these badgers were just not behaving as Kruuk had led me to expect. First, the sow that I was radio-tracking should not have been out of her territory and, second, even if she was, a member of the neighbouring group should not have tolerated her presence. However, during the years that followed, I and other members of my research group made many similar observations involving badgers of both sexes. As a result, whereas the territories of our badger groups, as defined by bait-marking and by the presence of latrines and paths, showed no overlap, the home ranges of

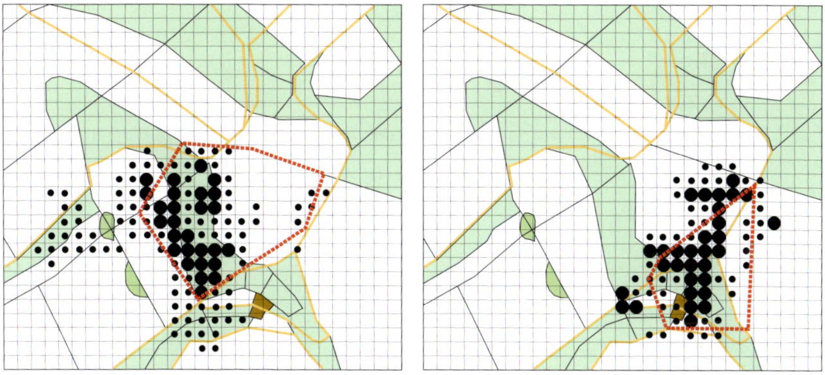

FIG 160. Home ranges (black circles) and territory boundaries (dashed red lines) of two adjacent social groups in the South Downs, East Sussex. Large black circles denote grid squares (0.25 ha) in which badgers frequently foraged ('core foraging areas'); small circles denote grid squares in which they occasionally foraged. Note that badgers foraged well outside their own territories.

neighbouring groups overlapped extensively (Fig. 159). In some cases, even the 'core' foraging areas of a particular group (that is, foraging areas that were used especially frequently) were located within the territory of a neighbouring group.

With the accumulation of more data, we found that these unchallenged extra-territorial excursions, which were clearly for foraging purposes, showed a strong seasonal pattern: they were most frequent in summer, happened to some extent in autumn and were rare in spring. (They were also rare in winter, but this was because badgers are more or less inactive in winter.) Now, we had already observed that latrine use showed the reverse pattern, with a major peak in spring, a minor peak in autumn and a trough in summer (see Chapter 6). Putting these two observations together, therefore, we concluded that territoriality in badgers is seasonal: it is relaxed, and extra-territorial excursions are permitted, in summer and, to a lesser extent, in autumn. This also provided us with the first clue that territoriality might have more to do with mating than with the defence of food resources, since spring and autumn, when territorial behaviour was apparently strongest, are the main times of year for mating (see Chapter 8 for further discussion).

Frustratingly, our observations of extra-territorial ranging behaviour remain unreplicated, because surprisingly few intensive radio-tracking studies of badgers have been conducted on high-density populations subsequent to Kruuk's own work. For example, the long-term studies at Woodchester Park and

Wytham Woods have mainly involved capture–recapture or observations of badgers at their setts. In low-density populations, such as those carried out in Poland and Spain, home ranges of neighbouring groups are not contiguous in the first place, so the issue of range overlap does not arise. Consequently, we do not know whether the movements of badgers in very high-density populations, such as that of Wytham Woods, really are as strictly confined to their own territories as Kruuk reported them to be.

Nightly ranging behaviour

Solitary versus social foraging

Despite the fact that the members of a social group share a communal home range, Kruuk reported that badgers forage solitarily. This latter observation has been confirmed in several subsequent studies and certainly fits with my own experience. In the 1980s, when my research group carried out intensive radio-tracking of badgers in the Sussex Downs, we sometimes had as many as four different observers tracking four different members of the same social group at the same time. Despite the fact that the group territories were quite small, it was astonishing how rarely different observers met one another during the course of the night. However, when we compared our data after a radio-tracking session, we would often find that when one badger (and its observer) left a particular foraging place, another would uncannily arrive a minute or two later. It was as if the different members of a group deliberately avoided foraging together.

In addition, we found that different group members had, to some extent, different favourite foraging areas. For example, Figure 161 shows the use of space by four male members of the same social group during the same period, with well-used (or 'core') foraging areas denoted by large filled circles. One can see, for example, that two of the males (M3 and M4) foraged a lot in a small triangle of rough ground in grid squares B2, C2, C3 and D4, whereas the other two males were never seen there. Similarly, M1 foraged often on a patch of pasture in grid squares J4 and J5, whereas the other three males used this area less intensively.

In the Białowieża Primeval Forest, Poland, something slightly different seems to happen. Here, individual badgers tend to use different segments of the communal home range on consecutive nights, as if their intention is to keep tabs on the whole of the group range during the course of a week or so (Fig. 162). Taken together with our own results, this suggests partitioning of the supposedly 'communal' home range on at least three levels: between individual group members within a single night; between individual group members over longer periods of time; and within a single individual between consecutive nights.

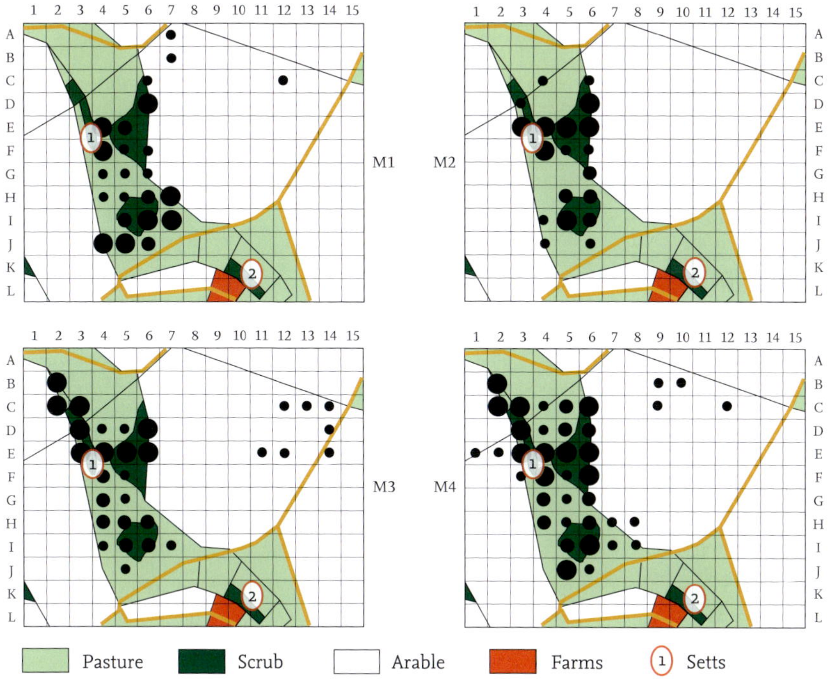

FIG 161. Areas used for foraging by four individual males from the same social group during the same period of time. Numbered circles show main setts. Black dots show areas used for foraging, with the size of the dot indicating the amount of time spent at that location. Grid squares are 0.25 ha in size. (Original from Shepherdson *et al.*, 1990. Copyright 1991, with permission from Elsevier)

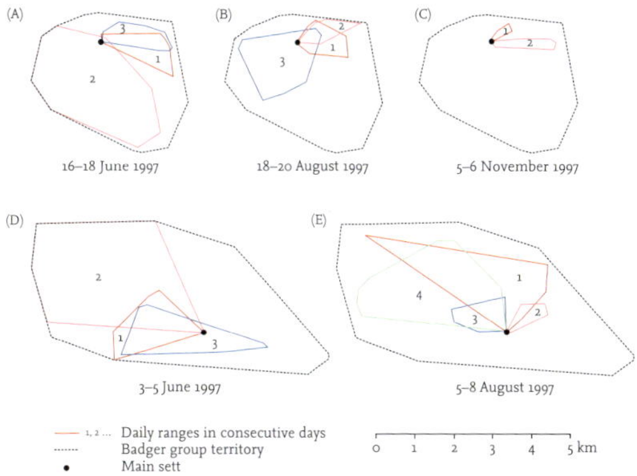

FIG 162. Home ranges of individual Białowieża Primeval Forest badgers on consecutive days (numbered 1, 2, 3, etc). Thick lines show the boundary of the group home range. A, B and C show data from a single male in different months; D and E show data from a single female. (Original from Kowalczyk *et al.*, 2006)

This is not to say, however, that foraging badgers cannot tolerate the presence of other animals, either from their own or from other social groups. During our study in the South Downs, one of the farmers on whose land we were working established a large slurry pit that provided, during the summer, an inexhaustible supply of rat-tailed maggots (*Eristalis* sp.). Every evening, up to 15 badgers from at least three social groups would congregate there, feeding peacefully together, often in very close proximity to one another. The only sign of aggression we ever saw was on a few occasions when one animal would threaten another, in which case the threatened badger would move a little further away and both would resume foraging. We also routinely saw badgers foraging communally when they were feeding on standing crops of wheat or maize. Similarly, David Macdonald and his colleagues observed hardly any signs of aggression between members of the same or neighbouring social groups when they deliberately provided food on shared territory boundaries (Macdonald *et al.*, 2002); and many householders who provision badgers in their gardens find that often, several members of a social group will arrive to feed at the same time (Fig. 163).

Almost certainly, the reason why badgers sometimes forage solitarily and at other times in groups has to do with the amount of food available at any one place and time. If there is a single, abundant supply of food at a particular location (what ecologists refer to as a 'clumped' form of food distribution), then badgers will tolerate one another's presence. The underlying logic of this is that if there is plenty of food for everyone, there is nothing to be gained by trying to exclude others. By contrast, if small amounts of food are scattered more widely (i.e. if food is 'dispersed'), badgers forage solitarily, because there is only enough food for one animal in any particular place at any one time. But whatever the explanation, it is clear that badgers are not intrinsically antisocial foragers: rather, solitary foraging is a response to particular ecological circumstances.

FIG 163. Family of badgers foraging together in a garden. (L. & P. Schofield)

Distance and speed of travel within the home range

Several studies have recorded the detailed routes taken by badgers as they move around their home ranges during the course of a single night (see Table 10). Average distance travelled per night ranges from 1.2 km (Bristol, England) to 7.0 km (Poland), with an overall mean of 4.0 km. These travel distances correspond to individual nightly range sizes varying from 0.9 km^2 (Spain) to 2.1 km^2 (Poland), with an overall mean of 1.4 km^2. As we might expect, both nightly travel distances and nightly range sizes correlate with group home-range size, both within a single study and between different studies. That is, the lower the population density, and therefore the larger the communal home range, the further individual badgers travel in a single night. In addition, individual nightly travel distance varies to a considerable degree with season, being largest in summer and autumn and smallest in winter (Fig. 164).

TABLE 10. Year-round group home-range size, plus daily movement distance, speed of movement and daily range size of individual badgers.

Country	Location	Home range (km^2)	Daily movt distance (km)	Speed (km/hr)	Daily range (km^2)	Source
England	Bristol *	0.3	1.2	0.6		Cresswell & Harris (1988)
Norway	Trondheim *	7.6	4.4	0.4	1.1	Johansen (1993) **
Poland	Białowieża	9.3	7	0.9	2.1	Kowalczyk *et al.* (2006)
Poland	Rogow		3.5	0.9		Goszczyński *et al.* (2005)
Portugal	Serra de Grândola	5.3	4.4			Rosalino *et al.* (2005)
Spain	Doñana	4.1	4.6	0.3	0.9	Revilla & Palomares (2002)
Spain	Urdaibai		1.6	0.4		Zabala *et al.* (2002) **
Switzerland	Jura	3.2	5.1	1		Do Linh San *et al.* (2007b)
Mean		***4.9***	***4***	***0.6***	***1.4***	

* Urban study areas
** Studies cited in Kowalczyk *et al.* 2006

Average speed of movement varies from 0.3 km/hr to 1.0 km/hr, with an overall mean of 0.6 km/hr (Table 10). However, average travel speeds are somewhat misleading, because a badger's night usually consists of periods of relatively slow travel interspersed with bursts of more rapid movement. For example, badgers travel rapidly early in the night, when they leave the sett

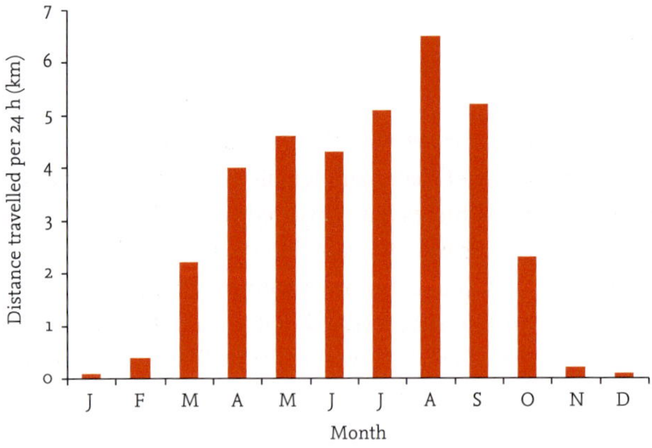

FIG 164. Nightly distance travelled by badgers in different months of the year. (From Goszczyński *et al.*, 2005)

and move to a foraging area, late in the night when they return home again, and during the night when they move between different foraging areas or visit latrines. At these times, the animal also takes a more or less direct route to wherever it is going. During bouts of foraging, by contrast, travel speed is slow and the animal's path tends to become more convoluted (see also Chapter 4).

Nocturnal resting periods

In his original studies carried out in Wytham Woods and in Scotland, Hans Kruuk noted that badgers would sometimes rest during the night, either in an outlier or by returning to the main sett. Again, this observation has been substantiated, though the frequency of resting seems to vary from place to place. Emmanuel Do Linh San and others (2007b) report that in Switzerland, resting is infrequent and the duration of rests is generally rather short (average 0.8 hr). We have found the same in Sussex. Alejandro Rodríguez and his colleagues (1996), by contrast, report that Portuguese badgers rest on 44 per cent of nights and that the duration of these rests is relatively long (average 1.7 hrs, and sometimes as long as 5 hrs). The most obvious explanation of these rest periods is that they serve the purposes of digestion when a badger has eaten as much as it can, in which case the variations in frequency and duration of resting between different studies could reflect differences in food availability. For example, it will take a badger much longer to fill its stomach if it is foraging on a dispersed food resource such as insects than if it is feeding on a clumped food such as fruit or cereals.

SOCIAL STRUCTURE

Sex ratio and age structure

Most badger populations that have so far been studied have been found to contain approximately equal numbers of males and females. However, a word of caution is needed here, because most studies have involved relatively few animals, so their sample sizes may have been too small to detect biased sex ratios. A uniquely large-scale analysis of data from the Woodchester Park population over the period from 1978 to 1993 revealed that the adult population was biased towards females in almost every year, with an overall average sex ratio of 39 per cent males to 61 per cent females. Among cubs, however, the sex ratio was not biased (Rogers *et al.*, 1997).

If equal numbers of male and female cubs are born but there are more adult females than males, this can only mean that males suffer a higher rate of mortality than females. This is verified by data on age distribution from the same Woodchester Park study, showing that females outnumber males in every age class and that the difference between the sexes increases with age (Fig. 165). The same data also show that, as would be expected, the number of animals of a given age in the population decreases as age increases: for example, there are only about half as many four-year-olds as two-year-olds. However, on average, about a quarter of all social groups contain a male, and about half a female, aged seven years or more, so the presence of quite elderly group members is not that unusual.

From these data, we can construct a picture of a 'typical' Woodchester Park group. This contains three cubs (either two males and one female, or one male and

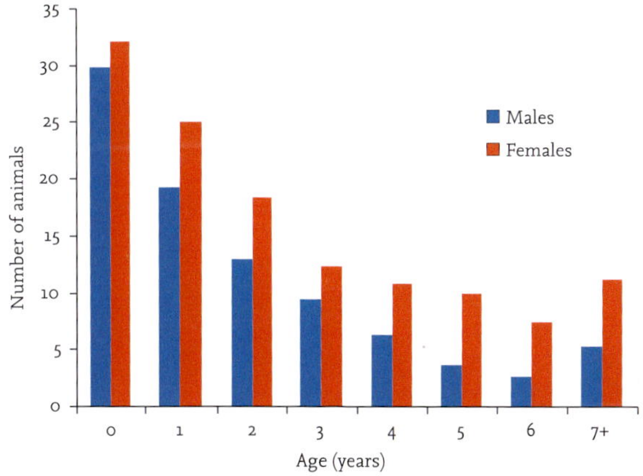

FIG **165.** Number of males and females of different ages in the Woodchester Park population. Data show the annual total for each age and sex category in 21 social groups, summed over the period 1985–93. (Based on data in Rogers *et al.*, 1997)

two females), two yearlings (most probably, one of each sex), two adult males and three adult females. Overall average group size is then five adults, or ten animals in all, including cubs and yearlings. In lower-density populations, where there are fewer adults per group, the ratio of cubs and yearlings to adults is likely to be higher, such that perhaps 70 per cent of group members will be reproductively immature and only 30 per cent mature. However, we lack the data to confirm this.

Kinship

As we saw in Chapter 5, the mating system of badgers is complex. Consequently, the pattern of genetic relatedness within groups is also complex. Because badgers do not disperse until they are reproductively mature, juveniles and cubs will be offspring of one or more adult females belonging to the same social group as themselves. However, their father could be from the same or from a different group. Consequently, any two cubs or juveniles could be siblings, half-siblings or, if they are the progeny of different mothers as well as of different fathers, completely unrelated. Similarly, any two adult members of the same group could themselves be siblings or half-siblings; one could be a direct descendant of the other (for example, a group might contain a grandmother and a mother, or a mother or father plus reproductively mature offspring); or, if at least one of them has immigrated from a different social group, they could be completely unrelated. Molecular genetics studies have found that the overall degree of genetic relatedness (R) between members of the same social group, in high-density badger populations such as Woodchester Park, is about 0.15 (Carpenter, 2002) to 0.2 (Dugdale *et al.*, 2008): that is, members of the same group are on average somewhat more related than cousins ($R = 0.125$) and less related than, say, a grandparent to its grandchild ($R = 0.25$). So far, however, we do not know the relative frequencies of the different types of relationship (parent/offspring, sibling, half-sibling, cousin, etc.) that contribute to this overall average.

To summarise, badger social groups are family groups, in the sense that most group members are genetically related to some degree. They do not, however, correspond to our idea of a nuclear family, except in places like the Białowieża Primeval Forest, where groups consist of a single adult male and female plus their offspring.

Dominance

The concept of dominance is fundamental to our understanding of how animal societies function. In common parlance, when we say that an individual is 'dominant', we mean that he or she is the boss, able to dictate to others and get what they want for themselves; and this is not too far removed from what biologists mean by the term. To a biologist, the concept of dominance arises from the fact that altercations between any two members of the same social group often have a predictable outcome: that is, if A repeatedly quarrels with B, one of them is observed to win consistently, while the other is observed to lose consistently. The individual that consistently wins is then said to be the dominant member of that particular pair or 'dyad', while the consistent loser is said to be subordinate.

In mammals in general, the most common kind of dominance system is a so-called 'linear' hierarchy in which A is dominant over all other members of the group, B over all other members except A, C over all except A and B, and so on. The individual at the top of the hierarchy is referred to as the dominant or 'alpha' individual. What enables an individual to become dominant varies from species to species, but dominance is often associated with body size or age (the larger and older the individual, the more likely it is to be dominant) and sex (males are generally dominant over females). This makes sense, because if dominance is achieved and maintained by physical force and intimidation, characteristics such as body size, age and sex will obviously be relevant.

Research suggests that most animal societies exhibit dominance systems of one kind or another, so it is natural to ask whether the same is true of badgers. We can be fairly sure that it is in at least one context: namely, that of reproduction in females. Indeed, Hans Kruuk and others have treated the term 'dominant female' as synonymous with 'breeding female' (e.g. Kruuk, 1989). The argument goes as follows. Within any one social group, it is common for only one reproductively mature female to breed (see Chapter 5), whereas the theory of natural selection leads us to expect that all mature females should try to breed. Hence, there must be competition between females for breeding status. Since, by definition, the winner of this competition within any one social group is the individual that does succeed in breeding, we are justified in referring to the breeder as the 'dominant' female. Observations of direct aggression on the part of breeding females towards non-breeders, plus the fact that breeding females are often the largest and oldest females in the group, add further support to the idea that a female achieves breeding status by becoming dominant (see Kruuk, 1989; and Chapter 5). By the same logic, males that achieve a disproportionate share of matings can also be termed dominant, though less is known about the relative mating success of different males within a social group.

The concept of dominance may also apply in contexts other than competition over breeding. Eloy Revilla & Francisco Palomares (2001), working in the Doñana reserve, asked whether individual badgers that had achieved breeding status, and were therefore by that criterion dominant, gained preferential access to good food resources. In Doñana, the staple food of badgers

FIG 166. An instance of 'directed aggression'. A male badger lunges towards the neck of a female, which flinches away. (Photograph reproduced courtesy of Julia Hurst of Boo's Photos)

is young rabbits, which are found mainly in a type of habitat known as 'Mediterranean scrub'. Revilla & Palomares found that in a year when rabbits were scarce owing to unusually heavy rainfall, dominant badgers used Mediterranean scrub habitat more than usual, while subordinates used it less than usual. The obvious inference is that when times were hard, dominants excluded subordinates from the best habitat.

However, the best evidence for some kind of generalised system of dominance in badgers comes from a study by Stacey Hewitt and others at Wytham Woods (Hewitt *et al.*, 2009). They stationed video-recording equipment at the main setts of three social groups of badgers, in order to record, and subsequently analyse, social interactions between the members of these groups at around the time of emergence. The study focused especially on instances of so-called 'directed aggression': that is, cases in which one badger bit, nipped or charged at another, and in which the recipient backed down rather than responding in kind (Fig. 166). The question was whether certain individuals were consistently aggressive while others consistently gave way.

Analysis of over 11,000 hours of video recordings revealed the existence of linear dominance hierarchies in which adult females tended to have higher rank than adult males, and breeding females higher rank than non-breeders. There was also some indication that these dominance hierarchies affected other behaviours such as allo-grooming and allo-marking, insofar as subordinate individuals tended to groom dominants more than vice versa, while dominants tended to allo-mark subordinates more than vice versa.

These are exciting results but, unfortunately, the picture is complicated by the fact that statistically significant dominance hierarchies were only found in some social groups in some years. Dominance may therefore only become manifest in certain circumstances and it is unclear what these are. In addition, Hewitt's study was carried out during the mating and cub-rearing season, so we do not know whether the dominant status of breeding females is specific to this time of year. And, finally, there is always the suspicion that, owing to the very large sizes of the social groups found in Wytham Woods, together with the very small territories that these groups occupy, the rate of aggressive interactions between group members could be unnaturally high. Indeed, another Wytham study has shown that the frequency of bite-wounding in this population has increased with a rise in population density, and that the members of large social groups are more likely to show evidence of having been in fights (Macdonald *et al.*, 2004b). If this is so, then the appearance of dominance hierarchies in this population could be an artefact of the crowded conditions under which the Wytham badgers live.

Nevertheless, Hewitt's work constitutes the best attempt so far to shed light on the social structure operating within badger groups. It also demonstrates that when it comes to understanding the subtleties of social behaviour, you do not necessarily need high-tech methods: you just need simple observation and lots of patience. Perhaps this message will stimulate others to replicate Hewitt's study on more typically sized social groups.

Fighting

In any species, social relationships find their most dramatic expression in the form of full-blown fights. Badgers are no exception: fights can be fierce, prolonged and accompanied by a great deal of noise and commotion (see Chapter 6 for an eye-witness account). They can also result in serious bloodshed and even death.

Since badgers fight with their teeth, they initially confront one another face to face, each snapping and biting at the head and neck of its opponent. But fights often escalate into skirmishes in which the two animals chase one another around in a circle, biting at one another's hindquarters. As a result, badgers that have been involved in fighting show a very distinct pattern of wounding, involving the face, neck and shoulders, and the rump (see Fig. 167). Wounds, especially on the rump, can be severe, sometimes involving great patches of skin being torn open. Sometimes, when badgers exhausted by fighting have been found and rescued, they have been so badly injured that euthanasia has been the

FIG 167. Typical patterns of scarring as a result of fighting: (left) on the rump (T. Roper); (above) on the head and neck. (M. & K. Blackman)

only option. However, like other wild animals, badgers exhibit a stoic indifference to what we would regard as horrific wounds, accompanied by remarkable powers of recovery. I have trapped badgers suffering from serious, and sometimes badly infected, bite wounds, only to catch the same animals a year later and find no evidence of the previous injuries other than a few scabs or scars. Other investigators have reported the same thing.

Four studies have recorded the incidence of bite wounds: two using data from road-killed badgers and two from capture–recapture studies, including the long-term capture–recapture studies carried out at Woodchester Park and Wytham Woods (for references, see Delahay *et al.*, 2006). Taking the results of these studies together, it is clear that bite-wounding is more frequent in males than in females: on average, over half of all males and about a third of all females show evidence, in the form of wounds or scars, of having been bitten relatively recently. Given that these figures constitute a snapshot of the prevalence of injuries at a single point in time, it seems likely that a majority of badgers of both sexes become involved in fights at some point in their lives. The prevalence of fresh wounds is naturally rather less, at about a quarter of all males and a fifth of all females at any one time; and the prevalence of severe wounds is less still, at about a sixth of all males and a tenth of all females. Prevalence is related to age, so that older badgers of both sexes are more likely to bear wounds (Fig. 168), and it is related to season, being most frequent in both sexes in winter and spring (Fig. 169). Interestingly, males are more likely to be bitten on the rump, while females are more likely to be bitten on the face and neck, perhaps indicating a difference in the way the two sexes fight. However, if there is such a difference, it is only one of degree, since wounds of both kinds are found in both sexes.

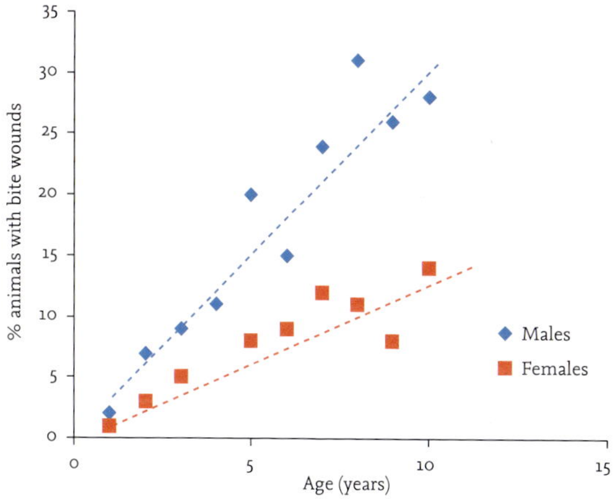

FIG 168. Percentage of badgers with bite wounds, at different ages and for each sex. Probability of wounding increases with age in both sexes and is higher in males than in females at all ages. (From Macdonald *et al.*, 2004b)

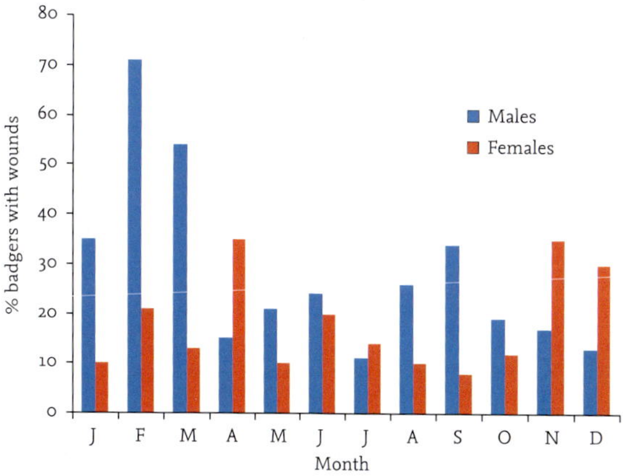

FIG 169. Percentage of male and female badgers with bite wounds, in each month of the year. (Based on data in Cresswell *et al.*, 1992)

These studies of bite-wounding show that both males and females get involved in fights and that fighting is mainly associated with the reproductive season. However, they do not tell us where fights take place, who is fighting whom, or why. In his 1978 paper, Hans Kruuk reports fierce fighting between members of neighbouring social groups that had met one another at a territory boundary, and others (including myself) have made similar observations. However, such fights seem to be relatively rare and fighting also occurs, perhaps more frequently, at the main sett (see, for example, Christian, 1995). As regards who fights whom, Kruuk only ever observed badgers of the same sex fighting one another, and members of my own research group, studying badgers in Sussex over a five-year period, recorded only one fight between a male and a female, compared with eight fights between members of the same sex. Fighting does, therefore, seem to be largely between pairs of males or pairs of females.

Since fighting is associated with the breeding season, differs in frequency and kind between the sexes, and usually involves two animals of the same sex, it seems likely that it is associated, at least primarily, with reproduction. In addition, the fact that badgers are willing to risk serious injury or even death indicates that they are fighting over something important – and the opportunity to reproduce is the most important thing in any animal's life.

In the case of males, it seems likely that the main cause of fighting is competition for access to an oestrus female – in which case, it could in principle involve members of the same social group or of different ones. In reality, several observers have commented on the fact that males from the same social group usually show surprisingly little reaction when one of their number is mating with a female. Therefore, within-group competition for mates seems not to be a major source of male–male conflict. By contrast, there have been several accounts of fierce fighting between a resident male and an intruder, when the latter turns up at a sett containing an oestrus female (e.g. Christian, 1993); and boundary fights between male members of different groups could also be attempts to deter intrusion for mating purposes. It seems likely, then, that most fighting between males involves individuals from neighbouring social groups, though this needs verifying by direct observations.

The situation is different for females, because although oestrus sows do sometimes visit neighbouring setts for mating purposes (see Chapter 5), there is no reason why a resident sow should object to this. An alternative possibility is that females sometimes fight intruders in order to defend the food resources within their own territories. However, this seems unlikely in practice, since, as we have seen, intrusions into a neighbouring territory for feeding purposes seem generally to be tolerated.

On the other hand, females do compete with other female members of their own social group for breeding status, so this may be the source of most female–female aggression. In other words, most fighting among females may come about because dominant sows try to prevent subordinates from successfully rearing cubs (see also Chapter 5). This could also be the cause of the relatively rare cases in which cubs get bitten. And, if females are fighting mainly within the confines of the sett rather than out in the open, this could explain why they are more likely than males to display wounds to the face and neck. However, this hypothesis, relying entirely as it does on circumstantial evidence, badly needs verification in the form of direct observations of female–female disputes.

URBAN BADGERS

I shall consider urban badgers separately, because urban environments differ in various fundamental ways from rural ones. For example, human influences are obviously much greater in towns and cities than in the country; road mortality is likely to be higher; travel from place to place is more difficult owing to the presence of barriers of one kind or another; suitable sites for setts are likely to be harder to find; different kinds of food will be available, and so on. As we shall see, the net result of these factors is that urban badgers do behave in various respects differently from rural badgers, though there are also some striking similarities.

Badgers in Bristol

The classic study of urban (or, more accurately in this case, suburban) badgers was undertaken in the Clifton area of Bristol in the 1980s, by Stephen Harris and Warren Cresswell (Fig. 170a: see Harris *et al.*, 2009, for a summary and references). They studied 15 social groups of badgers living in an area of about 8 km^2, using sett surveys, capture-mark-recapture and radio telemetry as the main methods of data collection. The total number of adults in the population ranged from 35 to 60 in different years, which means that average group sizes ranged from 2.3 to 4.0 adults. This is small by comparison with rural south of England populations such as those of Woodchester Park and Wytham Woods, and slightly smaller than the average for southern England as a whole. However, since group ranges were also small, averaging about 50 ha, the overall population density was moderate, varying from year to year between 4.4 and 7.5 adults/km^2. This is lower than at Woodchester Park or Wytham Woods but comparable to the average for southern

FIG 170. Sites of two studies of urban badgers: (above left) Clifton area of Bristol; (above right) Kemptown area of Brighton. (J. Davison)

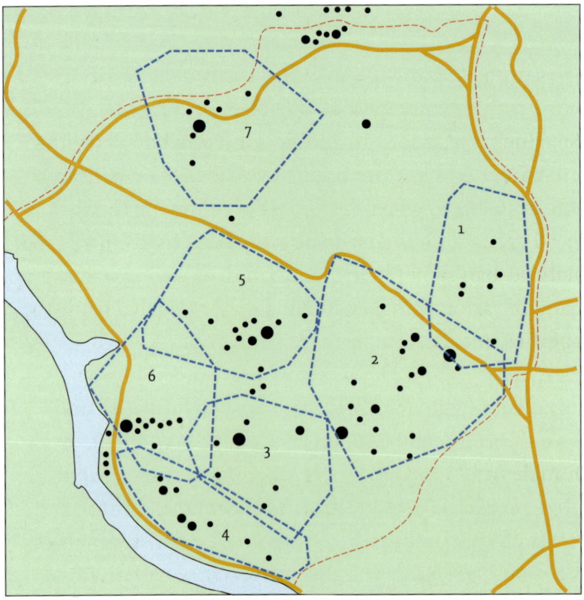

FIG 171. Setts and group home ranges (dashed blue lines) of badgers in the Clifton area of Bristol. Small, medium-sized and large black circles denote setts with fewer than 5 entrances, 5–10 entrances and more than 10 entrances, respectively. (Original from Harris, 1982. Copyright Zoological Society of London, reproduced by permission of the copyright holder)

England as a whole and also to population densities in northern England, Germany and Luxembourg (see Table 9 above).

Although the Bristol badgers typically lived in social groups containing mature adults of both sexes, their social organisation seems to have been somewhat looser than is typical of rural populations. One symptom of this was that the Bristol population contained a number of solitary animals – usually, young badgers that had dispersed from the group they were born into but had not managed to join another group. These seem to have survived as 'floaters', living in sub-optimal habitat in the gaps between established group territories. In addition, the rate of dispersal in the Bristol population was substantially higher than has been found in rural populations, with 80 per cent of males and 44 per cent of females switching groups every year.

As regards territoriality and ranging behaviour, social groups in Bristol, like rural badgers, occupied communal home ranges that varied in size from season to season. In some cases, neighbouring group ranges were non-contiguous (i.e. there was space between them), while in other cases they partially overlapped (Fig. 171). Latrines were mainly clustered around main setts and were apparently absent from range boundaries. The pattern of sett use was not examined in any detail, but it is clear that there were main setts, some of which were very large, plus a scattering of secondary setts, of various sizes, throughout each home range.

Badgers in Brighton

A few years ago, two members of my research group, John Davison and Maren Huck, undertook a three-year study of a population of badgers in Brighton (Davison *et al.*, 2008a, 2008b; Huck *et al.*, 2008). In addition to radio telemetry, the study involved estimating social group sizes and population density by analysing DNA obtained from badger hairs (see the Appendix for details of the method). Most of the work involved six social groups occupying an area of about 1 km^2 in a part of Brighton that was indisputably urban rather than suburban in character, containing as it did high-density housing of various kinds, schools, a major hospital complex, commercial and retail properties, and some busy roads (Fig. 170b).

The badgers in this population lived in stable social groups containing, on average, 5.5 animals including cubs, which is about the same as in Bristol and slightly lower than in the south of England as a whole. Groups contained, on average, equal numbers of males and females, and each group was associated with what clearly constituted a main sett. In addition, group ranges contained, on average, 3.5 secondary setts of various sizes. Movements (either temporary or permanent) of individual badgers between one group and another were somewhat more frequent in the urban population than in comparable rural populations, but not as frequent as Harris and Cresswell had found in Bristol.

When it came to ranging behaviour, however, there were some real surprises. The group ranges of the Brighton badgers were extremely small, averaging a mere 9.3 ha, while individual home ranges were smaller still at 4.9 ha (see Fig. 172). These are by a considerable margin the smallest ranges ever recorded in badgers

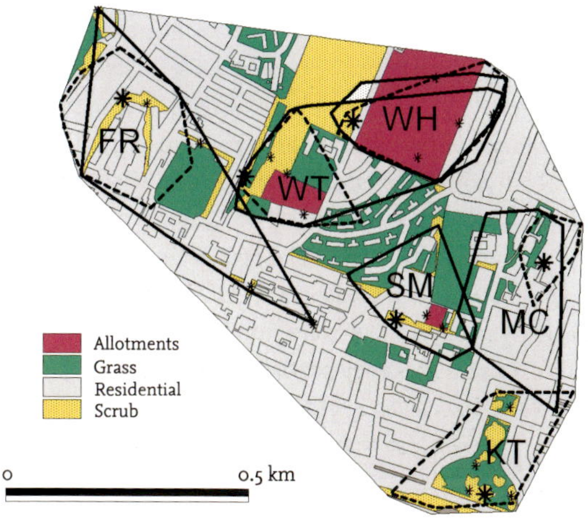

FIG 172. Home ranges of ten individual badgers from six different social groups, in the city of Brighton, UK. Capital letters (FR, WT etc.) denote different social groups. (From Davison *et al.*, 2008b)

anywhere. In addition, the ranges of neighbouring social groups were even less contiguous than were those of the Bristol population; and, as in the Bristol study, there was no evidence of range boundaries being demarcated by latrines. Because of the extremely small group range sizes, the Brighton population had the highest population density ever recorded in badgers, of about 33 adults/km^2.

Similarities and differences between the Bristol and Brighton studies

In both Bristol and Brighton, badgers formed mixed-sex social groups that lived in well-established main setts and ranged over more or less exclusive, communal territories. To this extent, they followed the typical rural pattern. However, in both studies, group ranges were small (very small in the case of Brighton) and tended to be non-contiguous, and there was no sign of overt territorial behaviour. Social groups also tended to be on the small side and were less stable, in the sense that there was a higher rate of movement between groups (very high in the case of Bristol). The only qualitative difference between the two studies is that we found no sign of individuals living solitarily as 'floaters' in Brighton, but nor has such behaviour been reported in any study of rural badgers.

At the time of Cresswell and Harris's study, rural badgers had mainly been studied in high-density populations such as those at Wytham Woods and Woodchester Park. In this context, various aspects of the behaviour of the Bristol badgers, such as the non-contiguity of their home ranges, the lack of boundary latrines and the relaxed social structure, seemed distinctly unusual. It looked, therefore, as though urban badgers organised themselves, socially and spatially, in a rather different way from rural badgers. However, now that we know much more about how rural badgers live at moderate and low population densities, the behaviour of the Bristol badgers seems less exceptional. For example, small group sizes, overlapping or non-contiguous home ranges and the partial or complete absence of boundary latrines are all characteristic of moderate- or low-density rural populations. It is therefore tempting to suggest that the unusual features of the Bristol population could be a consequence of moderate population density rather than of the urban environment per se. The same could also be true of the relatively high rate of dispersal, though in this case we cannot be sure, because dispersal rates have never been measured in moderate- or low-density rural populations. On the other hand, the small range sizes of the Bristol population cannot be attributed to moderate population density, since, in rural environments, lower population densities are associated with larger range sizes.

When we consider the Brighton population as well, the picture becomes even more complicated. Here, home ranges were even smaller and less contiguous than in Bristol, boundary latrines were again absent and there was a high rate of

FIG 173. Badgers feeding in a back garden. (R. Dixon)

movement between social groups. Yet population density in Brighton was the opposite of moderate or low – it was the highest ever recorded. This means, then, that the characteristics in question cannot be attributable to urban population densities being lower than rural ones. Rather, they seem to reflect differences in the intrinsic nature of urban and rural environments.

Although we still have much to learn about urban badgers, one thing seems fairly certain: namely, that their small range sizes result from the presence of concentrated, easily available food resources provided, either intentionally or unintentionally, by householders (Fig. 173). Unpublished surveys carried out independently by Stephen Harris and John Davison show that a significant number of residents deliberately provide food for badgers, while others report badgers raiding bird-feeders, taking food put out for household pets, raiding dustbins or eating garden fruits and vegetables. The importance of these sources of food is confirmed by a study of the diet of the Bristol badgers, about 50 per cent of which consisted of scavenged material (Harris, 1984).

The point about these kinds of foods is that they are so readily available in urban environments, and present in sufficient quantities, that urban badgers do not need to venture far away from their setts in order to get enough to eat. Hence, home-range sizes can be small. This was particularly evident in our Brighton study area, where the range of one social group was essentially restricted to just two back gardens immediately adjacent to the main sett. The owners of these gardens provided the badgers with so much food, and so regularly, that they hardly ever needed to go further afield.

However, some of the other characteristics of urban badgers, such as the non-contiguity of home ranges, the relatively high rate of movement between groups and the small group sizes still require explanation. First, if food is so readily available, why are there unoccupied spaces in between the home ranges of established groups? The most likely answer is that what limits the density of social groups is the availability of suitable sites for setts rather than the availability of food. In our Brighton study area, most main setts were located in small corners of wasteland rather than in the gardens of occupied houses, and such sites are rare in a densely occupied townscape.

Second, if food is so plentiful, why do urban badgers not form larger groups and why are these groups apparently less stable? Here, the answer may lie in yet another factor: namely, a high rate of mortality, which would both limit group size and, by increasing the rate at which breeding opportunities become available, encourage higher rates of dispersal. Unfortunately, no one has yet measured the survival rates of urban badgers, but it seems likely that road traffic, which is the single most important cause of death in UK rural populations (see Chapter 1), is even more of a hazard in urban environments.

Other studies of urban badgers

Little is known about the ranging behaviour or social structure of urban badgers outside the UK. However, one study in Trondheim, Norway, and two studies in Japan, in Yamaguchi City and Hinode respectively, provide a limited amount of relevant information.

In Trondheim, group ranges were considerably larger than in either Bristol or Brighton and varied enormously in size, from about 1.5 to 18 km^2. Some of this variation in range sizes was seasonal, but there was also a tendency for ranges in the central part of the city to be larger than those in the suburbs (Johansen, 1993, cited in Harris *et al.*, 2009; Bevanger *et al.*, 1996). It is perhaps worth noting that the ranges of rural badgers are also much larger in Norway than in the UK, suggesting that socio-spatial organisation may differ more between countries than it does between urban and rural environments within any one country.

The study of Japanese badgers living in an outer suburb of Yamaguchi City (Tanaka *et al.*, 2002) is intriguing, because it suggests the existence in badgers of a completely different system of socio-spatial organisation, of the kind known as 'solitary intra-sexual territoriality'. Here, single adult females occupy exclusive, non-contiguous ranges shared only with their cubs, while single males occupy larger ranges surrounding those of two or more females (Fig. 174). This finding is of considerable interest, because solitary intra-sexual territoriality, although

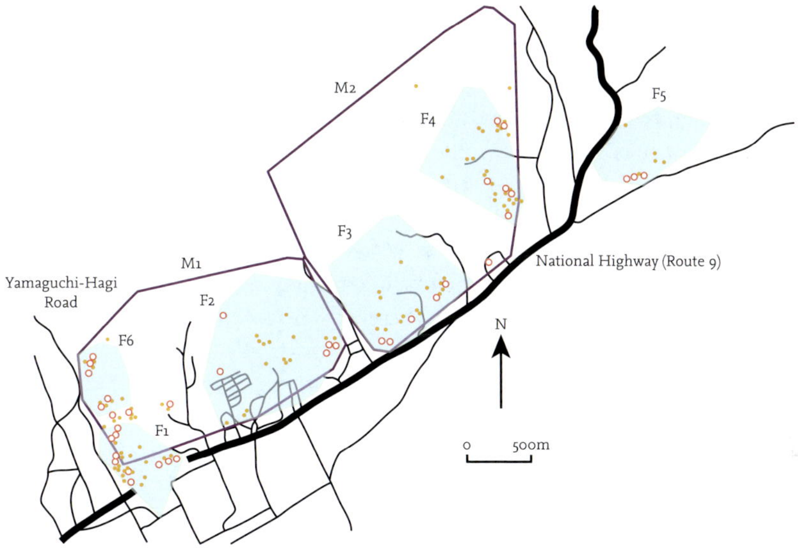

FIG 174. Home ranges of two male and six female Japanese badgers, *Meles meles anakuma*, in a suburb of Yamaguchi City, Japan. Yellow dots: small setts. Red circles: larger setts. Thick and thin black lines show major and minor roads. (Redrawn from Tanaka *et al.*, 2002, with permission of the publisher)

qualitatively different from the communal territoriality of Eurasian badgers, is characteristic of most other members of the mustelid family (see Chapter 8 and Powell, 1979). The second study of suburban Japanese badgers, carried out in Hinode, also revealed a striking sex difference in range size, with male ranges being on average about four times as large as those of females (Kaneko *et al.*, 2006). Unfortunately, it is not clear whether these badgers were living solitarily or how their home ranges related to one another in spatial terms.

These studies raise the question as to whether solitary intra-sexual territoriality reflects a difference between Japanese and European badgers or is a consequence of urbanisation. The latter explanation seems unlikely, given that urban European badgers, as we have seen, live in groups. Also, it is debatable whether the Yamaguchi City study site could reasonably be described as urban or even suburban, since 70 per cent of the area was forested and houses seem to have been well spaced out. It is therefore more likely that solitary intra-sexual territoriality is a subspecies-specific characteristic of *Meles meles anakuma*. However, further studies of Japanese badgers, especially in genuinely rural environments, are needed to confirm this.

Summary

The socio-spatial organisation of urban European badgers resembles that of rural badgers in many important respects, but there are also some significant quantitative differences, for example in group sizes, range sizes and dispersal rates. Some of these differences are almost certainly attributable to the presence, in urban environments, of rich anthropogenic food resources, while others may reflect the relative rarity of suitable sett sites and a high rate of mortality. However, urban badgers remain relatively unstudied and there is much to be discovered about their habits, both within and outside the UK. In addition, it is worth remembering that urban environments are themselves extremely heterogeneous, varying as they do from city centres at one end of the spectrum to urban fringes and villages at the other. Almost nothing is known about how badger behaviour might differ between these different kinds of 'urban' habitat.

CONCLUSIONS

Much has been made in the scientific literature of the supposed 'flexibility' of the badger's socio-spatial organisation. Badgers, it is often said, can live either solitarily or in groups containing from as few as two to as many as 30 adults, and they can occupy territories varying in size from a few hectares to several square kilometres. There are, however, two reasons for thinking that this emphasis on 'flexibility', at least with respect to social group size and composition, has been somewhat overstated.

First, there is no good evidence that European badgers live solitarily, the sole basis for this claim being a much-cited but questionable PhD project by Pigozzi (1987). The Japanese badger does appear to live solitarily, but since it is a different subspecies (or perhaps even a different species; see Chapter 1), it would not be surprising if it behaved differently from the European badger.

Second, even in the UK, where groups seem to be larger than elsewhere, group size peaks at only three adults (see Fig. 151 above) and averages only five to six adults. Although it is true that very large groups do occur, they are only found in a few UK populations, where conditions are clearly exceptionally favourable and where artificial provisioning may be a factor. In the UK, therefore, the majority of groups contain from two to eight adults, while, over most of the remainder of their geographical range, European badgers probably live in groups containing two or three adults. This is not such a remarkable degree of variation, either in absolute terms or by comparison with other social species, though it does attest to the ability of badgers to adapt their social behaviour to a wide range of ecological conditions.

Territory size, on the other hand, varies by at least two orders of magnitude, which seems like a lot by any standards. Over most of their geographical range, badgers probably occupy territories several square kilometres in size, though more studies are needed from central and eastern Europe, and from Asia, to confirm this. Territories occupying less than 1 km^2 have so far been reported only in the UK, Ireland and Luxembourg, so are probably confined to the northwestern corner of the species' range. The fact that territory size and group size covary geographically, such that smaller territories tend to contain larger social groups, suggests that both variables reflect the overall suitability of a particular region from the badger's point of view. However, we still do not understand what factors determine 'overall suitability' in this sense. Thinking so far has concentrated almost exclusively on differences in food availability, but it seems likely that other factors also enter into the equation (see Chapter 1).

CHAPTER 8

The Origins of Social Territoriality in Badgers

QUESTIONS ABOUT THE SOCIO-SPATIAL ORGANISATION OF BADGERS

During the course of his pioneering studies of badger behaviour, first at Wytham Woods and then in Scotland, Hans Kruuk realised that the socio-spatial organisation of badgers was unusual in two respects. First, badgers live, as we have seen, in mixed-sex groups, each of which defends a common territory (see Chapter 7 and Fig. 175b). This is in contrast to most members of the mustelid family, which operate a system known as 'solitary intra-sexual territoriality', in which individuals of each sex live alone, defending their territories against other individuals of the same sex but not against individuals of the opposite sex (see Fig. 175a). Kruuk therefore found himself asking why badgers live socially while most of their closest taxonomic relatives live solitarily.

Second, Kruuk considered badgers to be less highly social than many other carnivores. One symptom of this was that for a group-living species, badgers seemed to Kruuk to be relatively uncommunicative (see Chapter 6); another was that they behaved like solitary animals as soon as they left the vicinity of the sett, foraging alone for most of the time and rarely taking much notice of one another even when they did meet (see Chapter 7). But what really seemed odd to Kruuk was the badger's lack of cooperative behaviour. Unlike most other socially living carnivores, the members of a badger group do not assist one another in finding food, defending themselves against enemies or caring for young.

This lack of cooperative behaviour did not just make badgers appear unusual by comparison with many other social carnivores; it also gave rise to an important theoretical insight. At the time of Kruuk's badger studies, in the late 1970s and early

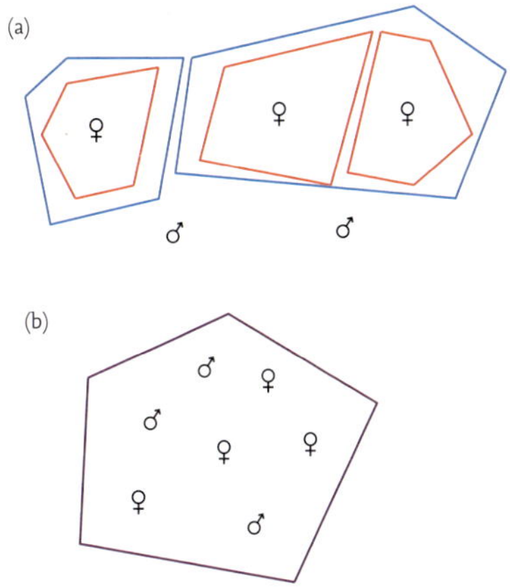

FIG 175. (a) System of solitary intra-sexual territoriality, as observed in most mustelids. (b) System of mixed-sex communal territoriality, as observed in badgers.

1980s, it was generally supposed that a primary benefit of group living, at least in carnivores, was that it allowed cooperation. However, the fact that badgers lived in social groups but were not cooperative suggested that sociality could arise for other reasons. In other words, it occurred to Kruuk that cooperation could be a consequence, not a cause, of sociality. This insight led in turn to the idea that badgers might represent a relatively 'primitive' stage in the evolution of sociality, in which group formation had occurred but cooperative behaviour had yet to appear.

This view of the evolution of sociality raises the obvious question as to why badgers live in groups in the first place, if not because of the benefits to be gained from cooperation. In an attempt to answer this question, Kruuk proposed that group formation had an ecological rather than a behavioural basis: more specifically, he suggested that it was linked to the spatio-temporal pattern of food availability. This idea was subsequently formalised and extended by David Macdonald and others, who have termed it the Resource Dispersion Hypothesis, or RDH for short (e.g. Macdonald, 1983; Woodroffe & Macdonald, 1993).

In this chapter, I shall describe the Resource Dispersion Hypothesis and ask to what extent it sheds light on the evolution of social territoriality in badgers. I should perhaps warn the reader that this involves venturing further into the realms of theory than has been necessary in previous chapters. However, I will endeavour to keep the discussion simple and to avoid becoming so caught up in the pursuit of ideas as to lose contact with reality.

THE RESOURCE DISPERSION HYPOTHESIS (RDH)

In its original form, the Resource Dispersion Hypothesis (RDH) grew directly out of Kruuk's studies of badger diet (see Kruuk, 1989, for references). Four findings from these studies were relevant, as follows. First, Kruuk had found that badgers

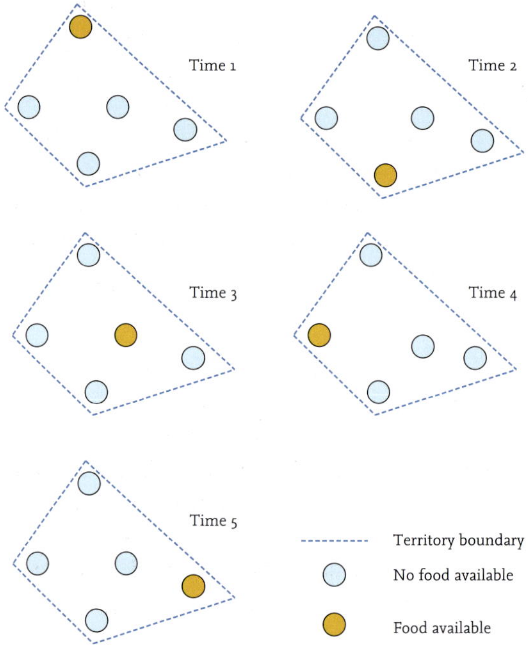

FIG 176. The Resource Dispersion Hypothesis. Different patches provide food at different times. Therefore, a territory has to contain several patches in order to provide a continuous supply of food.

in the UK fed mainly on earthworms, and that their main method of foraging was to pick these worms off the surface of the ground when they had emerged from their burrows to feed (the behaviour that Kruuk called 'worming': see Chapter 4). Second, he showed that the availability of earthworms on the surface was related to local, and sometimes rapidly changing, climatic conditions: worms only come out of their burrows in large numbers on warm, relatively still nights when the ground is moist. Hence, the availability of earthworms, from the badgers' point of view, is unpredictable. Third, Kruuk found that only certain kinds of habitat yielded worms in abundance, short-grass pasture and deciduous woodland being the most fruitful. That is, earthworms were patchily distributed in space. Finally, he showed that on a 'good' worm night, a small area of suitable habitat (pasture or woodland) could yield a super-abundance of worms – more than enough to feed the members of an entire social group of badgers.

Based on these observations, the argument underlying the RDH was as follows. Because earthworm availability is related to local climatic conditions, different places ('patches') will yield earthworms at different times. For example, because worms do not surface in windy conditions, the southern edge of a block of woodland might be sufficiently sheltered to yield worms when the wind was from the north, and the northern edge when the wind was from the south. Or, a part of a field that was slightly lower than the rest, and hence moister, might yield worms when the rest of the field was too dry. Therefore, because different earthworm 'patches' will provide worms at different times, a badger needs to have access to several patches in order to guarantee a continuous supply of food (see Fig. 176). More specifically, Kruuk calculated that a badger territory, in order to be viable, would need to contain about five separate worm 'patches'. This gives rise to an important prediction of the RDH: namely, that territory size and shape should depend on the spatial distribution of worm patches. Specifically, the further apart earthworm patches are, the larger the territory will need to be to contain enough of them (see Fig. 177).

So far, we have been considering how large a territory needs to be to feed a single badger. However, because earthworm biomass in suitable habitat is so high, each earthworm patch, provided that local climatic conditions favour worm emergence, will yield enough food for many badgers. Therefore, the RDH argues, a territory that is large enough to feed a single badger (i.e. a territory containing about five worm patches) will feed additional badgers at no extra cost. This leads to a second important prediction of the RDH: namely, that group size should depend on the 'richness' of worm patches – that is, on how many badgers an individual worm patch can support.

To summarise, the original form of the RDH proposed that territory size and shape on the one hand, and group size on the other, are determined by different aspects of earthworm availability: namely, worm patch distribution and patch richness, respectively. But the hypothesis also had wider significance. First, it helped to shift thinking about the evolution of sociality away from an emphasis on cooperative behaviour and towards an emphasis on ecological factors such as food availability. And, second, it was innovative insofar as it constituted a kind of

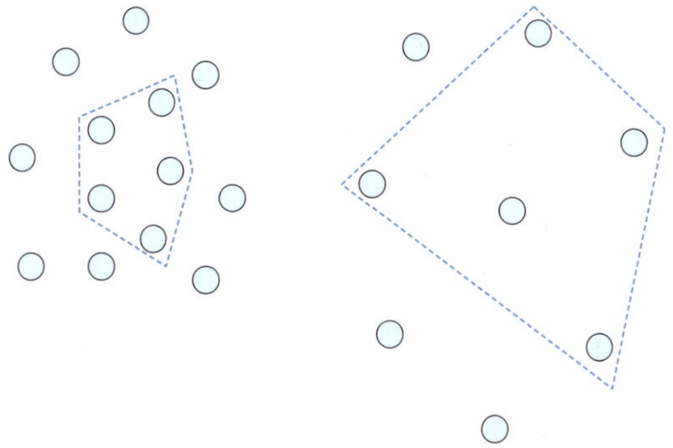

FIG 177. Predicted relationship between food-patch density and territory size. The greater the average distance between food patches, the larger the territory needs to be to contain a sufficient number of patches.

'default' model of sociality: it suggested that group living can arise not because it offers special advantages by comparison with a solitary lifestyle, but because it does not incur any additional costs.

Following this original formulation, the RDH has been modified and extended in various ways to make it applicable to species other than badgers and to resources other than earthworms. In the process, however, it has become both less intelligible to an ordinary reader (later versions take the form of mathematical models) and more divorced from reality. What I like about the original version is that it is easy to understand and arises in a very direct way from real observations of real badgers. And, since the basic principles of the RDH have remained unchanged, the original version still serves to illustrate them. In what follows, therefore, I shall use the original version of the hypothesis as a basis for discussion.

PROBLEMS WITH THE RDH

There is no disputing that the RDH was an original and ingenious idea but does it hold up to scrutiny? This is still a matter of debate. Various criticisms of the RDH have been made over the years along with attempts to refute them (e.g. Woodroffe & Macdonald, 1993; Revilla, 2003a, 2003b; Johnson and Macdonald, 2003). However, rather than getting bogged down in the details of these, I will confine myself to touching on what I see as the RDH's two most important deficiencies.

First, although the RDH seems to make rather concrete predictions about the factors that determine the size of social groups and the size and shape of territories, these have proved, in practice, difficult to test. One problem is that neither Kruuk nor anyone else has ever said precisely what they mean by a food 'patch'. Sometimes, Kruuk writes as if an earthworm patch could be an area covering only a few square metres, such as a corner of a field that is sheltered by a hedge or a place in a wood where the soil is especially rich and moist. At other times, however, it seems that a patch could be an entire field of pasture or block of woodland. Consequently, it is hard to evaluate the assertion that food patches, in the sense required by the RDH, exist, let alone that their spatial distribution and richness determine, respectively, territory size and group size. The same objection applies to later versions of the RDH, which, although they do not necessarily require food patches, do demand that some resource or other be distributed in a spatio-temporally unpredictable manner. Indeed, even the most enthusiastic proponents of the RDH admit that its main predictions have so far not been tested (Johnson *et al.*, 2003).

The second major drawback of the RDH is that it is based on the idea that sociality in badgers is cost-free. This may indeed be valid when it comes to food resources (i.e. there may be little or no competition for food within badger social groups) but is certainly not valid when it comes to reproduction. As we have seen, there is competition between adult females for breeding status so that, often, only a single female can breed within any one social group in any one year. This means that subordinate females suffer a reproductive cost from being members of a group, because they are prevented, at least temporarily, from breeding. Consequently, their fitness (the number of offspring they are able to have in their lifetime) will be lower than if they lived solitarily.

This second point cuts to the heart of any form of the RDH. As Eloy Revilla (2003a) has pointed out, the RDH can only, at best, explain why dominant individuals allow subordinates to remain in the social group (i.e. because the territory contains enough resources for everyone). It cannot, by contrast, explain why those subordinates want to stay, if they could have more offspring by dispersing. In reply to this criticism, advocates of the RDH have stated that it was never intended to explain why subordinates remain in their natal group; it was only intended to suggest a set of ecological conditions that would enable them to do so (Johnson *et al.*, 2003). This, however, is disingenuous. The RDH was originally presented as a self-sufficient explanation of why badgers sometimes form social groups, not just as one of a set of factors that might make group formation possible.

Be that as it may, we can now see that group formation requires an answer to two questions. First, why does a territory that was set up in the first place by a single badger, or at most a pair of badgers, contain enough resources to support an entire social group? And, second, why do offspring fail to disperse, or only disperse late in life, in some badger populations, despite the fact that this reduces their fitness? Having identified these as the key questions, we can now try to answer them.

GROUP FORMATION AND SIZE

The problem of excess resources

According to the RDH, a badger setting up a territory *de novo* defends an area just large enough to ensure a continuous supply of food for itself; but the pattern of food distribution is such that a territory large enough to support a single individual will, *ipso facto*, support additional individuals at no extra cost. However, there is another way of explaining why territories contain more food than is required by a single badger. This involves questioning the assumption, intrinsic to the RDH, that the founding territory holder only defends the minimum area that is needed to feed itself.

The standard rationale for this assumption is that because territory defence is costly, in terms of time and energy, no territory holder should defend a larger territory than it needs. However, this argument has always seemed to me to be simplistic. Imagine a single badger wanting to set up home in an unoccupied, or only sparsely occupied, region. Should it really only try to lay claim to the minimum area that it needs in order to support itself at that time? Badgers are long-lived animals and badger groups can be very long-lived indeed; and it seems fair to assume that badgers are no better than the rest of us at predicting the future. If I were a badger, therefore, setting up home in an area of low population density, I would lay claim to as much territory as I could reasonably expect to hold at that time. That way, I or my descendants would still be able to survive if, at some future time, food availability declined or increasing population density forced a degree of retrenchment. What I am suggesting, then, is that badgers should try to grab as much as they can while the going is good, as an insurance against future hard times.

This idea, unlike the RDH, can explain the results of the study carried out by Jessica Ostler (see Chapter 7). She found that in the 20-year period between two surveys, the number of main setts in her South Downs study area more than doubled, while average territory size more than halved. According to the RDH, this could only have happened if food-patch density had doubled during the same period, so that the requisite minimum number of food patches could be encompassed within smaller territories. However, during the period in question, there was little change to the agricultural regime and, therefore, no reason to suppose that the pattern of food availability changed. A much more straightforward explanation is that at the time of the first survey, when population density was relatively low, territories were larger than they needed to be.

The same conclusion also emerges from a study of the recolonisation of areas from which badgers had been removed by culling (Cheeseman *et al.*, 1993). Females that moved into vacated setts initially occupied large, overlapping home ranges incorporating several of what had previously been main setts. Only after a few years, when they started to breed, did these foundress females reduce their range sizes and settle permanently in a single main sett. Eventually, as social groups containing multiple adults of both sexes developed, territory boundaries contracted to the size they had been prior to culling, presumably owing to a gradual increase in intruder pressure.

Of course, this process of contraction of territories as population density increases cannot go on for ever – eventually, territory size will be forced down to a minimum, and what constitutes that minimum will depend on the availability of the resources, including food, that are needed for survival. This situation seems to have been reached in places like Wytham Woods and Woodchester Park. But by that time, the badgers in question will all be living in groups, so the minimum territory size will be determined by the requirements of a whole group, not just by the needs of an individual.

Why do offspring not disperse?

Genetic and other evidence shows that social groups form, in badgers as in almost all other social animals, because offspring remain within the group in which they were born. What we want to know, then, is why offspring fail to disperse, or only disperse late in life, in some badger populations. The question is especially acute in relation to females, because subordinate males have the chance of stealing at least a few copulations from dominant males within their own social group or from males in neighbouring groups. Therefore, competition for the opportunity to reproduce is likely to be greater among females than among males.

Since groups containing multiple adults of both sexes only form in moderate- and high-density populations, the obvious explanation is that offspring fail to disperse because of 'habitat saturation': that is, because the environment is already so full of established territories that there is nowhere for a young dispersing female to set up home on her own, attract a mate and start breeding (da Silva *et al.*, 1994). Ideally, this hypothesis could be tested experimentally by removing some social groups from a high-density population and seeing whether the rate of dispersal increases. Such experiments have not been done on badgers, though they have been carried out, with the predicted result, in other species of group-living animals.

As already noted, however, there are several cases in which populations of badgers have been culled for purposes of bovine tuberculosis control and we can treat these as quasi-experiments with which to evaluate the habitat saturation hypothesis. From what is known, it does seem as if setts that have become vacant as a consequence of culling are reoccupied rather rapidly, usually by single females, who must presumably be dispersers from surrounding non-culled areas (Cheeseman *et al.*, 1993; Tuttyens *et al.*, 2000). This is precisely what the habitat saturation hypothesis would predict. There is, then, some direct evidence that habitat saturation acts as a bar to dispersal in badgers. However, the main reason for thinking that it does so comes from the abundance of convincing evidence from other species.

Some time ago, I suggested another possible cause of non-dispersal in badgers, which has to do with the availability of setts that are suitable for breeding (Neal & Roper, 1991; Roper, 1993). Struck by the size and complexity of many main setts in the UK, I proposed that it might take several years for a female disperser to dig a sett that was large enough to rear cubs in. Therefore, I argued, it might be better for a young female to remain in the group where she was born, and hope eventually to inherit breeding status together with an existing main sett, rather than to try to establish a new main sett on her own. However, there is no evidence that breeding can only occur when a sett reaches a certain level of size and complexity; rather, evidence has since accumulated that badgers breed successfully in quite small setts in many parts of their geographical range (see Chapter 3). In addition, setts can sometimes sprout new entrances and spoil heaps at a surprising rate, suggesting that badgers can excavate extensively, in a relatively short period of time, when they really want to (da Silva *et al.*, 1994). Consequently, I no longer set much store by the idea that the difficulty of constructing a new breeding sett acts as a significant bar to dispersal.

To summarise, if we are looking for factors that limit dispersal in badgers, then habitat saturation is the most likely candidate.

Social group size

This still leaves the question of what determines social group size. Ultimately, group size must reflect the balance between the production of offspring on the one hand and the rates of mortality and dispersal on the other. In high-density badger populations in the UK, where the level of predation (other than by road traffic) is low, the climate is moderate, badgers are not hunted and opportunities for dispersal are limited, the main factor affecting this balance may well be food availability. Some evidence of this is provided by Kruuk, who compared social group size and the biomass of earthworms per territory in Scottish badgers. Groups were indeed larger where earthworms were more abundant (see Fig. 178). In addition, there is anecdotal evidence from householders that when badgers are artificially fed, their numbers increase. Indeed, it would be surprising if this were not so.

Conversely, there is also some (albeit rather slight) evidence that reductions in food availability can impact negatively on group size. For example, Kruuk & Parish (1987) reported that when earthworm availability was reduced by agricultural changes in one of their Scottish study areas, social group sizes did decline, though the effect was not statistically significant. Similarly, Nolet & Killingley (1987) provide anecdotal evidence of a decline in the size of a group of badgers that lost part of its territory owing to a change in land use. The trouble with these kinds of 'natural experiments', however, is that changes in land use

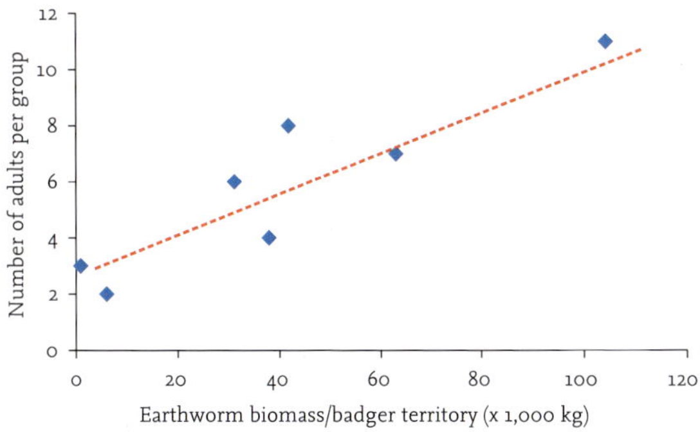

FIG 178. Relationship between social group size and the abundance of earthworms in the corresponding territory. (From Kruuk & Parish, 1982)

usually affect the spatial distribution as well as the abundance of food, so the effects are likely to be more complex than a simple reduction in group size. For example, in the study by Kruuk & Parish, the decrease in average group size was complicated by a simultaneous increase in the number of groups, making the results of the study difficult to interpret.

Overall, then, there is some evidence that food abundance impacts on social group size, which seems like good news for advocates of the RDH. However, the existence of a link between food availability and group size does not require food to be distributed in the patchy, unpredictable manner suggested by the RDH (see Fig. 176 above). On the contrary, food could limit population density however it is distributed in space and time.

Conclusions

To summarise the argument so far, the Resource Dispersion Hypothesis is a possible explanation of why badger territories can support a whole social group, as opposed to supporting only a single foundress female. However, an alternative explanation is that when population density is low, foundress females commandeer larger territories than they need at the time. With respect to the issue of why young badgers sometimes do not disperse, the RDH is irrelevant, and habitat saturation is the most likely explanation. With respect to the issue of group size, the RDH may well be right in proposing a link between group size and food availability. However, this does not require food to be distributed in the manner suggested by the RDH. In addition, it is perfectly possible that outside the relatively badger-friendly conditions that obtain in southern England, group size may be limited by any of the host of other factors that impact on reproductive rate and mortality. In short, the RDH could be part of the explanation as to why badgers form groups and how the sizes of these groups are determined, but other, simpler explanations are at least as plausible.

TERRITORY SIZE AND SHAPE

As already noted, the RDH predicts that badger territories will be just large enough to contain the number of food patches needed to guarantee survival – five patches, according to Kruuk, when the staple food is earthworms. Therefore, both the size and the shape of individual territories should be determined by the pattern of patch distribution in space (see Fig. 177, above). How well do these predictions stand up to the available evidence?

Territory size

There is quite good support for the prediction that territory size is related to the distribution of good foraging habitat. For example, Brøseth *et al.* (1997) found that in Norway, where badgers eat mainly earthworms, territory size was inversely related to the density of earthworm-rich patches of deciduous forest (see Fig. 179). Other examples are a study in Portugal by Rosalino *et al.* (2004) and one in the Doñana reserve, Spain, by Rodriguez *et al.* (1996). In Portugal, where badgers fed mainly on fruit, home-range size was proportional to the average distance between fruit-providing areas such as olive groves, orchards and vegetable gardens. In Spain, where badgers fed mainly on young rabbits, territory size was inversely related to the amount of dense scrub and pasture, which were the types of habitat in which rabbits were most abundant.

However, although these findings look like convincing evidence in favour of the RDH, they do not necessarily show that there is a direct connection between food-patch dispersion and territory size – a point to which I return below. In addition, although they show an association between territory size and the spatial distribution of food patches, they do not address the rather more critical

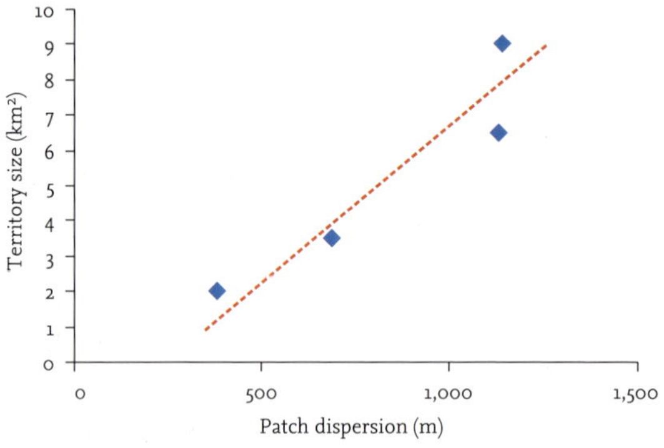

FIG 179. Relationship between territory size and food-patch dispersion. (From Brøseth *et al.*, 1997)

requirement of the RDH that different patches provide food at different times, in an unpredictable manner (see Fig. 176, above). In the case of foods such as fruits or young rabbits, it is hard to see why this should be the case.

Territory shape

According to the RDH, badgers draw their territory boundaries around the minimum area needed to enclose a certain number of food patches. Consequently, since patches are by definition separated in space, adjacent territories should have gaps between them (Fig. 180). However, one of the most obvious features of territory boundaries in areas of high and moderate population density is that they are shared. This suggests that the precise location of territory boundaries is dictated not by the location of food patches but by the presence of (or, more precisely, the intruder pressure exerted by) adjacent social groups.

This idea, that the location of a territory boundary represents a point of balance between two adjacent social groups, each of which is exerting intruder pressure on the other, predicts that the territory boundary separating two groups should lie midway between the relevant main setts. In other words, territory boundaries should constitute a set of what are called 'Dirichlet tessellations' (see Appendix for further details). When two Oxford researchers, Patrick Doncaster and Rosie Woodroffe, tested this model using data on main sett locations from five different study areas, they found a good correspondence between predicted and actual territory boundaries in three of the five areas (Doncaster & Woodroffe, 1993). Coincidentally, one of my own students, Larissa Conradt, carried out a similar study at the same time, using data from our Sussex study area, with the same result (Conradt, 1993). In no case was the correspondence between predicted and actual territory boundaries exact, because actual territory

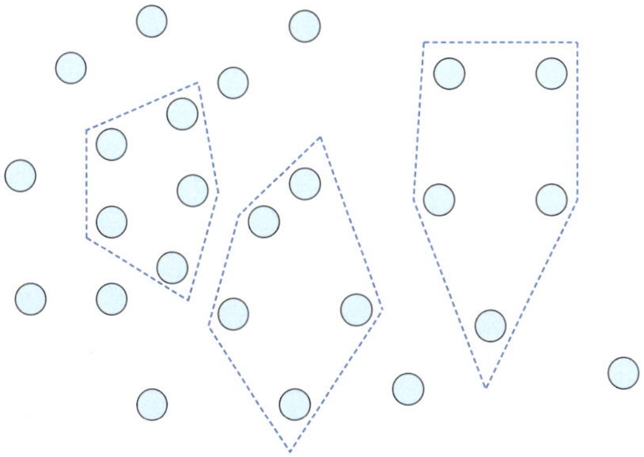

FIG 180. The Resource Dispersion Hypothesis. If territory size and shape are determined by the spatial location of food patches, then territories should be non-contiguous.

boundaries tend to follow landscape features such as fence lines, field edges and paths, rather than being situated precisely halfway between two main setts. However, the results of these studies are convincing enough to suggest that the location of a main sett in relation to that of its neighbours is an important determinant of the location of the relevant territory boundary.

There are other reasons for doubting the RDH explanation of territory shape. According to the RDH, there should be a food patch at every territory corner (see Fig. 180). In this case, the most heavily defended parts of the territory boundary should be the corners, and the corners of a territory should be the areas used most by badgers for foraging purposes. As regards territory defence, however, latrines tend to be most numerous along those parts of the boundary that separate two neighbouring main setts, especially when the main setts in question are close to one another (e.g. Nolet & Killingley, 1987). This is hard to explain in terms of defence of food resources but is exactly what we would expect if the amount of effort put into territory defence reflects the strength of intruder pressure.

With respect to foraging behaviour, there is no evidence that the corners of a territory are especially important: rather, territories often encompass large areas at their periphery that are seldom used for foraging purposes. Consider, for example, the map of individual territories provided by Brøseth *et al.* (Fig. 181). In their study area, the most important foraging habitat consisted of patches of deciduous forest, shown on the map as shaded areas. Each territory contains a certain amount of forest, but it is clear from the map that the locations of territory boundaries are not dictated by the locations of the relevant forest

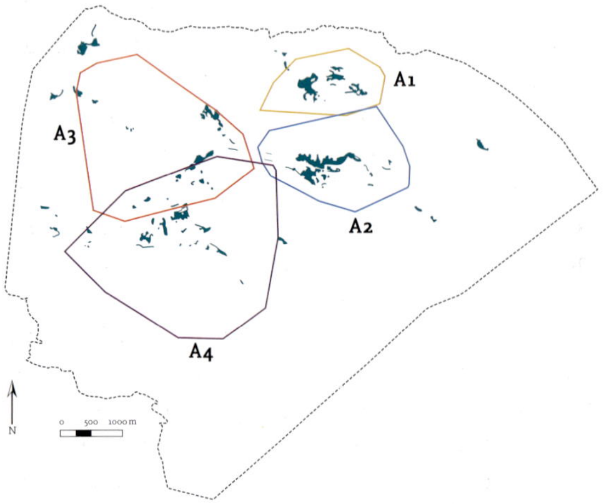

FIG 181. Territory boundaries of four adjacent badger groups in relation to the location of patches of deciduous forest (shaded areas) in central Norway. (Redrawn from Brøseth *et al.*, 1997. Copyright 1997, with permission from Elsevier)

patches. In territories A1 and A2, for example, all of the relevant patches of forest are located towards the centre of the territory, so each of these territories could be reduced considerably in size without losing access to any forest habitat. In A4, there is no forest habitat in the southern half of the territory and none towards the northeast corner, so this territory could be reduced in size by almost two-thirds without losing any important foraging habitat. In our study in Sussex, the same applies: territories often encompass, at their periphery, areas of arable land that are never used for foraging purposes (see Chapter 7, Fig. 160).

Conclusions

From what I have said, it would seem that the spatial distribution of food may determine territory size but does not account for the precise locations of territory boundaries. This may seems paradoxical, because the size of a territory must ultimately be determined by where its boundaries are.

The paradox can perhaps be resolved by further consideration of the map of individual territories shown provided by Brøseth *et al.* (see Fig. 181). As I have already pointed out, patches of forest do not, in this case, dictate the precise locations of territory boundaries. On the other hand, it does seem that territory sizes are inversely related to the density of patches of deciduous forest. In territories A1 and A2, deciduous forest occurs in dense clumps and these territories are indeed small, whereas in territories A3 and A4, clumps of deciduous forest are smaller and more scattered, and these territories are larger. However, the map also indicates a third conspicuous feature relating to territory size and conformation: namely, that neighbouring territories tend to meet one another. This suggests that territory boundaries are pushed out until they make contact with those of neighbouring groups, even if this means including in the territory a considerable amount of unproductive habitat.

Put together, these facts suggest the following explanation of territory size and shape. Areas where good places for feeding are relatively abundant, as for example the eastern half of Brøseth *et al.*'s study site, will support a higher *overall* population density of badgers. Consequently, intruder pressure on individual territories will be higher and those territories will be smaller. Conversely, areas where food-bearing habitat is more scattered, as in the western half of Brøseth *et al.*'s study site, will support fewer badgers overall, intruder pressure will be less, and so territories will be larger. According to this idea, the way in which food is distributed in space determines overall population density (that is, better habitat supports more badgers), but the size and shape of individual territories are dictated by the proximity of neighbouring social groups (i.e. by the strength of intruder pressure) and only indirectly by food distribution.

WHAT ARE TERRITORIES FOR?

A territory is, by definition, a defended area. Since territory defence is costly (it involves time, energy and the risk of being injured in fights with would-be intruders), it follows that if a territory is worth defending, it must contain something valuable. What, then, is the resource that badgers seek to defend by engaging in territorial behaviour?

All of the early thinking about territoriality in badgers, including the development of the RDH, was based on the assumption that badger territories serve to defend food resources (specifically, earthworm patches). Indeed, earthworms receive so much emphasis in some of Kruuk's early papers that he seems to have been more interested in them than in badgers. A few years later, however, I put forward the idea that territoriality in badgers might have more to do with sex than with food (Roper *et al.*, 1986) – an idea that has subsequently been given the rather forbidding name of the Anti-Kleptogamy Hypothesis, or AKH for short.

'Kleptogamy' means, literally, stealing sex. What I proposed was that in badgers, territoriality was primarily a male activity and that its function was to prevent neighbouring males from entering a territory in order to mate with resident females. My main reason for proposing this idea was the finding that latrine use peaked in spring and autumn, at around the times of year when females were most likely to be in oestrus (Roper *et al.*, 1986; see also Chapter 6). In addition, I and my co-workers had seen badgers routinely entering one another's territories for purposes of foraging (see Chapter 7), whereas we had seen ferocious fights breaking out when a male entered another territory in order to court a resident female (see Chapters 5 and 7). Since then, other evidence of various kinds has emerged that seems more readily explicable in terms of mate defence than in terms of food defence (e.g. Roper & Lüps, 1993; Revilla & Palomares, 1999).

But there was another reason why I found the AKH attractive: namely, that it made badgers look less anomalous by comparison with other mustelids. As has already been noted, most mustelids operate a system in which the territories of individual males encompass those of one or more females (see above, Fig. 175a). In such a system, males are self-evidently defending females, and why else would they do this except for purposes of mating? The AKH therefore suggests that the function of territoriality in male badgers is the same as in males of other mustelid species.

The AKH can be criticised on the grounds that it does not account for territoriality in females. In fact, however, there is very little direct evidence that female badgers participate in territorial defence and, as far as I am aware, no observation has ever been made of a female badger trying to actively exclude a neighbour from entering her territory. Sows do defecate and scent-mark at boundary latrines, but this could be to advertise their reproductive status to neighbouring males, not to deter would-be intruders (see Chapter 6). They also get involved in fights, but this could be in the context of reproductive competition with other females within their own social group, rather than in the context of territorial defence (see Chapter 5). However, there is clear evidence of territoriality in females of other mustelid species, and this suggests that female badgers are probably the same.

Assuming this is correct, what resource are females most likely to be defending? Food is probably a more critical resource for females than it is for males, because they need to meet the nutritional demands of pregnancy and lactation. Therefore, females might well be defending food resources. But I have also drawn attention to the importance of the main sett as a breeding resource for females, and have suggested that this could be the focus of their territorial behaviour (Roper, 1992). There is some evidence in favour of this suggestion, insofar as females scent-mark more at latrines close to the sett than they do at latrines located around the territory boundary (see Chapter 6).

When I first proposed what later became the AKH, the idea met with a surprising amount of resistance, at least within the UK. In some quarters, it was almost considered a crime to suggest that territoriality in badgers might be concerned with some resource other than food. However, it is now generally accepted that male participation in territory defence is at least partly for reasons to do with sex, rather than exclusively about food. On the other hand, if females also participate in territory defence, which seems quite likely, then the resource they are defending may well be food but could be the main sett.

THE EVOLUTION OF GROUP TERRITORIALITY IN BADGERS

If we accept that solitary intra-sexual territoriality is the basic form of socio-spatial organisation in mustelids, then badgers or their ancestors must, at some time, have conformed to this pattern. The question therefore arises as to how a system of solitary intra-sexual territoriality evolved into one of mixed-sex communal territoriality. In other words, how does one get from the kind of organisation shown in Figure 175a to the kind shown in Figure 175b? The crucial step that needs to be explained is why male and female badgers join up to form mated pairs, the members of which occupy the same burrow and the same home range (as is the case, for example, in the Białowieża Primeval Forest, Poland). Once we have explained pair formation in badgers, further expansion of the group to include additional adults is easily explicable in terms of habitat saturation.

One factor underlying pair formation may be that in areas of low population density, badgers occupy very large home ranges. Although they can travel quite rapidly when they want to, badgers are less mobile than most mustelids, so each male may only be capable of defending a single female if female home ranges are large. This, then, could explain why male and female badgers form mated pairs that share a common territory, rather than males having larger ranges that include those of more than one female, as sometimes happens in other mustelids (including the Japanese badger; see Chapter 7).

As regards cohabitation in a single burrow, this may be related to the fact that badgers undergo a period of winter dormancy. By huddling together in a single sett, a male and female would save energy, thereby improving their chance of surviving harsh winters (Fig. 182). In addition, since the sett is the site of most mating attempts, a male could best guard his partner from the attentions of other males by cohabiting with her. These ideas are consistent with the observed

FIG 182. Three badgers sleeping together in an artificial sett. The heat energy saved by huddling together may constitute an important benefit of group living. (H. Clark)

seasonal pattern of sett use, whereby the members of a social group share the same den in winter and early spring but tend to separate during the rest of the year (see Chapter 3).

Regardless of the precise series of steps through which badgers passed in order to become socially territorial, we can also ask whether social territoriality is an evolved trait or a facultative response to prevailing ecological conditions. If social territoriality is really universal in European badgers, as I have suggested, then the first stage of group formation, in which a single male and female cohabit, is probably an evolved trait. By contrast, the next stage of sociality, involving the augmentation of groups as a consequence of non-dispersal of offspring, seems definitely to be a response to local conditions, since it only occurs in high-density populations.

CONCLUSIONS

I began this chapter by saying that, according to Kruuk, badgers are unusual in two respects. They are unusual as mustelids owing to their system of socio-spatial organisation, and unusual as social carnivores owing to their lack of cooperative behaviour. To what extent do badgers still seem anomalous in these respects?

As regards the comparison with other mustelids, I now think that Kruuk overstated the differences. His crucial mistake was to assume that territoriality in badgers is concerned solely with the defence of food. As soon as we realise that territoriality in male badgers might be concerned with the defence of potential mates, the differences between badgers and the other mustelids more or less evaporate. Admittedly, we still need to employ some additional assumptions (such as, that a male badger can only defend the range of one female, and that cohabitation between the sexes offers thermoregulatory advantages in winter) in order to explain how the basic mustelid system of solitary intra-sexual territoriality evolved into one in which a male–female pair share a single territory and den. However, these assumptions do not seem implausible. And once we have a satisfactory explanation of pair formation, it is easy to see how this can give rise to larger groups containing multiple adults of each sex, owing to the constraints on dispersal imposed by habitat saturation.

As regards the lack of cooperative behaviour, however, Kruuk's characterisation of badgers has stood the test of time. He may have somewhat underestimated the species' communicative abilities (see Chapter 6), but it is still generally agreed that badgers forage solitarily most of the time. Even more importantly, no further convincing evidence of cooperative behaviour has emerged since Kruuk's studies in the late 1970s. To use Kruuk's own phrase, badgers are, indeed, 'primitively social' – not just in the sense that they lack certain aspects of social behaviour but also in the sense that they represent an intermediate stage in the evolution of sociality. Just why badgers have not evolved more in the way of cooperative behaviour and communication is another question, but the answer, almost certainly, is that multi-female, multi-male groups are a very recent, and still geographically localised, development in the species' history. Most Eurasian badgers still live in social units containing not more than one adult of each sex, where the necessity for cooperation and communication is limited.

Finally, what of the Resource Dispersion Hypothesis? The hypothesis was first suggested at a time when food availability was thought to be *the* key to understanding every aspect of socio-spatial organisation in every species, and when simplistic ideas about optimality exerted a disproportionate influence on thinking about issues like group and territory size. To that extent, it now seems dated. However, hypotheses tend to take on a life of their own, especially when they are given fancy names. I suspect, therefore, that the merits and demerits of the RDH will continue to be debated, despite the fact that simpler and, I would argue, more convincing explanations of social territoriality are now available.

CHAPTER 9

Badgers and People

THIS CHAPTER IS ABOUT the various ways in which the presence of badgers affects peoples' lives. Unfortunately, wildlife tends only to get noticed when it becomes a nuisance, so any discussion of the relationship between badgers and humans often focuses on badger-related problems and how they can be managed. Much of this chapter, therefore, will be about the conflicts of interest that sometimes arise between badgers and people. However, it is important to emphasise that most of the time, badgers go quietly about their business without being noticed, while most people, if they think about badgers at all, regard them as an asset worth preserving rather than a problem requiring some sort of solution. Furthermore, for some people, whether they be ordinary householders who enjoy watching badgers in their gardens, amateur naturalists, wildlife photographers or members of badger protection groups, badgers are a real and significant source of interest and pleasure.

Without a doubt, the most important badger-related problem in the UK and Ireland is that of bovine tuberculosis. However, the issues relating to badgers and bovine TB are so complex and contentious that I have given them a chapter on their own (Chapter 10), rather than discussing them here.

PROBLEMS RELATED TO BADGER FORAGING BEHAVIOUR

As we saw in Chapter 4, badgers eat a wide variety of foods including invertebrates, vertebrates, cereals, fruits and vegetables. Most of the time, they quietly glean these kinds of food off the surface of the ground without noticeable impact on the environment. Sometimes, however, their foraging habits can be a nuisance or even a cause of significant economic loss.

Damage to crops

When I first started studying badgers in East Sussex in the 1980s, most of the farmers to whom I talked said that they did not much mind having badgers on their land but that the badgers 'do get in the corn'. Our subsequent research confirmed that cereals, especially wheat, did indeed constitute an important part of the badgers' diet in this area (Shepherdson *et al.*, 1990). Badgers would start foraging on standing wheat in May, as soon as the young ears emerged, and they would go on doing so until the crop was harvested in August. In the process, they would flatten areas of crop so as to make them difficult to harvest, and would make paths through the standing crop in order to get from one part of their territory to another. There was no doubt, then, that badgers were responsible for a certain amount of crop damage (see also Chapter 4). On the other hand, the members of any one social group would repeatedly return to the same part of the same field to feed, so that the damage in any one territory was restricted to a few well-defined patches about 10–20 m in diameter. Consequently, it did not look to us as if the resultant crop losses were very great (Figs. 183 and 184).

This conclusion has been borne out by formal studies. Localised field surveys have shown that badgers damage from 1 per cent to 10 per cent of the total crop

FIG **183.** Damage to wheat by badgers. This is one of three patches in which the members of a single social group habitually fed. (T. Roper)

FIG 184. Sett located in a maize field in the Netherlands, with damaged maize in the background. (Dassenwerkgroep Brabant)

area of oats on individual farms in Devon, while the corresponding figures for wheat and barley in East Sussex are 0.25 per cent and 0.05 per cent, respectively (Wilson, 1993; Roper *et al.*, 1995). A questionnaire survey on a national scale, asking farmers themselves to estimate the amount of damage they suffer, has come up with roughly comparable figures of, on average, 5.1 per cent damage to oats, 4.9 per cent to maize, 2.9 per cent to wheat and 2.5 per cent to barley (Moore *et al.*, 1999). But because areas of crop damaged by badgers are not rendered completely unharvestable, the actual amount of grain lost is less: we estimated it to be less than 0.1 per cent of the crop in the case of wheat in East Sussex (Roper *et al.*, 1995). The general conclusion, then, is that although damage to cereal crops is quite common (nationally, it is reported by about 30 per cent of farmers who grow the crops in question), it is not economically significant, either to individual farmers or to the industry as a whole.

Insofar as data are available, the same seems to be true elsewhere in Europe. For example, in Luxembourg, where farmers are paid compensation for damage to crops, on average only about 30 farmers per year complain of damage by badgers, and these claims are for relatively small sums of money (Schley, 2000). Certainly, the losses, either in the UK or elsewhere, are not sufficient to justify the expense of excluding badgers from cereal crops, for example by means of electric fencing.

However, the situation can be different where more specialised, higher-value crops are grown on a relatively small scale. I first became aware of this when I was told that 'my' badgers were causing problems in a vineyard located within my study area in East Sussex. The farmer in question complained that badgers were not only eating the grapes but were also tearing holes in plastic netting that he had put over the vines in order to exclude birds. Consequently, pheasants and other birds were able to get to the vines, resulting in the loss of even more grapes. I soon found that both claims were indeed true. Remains of grapes turned up in samples of badger faeces collected from around the vineyard, and radio-collared badgers were observed entering the vineyard and consuming grapes from September until the harvest in early November. Indeed, during this period, grapes constituted 64 per cent by volume of the diet of the relevant badgers (Roper, 1987; Roper *et al.*, 1989: Fig. 185). The problem was exacerbated by the badgers' annoying habit of ripping fresh holes in the bird netting every night, even if the holes they had made on previous nights were still open. In addition, this particular vineyard had the bad luck to be located at the intersection of three different badger territories, making it vulnerable to the attentions of three separate social groups. Consequently, up to 20 badgers could be feeding there in a single night.

Curious as to whether this was an isolated instance, I carried out a questionnaire survey of all of the 100 vineyards that existed in England at the time. The replies suggested that badger damage was quite a common problem,

FIG 185. Remains of grapes in badger faeces found close to a vineyard in East Sussex. (T. Roper)

FIG 186. Wine labels from France and Austria, indicating that the association between badgers and grapes is neither recent nor confined to England.

affecting 20 per cent of growers. Estimates of the cost ranged mostly from £100 to £1,000 per annum, though one grower claimed that badgers were costing him £5,000 per annum and were driving him to bankruptcy. Having seen badger damage with my own eyes, and having calculated the weight of grapes that a single badger might be expected to consume over the course of the fruiting season, I concluded that even the largest of these estimates was not implausible (Roper, 1987). On the continent, badger damage to vineyards seems to be much less of a problem, probably because they have been more or less exterminated from major wine-making regions (Schley, 2000). However, it is clear that the association between badgers and vineyards is an old one (Fig. 186).

A subsequent, more rigorous and more detailed questionnaire survey conducted by Moore *et al.* (1999) suggests that if anything, the situation has got worse for vineyard owners since the time of our own study. In the later survey, badgers were reported to be present at 63 per cent of vineyards; and 40 per cent of respondents reported that badger damage had occurred during the previous 12 months, by comparison with 20 per cent in our survey. The average estimated cost for affected vineyards was about £540 per annum, but a cost of over £1,000 was claimed in 9 per cent of cases (Moore *et al.*, 1999). These may seem like modest sums but they are significant in the context of UK vineyards, most of which operate on a small scale.

There are several possible reasons why badgers are more of a problem for vineyard owners than for cereal farmers. For one thing, badgers probably prefer grapes to cereals; for another, grapes ripen in the autumn, when badgers are feeding most voraciously; for a third, grapes are a more valuable crop than cereals per unit area. The most important consideration, however, is probably the issue of scale. Where the landscape is dominated by arable farming, a single group of badgers, or even several groups, will not make much impact on the crop in percentage terms. By contrast, the same number of badgers can devastate a crop that is grown in small, isolated holdings. Grapes are not alone in this respect: the same is true of crops such as strawberries, and of fruit and vegetables grown by ordinary householders for their own consumption. For example, I can personally testify to the ability of a single group of badgers to lay waste to 50 sweetcorn plants in a single night. Consequently, although damage to commercial fruit crops is less frequent than damage to cereals on a national scale, it affects a greater percentage of the crop when it does occur. This makes it more costly, not only to individual farmers but also to the agricultural industry as a whole (Moore *et al.*, 1999).

Damage to lawns and pasture

Damage to pasture occurs when badgers are foraging for invertebrates, especially soil-dwelling insects such as the larvae of crane flies (Tipulidae) and chafers (Scarabaeidae). Badgers are powerful and untidy diggers, capable of ripping up sizeable chunks of turf when in pursuit of such prey. They can also damage turf when digging for earthworms, but their principle earthworm prey, *Lumbricus terrestris*, is mainly gleaned off the surface (see Chapter 4).

Damage to pasture is fairly frequent (it was reported by about 15 per cent of farmers in the survey conducted by Moore *et al.*, 1999) but is generally not very severe (on average, it was estimated to result in 3 per cent loss of grassland). In individual cases, however, it can be significant: for example, Milner (1967) reported that 10 per cent of upland pasture on a farm in Snowdonia was dug up by badgers. Golf courses, parks, playing fields and domestic lawns can also be a target (see Fig. 187), but damage to amenity grassland rarely amounts to a serious nuisance.

Predation on livestock

As noted in Chapter 4, badgers are sometimes accused of killing lambs and chickens, and many gamekeepers regard them as a significant threat to the rearing of pheasants. However, actual killing of livestock by badgers, as opposed to the consumption of animals that are already dead, is hard to verify. In the questionnaire survey of farmers carried out by Moore *et al.* (1999), only 7 per cent of respondents reported livestock predation and most of these incidents

FIG 187. Damage to grassland: (left) relatively mild damage to a lawn in the Netherlands (Dassenwerkgroep Brabant); (below left) more serious damage to a golf course in West Sussex. (H. Clark)

involved sheep. Perhaps not surprisingly, the evidence in most cases was circumstantial. Over England and Wales as a whole, Moore *et al.* estimated the total cost of livestock predation by badgers to be between £1 and £3 million per annum, which is considerably less than the cost of damage to crops. Similarly, a recent report by the Royal Society for the Protection of Birds concluded that badgers were not economically significant predators of game birds (Gibbons *et al.*, 2007). In short, it seems that badgers do occasionally prey on livestock but not to an extent that warrants preventive action.

Preventive measures

In many circumstances, the best way of keeping badgers out of an area, for whatever reason, is by means of electric fencing. Electrified sheep netting or rabbit netting will do the job, but the Department of Environment, Food and Rural Affairs (Defra) has also undertaken research on fences specifically designed

FIG **188.** Two-strand electric fence designed to keep badgers out of a vineyard in East Sussex. (T. Roper)

to exclude badgers. The most frequently used design consists of two parallel strands of electrified wire supported at heights of 10 cm and 20 cm above the ground, and a fence of this type successfully kept badgers out of the vineyard that my research group studied in East Sussex (Roper *et al.*, 1989; see Fig. 188). A four-strand fence, with wires at 10 cm, 15 cm, 20 cm and 30 cm above ground, is even more effective. Fence voltage needs to exceed 4 kV and better results are obtained if the wires are of plain steel rather than steel and plastic 'polywire' (for details of the relevant research, see Poole *et al.*, 2002, 2004).

Electric fencing, however, is not always a feasible solution. On a commercial scale, it is fairly expensive to install and its cost-effectiveness is further reduced by the need for maintenance (for example, the area beneath the fence has to be kept clear of vegetation in order to prevent shorting). In the case of domestic gardens and allotments, safety considerations can also arise, for example with respect to children and pets, unless the fence is switched off during the day. An alternative solution might be the construction of a physical barrier, in the form of a fence or wall, which requires no further maintenance once erected. However, because any barrier to badgers has to prevent them from burrowing under it as well as climbing over it (for further details, see below), physical exclusion on anything other than a limited scale is inordinately expensive. Nevertheless, some domestic gardeners have considered the trouble and cost of installing badger-proof fencing to be worthwhile. Yet another possible alternative, in the case of damage to lawns, is treatment with insecticides so as to remove the relevant prey, but this is ecologically undesirable except on a very small scale. A relatively cheap and effective solution in the case of new lawns is to lay wire or plastic netting just beneath the surface of the soil prior to seeding, in order to deter badgers from digging.

No commercially available chemical deterrent is licensed for use on badgers, so this option is ruled out. Research has been undertaken into the efficacy of other methods such as ultrasonic devices that emit a sound supposed to deter wildlife, and water-jet devices that spray the relevant area when a motion sensor is activated. Unfortunately, there is no evidence that any of these methods works, either alone or in combination. Indeed, badgers may use the devices as a cue that food is available (e.g. Ward *et al.*, 2008a).

Research has also been carried out into the use of 'learned aversion' as a way of deterring badgers from eating crops. The idea is to put badgers off, say, maize by allowing them to feed on cobs treated with a chemical that smells or tastes nasty, or that makes the animal sick when ingested. However, although badgers readily learn to avoid cobs that have been treated in this way, this does not deter them from subsequently eating untreated maize (e.g. Baker *et al.*, 2007).

To summarise, physical or electrical barriers are currently the only way of preventing damage caused by badger foraging behaviour. Deterrents do not work, and 'lethal control' methods such as snaring or poisoning, although sadly still practised by far too many gamekeepers, are neither morally justified nor legally permitted.

PROBLEMS RELATED TO BADGER MOBILITY

Roads and other transport corridors can impact on badgers by acting as a barrier to movement: that is, they can prevent badgers from getting from one part of their territory to another. This could disrupt contact with neighbouring groups for purposes of breeding or dispersal, or make part of a territory inaccessible for purposes of feeding. On a larger scale, transport corridors can result in what is called 'habitat fragmentation': that is, they can cause subpopulations of badgers to become isolated and hence more liable to inbreeding and extinction. And, finally, roads in particular are directly responsible for the deaths of large numbers of badgers (see Chapter 1).

This means that when new transport corridors are being planned, consideration should be given to their impact on wildlife movement. In the case of badgers, territories along the proposed route should ideally be mapped by means of bait-marking, so as to see precisely how individual social groups will be affected. A decision can then be taken as to how many safe badger crossings are needed and where precisely to install them. In the case of existing transport corridors, repeatedly finding dead badgers is an obvious indication that the location in question is a habitual crossing point.

Badger crossings

In the case of new roads and railways, safe badger (and other wildlife) crossings can take the form of underpasses or bridges (see Fig. 189). The most popular solution, and usually the most cost-effective, is an underpass formed of plastic or concrete piping. Consideration needs to be given to drainage, because badgers will not use a tunnel that contains standing water. Therefore, the piping needs to be laid in sections separated by drainage gaps, and the underpass as a whole should slope downwards from each side of the road towards a drainage sump in the centre. In addition, it is essential to fence off the road or railway, because if badgers can cross it on the surface they will continue to do so, regardless of the casualty rate. It may also help to arrange the fencing or to plant appropriate vegetation in such a way as to funnel wildlife towards the underpass. Follow-up studies have shown that provided these precautions are taken, badgers will

FIG 189. Underpass beneath a road (above left) and bridge over a road (left), both in the Netherlands. The underpass is designed specifically for badgers, whereas the bridge is for a variety of wildlife including badgers. (Dassenwerkgroep Brabant)

FIG 190. Installing an underpass beneath an existing road in the Netherlands. (Dassenwerkgroep Brabant)

FIG 191. Badger tunnel (above left) and badger pathways (left) beneath bridges in the Netherlands. (Dassenwerkgroep Brabant)

FIG 192. Bridge across a canal in the Netherlands, designed specifically to enable badgers to cross. (J. Vink)

quickly learn to use underpasses; and, provided that the underpasses in question are appropriately sited, disruption to the mobility of badgers and to the layout of their territories can be minimal.

Existing roads are more of a problem, because it is inconvenient and more expensive to install underpasses beneath them. Nevertheless, this has been done in the Netherlands (Fig. 190). A cheaper alternative, which is sometimes possible, is to use existing bridges or culverts as crossing points by installing badger pathways within them (Fig. 191). Even more cheaply, warning signs can be erected at places where significant numbers of badgers are killed. However, motorists are unfortunately not noted for their sensitivity to road signs of any description, let alone those that can be ignored with impunity. Other possible solutions have been trialled, such as reflectors that direct the headlights of an approaching vehicle towards the verge of the road, in order to warn any badgers that may be about to cross. These, however, have not proved successful.

Rivers and canals require a different approach, because underpasses cannot be installed beneath them and permanent bridges are expensive to construct and maintain. However, in the Netherlands, where significant numbers of badgers drown while trying to swim across canals (see Chapter 2), simple badger-sized bridges have proved effective (Fig. 192). Alternatively, the banks of canals can be made less steep, so as to enable badgers to climb in and out more easily.

Wildlife corridors

Large areas of inhospitable habitat, such as extensive, unbroken areas of arable crops, can also impede badger mobility and lead to subpopulations becoming isolated from one another. The solution in this case is to link the relevant subpopulations by means of a wildlife corridor. This is a linear 'street', intended explicitly for the use of wildlife, fenced in on either side and planted with appropriate cover in the form of trees and shrubs. Existing hedges, provided they have a narrow strip of uncultivated land alongside them, can also act as effective wildlife corridors, which is one reason why they should be preserved. The Netherlands has been particularly sensitive to the dangers of habitat fragmentation and has been active in the use of wildlife corridors to link isolated wildlife subpopulations, including those of badgers (e.g. Lankester *et al.*, 1991).

PROBLEMS RELATED TO BADGER SETTS

As we saw in Chapter 3, badger setts can be impressive structures. Their entrances and spoil heaps can spread over hundreds of square metres and can involve the excavation of, literally, tonnes of soil. Of course, not all setts are this big, but even a single-entrance outlier sett can make a significant impact on a small garden.

FIG 193. Sett that extends beneath a road (left). Note the spoil heap on the verge to the right. Sett in a railway embankment (below left). Both photographs were taken in the Netherlands. (Dassenwerkgroep Brabant)

Setts cause problems in several ways. They can be unsightly, for example in the context of a well-kept garden; they can constitute a danger to livestock or farm machinery, which might fall through the surface of a sett into the void beneath; and they can undermine structures such as buildings, roads and other paved surfaces, railway cuttings and embankments, and river dykes (Fig. 193). And, because they are legally protected, their presence has to be taken into account by developers seeking to build new structures on land that badgers already occupy.

The legal situation

The Protection of Badgers Act 1992 makes it illegal, in the UK, to interfere with a badger sett. This includes damaging or destroying a sett, obstructing access to it, deliberately putting a dog into it or disturbing the badgers that occupy it. Protection extends not only to the sett itself but also to the region immediately surrounding it, so that, for example, it is illegal to carry out construction or forestry work within a certain distance of a sett. However, the legislation does allow for action to be taken against a problem sett, provided that a licence has been obtained from the relevant authority.

Until recently, applications for licences had to be made to Defra if the sett in question was interfering with an existing structure or activity (for example, undermining a house or preventing a field from being ploughed), or to English Nature if it was hindering some future development (for example, a new road or housing scheme). Recently, however, Natural England (the successor to English Nature) became the relevant authority for all licence applications. A licence can be granted in order to prevent serious damage to land, crops, livestock or any other form of property; to prevent the spread of disease; to allow building works or agricultural or forestry operations to occur; to preserve or investigate scheduled monuments; and for various other purposes not relevant here. In the case of development projects, the granting or otherwise of a licence to interfere with a sett is independent of the granting or otherwise of planning permission: both have to be obtained if the development is to proceed. Penalties for unlicensed interference with a sett are potentially severe, with fines of up to £5,000, plus up to six months imprisonment, for each illegal sett interference or each badger killed or injured.

Whether or not a licence is granted depends on various factors, the most important of which are the nature of the sett and the seriousness of the problem. As regards the former, a licence to destroy an unoccupied outlier sett is unlikely to be refused (though precautions will still have to be taken to ensure that it really is unoccupied: see below). Conversely, permission to destroy a well-established main sett is unlikely to be granted unless there really is no alternative. As regards the seriousness of the problem, it is clear that dangerous undermining of, say, a house or railway embankment justifies action, whereas disturbance to the appearance of a garden may not. However, while cases such as these are relatively black and white, anyone working in this area soon learns that every sett, and every situation, is unique and that licensing decisions ultimately depend on individual judgement. For this reason, Natural England usually requires an independent report by a consultant or other knowledgeable person, or a site visit by one of its own staff, before making a decision. An additional complication is that licensed interference with a sett is unlikely to be permitted during the breeding season unless the problem is especially urgent.

Incidence of sett-related problems

During the years when Defra (or its precursor, MAFF) was one of the relevant licensing authorities, it kept records of licence applications and of other requests for advice about badgers. These records provide the best guide we have to the incidence of problems relating to badger setts. Various analyses of the Defra database, covering the period 1985 to 2004, have been published (Wilson & Symes, 1998; Matthews & Wilson, 2005; Delahay *et al.*, 2009), and I shall summarise their results here.

During the period 1985 to 1995, the number of requests to Defra for advice about badgers remained fairly stable, at about 500–550 per annum. During the period 1995 to 2004, however, it increased to about 900 per annum, indicating that badger-related problems were becoming more frequent (or, perhaps, that people were becoming more sensitive to them). Defra received licence applications from virtually the whole of England and Wales, but a disproportionate number came from the south and southwest of England, which is unsurprising, since these are the regions where badger population densities are highest. Most enquiries emanated from rural districts, but the number relating to urban problems more than doubled, from about 80 to about 190 per annum, during the five-year period between 1997/9 and 2002/4 (Fig. 194). For whatever reason, therefore, complaints about urban badgers have become more frequent.

In a large majority of cases (95 per cent), licence applications concerned badger setts, with most of the remaining 5 per cent relating to damage by badgers to gardens, pasture and livestock. The most frequent sett-related problem was damage to agricultural land, or to the farm machinery or livestock using it, but problems also arose with setts affecting roads, tracks, buildings, gardens, railways and watercourses. Between 1994 and 2004, a licence was granted for 78 per cent of applications, but about a third of these were to enable work to be carried out close

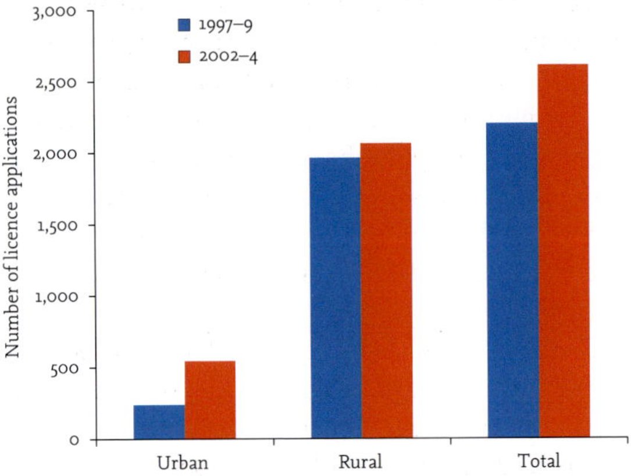

FIG 194. Number of licence applications related to badgers, received by Defra during the periods 1997–9 and 2002–4. Note that there was an increase in the total number of applications, including a disproportionate increase in the number originating from urban areas. (Based on data in Delahay *et al.*, 2009)

to a sett, rather than to directly interfere with a sett or its occupants. In the other two-thirds of cases, the licensed action almost always involved the destruction of all or part of a sett ('sett closure'), after excluding badgers from it. Licences to kill or translocate badgers were only granted in a handful of cases.

To summarise, badger-related problems, and especially problems relating to urban badgers, increased sharply in the early 2000s, such that licence applications are now being made at a rate of about 20 per week and licences granted at a rate of about 15 per week. About a third of these licences are to enable work to be carried out close to a sett, so are unlikely to involve significant disturbance to badgers. Most of the remaining two-thirds, however, involve evicting badgers from all or part of a sett and then destroying it. We can conclude, therefore, that there is licensed interference with about 500 setts per year. However, this does not cover licences issued in association with development work, which were not included in the Defra database and for which no data are available. Nor, of course, does it include illegal interference with setts, which undoubtedly occurs.

Mitigating action

If a sett is in the wrong place, what can be done about it? The answer depends mainly on the type of sett (main, annex, subsidiary or outlier) and on whether the disturbance is to an existing structure or to one that is still at the planning stage.

If the sett is an outlier or small subsidiary and shows no signs of recent occupation, then its destruction may be allowed without much further ado, whatever the nature of the problem. However, destruction of the sett should still be carried out carefully, either by hand or using a small mechanical digger, so as to avoid injury to any badgers that might be inside.

Main setts and annex setts, by contrast, are much more complex to deal with, because their loss will have more serious consequences for the social group to which they belong. If such a sett is in the way of a new development, then the developer will be required to leave it in situ if at all possible. For example, if the development in question is a new housing estate, the area containing the sett may have to be preserved intact and corridors provided to enable the occupants to access the rest of their territory. But badgers need food as well as a sett, so provision also needs to be made for their feeding requirements by leaving essential foraging habitat undisturbed.

In some cases, however, such as a major road development, the proposed structure cannot be relocated to take account of even a large main sett. And this is clearly also not possible where an existing structure, such as a railway embankment or house, is being undermined, or a garden destroyed. In such cases, the sett has to go, and there are now fairly standard procedures for achieving this.

Sett closure

The first step in sett closure is to exclude any occupants from the sett in question. This is usually achieved by installing one-way gates: that is, wooden or metal badger-sized doors, hinged horizontally at the top so as to allow animals through in one direction but not in the other (Fig. 195). In principle, if a gate of

FIG 195. One-way badger gate installed in a sett entrance. Note the wire mesh intended to stop badgers from digging around the gate. (M. Edwards)

FIG 196. Badgers inspecting a sett from which they have been excluded. The whole sett has been covered in wire mesh to prevent the badgers from digging their way back in. (Food and Environment Research Agency)

this type is fitted over every entrance, then badgers will not be able to re-enter the sett once they have left and, after a while, the sett will become vacant. In practice, however, badgers will do their utmost to reoccupy a sett that is important to them and will dig around the gates if they can. Consequently, the area around each gate, and in some cases the entire surface of the sett, has to be covered with some kind of badger-proof material, such as chain-link fencing pegged securely down (Fig. 196). In the case of a large sett with many entrances, it may be easier to surround the entire sett with a badger-proof fence, fitted with one-way gates at appropriate intervals.

Once the sett has been vacated, then it can be destroyed. But how does one know whether all the badgers have left? The best precaution is to leave the gates in place for as long as possible before excavation commences, but cases have been known in which live badgers have been recovered from setts some weeks after the entrances were gated. Consequently, excavation of a previously occupied sett should always be carried out carefully and cautiously, just in case there are still badgers inside. In addition, it needs to be done quickly, because the previous occupants may well re-enter a half-excavated sett.

Badger-proof fencing

Sometimes, after closing a sett, it is necessary to fence the area off to prevent any further incursion by badgers. For example, this will be desirable in the case of domestic gardens. This is not a trivial matter, since the fence in question must prevent badgers from digging under it as well as climbing over it (Fig. 197). A common recommendation is to use chain-link fencing at least 125 cm high and dug into the ground to a depth of 60 cm. For additional security, the fence can be lapped outwards at the top or surmounted with barbed wire. For domestic gardens, wooden closeboard fencing is a less aesthetically intrusive alternative, at least for the part of the fence that is above ground. However, something rot-proof and impenetrable to badgers still needs to be installed below ground.

In some parts of northern Italy, there are few places for badgers to dig setts other than in railway embankments, which can obviously be problematic. After

FIG 197. Badger-proof fence being erected beside a road in the Netherlands. The fencing material is dug in and lapped inwards at the base to prevent badgers from digging under it. (Dassenwerkgroep Brabant)

the closure of setts that threaten to undermine the railway, it has sometimes been necessary to cover an embankment with chain-link fencing in order to prevent badgers from digging another sett (Balestrieri *et al.*, 2006). Householders have even been known to hard-surface their entire gardens in order to deter badgers.

Providing alternative accommodation for badgers

The question obviously arises as to what will become of a group of badgers if a main sett is removed. The most desirable outcome is that the group moves into another sett in its existing territory – for example, the territory may already contain a subsidiary sett that could be converted into a new main sett. To evaluate the likelihood of this, the relevant territory should ideally be mapped by bait-marking prior to sett closure, in order to determine whether another suitable sett is available.

A second possibility is to provide an artificial sett. It would not be appropriate here to provide detailed instructions for constructing artificial setts, but the basic idea is to build one or more nest chambers in the form of wooden or concrete boxes, link them together and provide external access by means of sewer-pipe

FIG 198. Stages in the construction of an artificial badger sett. Constructing nest chambers from breeze blocks (above left); laying entrance tunnels (above); heaping earth (left) over the completed sett. (L. & P. Schofield)

FIG 199. An artificial sett constructed on level ground in the Netherlands. (Dassenwerkgroep Brabant)

'tunnels', and then cover the whole arrangement with soil (Fig. 198). Ideally, the artificial sett should be cited on a slope, which is dug out prior to building the sett and then backfilled. However, it is possible to build an artificial sett on level ground and then cover it with a mound of soil (Fig. 199). The main drawbacks to the use of artificial setts are the obvious cost and labour involved and the fact that there is no guarantee that the sett will be occupied. Sometimes, badgers move happily into an artificial sett and convert it into a permanent home; sometimes, they turn up their noses at it for no apparent reason and go elsewhere.

A third option is translocation: that is, capturing the badgers, taking them to a new location and releasing them. Although statistics are lacking, it seems that this was quite a popular way of dealing with problem badgers in the UK in the 1980s and 1990s and that it was, in at least some cases, successful (Brown & Cheeseman, 1996). More recently, however, it has become difficult to find suitable locations that are not already occupied by badgers, and, if such a location is identified, it usually turns out that there is a good reason why badgers have abandoned it, such as an overzealous gamekeeper or a nearby main road. Consequently, translocations have sometimes resulted in the deaths of the animals concerned. In addition, translocations risk spreading disease and disrupting genetic clines within the existing badger population. For all of these reasons, they are now seldom authorised by Natural England, though they are still sometimes attempted by local badger groups.

Finally, if all else fails, then a licence may be issued to enable the occupants of a problem sett to be trapped and killed. In some cases, this may be the most humane solution, but it can be difficult to convince members of the public of this. In a notorious case in Saltdean, East Sussex, a few years ago, a licence was issued for the capture and euthanasia of badgers occupying a sett that was thought to be undermining the foundations of a house. However, public outrage led to demonstrations, police presence, damage to community relations and questions in the House of Commons. The 'lethal control' plan was therefore abandoned and it was decided to build an artificial sett, which the badgers in question refused to use. It is not known what eventually became of them.

Overview

Dealing with a problem sett, especially if it is occupied, can be a time-consuming and expensive business, not least because there is no foolproof way of evicting the occupants or of ensuring their future welfare. If my own experience is anything to go by, the licensing system does its best to strike a fair balance between the interests of badgers and those of licence applicants, though the latter often complain that the law is tilted too far towards protecting badgers. Certainly, the process of obtaining a licence can sometimes seem cumbersome and protracted, though this is often owing to indecision on the part of the licence applicant(s) rather than to the complexity of the procedure per se.

Perhaps the most important deficiency in the licensing system as it currently operates is that insufficient attention is given to the issue of what will become of the occupants of a sett that has been closed. This has potentially serious welfare implications, because if the badgers in question have no alternative sett to move into, they are likely to be attacked by the occupants of neighbouring territories in which they try to settle, or killed by traffic while wandering around in search of suitable unoccupied habitat. Thus, sett closure may, in effect, constitute a death sentence for the evicted badgers. Alternatively, they may simply dig a new sett in an equally inconvenient location, such as a bit further along the same railway embankment or in a neighbouring garden, in which case the same problem will recur a year or two later. Proper consideration of the fate of the occupants should therefore be an essential part of all licensed operations that involve interference with a main or annex sett.

URBAN BADGERS

Urban badgers cause the same sorts of problems as rural ones (that is, problems resulting mainly from their foraging and burrowing behaviour), and these problems can in principle be resolved in the same sorts of ways (for example, by fencing off a foraging area or closing a problem sett). In practice, however, urban problems can be both more acute and more difficult to resolve; and, as we have seen, there has been a rapid increase in the number being reported during the last 15 years. For this reason, and also because urban landscapes bring badgers into especially close contact with people, urban badgers deserve special consideration.

Prevalence of urban badgers

Urban badgers seem first to have been noticed in the UK in the late 1960s and early 1970s, when they were reported in London, Durham and Southend-on-Sea (for references, see Table 11). However, a survey of all district councils in England and Wales undertaken by Stephen Harris in the early 1980s suggested that few towns and cities had permanent badger populations and that in most of these, the number of setts was small (Harris, 1984). Furthermore, affected towns were almost entirely restricted to the south of England.

Since that survey, it is clear that urban badgers have become more common. Large and well-established populations have now been studied in Brighton, Hastings, Swindon and Yeovil (Davison *et al.*, 2008a, b), and I am personally aware of permanent populations in Birmingham, Edinburgh, Exeter, Northampton, Nottingham and several south-coast towns, including Newhaven, Seaford and Bexhill-on-Sea. Furthermore, Defra has received complaints about urban badgers from every region in England, strongly suggesting they are now geographically widespread (Delahay *et al.*, 2009). Urban badgers seem especially common, and problems more frequent, in the south of England, probably owing to a combination of high overall badger numbers and a high degree of urbanisation of the human population.

Outside the UK, badgers have been reported living in various towns and cities (see Table 11), but many more examples have probably gone unreported. For example, when I visited Stuttgart recently, it did not take me long to notice a badger sett within easy walking distance of the central station, although badgers were far from my mind at the time. Most of the examples so far reported, both in the UK and elsewhere, involve badgers living in suburban or urban fringe areas, as opposed to town centres, and this probably reflects the general situation. For example, badgers were present in central Copenhagen in the 1930s but became

TABLE 11. Published reports of 'urban' badgers.

Country	Town/City	Habitat*	Reference
England	Greater London	S/R	Teagle (1969), Harris (1984)
	Durham	S	Stirling & Harper (1969)
	Southend-on-Sea	S	Cowlin (1972)
	Birmingham	?	Neal (1977)
	Bristol	S	Harris (1984)
	Bath	S	Harris (1984)
	Brighton	S/U	Davison *et al.* (2008)
	Hastings	S/U	Davison *et al.* (2008)
	Swindon	?	Davison *et al.* (2008)
	Yeovil	?	Davison *et al.* (2008)
Wales	Baglan	R	Tavecchia (1995)
Czech Republic	Brno	S	Pelikan *et al.* (1983)
Denmark	Copenhagen	S	Aaris-Sørensen (1987)
Norway	Trondheim	S	Bevanger *et al.* (1996)
Japan	Hinodecho, Tokyo	S/R	Kaneko *et al.* (1996)
	Hinode, Tokyo	S/R	Kaneko *et al.* (2006)
	Yamaguchi City	S/R	Tanaka *et al.* (2002)
Ukraine	Kiev	?	Zagorodniuk (2003)
Lithuania	Vilnius	S	Baranauskas *et al.* (2005)
Ireland	Ballincollig	S	Sleeman *et al.* (2006)
	Fota Estate	S	Sleeman *et al.* (2006)
	Abbotstown	S	Sleeman *et al.* (2006)
	Waterford	S	Sleeman *et al.* (2006)

* U = urban (i.e. resident in urban area); S = suburban (i.e. resident in suburban area); R = rural (i.e. visiting a built-up area but resident outside it).

gradually restricted to the suburbs during the period 1945 to 1975, presumably owing to increasing urbanisation of the city centre. However, I know of some setts, for example in Hastings, in heavily built-up areas with a high traffic density. As I pointed out in Chapter 1, badgers are remarkably adaptable animals, and their ability to colonise a wide spectrum of urban habitats provides a dramatic demonstration of this.

Although there is good evidence that badgers have become increasingly prevalent in urban environments, at least in the UK, the reason for this is less clear. In some cases, urban expansion has led to the incorporation, into built-up areas, of setts that were previously rural. In other cases, populations that have been present in urban areas for many decades may have increased in size, for the same sorts of reasons as have rural badger populations (see Chapter 1). In yet other cases, badgers may have immigrated into the suburbs from surrounding rural areas, looking for unoccupied places in which they can establish territories. As yet, we have no idea of the relative importance of these three processes, either in general or in the case of any particular population.

Problems related to urban badgers

Defra statistics show that the most frequent causes of complaint about urban badgers are damage to gardens (34 per cent), damage to buildings (27 per cent) and damage to recreational land (9 per cent) (Delahay *et al.*, 2009). Undoubtedly, the most serious problems, and the most difficult to resolve, relate to the presence of setts in inconvenient places. Sometimes this involves the

FIG 200. Urban badger setts in inconvenient places: (above left) beneath a summer house (Food and Environment Research Agency); (left) in a small front garden. (J. Davison)

undermining of buildings or other structures such as patios, but more usually it concerns damage to gardens (Fig. 200).

It is tempting to dismiss damage to gardens as a relatively trivial matter, but it can be a real source of heartache, anxiety and expense to some householders. An active badger sett in a small garden is not just unsightly, it can make the garden unusable. Even worse, some insurance companies now refuse to insure a house that has a sett in its garden, thus exposing the owner to serious financial risk and rendering the property unsaleable.

In principle, badgers can be removed from such setts and the setts themselves destroyed, using the procedures already described. In practice, however, this often proves difficult owing to disagreements between affected householders. I was recently involved in dealing with a main sett that had entrances in four adjacent gardens – three relatively small gardens side by side with one another and a fourth, larger garden that backed on to them. The owners of the three small gardens wanted the sett removed, but the owner of the large garden was opposed to this, pointing out, quite rightly, that the badger sett had existed before the houses in question were built. In the end, we were able to devise a way of destroying only those parts of the sett that were in the three small gardens and then proofing these gardens against subsequent badger incursion from the larger garden. However, reaching this compromise involved protracted negotiations.

Then, there is the issue of expense. What with consultants' fees, the cost of evicting badgers from a sett and excavating it, and the cost of badger-proof fencing, removing a sett and badger-proofing a garden can cost thousands, and perhaps even tens of thousands, of pounds. Not surprisingly, arguments erupt as to who should pay what percentage of the bill when the sett in question affects more than one property. Or, one householder may simply refuse to pay anything, in which case the whole operation can founder.

Finally, problems relating to urban setts can prove more complicated to resolve because of the difficulty of providing an alternative home for the badgers involved. Urban badger territories contain fewer secondary setts than rural ones, presumably owing to the general rarity of suitable sett sites in urban environments (Davison *et al.*, 2008a, b). Consequently, badgers evicted from a main sett may not already possess another substantial sett into which they can move. Usually, there is nowhere to put an artificial sett, so this option is also unavailable; and public outcry is likely to make lethal control impossible (see above). In practice, badgers are often excluded from urban setts with no thought about what will happen to them. However, this approach is short-sighted, because it may well lead to the badgers in question re-establishing themselves in a nearby garden, causing the whole problem to recur a few years later. This is probably why, according to the Defra database, the success rate for urban main sett closures is lower than for comparable rural operations (Delahay *et al.*, 2009).

Avoiding problems in the first place

If my experience is anything to go by, problems often arise in urban environments when householders start feeding badgers. This behaviour is surprisingly common and will probably increase as badgers become more urbanised. When one of my research students, John Davison, surveyed a part of Brighton containing a flourishing badger population, he found that 29 per cent of householders deliberately provided food for nocturnal mammals (badgers, foxes or hedgehogs), and of these, over half provided food every night (Davison, 2007).

FIG 201. Badgers as household pets: (above left) expecting food (R. Lowery); (left) being hand-fed. (B. Andrews)

In addition, householders may provide food for badgers inadvertently, in the form of bird food, pet food or the contents of their dustbins. In some cases, the amounts of food deliberately put out for badgers are substantial, and sometimes householders help badgers in other ways, for example by providing them with nest material in the winter. Davison found that urban badgers were significantly heavier than their rural counterparts, confirming that they are well fed.

It is easy to see why people feed badgers. They are handsome animals and being able to watch them regularly every evening, from the comfort of one's own sitting room, is an attractive proposition. They are also still sufficiently rarely seen to constitute a bit of a talking point, and they easily become tame enough to be hand-fed. To some people, they clearly provide a considerable amount of pleasure and become almost household pets (Fig. 201). However, the downside of this is that the animals may increase in number because they breed at a faster rate; and they may make themselves more welcome than was originally intended, by constructing a new sett in the garden in question or, perhaps, converting an outlier into a main sett. Or, they may cause a nuisance in a neighbouring garden, putting severe stress on community relations.

Perhaps, then, the best way of preventing badgers from becoming problematic in towns and cities would be to discourage people from feeding them, or at least increase awareness of the potential problems that this can cause. This would require a sustained propaganda effort, but it is practicably feasible and might well prove to be cost-effective. It would also be nice to see television wildlife documentaries adopting a more balanced stance, rather than giving the impression that having badgers in your garden is always something to be envied.

THE ECOLOGICAL IMPACT OF BADGERS

From what we know of the feeding and other habits of badgers, we would expect their ecological impact to be rather slight. Badgers do not prey on, or constitute prey for, any species that is of particular ecological importance, nor do they impact on the environment in other obvious ways, at least at anything other than a local level. For example, a badger sett may alter the topography and flora of a hillside or wood quite dramatically, but it does so only at the actual site of the sett (Neal & Roper, 1991). In addition, because badgers are territorial, even these local effects are dispersed across the landscape.

A more rigorous study in the UK has recently confirmed this impression of relative ecological neutrality. The study in question used the Randomised Badger Culling Trial, in which badgers were removed from ten areas of 100 km^2 (see

Chapter 10), to compare the abundance of various species of mammals and ground-nesting birds between control and culled areas (Trewby *et al.*, 2008; Defra, unpublished results). The only significant effects of badger removal turned out to be an increase in the abundance of hedgehogs and red foxes, and a decline in the abundance of brown hares *Lepus europaeus*. There was also some suggestion of an increase in the abundance of meadow pipits *Anthus pratensis* and skylarks *Alauda arvensis*, but this was difficult to interpret owing to a difference in habitat composition between the culled and control areas. Badger removal had no effect on rabbit numbers.

That badger culling resulted in an increase in hedgehog numbers was unsurprising, since there is plenty of other evidence that badgers prey on hedgehogs to an extent that limits their abundance and geographical distribution (see Chapter 4). By contrast, the effect on fox numbers was unexpected and is less easy to explain. Foxes may have benefited by taking over vacated badger setts, enabling a higher proportion of vixens to breed; or foxes and badgers may compete to some extent for food (Fig. 202). The decline in hare numbers was probably a secondary consequence of the increase in fox numbers.

FIG 202. Badger and fox. The two species usually tolerate one another, but a study in the UK has shown that removal of badgers from an area is followed by an increase in the fox population. (H. Clark)

To summarise, such evidence as is available suggests that the environmental impact of badgers, except insofar as it relates to hedgehogs, is relatively slight. Sometimes, as we have seen, badgers can inflict localised damage on the environment through their foraging or burrowing activities. On the other hand, they also do good by consuming some species of insect pests and acting as seed dispersers (see Chapters 3 and 4), though sadly these beneficial effects rarely get a mention. The fact that few people are aware of the presence of badgers, even in areas of relatively high population density, is itself a testament to their discreet and essentially benign habits.

REINTRODUCTION OF BADGERS

Reintroduction means attempting to establish a population in an area that is currently devoid of the species in question, by releasing animals brought in from elsewhere. Perhaps not surprisingly, this has rarely been contemplated in the case of badgers, because the species is already widespread. However, special circumstances have led to attempted reintroductions in the Netherlands in the early 1990s and in Italy during the period 2001 to 2004 (Mulder, 1996; Balestrieri *et al.*, 2006). In both cases, the animals to be reintroduced were held in an enclosure in the relevant locality for some weeks prior to being released (a so-called 'soft' release protocol) and were fitted with radio-collars so that their post-release behaviour could be monitored. However, the Dutch and Italian studies differed from one another in various other important respects, so I shall consider them separately here.

Reintroductions in the Netherlands

Owing to what appeared to be a catastrophic decline in the Dutch badger population prior to about 1980, the Dutch Ministry of Agriculture and Fisheries drew up a 'Badger Management Policy' that was approved by Parliament in 1985 (see also Chapter 1). This set out a '15-year plan' for the protection and encouragement of badgers, one element of which was to reintroduce badgers into parts of their previous range from which they had disappeared. The first reintroductions took place at two locations in the northeastern part of the Netherlands, in Overijssel and Friesland, respectively. Although badgers had been absent from these locations since at least the 1950s, they survived in surrounding regions. It was therefore hoped that if new breeding groups could be established at the reintroduction sites, their members would eventually make contact with badgers in the surrounding regions and form a single continuous population.

Since badgers seemed to be endangered throughout the entire Netherlands at the time, it was obviously undesirable to capture adults in the wild merely in order to reintroduce them elsewhere. The reintroduced animals were therefore either animals that had been captured as orphaned cubs and raised to maturity in captivity, or adults that had been injured by traffic and rehabilitated. This meant not only that the subjects of the Dutch reintroductions did not have recent experience of living in the wild but also that the reintroductions themselves had to take place in a piecemeal fashion, as and when suitable animals became available.

At Overijssel, 12 badgers were released in six different operations between 1991 and 1993. The size and composition of the groups of animals released at any one time were very varied: one group consisted of two males and two females, one of one male and one female, one of two males, and one of two females. In addition, one male and one female were released on their own. The results of this series of reintroductions were not encouraging: three years after the start of the project, only one of the reintroduced animals was still alive in the study area, though she had found a wild partner with whom she bred successfully. Of the remaining animals, three were killed by road traffic, one drowned in a canal and the rest left the area shortly after being released.

In Friesland, eight badgers were released within a relatively short period of time from three different release pens located a kilometre or so away from one another. This time, the result was more positive: three males and two females settled in the reintroduction area, forming two social groups with well-defined, neighbouring ranges. Of the remainder, one female settled outside the reintroduction area, one drowned and the fate of one animal is unrecorded.

Reintroduction in Italy

Badgers are relatively common over Italy as a whole but have become extinct, as a consequence of pest-control operations or hunting, in some localised natural areas. One such area, the Regional Park of Montevecchia and Curone Valley, about 30 km north of Milan in northern Italy, was chosen for badger reintroduction in order to restore natural biodiversity and promote conservation awareness among the general public. Badgers were known to have lived in the park until the 1980s, when they were hunted out in order to protect game species such as pheasants and hares.

Over a three-year period from 2001 to 2004, 12 badgers were released from a single site in 4 separate groups: 2 consisting of a male/female pair and 2 consisting of 1 male and 3 females. The animals in question were captured elsewhere in northern Italy, from setts that had been closed because they were undermining railway embankments. Of the released animals, two moved out of the study area, one died of unknown causes shortly after release and three could not be monitored owing to defective radio transmitters. However, the remainder seem to have established themselves into three separate groups, at least one of which bred successfully. At the end of the study, these groups together ranged over an area of about 10 km^2, corresponding to about 40 per cent of the area of the park.

Conclusions

Clearly, the Dutch reintroduction attempts were not an unqualified success: they failed, in the case of Overijssel, to establish a viable population in the reintroduction area and it is fair to assume that they caused significant suffering to at least some of the released animals. They also resulted in a number of badger deaths. Consequently, Mulder (1996) concluded that reintroduction was not a useful conservation measure in the Netherlands, suggesting instead that if impediments to badger mobility were removed (for example, by enabling badgers to cross roads and canals safely), members of surrounding populations would eventually discover vacant areas for themselves and recolonise them. In the event, subsequent conservation efforts in the Netherlands have indeed concentrated on reducing the impact of roads, railways and canals – a strategy that has been remarkably successful (e.g. Vink *et al.*, 2008).

By contrast, the Italian project seems to have succeeded in re-establishing badgers in a protected area; and, insofar as evidence is available, it seems that translocation attempts in England have also sometimes succeeded (see above). Taken together, the evidence suggests that reintroductions or translocations are more likely to succeed if they involve pre-established, wild-caught, mixed-sex groups of badgers rather than captive-reared individuals or single-sex groups. However, perhaps the areas chosen for reintroduction or translocation in Italy and England simply offered better habitat, from a badger's point of view, than either of the Dutch sites. Whatever the case, it is clear that any future attempts to reintroduce badgers need to be carefully thought through, given the potential costs not only in economic terms but also in relation to animal welfare. Provision should also be made for long-term post-release monitoring, without which we will be unable to learn what works and what does not.

FURTHER INFORMATION

My main aim in this chapter has been to broadly survey the ways in which badgers and humans interact, rather than to provide detailed practical instructions for dealing with specific badger-related problems. For those wanting advice of the latter kind, the Natural England website (www.naturalengland.org.uk) is a good place to start.

CHAPTER 10

Badgers and Bovine Tuberculosis

THIS CHAPTER FOLLOWS ON from the previous one, insofar as the control of bovine tuberculosis (TB) in cattle clearly involves a conflict of interest between humans and badgers. Indeed, TB is by far the most important badger-related problem at present in the UK and the Republic of Ireland, and shows every sign of remaining so for the foreseeable future. We have already looked at the epidemiology of TB in badgers in Chapter 2. Here, we turn to the question of how TB in badgers relates to TB in cattle and how the existence of TB in cattle impacts on badgers.

Within the UK, TB constitutes a serious livestock disease problem in parts of England and Wales, and in Northern Ireland. It is also problematic in the Republic of Ireland, Australia, New Zealand, parts of the USA and many developing countries (Cosivi *et al.*, 1998; Phillips *et al.*, 2003). By contrast, TB is now rare in cattle populations in continental Europe, although some countries have had high levels of the disease in the past. Here, I shall concentrate on the situation in Britain and Ireland, because these are the only countries in which badgers are strongly implicated in the transmission of TB to cattle.

BOVINE TUBERCULOSIS: A BRIEF HISTORY

The evolutionary origin of bovine tuberculosis

People often wonder where bovine tuberculosis came from in the first place and how it came to infect badgers. Bovine tuberculosis is caused by a bacterium, *Mycobacterium bovis* (Fig. 203). Although no one knows for sure how ancient the

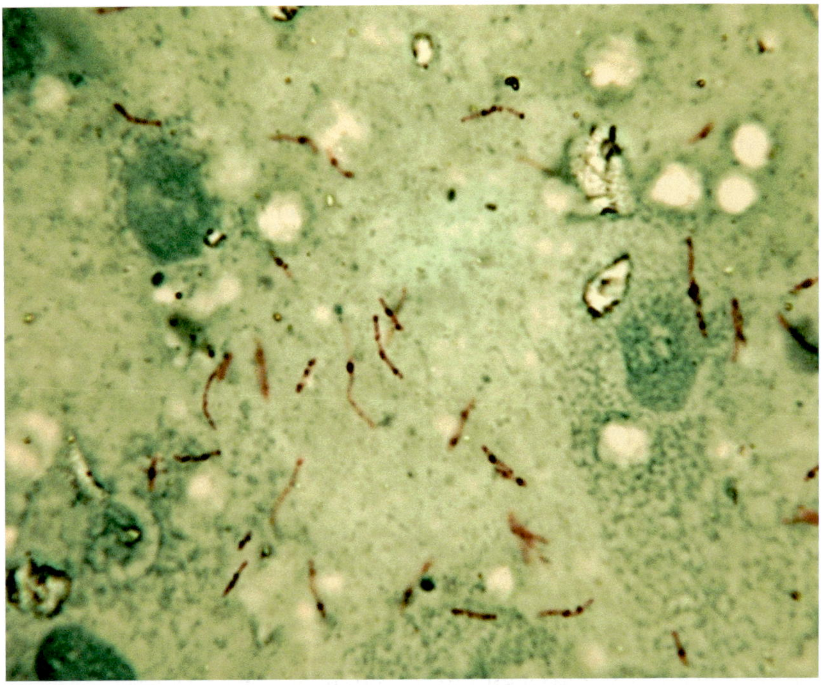

FIG 203. Ziehl Neelsen-stained smear of lung tissue showing large numbers of *M. bovis* bacilli (red). (© Crown copyright 2010, published with the permission of the Controller of Her Majesty's Stationery Office)

disease is, recent molecular genetic studies have revealed close similarities between *M. bovis* and the bacterium responsible for human tuberculosis, *M. tuberculosis* (Smith *et al.*, 2006). The most likely explanation is that the two organisms share a common ancestor.

What probably happened is that at some point in human history, presumably following the domestication of cattle, the ancestral precursor of *M. tuberculosis* mutated, giving rise to a form that was especially successful as a parasite of bovines. In other words, a genetic variant of *M. tuberculosis*, present in humans, 'jumped species', establishing itself in the cattle population and evolving into what we now know as *M. bovis*. Subsequently, cattle have passed this bovine form of the disease back to humans and on to other mammalian wildlife, including badgers. *M. bovis* remains, to this day, capable of infecting not only cattle but also humans and a variety of other mammals, including badgers.

Bovine tuberculosis in Britain

The history of TB in Britain has been described elsewhere, so I will confine myself here to a brief summary (for further details, see Neal & Cheeseman, 1996; Krebs *et al.*, 1997; Bourne, 2007).

In the 1930s, at least 40 per cent of UK dairy cattle were infected with TB, resulting in poor milk yields and premature death of the animals in question. In addition, the consumption of unpasteurised milk from infected cattle was estimated to cause about 2,000 human deaths annually. The human health problem was successfully addressed by the introduction of milk pasteurisation in the 1930s, which essentially eliminated bovine TB from humans. The cattle health problem, unfortunately, has proved far less tractable.

The first move towards eliminating TB from cattle, begun in 1935, was to encourage farmers to have their herds tested and to offer incentives for keeping stock TB-free. This scheme was strengthened in 1950 by the introduction of compulsory periodic testing of all herds plus compulsory slaughter of infected animals (the 'test-and-slaughter' policy). In addition, herds containing infected animals are subject to movement restrictions until repeated testing has shown them to be TB-free. Currently, cattle are compulsorily tested every one, two, three or four years, depending on how frequently TB occurs in the parish in question, and cattle in high-risk areas must also be tested prior to being moved.

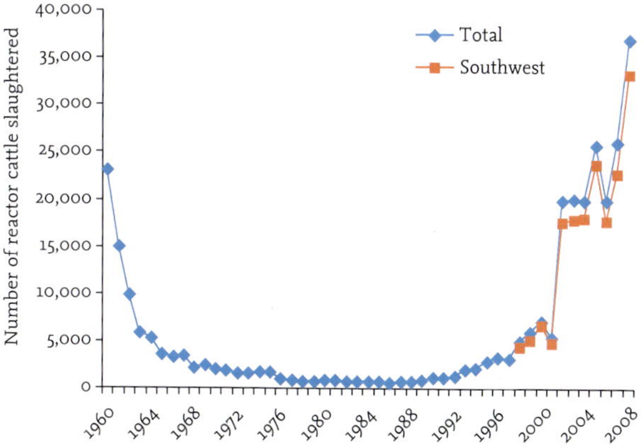

FIG 204. Number of reactor cattle (cattle testing positive for TB) slaughtered per year in the whole of England and Wales during the period 1960 to 2008, and number slaughtered in the southwest region during the period 1998 to 2008. Note that the southwest region accounts for a large proportion of the total number of cattle slaughtered. (Source of data: Defra)

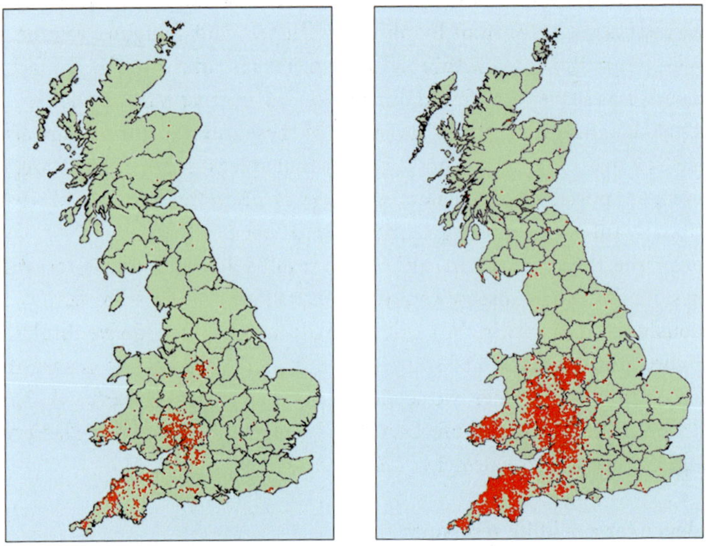

FIG 205. Locations of new TB incidents in Britain in 1999 (above left) and 2008 (above right). Although the disease remained largely confined to the southwest of England and parts of Wales during this period, the size of the 'hot-spot' areas increased considerably. (VLA, Weybridge)

Immediately following its introduction, the test-and-slaughter programme proved outstandingly successful: it produced a rapid decline in the percentage of herds testing positive each year, such that the annual incidence of TB had declined to less than one herd in a thousand in most of England and Wales by about 1980 (Fig. 204). At that point, it looked as though TB would soon be eliminated from British cattle. However, TB incidence remained stubbornly high in certain areas ('hot spots'), mainly in the southwest of England. And then, to make matters worse, it began to rise again in the early 1980s, especially in the southwest but also in the rest of England and Wales. In addition, the hot-spot areas started to increase in size, indicating that the disease was spreading geographically (Fig. 205). These trends have continued to the present day.

WHY ARE BADGERS IMPLICATED?

In theory, the test-and-slaughter programme should remove infected cattle from the system at an early stage, ideally before they have become infectious. However, because the sensitivity of the routine test for TB (the tuberculin test or 'skin test') is only about 80 per cent (i.e. the test fails to detect infection in about 20 per cent of cases), and because of various loopholes in the test-and-slaughter regime, some infected cattle remain within the system. This is confirmed by the fact that evidence of TB is sometimes found during the routine inspection of cattle carcasses at slaughterhouses. Just how many of these infected animals are also infectious is a matter of debate, but it is clear that at least some of them are, since it is sometimes possible to trace new outbreaks of TB to the purchase of what were evidently infected cattle (e.g. Gilbert *et al.*, 2005).

In principle, therefore, TB in cattle could result solely from cattle-to-cattle transmission: that is, the disease could persist, and even increase, by being continuously recycled within the cattle population. Why, then, do we think that badgers constitute an additional source of TB in cattle? In order to answer this question, we need to consider two separate issues. First, why do we think that there is a wildlife reservoir of infection at all? And, second, why do we believe that badgers constitute the principal reservoir species?

Evidence for a wildlife reservoir

The most compelling reason for suspecting a reservoir of infection is the fact that TB in cattle is, for the most part, geographically localised: that is, there are identifiable 'hot spots' of infection, mostly in the southwest of England and Wales, where the incidence of the disease has remained stubbornly high since the 1950s (Fig. 205). Now, if cattle were moved around only within localised geographical regions (for example, if all cattle bred in Devon remained in Devon for the rest of their lives), then it would be possible to explain these geographical hot spots in terms of cattle-to-cattle infection. However, cattle are transported throughout the length and breadth of the country. Consequently, if cattle-to-cattle transmission were the sole cause of infection, we would expect TB to have become geographically more widespread. Occasionally, of course, infected cattle from TB hot spots do take the disease with them when they are transported elsewhere (Gilbert *et al.*, 2005), but the degree to which TB has remained geographically localised suggests that this cannot have happened very often. Indeed, a recent mathematical model suggests that less than 25 per cent of all new incidents of TB in cattle are attributable to cattle movements (Green *et al.*, 2008).

Recent research on the genetic structure of the *M. bovis* population reinforces this line of argument by showing that the phenomenon of disease localisation extends to a finer geographical scale. It turns out that there are a number of different genetic strains of *M. bovis* (known as 'spoligotypes'), most of which are associated with specific, relatively localised geographical areas (Smith *et al.*, 2006: see Fig. 206). For example, TB in Devon is associated mainly with

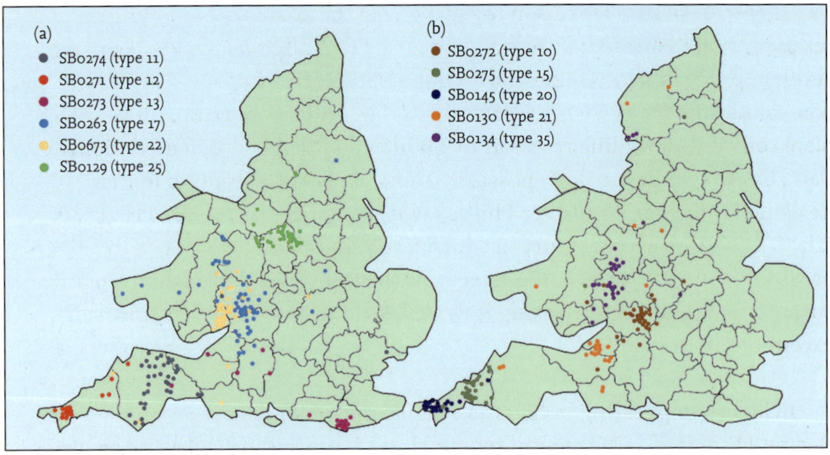

FIG 206. Spatial distribution of eleven major spoligotypes (genetic strains) of *Mycobacterium bovis* in cattle in Great Britain, illustrating how most individual spoligotypes are confined to a particular geographical area. A twelfth spoligotype (type 9, not shown) is more widely distributed. (From Smith *et al.*, 2006. Reproduced by permission of the publisher)

strain type 11, in East Sussex with strain type 13, in Gloucestershire and Worcestershire with strain type 17, and so on. Population genetic models show that it would take only a very low level of transfer of infection (i.e. movement of only a small number of infectious cattle each year) from region to region, over a period of years, to mix these strains up. Yet, most strains have remained confined, to a striking degree, to particular, relatively small and well-defined geographical areas.

The argument, then, is that if cattle-to-cattle transmission were the only cause of TB, neither the disease itself, nor the individual spoligotypes that make up the *M. bovis* population in the UK, would have remained geographically localised, given what we know about the scale and frequency of cattle movements. Rather, it seems that each of the hot-spot regions must contain a separate source of infection, external to the cattle population, which continually feeds the disease back into cattle herds faster than the test-and-slaughter programme eliminates it. In principle, that source of infection could be non-biological – for example, it could consist of infected cattle sheds or soil — but this cannot easily explain why test-and-slaughter has been sufficient to eradicate bovine TB in other parts of the UK and in continental Europe. A more likely explanation, therefore, is a wildlife reservoir involving a species that is especially prevalent in the UK.

There is also another reason for suspecting the existence of a wildlife reservoir, and that comes from experience of TB in other countries. There are several well-documented cases, outside the UK and Ireland, of wildlife reservoirs contributing to the persistence of bovine TB in cattle. For example, bison *Bison bison* constitute a wildlife reservoir of TB infection in Wood Buffalo National Park, Canada, while brushtail possums *Trichosaurus vulpecula* do so in New Zealand (for further details, see Phillips *et al.*, 2003; Corner, 2006). Indeed, it is fair to say that in every country in which test-and-slaughter has failed to eradicate TB in cattle, a wildlife reservoir has been either demonstrated or suspected. It would be surprising if the UK and the Republic of Ireland were exceptions to this rule.

Evidence implicating badgers as a significant wildlife host

Bovine TB can infect a variety of mammal species including rodents, carnivores and ungulates (Delahay *et al.*, 2002, 2007a). However, whether or not a particular species poses a risk to cattle does not just depend on whether it is susceptible to TB: it also depends on how many members of the species contract the disease (i.e. on the prevalence of the disease), how likely infected individuals are to become infectious (i.e. on the epidemiology of the disease) and how likely infectious individuals are to contact cattle (i.e. on the ecology and behaviour of the host species). In badgers, the rates of infection and infectiousness are both relatively high (see Chapter 2) and the ecology of badgers is such as to make contact with cattle likely (for example, they often forage in cattle pastures). Badgers seem, therefore, to exhibit all of the characteristics required of a wildlife reservoir species. Nevertheless, it is important to ask whether badgers are unique in this respect.

The most comprehensive available review of TB in wild mammals concluded that when the factors of prevalence, epidemiology and ecology were taken into account, only red deer *Cervus elaphus* and fallow deer *Dama dama* posed a risk to cattle comparable, in principle, to that posed by badgers (Delahay *et al.*, 2007a). In addition, some risk attaches to roe deer *Capreolus capreolus* and Reeves's muntjac *Muntiacus reevesi*. The reason for categorising these four species of deer as 'high risk' is that, like the badger, they have relatively high levels of infection and infectiousness, and they sometimes associate with cattle. In practice, however, these species of deer have not been sufficiently numerous in the past, or sufficiently geographically widespread, to explain the numerical incidence or geographical distribution of TB in cattle. Badgers, on the other hand, have been widespread for some time and are especially numerous in parts of the country where the incidence of TB in cattle is high. In short, although more information about the prevalence and epidemiology of TB in wild mammals other than the badger is desirable, the evidence currently available suggests that badgers are, and have been until now, the most likely wildlife reservoir species. Deer have the potential, however, to become a significant future source of TB in cattle.

An additional argument, also related to host behaviour and ecology, concerns the fact that cattle TB is localised in its distribution, both at the level of the disease in general and at the level of individual spoligotypes (see above, Figs. 205 and 206). This fits with what we know about the socio-spatial organisation of badgers. At the high population densities that obtain in most of the UK, badgers are relatively immobile animals, not given to long-distance migration for dispersal or other purposes (see Chapter 5). Consequently, if a particular *M. bovis* spoligotype became established in a particular badger population, we would expect it to remain geographically localised. Deer, by contrast, are more mobile animals and so would be expected to have spread TB more widely.

So far, we have considered circumstantial evidence identifying badgers as the most likely reservoir species. However, badgers are also implicated by compelling direct evidence derived from culling operations: that is, operations in which badgers have been completely or largely removed from a particular geographical area. Several such culls were carried out between 1975 and 1995, all of which resulted in reductions in the incidence of TB in cattle (see Carter *et al.*, 2007, and Table 12). These early culling operations can be criticised on the grounds that they were unreplicated and lacked control areas, leaving open the possibility that TB in cattle declined for reasons other than removal of badgers. However, these criticisms are less easily levelled at two more recent, more extensive and more carefully monitored operations: namely, the 'Four Areas' culling trial in Ireland and the 'Randomised Badger Culling Trial' (or RBCT) in the UK, both of which also resulted in a significant decline in the incidence of TB in cattle (see below for a more extended discussion).

TABLE 12. Results of early culling operations carried out in the UK and the Republic of Ireland. (Krebs *et al.*, 1997; Eves, 1999)

Location	Culling period	Area (km^2)	% decrease in TB in cattle
Steeple Leeze, Dorset, UK	1975–9	12	92
Thornbury, Avon, UK	1975–81	104	100
Hartland, Devon, UK	1984	62	73
East Offaly, Ireland	1989–94	528	76

Given this evidence that removal of badgers reduces TB in cattle, it is no longer possible to argue that badgers do not constitute a source of the disease. There remains, however, considerable uncertainty as to *how important* badgers are as a source of TB in cattle – a point to which I return below.

TRANSMISSION ROUTES

It is easy to see how TB might be transmitted from cow to cow or from badger to badger, because in both cases, members of the species in question spend a significant amount of time in close physical proximity to one another. Consequently, there is ample opportunity for what is called 'direct' transmission: that is, for bacteria to pass, in aerosolised form, directly from an infected animal to an uninfected one. The fact that almost all cattle and most badgers become infected via the respiratory route (i.e. they breath the infection in) lends further weight to this being the main transmission mechanism, though bite-wounding may also be important in the transmission of infection from one social group of badgers to another (Gallagher & Nelson, 1979; see also Chapter 2). The mechanisms underlying badger-to-cattle and cattle-to-badger transmission, by contrast, are much less well understood.

Transmission from badgers to cattle

The key question of how badgers transmit TB to cattle has proved remarkably hard to answer. Thinking to date has centred around two issues. First, is transmission direct (i.e. via respiratory contact between badgers and cattle) or indirect (i.e. via contamination of the environment by badgers)? And, second, does it occur while cattle are at pasture or while they are housed in farm buildings (Fig. 207)? Since these possibilities are non-exclusive and independent of one another, they yield a total of four possible transmission scenarios, any or all of which could, in principle, operate.

Transmission while cattle are at pasture

Badgers are known to favour short-grass pasture, including cattle pastures, for foraging purposes (see Chapter 4). Therefore, it seems reasonable to suppose that cattle might acquire TB from badgers as a result of both species using the same pastures. As regards direct transmission, it is likely that badgers sometimes come close enough to grazing or resting cattle to make this possible. However, the evidence is inconclusive. Early radio-tracking work suggested that badgers and cattle tend to avoid one another: for example, cases were convincingly described

FIG 207. Possible locations for badger-to-cattle transmission: (left) while cattle are at pasture; (below left) while cattle are housed on farm premises. (Food and Agriculture Research Agency)

of badgers taking detours in order to avoid passing through cattle herds, or running away if approached by a curious cow (Benham & Broom, 1989). More recent evidence, however, based on data from electronically tagged badgers and cows, suggests that individuals of the two species do, at least occasionally, come into close physical contact with one another (Böhm *et al.*, 2009). It seems, then, that direct transmission could occur while cattle are at pasture, but more research is needed to determine how often this occurs and in what circumstances.

Rather more attention has been given to the possibility of indirect transmission via badger urine or faeces. Badgers are known to defecate and urinate on pasture (see Chapter 6), and infected badgers can excrete live bacilli in their urine and faeces. Therefore, it has been suggested, cows could become infected while grazing on pasture contaminated in this way. Contamination of pasture with urine may constitute the greater risk, because live bacilli are found in greater numbers in urine than in faeces (MAFF, 1979). In addition, badgers urinate more frequently than they defecate, and urine is spread more widely in the environment because it is deposited both at and away from latrines (see Chapter 6).

Once again, however, the evidence is inconclusive. Early work suggested that cattle were reluctant to eat grass contaminated with badger excreta (Benham & Broom, 1991). However, subsequent evidence suggests that whether or not contaminated grass is avoided depends on the nature of the grazing regime (Hutchings & Harris, 1997; Smith *et al.*, 2009). If grazing pressure is high – for example, because cattle density is high or because most of the good grass in a pasture has already been eaten – cattle become less fussy about what they eat and consumption of contaminated grass becomes more likely.

However, there are other reasons for doubting whether indirect pasture-based transmission is an important phenomenon. For one thing, live bacilli probably do not survive for very long on open pasture, especially in dry, sunny conditions, though again the evidence is inconclusive. For another, almost all cattle contract TB via the respiratory route: that is, they inhale tuberculosis bacilli rather than ingesting them. It is perfectly possible that in the process of investigating a patch of contaminated grass, cows could aerosolise any bacilli present on it and then breathe them in; or bacilli could find their way into the respiratory tract while grass is in the mouth. But proof is needed that bacilli are frequently inspired in this way. And, finally, only a minority of tuberculous badgers excrete bacilli in their urine or faeces, so contamination of grass may not occur very often (Nolan & Wilesmith, 1994). In short, the idea that contaminated pasture constitutes an important source of infection is not as straightforward as might appear at first sight.

Transmission in and around farm buildings

An early paper by Chris Cheeseman and Peter Mallinson (1981), working at Woodchester Park, Gloucestershire, described three cases in which chronically infectious badgers left their social groups and took up residence elsewhere, including, in one case, in a cattle shed. During radio-tracking work in East Sussex in the early 1990s, I came across a small number of similar instances of badly debilitated, tuberculous badgers living in barns and cattle-feed stores. In addition, the Woodchester Park study has revealed that badgers found dead in and around farm buildings are more likely to test TB-positive than badgers found dead elsewhere. Taken together, these observations suggest that use of farm buildings by tuberculous badgers could put cattle at risk of infection.

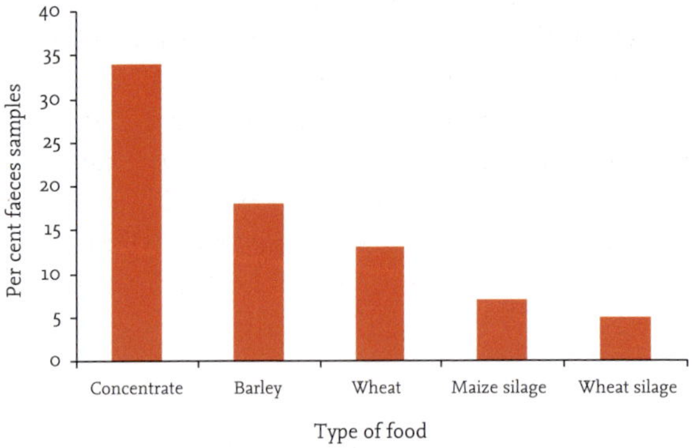

FIG 208. Percentage of badger faeces samples containing different types of food obtained in or around farm buildings. (Based on data in Tolhurst *et al.*, 2009)

Almost 20 years after the publication of Cheeseman & Mallinson's paper, I was able to collaborate with the Woodchester Park team in a more systematic investigation of the behaviour of badgers in and around farm buildings (Garnett, 2002; Garnett *et al.*, 2002). We found that some farms were, indeed, highly attractive to badgers, while others, for reasons that are still not clear, were rarely or never visited. Badgers visited farm buildings primarily for foraging purposes, the main places of interest being cattle-feed stores, barns, cowsheds and slurry pits, where badgers fed on concentrated cattle feed, stored grain and silage (Fig. 208). Some farms were positively alive with badgers: for example, one feed shed was visited on 55 per cent of nights by at least 12 different animals. However, visits to farms were generally restricted to dry, hot weather, indicating

FIG 209. Badger entering a cattle shed at night (above left), photographed by a surveillance camera; badger feeding on stored cattle food (above right), captured from a surveillance video. (Food and Agriculture Research Agency)

that badgers tended to turn to farm-based resources when their favourite natural food, earthworms, was unavailable. A second study has subsequently replicated and extended these findings (Ward *et al.*, 2008b; Tolhurst *et al.*, 2009).

These observations do not show that visits by badgers to farm buildings result in cattle becoming infected with TB. However, they certainly flag this up as a possibility. Infection could be direct or indirect, or both, since badgers sometimes come into close contact with cattle while foraging in cattle sheds or feeding from mangers, and they also urinate, defecate and scent-mark in and around feed stores (Fig. 209).

Other transmission scenarios

There have been anecdotal accounts of badgers feeding and drinking from cattle troughs, and I have seen this with my own eyes. Badgers are also attracted to mineral licks put out for cattle and there is a published account of badgers climbing into a trough containing concentrated feed and feeding from it at the same time as cattle (Garnett, 2002: see Fig. 210). In the latter case, badgers also defecated and urinated onto the feed contained in the trough, without any apparent deterrent effect on cattle feeding behaviour. Clearly, there was ample opportunity here for both direct and indirect transmission, but we do not know how common this kind of scenario is.

FIG 210. Cattle feed trough contaminated with badger faeces. (B. T. Garnett and Food and Environment Research Agency)

Researchers at Warwick University have recently reported the recovery of substantial amounts of *M. bovis* DNA from around badger setts and latrines, suggesting that such places could be heavily contaminated with TB (Courtenay *et al.*, 2006). At present, there remain doubts as to whether the DNA in question derives from live, viable bacteria or from dead ones. However, if the findings are substantiated, they would suggest that setts and latrines could be significant sources of infection. For example, when cattle are trampling around on badger setts, they might inhale dust particles carrying TB bacteria.

Transmission from cattle to badgers

Comparatively little attention has been given to the issue of whether TB passes from cattle to badgers or how it might do so. However, if cattle are capable of giving TB to other cattle, then presumably they could give it to badgers (and other wildlife) as well. Indeed, it is generally assumed that the bovine form of TB originated in cattle and only subsequently became established in wildlife.

A study by Rosie Woodroffe and others provides quantitative evidence of cattle-to-badger transmission. They showed that following an outbreak of foot-and-mouth disease in pigs, sheep and cattle in 2001, the prevalence of TB in badgers more than tripled (Woodroffe *et al.*, 2006b: see Fig. 211). The most plausible explanation is that during the foot-and-mouth epidemic, which lasted for about a year, the cattle test-and-slaughter programme was suspended. Consequently, tuberculous cattle remained in the population, free to spread the infection both to other cattle and to badgers. If this explanation is correct, then cattle constitute a significant ongoing source of TB in badgers.

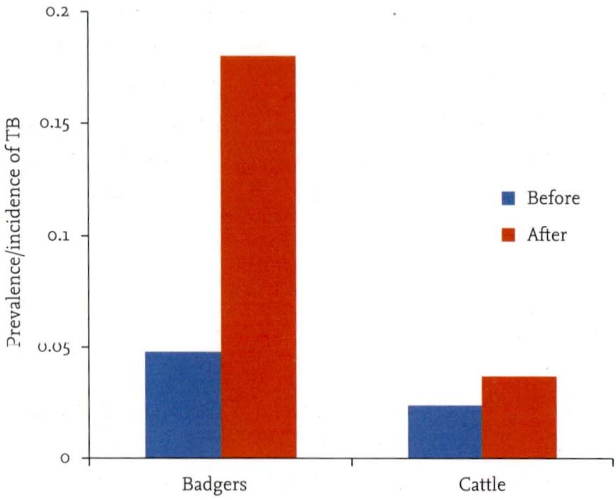

FIG 211. Prevalence of TB in badgers and incidence of TB in cattle before and after an outbreak of foot-and-mouth disease. (Based on data in Woodroffe *et al.*, 2006a)

IS TB IN BADGERS SELF-SUSTAINING?

The fact that cattle transmit TB to badgers, apparently to a significant extent, raises the question of whether TB in badgers is self-sustaining (or, to use the technical term, 'endemic'). In other words, if the disease were eliminated from cattle, would it still persist in the badger population or would it die out? This is an important question from a management point of view, because if elimination of TB in cattle would automatically eliminate TB in badgers, then control measures should clearly focus on cattle. If, on the other hand, TB is self-sustaining in badgers, then elimination of the disease in cattle will require control measures to be directed towards both species.

Frustratingly, this key question lacks a clear answer. Intuitively, it seems likely that TB is endemic in badgers, because their way of life, involving frequent close physical contact between the members of a social group, offers plenty of opportunities for disease transmission. Results from the Woodchester Park study lend further support to this view, insofar as they show that TB can remain for many years, at a relatively constant level, within a badger population; that individual badgers can remain infectious for long periods of time; that the mortality rate due to TB is low; and that cubs can contract TB, apparently from their mothers, at an early age (see Chapter 2). All of these factors make badgers an ideal maintenance host for TB. However, the fact is that some social groups in the Woodchester Park population range over land that is used by cattle and some of the relevant cattle herds have a history of TB. Consequently, it is conceivable that without input from infectious cattle, TB in the Woodchester badgers would die out.

An additional piece of evidence, again consistent with endemism, is that tuberculous road-killed badgers have been collected from parts of the country where no TB has been detected in cattle (see Krebs *et al.*, 1997). However, the sample sizes in these cases were small and the fact that TB had not been detected in cattle in the relevant areas does not necessarily mean that it did not exist. In short, there is no absolute proof that TB is self-sustaining in badgers but the evidence points strongly in that direction.

CONTROL MEASURES

As we have seen, there is good evidence for the transmission of TB both from badgers to cattle and from cattle to cattle. In principle, therefore, the surest policy for reducing the disease in cattle would be to target both of these transmission routes. And, in practice, this is what has happened. As regards badger-to-cattle transmission, three management tools have been used in the past or are being developed for use in the future: namely, culling of badgers, vaccination of badgers and enhanced farm biosecurity (i.e. measures aimed at reducing contact between badgers and cattle). As regards cattle-to-cattle transmission, the principle method of control has always been, and continues to be, test-and-slaughter combined with movement controls, and steps have recently been taken to make this approach more rigorous (see below). In addition, vaccination of cattle is under consideration as a future means of disease control, while husbandry measures, such as the double-fencing of fields, have been suggested in order to prevent infection passing directly from one herd to another.

Badger culling

One way or another, badgers in Great Britain have been subjected to culling almost continuously since the early 1970s (see Neal & Cheeseman, 1996; Bourne, 2007, for further details). In 1973, the Ministry of Agriculture, Fisheries and Food, having decided that badgers were a threat to cattle, advised farmers on methods of killing the animals, on their own land, in areas where TB was especially problematic and where badgers were a potential cause. Soon afterwards, however, and in response to public disquiet, legislation was enacted allowing badger setts to be gassed with hydrogen cyanide. However, only government officials were allowed to gas setts, meaning that the responsibility for badger culling passed from farmers to the government itself – a situation that has continued until the present. Gassing of setts commenced in 1975 and continued until 1982, during which period badgers were culled in 166 different areas, averaging 7 km^2 in size, distributed throughout the southwest of England. This included the repeated gassing of setts in a 104 km^2 area near Thornbury, in Gloucestershire, which effectively eliminated both the badger population and the occurrence of TB in cattle (Clifton-Hadley *et al.*, 1995: see Table 11 above).

Public opposition to gassing led to a review of the policy by Lord Zuckerman, during which gassing was suspended. This review recommended that gassing be resumed if it could be shown to kill badgers effectively and humanely (Zuckerman, 1980). However, subsequent research suggested that lethal concentrations of gas might not reach the most distant parts of a large main sett, in which case some badgers might suffer a lingering death. In addition, scientists and others criticised gassing on the grounds that it failed to yield carcasses for testing, so there was no way of knowing how many slaughtered badgers were, in fact, infected. As a result of these concerns, gassing was never resumed. Instead, it was replaced by a policy of live-trapping and shooting of badgers, which has continued to operate, in one form or another, until the present.

In 1986, the control strategy changed yet again, following a report by an independent advisory committee under the chairmanship of Professor George Dunnett (Dunnett *et al.*, 1986). By this time, it was evident that large numbers of healthy badgers were being killed in culling operations, which was clearly undesirable and was a major source of public opposition to culling. One of the Dunnett Report's recommendations, therefore, was that a method of testing for TB in live badgers should be developed, so that healthy individuals could be spared in culling operations. Meanwhile, an 'interim strategy' was implemented, in which badger culling (by trapping and shooting) was restricted to individual farms or to parts of farms on which cattle had become infected.

Towards the end of 1993, a test for TB in live badgers became available but its sensitivity (i.e. its ability to correctly diagnose individual infected badgers) was low (about 40 per cent). Nevertheless, it was decided to trial the new test by culling all of the badgers in a sett if at least one of them tested positive. Meanwhile, the interim strategy was continued outside the designated trial areas. In the event, the prevalence of TB in badgers culled in live-test trial areas was not significantly different from that of badgers culled in interim-strategy areas, meaning that the live-test procedure did nothing to protect healthy badgers. Both the live-test trial and the practice of interim culling were suspended in 1996.

The Randomised Badger Culling Trial (RBCT)

In 1996, the Ministry, alarmed by the rising incidence of TB in cattle, commissioned yet another independent review of TB control, this time under the chairmanship of Professor John Krebs. Krebs's committee found 'compelling' evidence that badgers were 'a significant source of infection in cattle' (Krebs *et al.*, 1997, p. 6). However, the committee also acknowledged that most of the evidence was circumstantial, not least because previous culls had failed to include 'no cull' control areas. Consequently, the reductions in incidence of cattle TB demonstrated by those culls (see Table 11 above) could have been caused by factors other than badger removal.

One of the Krebs committee's many recommendations, therefore, was that a properly controlled culling trial should be carried out, with the explicit aim of determining the extent to which removal of badgers reduces TB in cattle. Two culling regimes were tested: a 'proactive' regime in which badgers were eliminated, as far as possible, from the whole of a designated area, and a 'reactive' regime where culling only occurred locally and in response to an actual TB outbreak on an individual farm. An equal number of 'no cull' areas were designated as controls. The trial was designed on a heroic scale: ten proactive cull areas, ten reactive cull areas and ten control areas were identified, each about 100 km^2 in size. These areas were grouped into ten 'triplets', each containing one proactive, one reactive and one control area, such that the three areas within any one triplet were located close to one another, while the different triplets were geographically separated, although all were situated in parts of the country historically associated with high rates of TB in cattle (Fig. 212). The trial was overseen by a committee called the Independent Scientific Group on Cattle TB, or ISG for short, under the chairmanship of Professor John Bourne. The trial itself was named the 'Randomised Badger Culling Trial', or RBCT, and it ran from 1998 until 2005. During the RBCT, no other form of badger control was attempted, the interim strategy (see above) having been suspended.

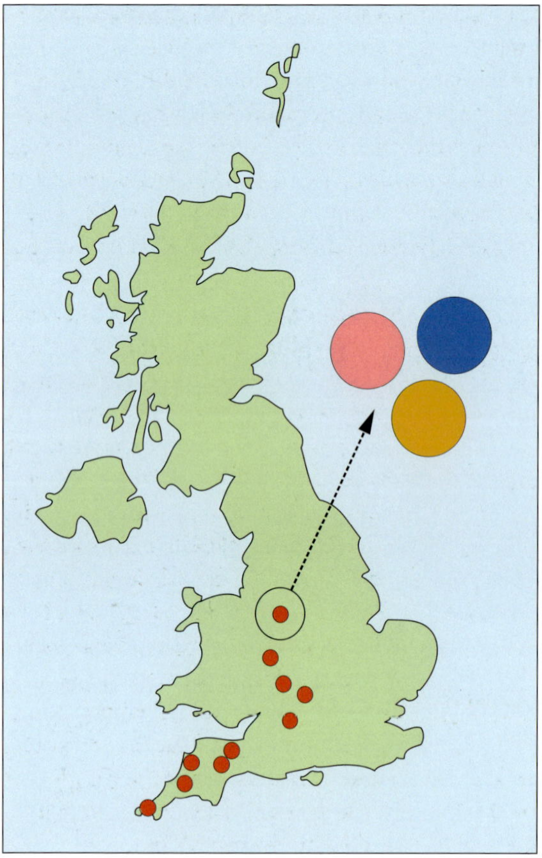

FIG 212. Locations of the ten triplet areas (red) comprising the Randomised Badger Culling Trial. Each triplet contained three treatment areas: a proactive culling area (pink), a reactive culling area (blue) and a control area (yellow), separated from one another by a distance of at least 3 km. Treatment areas were roughly circular in shape and about 100 km^2 in extent.

The whole idea of the RBCT met with a good deal of scepticism from scientists, badger protection groups, farmers and others. Scientists doubted whether a trial on such a scale would be practicably feasible; badger protection groups objected to the trial on the grounds that it meant killing more badgers when, in their view, culling had already been discredited as a TB control strategy; and farmers objected on the grounds that there would be no culling of badgers outside the triplet areas while the trial was in progress. And, right from the start, the trial ran into trouble. Some landowners refused to take part; there were problems assembling the enormous resources needed to undertake the work; vigilantes threatened to disrupt trapping operations, and so on. Culling even had to be suspended for almost a year in the middle of the trial owing to an outbreak of foot-and-mouth disease. Nevertheless, it is a tribute to the tenacity of Bourne and his colleagues that the trial did get up and running, was seen through to completion and delivered meaningful results, albeit somewhat behind schedule.

The results of the RBCT were, to say the least, unexpected. The first bombshell came in the form of a paper showing that reactive culling, far from reducing the incidence of TB in cattle, actually increased it, on average by 27 per cent (Donnelly *et al.*, 2003). Although these were only interim results and the trial had been scheduled to continue for some further time, the Minister decided (understandably, given the results) to abort this part of the trial there and then. Accordingly, reactive culling ceased in November 2003. The proactive part of the trial, however, was allowed to continue.

The results of proactive culling, released three years later, were more complex but in some respects just as surprising (Donnelly *et al.*, 2006, 2007). This time, the incidence of TB in cattle was lower in culled areas than in control areas, showing that removal of badgers did reduce TB in cattle. However, the reduction was comparatively modest, being only about 33 per cent by the end of the trial and only about 20 per cent when averaged over the course of the trial. Furthermore, incidence of TB in cattle *increased*, by about 25 per cent on average, in a 2 km-wide band around the outside of each culled area (Fig. 213). This increase in cattle TB outside the culled areas more or less cancelled out the decline within the culled areas, so that the net effect of proactive culling was far too small for culling to be worthwhile.

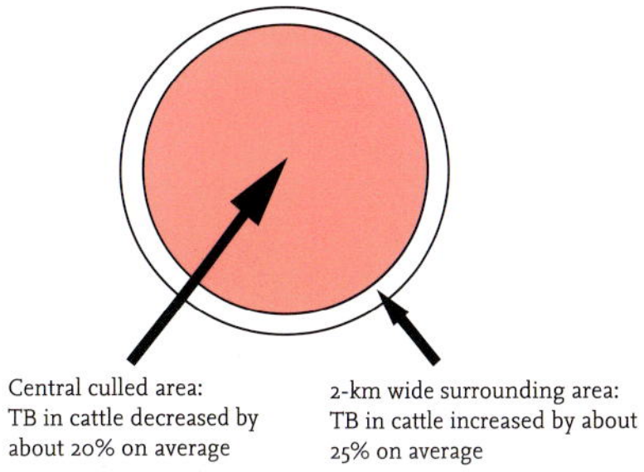
Central culled area:
TB in cattle decreased by about 20% on average
2-km wide surrounding area:
TB in cattle increased by about 25% on average

FIG 213. Diagram summarising the results of the proactive culling component of the Randomised Badger Culling Trial.

The 'perturbation effect'

Why should the incidence of TB in cattle have increased within the reactively culled areas and around the proactively culled areas? The most plausible explanation of these unexpected phenomena is in terms of what has come to be called the 'perturbation effect'. According to this idea, when badgers are culled, their socio-spatial organisation, and that of their neighbours in surrounding regions, is disrupted, causing an increase in ranging and dispersal movements between any remaining social groups and into vacated territories. This increase in badger movements is thought to lead both to an increase in the prevalence of TB in badgers and to an increased rate of contact between badgers and cattle. As a consequence of these two factors, more cattle become infected.

Various lines of evidence support the perturbation hypothesis (for a review, see Carter *et al.*, 2007). First and foremost, radio-tracking and bait-marking studies have shown that culling does indeed lead to an increase in the mobility of any badgers remaining within the culled area and also within the population immediately outside the culled area. Their territories become larger and less distinct, those of adjacent groups overlap more than is usual, and dispersal occurs more often and over longer distances (Tuyttens *et al.*, 2000; Woodroffe *et al.*, 2006a). Genetic studies have backed up these findings by showing that after culling, there is more genetic mixing within the remaining population, again implying that badgers are dispersing more often and further (Pope *et al.*, 2007). In short, there is good evidence that culling destabilises the pattern of communal territoriality that is so characteristic of badgers in undisturbed high-density populations.

The next step in the perturbation argument is that owing to this increase in badger movements, the prevalence of TB in badgers increases. Again, there is compelling evidence that this happens. The prevalence of TB in badgers rose with successive culls in both reactively and proactively culled areas, approximately doubling between the first and fourth proactive culls. Furthermore, this increase was especially marked in trial areas that were not bounded by geographical barriers such as rivers or motorways, suggesting that it was associated with immigration into the culled areas (Woodroffe *et al.*, 2006b). Proactive culling also resulted in TB in badgers becoming less clustered, which fits with the idea that the badger population within and just outside the culled areas became more mobile, carrying the infection outside their normal territorial boundaries (Jenkins *et al.*, 2007). And, finally, data from the Woodchester Park study show that the prevalence of TB in an undisturbed badger population increases following periods when there is a higher than

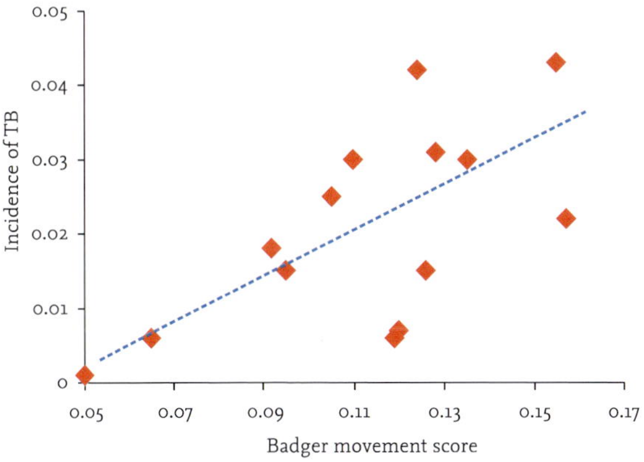

FIG 214. Relationship between the amount of movement between groups in the Woodchester Park badger population and the incidence of TB in badgers in the following year. (Based on data in Rogers *et al.*, 1998)

normal degree of movement between social groups (Rogers *et al.*, 1998; Vicente *et al.*, 2007: see Fig. 214). Precisely why periods of social instability result in more TB remains, however, a matter of speculation. One possibility is that increased ranging behaviour increases the rate at which badgers from different social groups contact one another, leading to increased transmission between groups. Another is that owing to the stress of social perturbation, the disease progresses in individuals that were already infected but in which the disease was dormant.

Despite this supporting evidence, however, the perturbation effect has been questioned, mainly owing to the rapidity with which it apparently operates. Consider the sequence of events that has to occur for culling to produce an increase in the incidence of TB in cattle. First, culling has to disrupt the spatial organisation of badgers, producing an increase in badger movements; then, this increase in movements has to result in more badgers developing TB to the extent that they become infectious; then, the disease has to be passed on to cattle; then, infected cattle have to develop the disease sufficiently for it to be detectable by routine testing; and, finally, the cattle have to be tested. Bearing in mind that all these things have to happen, that TB infection is usually slow to develop in both badgers and cattle, and that cattle are only tested once per year, it is hard to see how badger culling could produce a measurable increase in TB in cattle in a short space of time. Yet, in two of the reactive cull areas, culling only began seven months and four months, respectively, before the trial was terminated. It seems implausible that such short periods of culling provided sufficient time for all of the events listed above to have occurred, or that the extent of culling in these cases produced sufficient increase in TB in badgers, and sufficiently frequent onward transmission to cattle, to produce a measurable increase in the incidence of TB in cattle (Godfray *et al.*, 2005; More *et al.*, 2007).

Despite these misgivings, however, the fact remains that TB in cattle did increase, both within the reactively culled areas and outside the proactively culled areas, as a consequence of badger culling. In the absence of any alternative suggestion, the perturbation hypothesis remains the most plausible explanation of these findings.

The ISG Final Report and subsequent developments

Following completion of the RBCT, the Independent Scientific Group produced a comprehensive Final Report, providing a detailed analysis of the RBCT data and making policy recommendations (Bourne, 2007). As regards culling, the ISG concluded that since reactive culling increased the incidence of TB in cattle, while proactive culling had little net effect, culling should be abandoned as a component of the nation's TB control strategy. This recommendation resulted in considerable further discussion, involving reports by the House of Commons Environment, Food and Rural Affairs Committee and by a group of experts convened by the government's Chief Scientific Advisor, Sir David King. Eventually, however, the Secretary of State for Environment, Food and Rural Affairs, Hilary Benn, accepted the recommendation of the ISG that the culling of badgers be abandoned. However, Benn did leave open the possibility of revisiting his decision in 'exceptional circumstances' or in the light of new scientific evidence.

Benn's decision, however, did not apply to Wales. Badger lovers had hardly begun to celebrate the cessation of culling in England when the Minister for Rural Affairs in the National Assembly for Wales, Elin Jones, recommended a 'targeted cull of badgers' in those parts of Wales where the incidence of TB in cattle was especially high. Consultations are now under way as to how and where this cull will be carried out.

On the scientific side, the main development since the publication of the ISG's Final Report has been the emergence of further data relating to the proactive part of the RBCT. As we have seen, analysis of the RBCT data carried out shortly after the cessation of the trial showed two effects of proactive culling: a reduction in the incidence of cattle TB of about 20 per cent within the culled area, and an increase of about 25 per cent just outside the culled area. However, it has subsequently become clear that this is not the end of the story. Although actual culling of badgers ceased in 2005, the incidence of TB in cattle within the proactively culled areas continued to decline, while the 'peturbation effect' also declined and eventually, by the first year after the cessation of culling, went into reverse. The maximal effect of culling was seen two years after culling ceased, by which time the decrease in the incidence of TB in cattle was about 61 per cent on average within the culled areas and about 30 per cent in the surrounding regions (Jenkins *et al.*,

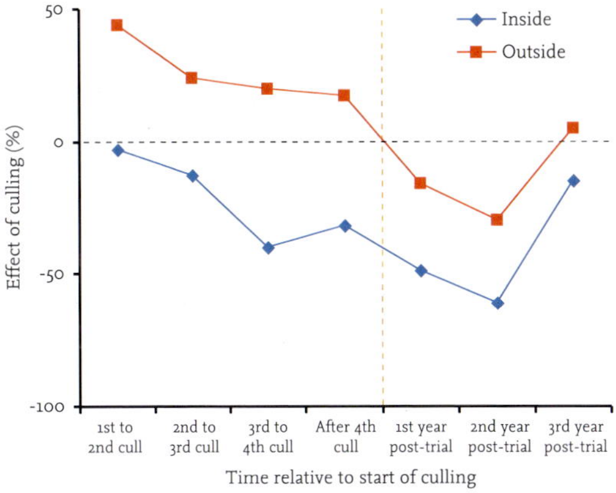

FIG 215. Effect of proactive culling on incidence of TB in cattle inside, and up to 2 km outside, trial areas. The yellow vertical line indicates the time at which culling ceased. By the second year after the cessation of culling, TB in cattle had decreased by 30% outside the trial areas and by 61% inside them. However, it increased again during the third year after cessation of culling. (Based on data in Jenkins *et al.*, 2008, 2010)

2008). By the end of the third year after the cessation of culling, however, incidence of TB in cattle had returned to baseline level, both within and outside the culled areas (Jenkins *et al.*, 2010; see Fig. 215). We can now conclude, therefore, that while proactive culling of the type implemented in the RBCT does produce a reduction, of more than 50 per cent, in the incidence of TB in cattle, the full magnitude of this effect not only takes time to develop, but also disappears again fairly rapidly once culling has ceased.

Modifications to the test-and-slaughter policy

In addition to reviewing evidence relating to badger culling, the ISG Final Report also made recommendations relating to cattle-based methods of TB control. Their most striking conclusion in this respect, based partly on the results of a mathematical model and partly on the effects of TB control policy in Northern Ireland (see below), was that significant progress towards solving the TB problem could be achieved through cattle-based measures alone (Bourne, 2007).

Accordingly, various changes have been made to the test-and-slaughter regime. One new measure has been the introduction of compulsory pre-movement testing of cattle in high-risk areas, with the aim of reducing the spread of TB to uninfected herds. Another has been the use of a new, more sensitive test for TB in cattle (the γ-interferon or IFN test) in addition to the traditional tuberculin test (the 'skin test'), with the aim of reducing the number of infected cattle that go undetected. It remains to be seen how effective these measures will be.

Other possibilities, still under discussion, are the introduction of 'zoning', which would prevent altogether the movement of cattle from high-risk to low-risk areas, and the slaughter of entire herds (as opposed to individual infected cattle) in cases where TB has been repeatedly diagnosed over a period of time. Research is also continuing into the development of better (i.e. more sensitive and more specific) diagnostic tests for use on cattle.

Vaccination

The ideal way of eliminating TB from cattle, badgers or both would be by vaccination. Apart from the fact that prevention is always better than cure, the major attractions of vaccination in the case of badgers are that it would be more acceptable to all parties than culling and would avoid perturbation of badger populations. In the case of cattle, vaccination could in principle be more effective than test-and-slaughter.

A 10- to 15-year research programme aimed at developing a badger vaccine was one of the key recommendations in a 'six-point plan' adopted by MAFF in 1993. Four years later, by contrast, the Krebs Report concluded that the best long-term prospect for control of TB was the development of a cattle vaccine, though it also recommended that research into the development of a badger vaccine should continue. Since then, work on both types of vaccine has proceeded and significant advances have been made. Defra's long-term goal is now to control TB by vaccination of badgers or cattle, or both, to which end it is spending over £1 million per year on research (Reynolds, 2006).

Vaccination of cattle

At first sight, vaccination of cattle seems preferable to vaccination of badgers for a number of reasons. First, TB is problematic primarily because it is a disease of cattle, not because it is a disease of badgers. Therefore, it seems logical to attack the disease in cattle directly, rather than via badgers. Second, it would be far easier, from a purely practical point of view, to vaccinate cattle rather than badgers. Third, vaccination of cattle would protect them not just from infectious badgers but also from any other external source of infection that might exist now or arise in the future. Fourth, research is easier to carry out on cattle than on badgers. And, finally, more of the sort of background information needed to develop a vaccine, such as knowledge of the detailed epidemiology of TB and of the host's immune system, is available for cattle than for badgers.

Unfortunately, however, there are two major stumbling blocks to the use of a cattle vaccine, both of which arise from the fact that because no vaccine is ever

100 per cent effective, vaccinated herds would still have to be monitored for TB. This would be impossible using any of the tests currently available, because vaccinated cattle would be diagnosed as TB-positive. Consequently, the development of a cattle vaccine requires the parallel development of a new test for TB (a so-called DIVA test), able to distinguish between a vaccinated animal and a diseased one. The first problem with cattle vaccination, then, is a scientific one: namely, the challenge of developing a suitable combination of vaccine and cattle test that would meet these requirements.

The second problem is a political one: namely, that EU legislation (in the form of EU Council Directives 64/432 and 78/52) currently forbids the vaccination of cattle, for precisely the reason that vaccinated cattle cannot be tested for TB. Before a vaccine programme could be implemented, therefore, the rest of the EU would have to consent to the withdrawal of this legislation. This would require proof that meat and dairy products from vaccinated cattle are safe.

Since the Krebs Report in 1997, Defra scientists and others have tested about 60 candidate vaccines on laboratory animals and ten of these on cattle. The most promising candidate is Bacille Calmette-Guérin (BCG), the vaccine that has been used for decades on humans. This has the advantages of having been thoroughly studied at a molecular level and acknowledged as safe, not just in humans but also in various other species. However, BCG alone does not offer a sufficiently high level of protection to cattle (it is estimated to offer complete protection to only 50 per cent of cattle and partial protection to a further 30 per cent). Consequently, current research is investigating the use of a so-called 'prime-boost' strategy in which BCG would be combined with some other vaccine, possibly providing complete protection to about 70 per cent of cattle and partial protection to a further 20 per cent. Progress is also being made towards the development of a cattle test that would distinguish between a BCG-vaccinated bovine and one infected with *M. bovis*. Probably, such a test will be based on antigens absent from BCG but present in live bacilli.

Nevertheless, a significant amount of research remains to be done. For example, although various vaccine candidates, including BCG, have been shown to limit transmission in the laboratory, it is not known whether they will be equally effective in natural conditions. Research is under way to address this issue by introducing vaccinated cattle into a herd containing naturally infected animals. But even if these experiments are successful, large-scale field trials will still be necessary for the licensing of a vaccine. And, there still remains the political problem of getting EU approval for a cattle vaccination programme. In view of these and other obstacles, it is unlikely that a cattle vaccine will be available before 2016 (Reynolds, 2006).

Vaccination of badgers

While the goal of cattle vaccination is to prevent healthy animals from becoming infected with TB, that of badger vaccination is to prevent already infected animals from developing the disease to a stage at which they become infectious. As is the case for cattle, the most promising candidate vaccine for badgers is BCG, which has already been shown to be safe in badgers and to limit disease progression in artificially infected animals in laboratory conditions. The next stage is to investigate the logistics of vaccinating naturally infected badgers in field conditions, to which end a 'Badger Vaccine Deployment Project' has been set up to begin in 2010 (see Fig. 216). This will involve live-trapping and vaccinating badgers repeatedly over a five-year period in six catchment areas of about 300 km^2. Within each of these catchment areas, vaccination will be targeted towards cattle farms and their immediate surroundings, which are expected to amount to about a third of the total land area (i.e. to about 100 km^2 within each 300 km^2 catchment area).

FIG 216. Cover of a booklet providing information about the Badger Vaccine Deployment Project. (Copyright © Defra, 2009, reproduced by permission)

Nevertheless, serious practical and scientific problems remain with respect to the large-scale delivery of a vaccine to wild badgers. Trials so far, and the Badger Vaccine Deployment Project that is about to begin, have used an injectable form of BCG, but it would be prohibitively expensive to vaccinate wild badgers on a large scale by live-trapping and injecting them. Rather, an oral form of the vaccine, to be delivered in bait, will be required. One problem with oral vaccines is that they have to survive the acid conditions of the stomach in order to still be viable when they reach the site of absorption: namely, the duodenum. This means packaging the vaccine in some sort of acid-resistant matrix, usually formed of lipid (fatty) material. Commercial drug companies have developed vaccine-packaging substances that are safe and effective in humans, but these will need to be adapted for use on badgers and tested for their efficacy. These sorts of considerations mean that a licensed oral vaccine for badgers is not expected to be available before 2015.

Other problems related to vaccine delivery are more prosaic. A bait needs to be found that is palatable to badgers; a method needs to be found of presenting this bait so that it gets consumed by most or all of the badgers in a social group, not just by the greediest individual; trials need to be carried out to determine the optimum number of baits to be made available at any one sett and the optimum length of time for which baiting should continue; the bait needs to be accessible to badgers but inaccessible to other species, and so on. It is especially important that cattle be unable to consume any bait, because if they did so they would subsequently test positive for TB. All of these problems are being addressed by current research and none should be insoluble. However, carrying out this kind of painstaking behavioural research on adequate numbers of wild badgers is inevitably a slow business.

Finally, there remains the problem that because we do not know how important badgers are as a source of TB in cattle, or how effective vaccination will be in field conditions, we do not know to what extent it would reduce the incidence of TB in cattle. Consequently, the cost-effectiveness of a vaccination programme cannot be accurately estimated. But at least, unlike culling, vaccination will not do badgers any harm and has the potential to rid them of a nasty disease.

Preventing contact between badgers and cattle

The transmission of TB between badgers and cattle requires that the two species contact one another, either directly or indirectly. Preventing contact from occurring would therefore be an obvious way of controlling the disease. This is the logic behind what has come to be called the 'biosecurity' approach to TB management.

The biosecurity approach is attractive in principle, because the cost of implementing it would be relatively small by comparison with policies such as badger culling or vaccination and because the responsibility for implementing it could be passed on, at least partly, to farmers rather than resting entirely with the government. Unfortunately, however, biosecurity measures are presently hard to justify owing to the fact that we do not know how transmission occurs. For example, if we knew for certain that badgers transmit TB to cattle when they go looking for food in and around farm buildings, then it would be worth making the relevant buildings more secure. Or, if we knew that cattle troughs were a significant locus of transmission, then we could find ways of preventing badgers

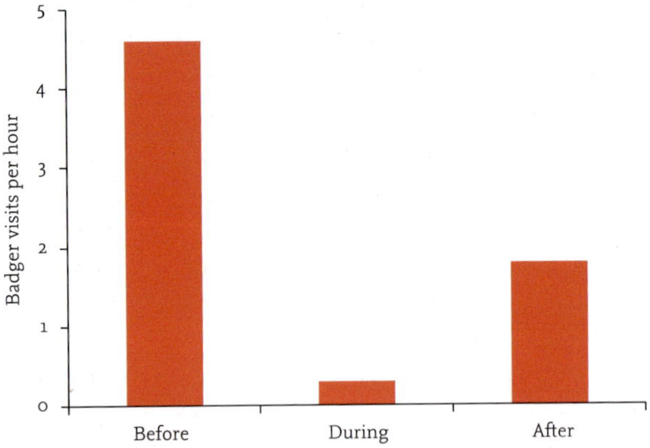

FIG 217. Number of badger visits per hour to farm buildings before, during and after the installation of electric fencing. The presence of electric fencing almost completely eliminated visits by badgers. (Based on data in Tolhurst *et al.*, 2008)

from climbing into them. Or, if we knew that cattle breathe in live *M. bovis* bacilli when they are investigating badger setts, then setts could be fenced off. The problem is that although there is circumstantial evidence for all of these transmission scenarios, there is no proof that any of them makes a significant contribution to the problem of TB in cattle. Consequently, it is hard to persuade farmers to adopt biosecurity measures.

FIG 218. An example of farm biosecurity: cattle feed stores fitted with badger-proof doors that can be shut at night. (Food and Agriculture Research Agency)

Nevertheless, if a cattle shed or feed store is being regularly visited by badgers on a farm that has experienced repeated incidents of TB in its cattle, then it seems only common sense to try to prevent this from occurring – especially if the economic cost of doing so is relatively low. On this basis, Defra has financed further research into ways of preventing badgers from gaining entry to farm buildings: for example, by installing electric fencing or by badger-proofing the gates of cattle sheds (e.g. Tolhurst *et al.*, 2008: see Fig. 217). This research shows that it is indeed possible, often at relatively modest cost, to make farms more biosecure (Fig. 218). However, the research also suggests that because every farm is unique, exclusion measures need to be tailor-made for the individual circumstances. This makes it difficult for Defra to issue generic advice to farmers about biosecurity measures. In addition, the same research has shown that individual farms differ enormously in the extent to which they are visited by badgers but has failed to discover why this is so. Consequently, there is no way of determining which farms are most at risk and which, therefore, stand to gain most from enhanced biosecurity.

TB IN IRELAND

It might seem sensible to consider the TB problem in Ireland as a whole, since diseases do not respect arbitrary national boundaries. In practice, however, there are significant differences both in farming practice and in the way TB has been managed between Northern Ireland and the Republic of Ireland, making it impossible to directly compare the situation in the two countries (or to compare either of them with England and Wales). I shall therefore consider Northern Ireland and the Republic of Ireland separately.

Northern Ireland

Prior to about 2002, the story of TB was more or less the same in Northern Ireland as in Great Britain. A majority of herds were infected in the 1940s but the introduction of a test-and-slaughter policy brought about a rapid reduction in the incidence of the disease. This reached a minimum in 1986, when only 0.06 per cent of tested cattle were diagnosed as TB-positive. Thereafter, however, the situation began to deteriorate, just as it did in Britain. Levels of TB in cattle rose, slowly at first but more rapidly after about 1997, reaching a peak in 2002 when the herd-level incidence of TB reached about 10 per cent (Fig. 219). At this point, Northern Ireland was thought to have the highest levels of TB in Europe (NIAO, 2009). Since then, however, and in contrast to what has happened in Great

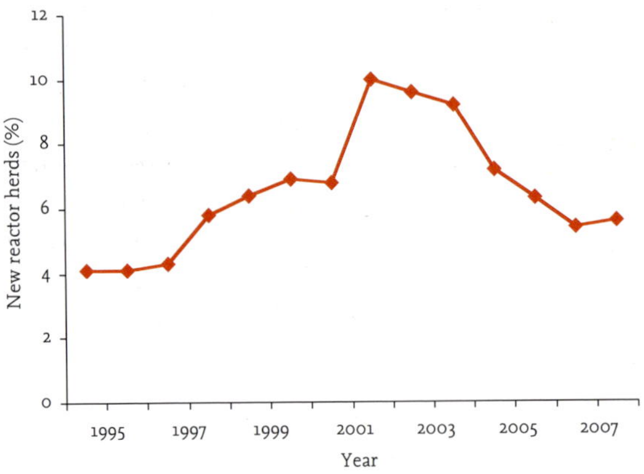

FIG 219. Percentage of new cattle herds testing positive for TB ('reactor herds') in Northern Ireland each year from 1995 to 2008. (Department of Agriculture and Rural Development)

Britain, the level of TB has dropped again, such that in 2007 just under 7 per cent of herds tested positive. From the British perspective, therefore, it is important to know what has brought about this recent decline in the level of the disease. What is clear is that it cannot have anything to do with control of badgers, since there has never been any badger culling in Northern Ireland.

In 1992, an 'Enhanced TB Eradication Programme' was launched in Northern Ireland, involving additional testing of cattle, improved education of farmers and improved training for the veterinarians responsible for cattle testing. Although this programme did seem to result in an initial reversal of the upward trend in TB, levels were still higher at the end of the programme, in 1995, than they had been five years earlier; and, as we have seen, they began to rise again after about 1996.

A further review in 2002 called for urgent action and recommended 17 new TB-control measures (NIAO, 2009). None of these constituted a radical break from previous policy: rather, they sought to improve the effectiveness of the control measures that were already in place. For example, herds were already being tested annually but measures were introduced to tighten up the regime in various ways, to employ more veterinary officers to test cattle and to provide farmers with an annual test certificate stating when the next test was due. In addition, the compensation system was changed and farmers were given further encouragement to fence off their land in such as way as to prevent nose-to-nose contact between their own cattle and those on adjoining farms.

As we have seen, these new measures produced a substantial reduction in the level of TB in cattle. However, the reduction now seems to have stalled and the level of TB is still considerably above target. Consequently, calls for action

FIG 220. Opposition in Northern Ireland to a recent decision to carry out a trial badger cull. (Mike Rendle, Northern Ireland Badger Group, and Ian Knox. Reprinted by permission of the artist)

against the wildlife reservoir have gained in strength and the Minister for Agriculture in Northern Ireland has recently announced her intention to carry out a badger-culling trial. We may yet, therefore, see culling implemented as a TB control strategy in this part of the UK (Fig. 220).

The Republic of Ireland

In the Republic of Ireland, as in the UK, TB eradication efforts begun in the 1950s were initially successful, leading to a substantial reduction in disease incidence by the late 1960s (see Fig. 221). However, this reduction was not as great as the results achieved by the introduction of test-and-slaughter in Britain. Since the 1960s, there has been no further decline in the level of TB in the Republic of Ireland, but, in contrast to the situation in Northern Ireland and Britain, nor has

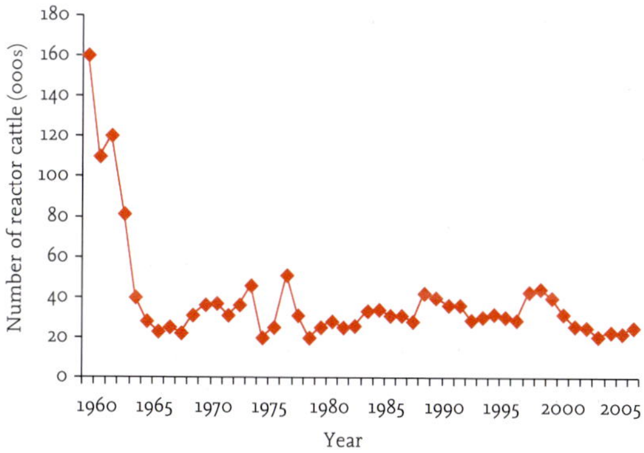

FIG 221. Number of cattle testing positive for TB ('reactor cattle') each year in the Republic of Ireland, during the period 1960–2007.

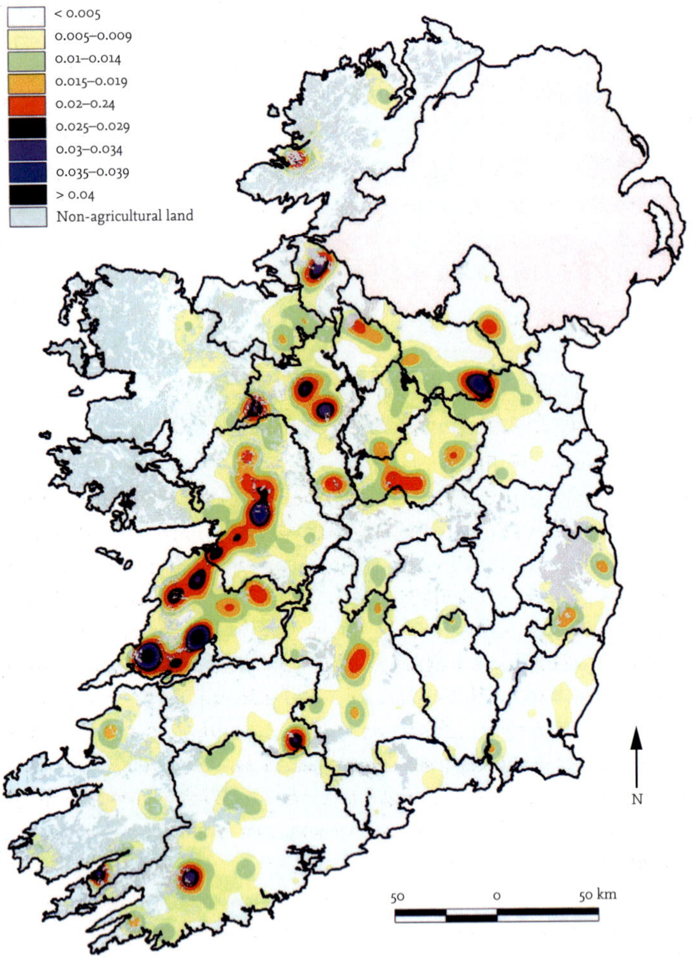

FIG 222. Incidence of TB in cattle in the Republic of Ireland in 2007. (Centre for Veterinary Epidemiology and Risk Analysis, University College Dublin)

there been any increase. In terms of its geographical spread, TB is present across most of the Republic but its incidence is greatest in a region stretching diagonally across the country from Monaghan to Clare (Fig. 222).

As regards disease-control measures, the biggest difference between Northern Ireland and the Republic is that during the last two decades the latter has made badger culling a significant part of its TB control strategy. In 1989, the Eradication

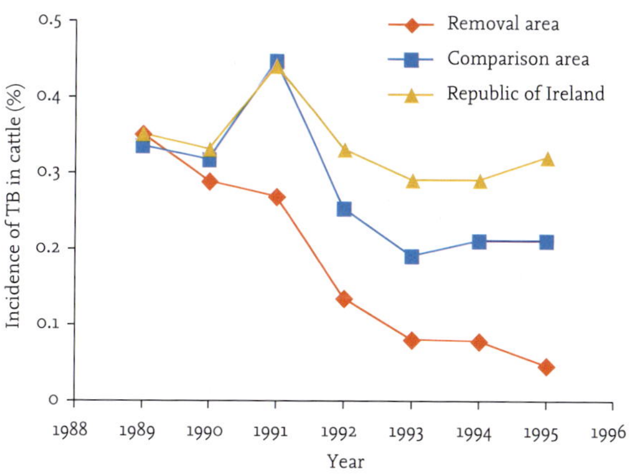

FIG 223. Results of the East Offaly Project, showing incidence of cattle TB in the removal area, the comparison area and the Republic of Ireland as a whole. Culling began in 1989 and ended in 1994. (Based on data in Eves, 1999)

of Animal Disease Board (ERAD) initiated a three-phase TB eradication programme, one element of which was a badger-culling trial. This trial, the East Offaly Badger Research Project, involved the repeated removal of badgers from a single 528 km^2 area in central Ireland during a six-year period from 1989 to 1994. The incidence of TB in cattle within this culled area was compared with the incidence in a surrounding, 1,456 km^2 comparison area in which there was limited, localised removal of badgers. Culling produced a systematic, year-on-year decline in the incidence of TB in cattle within the removal area, though there was also some decline in the comparison area, possibly owing to the limited culling that took place there (Eves, 1999: see Fig. 223). By the end of the study in 1995 (i.e. one year after the cessation of culling), incidence of TB in cattle was 76 per cent less in the removal area than in the comparison area and 86 per cent less in the removal area than in the Republic of Ireland as a whole. Clearly, then, culling of badgers had a substantial impact on levels of TB in cattle. However, since the trial involved only one experimental and one control area, it is not possible to generalise from the results.

In order to see whether culling would be equally successful in other parts of Ireland, a second and more extensive trial, the Four Areas Project, was carried out during a five-year period from 1997 to 2002. As the name suggests, this trial involved removal of badgers from four different areas, ranging from about 200 to 300 km^2 in size and located in Donegal, Monaghan, Kilkenny and Cork, respectively (Fig. 224). Each removal area was paired with a 'reference area' of roughly equal size, located close to the removal area but separated from it by a 'buffer area' up to 6 km wide. As in the East Offaly Project, the reference areas were not 'no-cull' areas: they were subjected to the same limited reactive culling

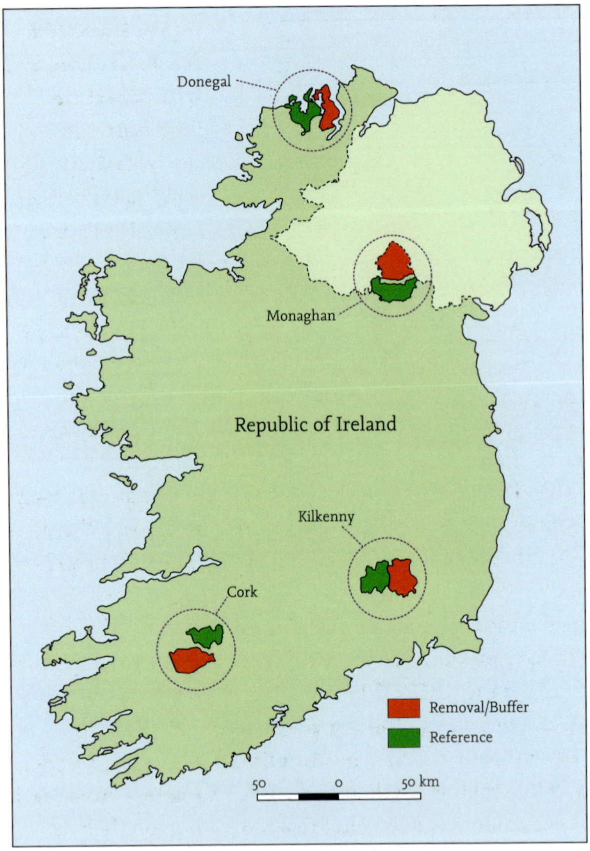

FIG 224. Locations of paired removal and reference areas in the Irish Four Areas Project.

regime as the rest of the Republic, involving culling of badgers on individual farms that suffered 'severe' TB outbreaks and where the source of the outbreak appeared to be badgers.

The results of the Four Areas Project indicate a progressive, year-on-year reduction in the relative incidence of TB in cattle within the experimental areas, such that TB levels had been substantially reduced by the end of the trial (Fig. 225). However, as in the East Offaly Project, analysis of the data is complicated by the fact that some culling occurred in the reference areas and by a variety of other methodological anomalies (see Bourne, 2007). Consequently, the exact extent of the reduction in cattle TB is controversial. Analysis of the data by Irish researchers claimed a reduction of about 60 per cent in Monaghan, 75 per cent in Cork and Kilkenny, and 96 per cent in Donegal (Griffin *et al.*, 2005), while analyses by UK researchers suggest a more modest overall reduction of about 50–75 per

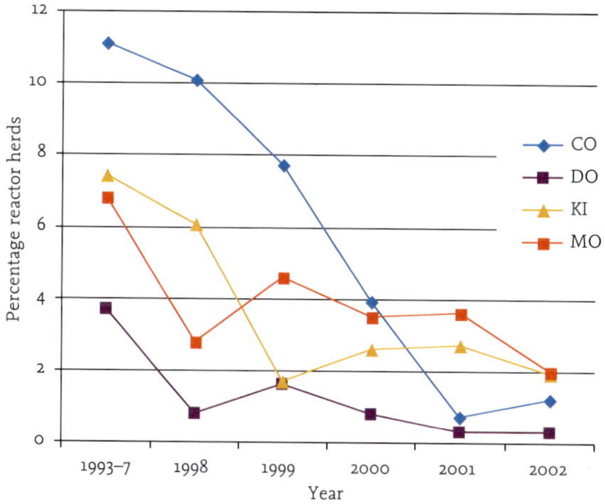

FIG 225. Results of the Four Areas culling trial. Percentage of cattle herds that tested positive for TB ('reactor herds') in each of the four trial areas, in the five years prior to, and during, the trial. Culling started in 1998 and ceased in 2002. (Based on data in Griffin *et al.*, 2005)

cent in the different areas (Godfray *et al.*, 2005; Bourne, 2007). Either way, it is clear that culling had a significant impact on levels of TB in cattle but also that there were considerable differences between the four removal areas in the extent and time-course of that impact.

Whichever figures one chooses to believe, the East Offaly Project and the Four Areas Project seem to have produced more rapid and more convincing reductions in cattle TB than did the RBCT. There has been much debate as to why this should be so (see Bourne, 2007). One probable reason is that badger removal was more complete in the Irish trials, partly owing to the use of snaring, rather than live-trapping, as the capture method and partly owing to a lower level of non-compliance (i.e. fewer landowners refusing to allow culling on their property). Another is that the boundaries of the Four Areas trial locations were specifically placed so as to incorporate natural barriers to badger movement, in the form of rivers, major roads, etc. Consequently, any perturbation effect, caused by immigration of neighbouring badgers into the culled areas, would have been minimised. But there are also differences in badger social organisation and population density between Britain and Ireland, as well as differences in farming practice, which almost certainly make the relationship between badgers and cattle different in the two countries. And, finally, the explanation may simply be that badgers cause a higher proportion of cattle TB incidents in Ireland than they do in Britain. For all of these reasons, the results of the Irish trials are not straightforwardly applicable to the British situation. Consequently, it is simplistic to argue, as some have done, that if proactive culling of badgers in the RBCT had been more thorough, there would have been a larger and more rapid decline in the incidence of cattle TB.

Whatever the case, the results of the East Offaly and Four Areas trials have been used to justify further culling of badgers in the Republic. Currently, a large-scale reactive culling programme is under way, whereby badgers are culled whenever, following an outbreak of TB in cattle, they are considered to be a likely cause. At first sight, the decision to implement reactive culling seems strange, since the RBCT showed that reactive culling was counterproductive and data from the reference areas of the East Offaly and Four Areas projects suggest that it had little effect. However, since, under the current policy, culling at a particular location can be repeated, it can result in the removal not just of badgers that were in that location to start with but also those that immigrate into the area from surrounding regions, once the original occupants have been culled. Over time, therefore, significant areas of the Republic of Ireland could be effectively cleared of badgers and there are fears that this is happening.

So far, culling has covered about 20 per cent of the Republic's total agricultural area, from which it is estimated that about two-thirds of badgers have been removed. The eventual aim is to maintain badger populations at less than 20 per cent of their original densities over 30 per cent of all agricultural land, which is predicted to correspond to a reduction of 25–30 per cent in the total national badger population (J. O'Keefe, cited in White *et al.*, 2008). In the longer term, however, the stated policy is to control TB in badgers by means of vaccination, and the Republic of Ireland is actively pursuing research into vaccine formulation and delivery (e.g. More & Good, 2006). In contrast to current policy in the UK, Ireland does not seem much interested in cattle vaccination as a control option.

TB AND BADGERS: THE FUTURE

Scientific considerations

It will be clear from the above account that a number of basic scientific questions relating to TB in badgers and cattle remain unanswered. Most importantly, although there is now indisputable evidence that cattle-to-cattle and badger-to-cattle transmission both occur, we do not know the relative importance of these two sources of infection. Given that proactive culling in the RBCT produced a decline of about 60 per cent in the incidence of TB in cattle (see Fig. 215), it looks as though at least 60 per cent of new cases of TB could be attributable to badgers. However, mathematical models suggest that the percentage could be as high as 75 per cent (Green *et al.*, 2008), and some have suggested that it could be as high as 95 per cent within hot-spot areas. However, we still cannot accurately predict the extent to which either badger-oriented management policies, such as vaccination of badgers or improvements to farm biosecurity, or cattle-oriented policies, such as improvements to the test-and-slaughter regime, are likely to impact on the problem of TB in cattle.

In addition, we do not know how badgers transmit TB to cattle; how close is the spatial association between the prevalence of TB in badgers and its occurrence in cattle; whether TB is self-sustaining in badgers; what proportion of infected badgers or cattle are infectious; or whether environmental contamination, for example of the soil surrounding latrines or setts, is a significant factor. It may seem absurd that fundamental questions such as these remain unanswered after decades of research, but disease problems involving wildlife reservoirs are notoriously difficult to tackle. In addition, TB is an intrinsically complex disease in terms of its epidemiology and there are serious practical difficulties in carrying out research on large numbers of either badgers or cattle. Not for nothing has TB been described as 'the most difficult animal health problem we face in Great Britain' (Reynolds, 2006). We have come a long way in terms of scientific understanding of the disease but there is still much to be learned.

Management considerations

As far as the UK is concerned, TB policy has entered, for the first time for many years, a period of relative stasis. The RBCT is over and culling in England has ceased. Badger and cattle vaccines are under development, but it will be some time before either is ready to be rolled out on a large scale. Modifications have been made to the test-and-slaughter regime, but it is not yet clear what impact they are having on the incidence of TB in cattle. The only disturbance to this sense of respite is that badger culling is under discussion once again in Wales and Northern Ireland. In the case of Northern Ireland, planning is still at an early stage but in Wales, agreement has already been reached as to the location of the area to be culled and the method to be used (i.e. live trapping followed by shooting, as in the RBCT). However, at the time of writing the decision to cull in Wales is being challenged in the courts and it would not be too surprising if, in the end, the plans come to nothing. In the Republic of Ireland, meanwhile, a major culling operation is in progress, but it is too early to say how this is affecting the incidence of TB in cattle.

The ISG Final Report predicted that cattle-oriented policies would be sufficient in and of themselves to bring about a decline in TB in Great Britain (Bourne, 2007). However, it remains to be seen whether this expectation is realised and, if it is, how great the decline will be. Improvements to the test-and-slaughter regime may curtail the further geographical spread of TB in cattle. However, if TB is self-sustaining in badgers (which is virtually certain) and if the percentage of new cattle TB incidents attributable to badgers exceeds 50 per cent (see above), then it seems self-evident that some kind of action against the wildlife reservoir will be necessary, at least in the hot-spot areas.

Almost certainly, therefore, effective management of TB will require a combination of different approaches targeted towards both badgers and cattle, and towards the interactions between them. In other words, there will be no single 'silver bullet' (White *et al.*, 2008). This, at any rate, seems to be the assumption underlying Defra policy, since research into vaccines for both badgers and cattle is being strongly supported and other options involving both badgers and cattle, such as enhanced biosecurity measures and further strengthening of the test-and-slaughter regime, are under active consideration.

And what about badger culling, which is, of all the possible management options, the one of most interest to readers of this book? It is easy to understand why farmers are frustrated by the lack of progress towards controlling what is, by any account, a serious disease situation. It is also easy to understand why this frustration results in calls for the resumption of badger culling. Culling has a strong intuitive appeal: it seems only common sense, when faced with a disease reservoir, to try to eliminate it; and the most obvious way of doing this is by eliminating the host species. However, the RBCT has shown that things are not that simple. At best, culling may not have much of an effect and, at worst, it may have unintended and counterproductive side-effects. And, despite the multiplicity of trials, the long-term effects of culling on the prevalence of TB, in either cattle or badgers, are still not known. From a political point of view, culling is hard to defend because of its unpopularity with the general public and because the economic costs of doing it are substantially greater than the immediate economic benefits that the expected reduction in cattle TB would bring (Jenkins *et al.*, 2010). It is still possible that culling would contribute usefully to TB control in certain well-defined circumstances or in combination with other measures such as vaccination or enhanced biosecurity (White *et al.*, 2008). However, the scientific case against isolated, one-off, spatially restricted culls of limited duration, such as were carried out in the RBCT, is very strong.

Appendix: Surveying for Badgers

IN COUNTRIES SUCH AS THE UK, where badgers enjoy a substantial level of legal protection, developers must take them into account when planning new road or housing schemes (see Chapter 9). This means, in the first instance, determining whether badgers are present in the area to be developed. Specialist consultancy firms or members of local badger groups are often called in to carry out an assessment of this type, which involves surveying the relevant area for the presence of setts, latrines, badger paths and runs, footprints, hair caught on barbed-wire fences, and snuffle holes. Most of these signs have been described and illustrated in previous chapters and all are relatively easy to recognise, so I shall not say much more about them here.

In some circumstances, however, more detailed information than the mere presence or absence of badgers is required. For example, the loss of a main sett will threaten the existence of an entire social group of badgers, whereas the loss of an outlier may be of little consequence. Therefore, it will be necessary, if a sett is threatened by a new development, to decide what type of sett it is. It may also be helpful to know how many animals use the sett in question, which requires some method of counting individual badgers. On a larger scale, badger counts may be needed to determine population size and population density for conservation or management purposes (see Chapter 1).

In yet other cases, it may be useful to know what fraction of a badger territory is occupied by an area scheduled for development, or whether the construction of a new road would result in part of an established territory becoming inaccessible. This requires that the boundaries of the territory be determined. Information about both territory sizes and social group sizes is also useful to scientists interested in the factors underlying differences in population density (see Chapter 7).

The purpose of this appendix is to provide a brief account of the methods available for determining the status of a particular sett, for measuring the size of a social group or population and for locating territory boundaries. One aim is to provide, in conjunction with Chapter 9, a succinct practical guide to the available methodology for would-be badger surveyors and others concerned with practical aspects of badger management. However, I also discuss the accuracy of the available methods and ask how important absolute accuracy is from a scientific point of view. In this respect, the contents of this appendix can be viewed as a methodological supplement to Chapters 1, 3, 7 and 8, describing, in more detail, how some of the data cited in those chapters were collected.

ASSESSING THE STATUS OF A SETT

As we saw in Chapter 3, UK surveyors recognise four different types of sett: main, annex, subsidiary and outlier. These are distinguished on the basis of their size and the manner in which they are used.

A main sett is the primary, year-round residence of an entire social group of badgers, and is used for breeding and overwintering. Main setts usually have multiple entrances; these entrances are often linked by obvious paths; there may be a scratching tree or playing area at the sett; and there is usually a sizeable latrine nearby. In addition, since main setts are relatively permanent structures and can be very old, their spoil heaps tend to be large. As a main sett is occupied year-round and by a whole group of badgers, several entrance holes may show signs of use – for example, they should be clear of debris, there may be fresh footprints, and there may be signs of recent digging or of bedding collection (Fig. 226a). Other signs that a sett is occupied are that in summer; flies may be seen buzzing in and out of the entrances, attracted by the odour of the occupants. In winter, steam may be seen rising from the entrances of an occupied sett or frost may have accumulated around them as a consequence of condensation (Fig. 226b and c).

Annex, subsidiary and outlier setts are less easy to define and, as a consequence, more difficult to distinguish. An annex sett is a kind of satellite main sett: it usually has several entrances, is close to (< 50 m from) a main sett and is occupied for most or all of the year. It may well be used for breeding and is typically connected to the main sett by an obvious path. Subsidiary setts share some of these features: they often have several entrances and may be semi-permanently occupied and used for breeding. However, they are located further away from the main sett and there is less coming and going between a main sett

FIG 226. Signs that a sett is occupied: (a – top left) fresh footprints in an entrance (E. Do Linh San); (b – top right) steam rising from an entrance (M. Clark); (c – above) frost around an entrance. (Dassenwerkgroep Brabant)

and a subsidiary sett than between a main sett and an annex. Outliers are usually single-entrance setts and are only used sporadically, by one animal at a time, for purposes of emergency refuge, for resting during the night, as a temporary dwelling place during the process of dispersal or as a temporary sleeping place during the summer. They may remain completely unused for long periods of time. Outliers are also more numerous than subsidiary setts or annexes, since a typical territory contains several outliers but only one main sett, one subsidiary sett and, at most, one annex.

Recorders in UK and Irish national sett surveys have been instructed to take into account all of these criteria when classifying setts (e.g. Cresswell *et al.*, 1990). However, there are obvious problems, both in principle and in practice, with this approach. First, it is clear that some of the criteria are arbitrary (for example, the stipulation that an annex must be within 50 m of a main sett), while others are subjective (for example, there is no definition of what constitutes 'sporadic' use). Second, criteria based on continuity of use are impossible to apply in a single visit, which may be all that is possible in the context of a one-off survey. Third, and perhaps most importantly, it is clear that the setts within any one category cover a wide range in terms of both appearance and use, and that there is overlap between the different categories. For example, main setts with only one or two entrances are not uncommon in areas of low population density, or in upland habitat where the geology puts constraints on digging. Conversely, subsidiary setts and annexes in areas with easily dug soil can have more entrances than many main setts have elsewhere.

Consequently, while it is easy to distinguish setts at the extreme ends of the continuum (e.g. an ancient multi-entrance main sett versus a disused single-entrance outlier), problems arise in the case of intermediates (e.g. a small main sett versus a large subsidiary sett). Additional insights can be gained from considering the pattern of setts over a wider area, since a typical territory contains multiple outliers but only one main sett, one subsidiary sett and, at most, one annex. So, for example, a well-used multiple-entrance sett is more likely to be an annex than a main sett if there is an even larger sett nearby. But even so, ambiguous cases sometimes arise, such as when a single social group uses more than one main sett.

In cases where the status of a sett is unclear, bait-marking can provide confirmatory information. Consider, for example, a case in which a sett of ambiguous status occurs between what appear to be two main setts (Fig. 227). By bait-marking each of the three setts, it is possible, at least in principle, to determine whether the sett in question is a main sett (Fig. 277a) or a subsidiary (Fig. 277b). However, bait-marking suffers from some serious practical

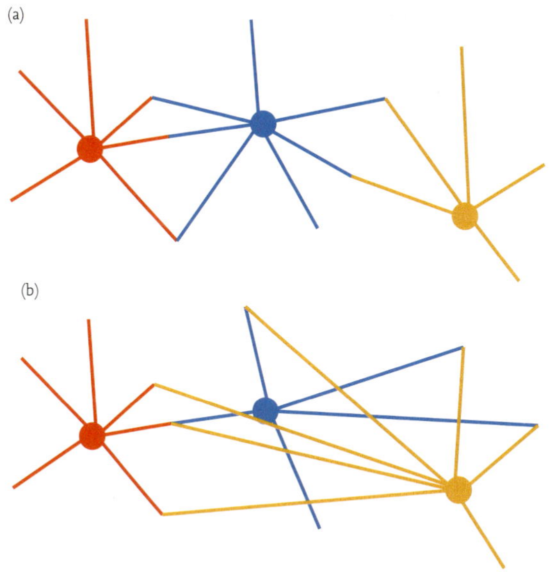

FIG 227. Use of bait-marking to determine the status of a sett. In (a) the blue sett is a main sett, because it is surrounded by its own territory. In (b) it must be a subsidiary sett, because it is within the territory of a larger sett (the yellow sett).

limitations. First, it is relatively time-consuming and labour intensive, so is only worthwhile when special importance attaches to the sett in question and when no decision can be reached on the basis of a simple survey. Second, bait-marking can only be carried out in the spring and autumn when boundary latrines are in frequent use and it cannot be used at all in urban areas or where badger population density is low. Consequently, it not always feasible, even in principle.

Given that the vast majority of sett surveys base their results on the external appearance of individual setts, it is important to ask how accurate this method is. In fact, it seems to work reasonably well. Surveyors report little practical difficulty in classifying setts, suggesting that ambiguous cases are rare. In addition, surveys in England, Northern Ireland and the Irish Republic have produced remarkably similar results with respect to the overall number of annex setts, subsidiary setts and outliers per main sett, suggesting that repeated applications of the same methodology produce consistent results (see Wilson *et al.*, 1997). There has also been one attempt, in the Republic of Ireland, to validate survey results independently, by means of follow-up trapping operations. This study showed that setts previously classified as main setts were indeed, in most cases, occupied by an entire social group of badgers (Smal, 1995). On the whole, then, sett surveys probably do a reasonable job of distinguishing main from secondary setts.

MEASURING POPULATION DENSITY

Like many mammals, badgers are hard to count directly: they are nocturnal, shy and, in many places, not very numerous (Wilson & Delahay, 2001). Attempts have been made to estimate population density directly by what is called 'distance sampling', which means driving along a predetermined route at night, spotlighting any badgers that are within range of the vehicle and estimating their distance from the vehicle. From this information, it is possible, using various algorithms, to estimate the number of badgers in the area as a whole. However, this method can only be used in relatively open landscapes and depends on animals not being scared off by the approach of a vehicle. At best, it provides only a rough, comparative indication of badger abundance (Hounsome *et al.*, 2005).

Badger setts, by contrast, are often known to local residents, gamekeepers, foresters and hunters or, if not known, are relatively easy to find and record. For these reasons, counting setts has often been used as a substitute for counting badgers. There are, however, two problems with this approach. First, in order to know how many social groups of badgers occupy a given region, it is necessary to distinguish 'main' setts (setts that constitute the permanent home of a social group – see above) from 'secondary' setts (setts that are used only occasionally). This distinction is crucial, because a social group of badgers almost always has only one main sett, whereas the number of secondary setts per social group is unpredictable. Hence, the number of main setts in a given area reflects fairly accurately the number of social groups, whereas the total number of setts does not. Guidelines have been developed to enable surveyors to distinguish main setts from secondary setts (see above), and these seem to work well in practice. However, estimates of the number of main setts in a region are unlikely to be completely accurate, not only because some setts may be misclassified but also because some may be missed altogether.

The second problem is that even if we know the number of main setts in an area, and therefore the number of social groups, we also need to know the average number of badgers per social group in order to arrive at an estimate of population density. How, then, can social group size be determined?

Methods of counting badgers at setts

The simplest way of estimating social group size is to sit at a main sett in the evening and count the badgers as they emerge. However, since badgers have the annoying habit of emerging from and disappearing back into a sett repeatedly before going off to forage, and since individuals are rarely distinguishable from one another, it is easy to count the same badger more than once using this method. Consequently, direct observation can only provide a figure for minimum group size, defined as the largest number of badgers seen simultaneously. The accuracy of the estimate can be increased by using video surveillance (i.e. monitoring the sett with the type of night-vision camera used for security purposes), but even then, some individuals may be missed (Scheppers *et al.*, 2007).

As an alternative to direct observation, attempts have been made to estimate social group size using field signs such as the number of used entrances per main sett or the rate of deposition of fresh faeces at latrines. However, these methods have proved unsatisfactory (Wilson *et al.*, 2003; Sadlier *et al.*, 2004). A more promising approach may be the use of what is called 'remotely collected DNA', which means DNA that can be obtained without trapping the animal and

FIG 228. Hair trapping as a method of counting badgers: (above left) a barbed-wire hair trap placed over a badger path – note the tufts of hairs caught on the wire; (left) badger passing beneath a hair trap. (T. Scheppers)

taking a tissue sample. One such source of DNA is faeces, which contain, on their surface, cells from the intestinal lining of the animal that left the faecal deposit. It is possible to extract DNA from these cells and to obtain from it a genetic profile or 'fingerprint' that identifies the individual in question. Consequently, if samples of faeces are collected from a badger latrine over a period of time, and DNA is extracted from them and genotyped, the number of individual genetic profiles corresponds to the number of badgers using the latrine. One of my postgraduate students, Alain Frantz, developed a procedure for extracting and genotyping DNA from badger faeces and showed that this method could indeed provide an accurate estimate of badger social group size (Wilson *et al.*, 2003; Frantz *et al.*, 2004). However, the procedure is prohibitively expensive for most purposes, owing to the laboratory costs involved in analysing the DNA.

Alternatively, DNA can be obtained from hairs plucked remotely from the animal using a 'hair trap' – which simply means positioning a strand of barbed wire or sticky tape above a badger path, so that any badger using the path leaves a few hairs behind (Fig. 228). The follicles attached to these plucked hairs yield DNA that is of better quality, and hence easier to analyse, than DNA obtained from faeces. Thus, by 'trapping' hairs at a main sett over a period of a few weeks and counting up the number of individual genetic profiles that these hairs represent, one can count the number of badgers present at the sett (Frantz *et al.*, 2004; Scheppers *et al.*, 2007). This method is at least as accurate as using DNA from faeces and is somewhat less expensive, but is still too costly for use on anything other than a local scale.

A final method of counting badgers is by what is called 'capture-mark-recapture'. This method involves repeatedly trapping as many badgers as possible from a main sett and marking each one, the first time it is captured, with some kind of permanent identification. This can be done by tattooing a number on the inside of the animal's hind leg or by injecting, subcutaneously, a small capsule containing a 'bar code' that can be read electronically. The expectation is that, provided trapping continues for long enough, all of the resident badgers will be trapped. However, this expectation is seldom justified in practice, owing to the existence of 'trap shy' individuals. Consequently, an estimate of group size has to be arrived at by a process of extrapolation, and various computer programs are available for doing this. In addition, capture-mark-recapture is very labour intensive and inevitably impacts, at least to some degree, on the welfare of the animals involved. In short, there is currently no way of counting the number of badgers in a given area, or the number using a particular sett, that is accurate, cost-effective and non-invasive.

Problems with recording social group sizes

Unfortunately, the difficulties involved in estimating social group sizes are not solely due to imperfections in the methods available for counting badgers: there are also problems relating to sample sizes and to the reporting of data. These problems are unlikely to matter from a practical, management point of view but they are troublesome for scientists interested in comparing data on social group sizes from different studies (see Chapters 7 and 8).

One such complication is that group size varies seasonally, being highest in spring when new cubs have been recruited. For this reason, the best measure of group size is the number of adults per group. However, many studies just report the total number of badgers per group, making it unclear how many of these were cubs of the year in question.

A second factor is that large-scale long-term studies, such as those undertaken at Woodchester Park and Wytham Woods, have revealed a considerable degree of year-to-year variation in social group sizes (see Fig. 229), and they have also shown that different groups, in the same study area, can differ considerably in size from one another within a single year. Consequently, estimates of average group size should ideally combine data from several years and be based on a reasonably large number of groups. Unfortunately, few studies meet either of these requirements.

Estimating population density at a regional or national level

Despite the problems inherent in estimating social group size using the method of capture-mark-recapture (see above), the best available data on population density at a local level come from several relatively long-term capture-mark-recapture studies

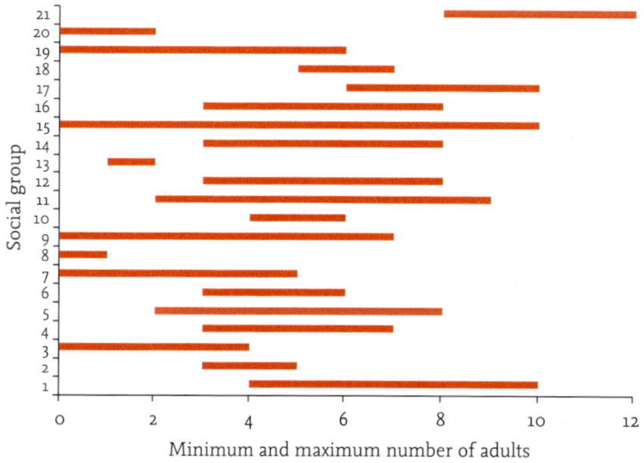

FIG 229. Variation in the size of individual social groups at Woodchester Park between 1980 and 1985. For example, Group 1 contained from four to ten adults during the period in question. (Based on data in Cheeseman *et al.*, 1987)

carried out in the UK. These mostly revealed average group sizes of about five to six adults (see Krebs *et al.*, 1997, for references), and it used to be assumed that this was typical of the species as a whole. More recently, however, it has become clear that social group size varies from region to region and from country to country (see Chapter 7). Consequently, in order to estimate population density at a particular locality, it is necessary both to survey the relevant area for main setts and to estimate average social group size: one cannot simply assume that group size is the same everywhere.

A careful study of badgers in Northern Ireland by Sarah Feore and Ian Montgomery provides a telling illustration of the extent to which estimates of national population size depend on assumptions about social group size. Prior to this study, the population of badgers in Northern Ireland had been estimated to contain 52,000 adults, based on the assumption that there were, on average, 5.9 adults per main sett. (This assumption was derived from trapping studies carried out previously in the UK.) However, when Feore and Montgomery observed a sample of setts in Northern Ireland, she found average group sizes of 6.5 adults in parkland habitat, 2.5 in upland and 2.0 in an agricultural region. When these data on average group sizes were combined with information about the relative areas of parkland, upland and agricultural habitat in Northern Ireland as a whole, the total estimated population of badgers dropped to 38,000: that is, about 25 per cent less than the previous estimate of 52,000 (Feore & Montgomery, 1999). A similar recent study in the Republic of Ireland has resulted in an even more dramatic reduction in the population estimate, from 200,000 to 84,000 badgers (Sleeman *et al.*, 2009). These studies therefore call into question the accuracy of most data on regional and national population densities.

ESTIMATING TERRITORY SIZE AND SHAPE

Bait-marking

The best method of determining where the boundaries of a territory lie is bait-marking, the practical application of which was described in Chapter 6 (see also Delahay *et al.*, 2000a, for further details). As we have seen, however, bait-marking is by no means universally applicable, since it only works at certain times of year and in rural habitats where the population density of badgers is relatively high.

It is less commonly realised that bait-marking, on its own, can give a misleading impression of territory size, even when it is applied in optimal conditions. Ideally, the members of a social group defecate only in the latrines surrounding their own territory, in which case bait-marking will provide a good

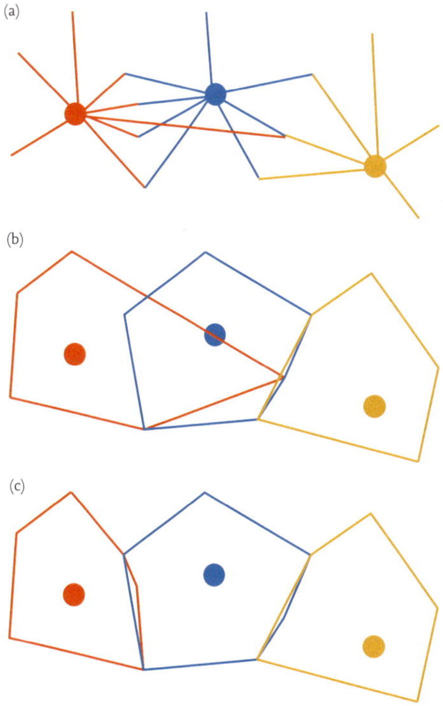

FIG 230. Problems involved in the interpretation of bait-marking data. (a) A badger from the red sett has defecated on the far side of the blue territory, producing an anomalous marker return. (b) Inclusion of this anomalous marker return suggests a considerable degree of overlap between the red and blue territories. (c) Excluding the anomalous marker return suggests a pattern of non-overlapping territories.

indication of the territory boundaries. In practice, however, badgers sometimes make forays into neighbouring territories, especially during the spring mating season, which happens also to be the time of year when bait-marking is most effective. During the course of such forays, the animals in question may defecate, and therefore deposit bait-markers, in 'foreign' latrines (Fig. 230a).

Incorporating these occasional extra-territorial forays into the bait-marking map (Fig. 230b) would clearly give a misleading impression of territory size and of the extent to which neighbouring territories overlap, so it is general practice to exclude them (Fig. 230c). It is important to realise, however, that this process of exclusion relies on intuitive judgement as to what constitutes an 'anomalous' result. In other words, it is a kind of subjective massaging of the data, making bait-marking a less objective method than it appears to be on the surface. If additional information about the true location of territory boundaries is available in the form of boundary paths, this can be used as an aid in interpreting bait-marking data. However, such information is only available when population density is high.

The Dirichlet tessellation method

An alternative, less labour-intensive and in some respects more objective method of locating territory boundaries is by the Dirichlet tessellation method. This depends on the assumption that territory boundaries lie at the halfway point between adjacent main setts (see Chapters 7 and 8). In practice, all you need to do is to take a map of the main setts in a given area, draw a line between each pair of adjacent main setts and then bisect each of these lines with another line at right angles to it (Fig. 231a). By doing this between all pairs of neighbouring main setts and joining up the relevant lines, you end up with a set of irregularly shaped polygonal areas or 'tiles', which are technically known as 'Dirichlet tessellations' (Fig. 231b).

On the face of it, this method provides an easy way for surveyors to determine, say, where an area scheduled for development, or the route of a new road, lies in relation to existing territory boundaries. However, caution is required for two reasons. First, the method depends crucially on main setts being correctly identified in the first place, and, as we have seen, this is not always straightforward. Second, although territory boundaries estimated by the Dirichlet tessellation method correspond well with bait-marking results in some

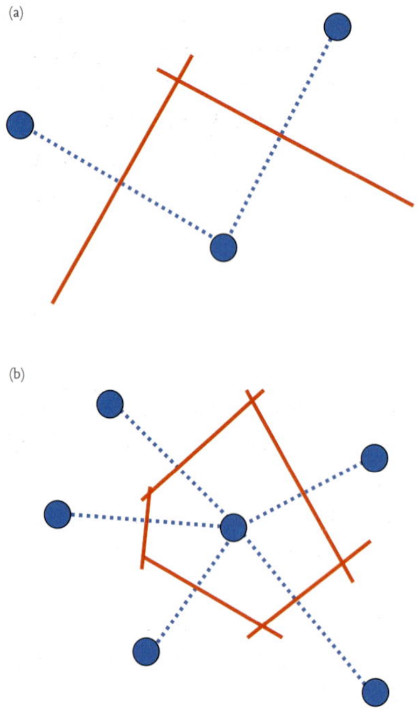

FIG 231. Estimating territory boundaries using the Dirichlet tessellation method. (a) Each pair of adjacent main setts (blue circles) is connected by a line (blue dashed lines). Territory boundaries (red) are then drawn at right-angles to, and bisecting, these lines. (b) A complete territory boundary constructed by this method.

areas, the match is less convincing in others (Doncaster & Woodroffe, 1993). Probably, the method performs best in areas of high population density, where main setts are relatively close together.

Radio telemetry

Radio telemetry is unlikely to be an option in the context of small-scale management of badgers owing to the cost of the requisite equipment, the necessity of trapping animals in order to fit radio transmitters and the labour intensiveness of the process of data collection. However, it has been the method of choice for scientists wanting to investigate the structure of badger populations in areas where bait-marking is impossible.

Strictly speaking, radio telemetry provides data on badger ranging behaviour, not on territoriality. That is, it relates to where badgers go, not to the area of land that they defend. Although it is generally assumed that range boundaries are the same as territory boundaries, this was not the case in the population of badgers that my research group studied in Sussex, where ranges were considerably larger than territories (see Chapter 7). In addition, as is the case for bait-marking, decisions have to be made concerning the inclusion or exclusion of data resulting from occasional forays into what appear to be neighbouring territories. Various computer programs are available for doing this but they yield different results, and there is no consensus as to which is the best. Finally, the problem of sample size is just as acute with respect to territory size estimation as it is with group size estimation, yet some studies are based on data from as few as three individuals or groups. Altogether, then, determination of range sizes from radio-tracking data is far from straightforward, making it difficult to compare the results provided by different studies

CONCLUSIONS

It is relatively easy to detect the presence of badgers in an area, because they leave various signs that are both conspicuous in themselves and, in most cases, easily distinguishable from those of other species. Problems arise, however, in determining the status of setts and in estimating social group sizes, population densities and territory sizes. How important are these problems from a practical and scientific point of view?

Misclassification of setts has important implications in the context of planning applications, because the decision as to how a sett and its occupants should be treated hinges mainly on the status of the sett in question (see

Chapter 9). Since mistaking a main sett for a secondary sett might result in the destruction of an entire social group of badgers, decisions concerning the status of a threatened sett should always be conservative. That is, a sett whose status is uncertain should be given the benefit of the doubt, and assumed to be a main sett. In addition, if a sett is to be destroyed, it should always be excavated cautiously, because even what appears to be a disused outlier might have a badger inside it.

Misclassification of setts also has adverse consequences for the estimation of population density, because the latter is usually based on counting the number of main setts per unit area. But estimation of population density also requires accurate information about average social group size, which is considerably more difficult to obtain. This has implications from the point of view of conservation, because it means that national and regional estimates of population density are unlikely to be accurate.

Finally, the same problems, and also those affecting the estimation of territory sizes, undermine attempts to compare different scientific studies with respect to the variables of social group size, territory size and population density. Consequently, the estimates of national population density cited in Chapter 1, and the data on social group sizes, territory sizes and local population densities cited in Chapter 7, should be treated with caution.

References

Aaris-Sorensen, J. (1987). Past and present distribution of badgers *Meles meles* in the Copenhagen area. *Biological Conservation* **41**: 15–165.

Aaris-Sorensen, J. (1995). Road-kills of badgers (*Meles meles*) in Denmark. *Annales Zoologici Fennici* **32**: 31–6.

Abramov, A. V. (2002). Variation of the baculum structure of the Palearctic badger (Carnivora, Mustelidae, *Meles*). *Russian Journal of Theriology* **1**: 57–60.

Abramov, A. V. (2003). The head colour pattern of the Eurasian badgers (Mustelidae, *Meles*). *Small Carnivore Conservation* **29**: 5–7.

Abramov, A. V. & S. G. Medvedev (2003). Notes on zoogeography and taxonomy of the badgers (Carnivora: Mustelidae: *Meles*) and some of their fleas (Siphonaptera: Ceratophyllidae: *Paraceras*). *Zoosystematica Rossica* **11**: 397–402.

Abramov, A. V. & A. Y. Puzachenko (2005). Sexual dimorphism of craniological characters in Eurasian badgers, *Meles* spp. (Carnivora, Mustelidae). *Zoologischer Anzeiger* **244**: 11–29.

Ahnlund, H. (1980). Sexual maturity and breeding season of the badger, *Meles meles*, in Sweden. *Journal of Zoology, London* **190**: 77–95.

Andersen, J. (1954). The food of the Danish badger (*Meles meles* Danicus Degerbol) with special reference to the summer months. *Communications from Vildtbiologisk Station Kalo No. 12*. Copenhagen, Vildtbiologisk Station Kalo: 1–75.

Anderson, R. M. & W. Trewhella (1985). Population dynamics of the badger (*Meles meles*) and the epidemiology of bovine tuberculosis (*Mycobacterium bovis*). *Philosophical Transactions of the Royal Society of London Series B: Biological Sciences* **310**: 327–81.

Apeldoorn, R. C. v. *et al.* (2006). Dynamics of a local badger (*Meles meles*) population in the Netherlands over the years 1983–2001. *Mammalian Biology* **71**: 25–38.

Asprea, A. & A. M. De Marinis (2005). The diet of the badger *Meles meles* (Mustelidae, Carnivora) on the Apennines (central Italy). *Mammalia* **69**: 89–95.

Baker, P. J. & S. Harris (2007). Urban mammals: what does the future hold? An analysis of the factors affecting patterns of use of residential gardens in Great Britain. *Mammal Review* **37**: 297–315.

Baker, S. E. *et al.* (2007). Learned food aversion with and without an odour cue for protecting untreated baits from wild mammal foraging. *Applied Animal Behaviour Science* **102**: 410–28.

Balestrieri, A. *et al.* (2004). Diet of the Eurasian badger (*Meles meles*) in an agricultural riverine habitat (NW Italy). *Hystrix Italian Journal of Mammalogy* **15**: 3–12.

Balestrieri, A. *et al.* (2006). Reintroduction of the Eurasian badger (*Meles meles*) in a protected area of northern Italy. *Italian Journal of Zoology* **73**: 227–35.

Baranauskas, K. *et al.* (2005). Vilnius city theriofauna. *Acta Zoologica Lituanica* **15**: 228–38.

Barer, M. *et al.* (2008). *The Society for General Microbiology Independent Overview of Bovine Tuberculosis Research in the United Kingdom: A Defra Sponsored Review.* Department for Environment, Food and Rural Affairs, London: 77.

Benham, P. F. J. & D. M. Broom (1989). Interactions between cattle and badgers at pasture with reference to bovine tuberculosis transmission. *British Veterinary Journal* **145**: 226–41.

Benham, P. F. J. & D. M. Broom (1991). Responses of dairy cows to badger urine and faeces on pasture with reference to bovine tuberculosis transmission. *British Veterinary Journal* **147**: 517–32.

Bevanger, K. (1990). Grevling som konfliktfaktor i et urbant miljo. *NINA Forskningsrapport* (Trondheim.) **11**: 1–22.

Bevanger, K. & H. Brøseth (1998). Body temperature changes in wild-living badgers *Meles meles* through the winter. *Wildlife Biology* **4**: 41–5.

Bevanger, K. & E. R. Lindström (1995). Distributional history of the European badger *Meles meles* in Scandinavia during the 20th century. *Annales Zoologici Fennici* **32**: 5–9.

Bevanger, K. *et al.* (1996). Økologi og populasjobsbiologi hos europeisk grevling *Meles meles* L. i en urban-rural gradient i Sør-Trøndelag. *NINA Fagrapport* (Trondheim) **23**: 1–48.

Biancardi, C. M. *et al.* (1995). Analisi della alimentazione del tasso, *Meles meles* (L.), nell' Alto Luinese (Provincia di Varese, Italia). *Atti della Società Italiana di Scienze Naturali e del Museo Civico di Storia Naturale di Milano* **134**: 265–80.

Blakeborough, J. F. & A. E. Pease (1914). *The Life and Habits of the Badger.* 'The Foxhound' Offices, London.

Bock, W. F. (1988a). Die Bedeutung des Untergrundes für die Grösse von Bauen des Dachses (*Meles meles*) am Beispiel zweier Gebiete Südostbayerns. *Zeitschrift für Säugetierkunde* **53**: 49–57.

Bock, W. F. (1988b). Untersuchungen zur Lage und zum Mikroklima von Dachsbauen (*Meles meles*). *Zeitschrift für Jagdwissenschaft* **34**: 141–52.

Boesi, R. & C. M. Biancardi (2002). Diet of the Eurasian badger *Meles meles* (Linnaeus, 1758) in the Natural Reserve of Lago di Piano, northern Italy. *Mammalian Biology* **67**: 120–5.

Bohm, M. *et al.* (2009). Contact networks in a wildlife-livestock host community: identifying high-risk individuals in the transmission of bovine TB among badgers and cattle. *PLoS One* **4**: 1–12.

Bourne, F. J. (2007). *Bovine TB: The Scientific Evidence. Final report of the Independent Scientific Group on Cattle TB.* Department for Environment, Food and Rural Affairs, London.

Brøseth, H. *et al.* (1997). Spatial organization and habitat utilization of badgers *Meles meles*: effects of food patch dispersion in the boreal forest of central Norway. *Zeitschrift für Säugetierkunde-International Journal of Mammalian Biology* **62**: 12–22.

Brown, J. A. & C. L. Cheeseman (1996). The effect of translocation on a social group of badgers (*Meles meles*). *Animal Welfare* **5**: 289–309.

Brown, J. A. *et al.* (1993). *The development of field techniques for studying potential modes of transmission of bovine tuberculosis from badgers to cattle.* In: *The Badger* (Ed. Hayden, T. J.). Royal Irish Academy, Dublin: 139–53.

Buesching, C. D. & D. W. Macdonald (2001). *Scent-marking behaviour of the European badger (*Meles meles*): resource defence or individual advertisement?* In: *Chemical Signals in Vertebrates 9* (Eds Marchlewska-Koj, A., Lepri, J. P. and Muller-Schwartze, D.). Kluwer Academic/Plenum Publishers, New York: 321–7.

Buesching, C. D. & D. W. Macdonald (2004). Variations in scent-marking behaviour of European badgers *Meles meles* in the vicinity of their setts. *Acta Theriologica* **49**: 235–46.

Buesching, C. D. *et al.* (2002a). Variations in colour and volume of the subcaudal gland secretion of badgers (*Meles meles*) in relation to sex, season and individual-specific parameters. *Mammalian Biology* **67**: 147–56.

Buesching, C. D. *et al.* (2002b). Gas-chromatographic analyses of the subcaudal gland secretion of the European badger (*Meles meles*). Part I: Chemical differences related to individual parameters. *Journal of Chemical Ecology* **28**: 41–56.

Buesching, C. D. *et al.* (2002c). Gas-chromatographic analyses of the subcaudal gland secretion of the European badger (*Meles meles*) Part II: Time-related variation in the individual-specific composition. *Journal of Chemical Ecology* **28**: 57–69.

Buesching, C. D. *et al.* (2003). The social function of allo-marking in the European badger (*Meles meles*). *Behaviour* **140**: 965–80.

Buesching, C. D. *et al.* (2009). Seasonal and inter-individual variation in testosterone levels in badgers *Meles meles*: evidence for the existence of two endocrinological phenotypes. *Journal of Comparative Physiology A* **195**: 865–71.

Butler, J. M. & T. J. Roper (1995). Escape tactics and alarm responses in badgers *Meles meles* – a field experiment. *Ethology* **99**: 313–22.

Butler, J. M. & T. J. Roper (1996). Ectoparasites and sett use in European badgers. *Animal Behaviour* **52**: 621–9.

Butler, J. M. *et al.* (1994). Investigation of badger (*Meles meles*) setts using soil resistivity measurements. *Journal of Zoology, London* **232**: 409–18.

Canivenc, R. (1966). A study of progestation in the European badger (*Meles meles* L.). *Symposia of the Zoological Society of London* **15**: 15–26.

Canivenc, R. & M. Bonnin-Laffargue (1981). Environmental control of delayed implantation in the European badger (*Meles meles*). *Journal of Reproduction and Fertility* **29**: 25–33.

Carpenter, P. J. (2002). A study of mating systems, inbreeding avoidance and TB resistance in the Eurasian badger (*Meles meles*) using microsatellite markers (PhD thesis, Molecular Ecology Laboratory, University of Sheffield, Sheffield).

Carpenter, P. J. *et al.* (2005). Mating system of the Eurasian badger, *Meles meles*, in a high-density population. *Molecular Ecology* **14**: 273–84.

Carter, S. P. *et al.* (2007). Culling-induced social perturbation in Eurasian badgers *Meles meles* and the management of TB in cattle: an analysis of a critical problem in applied ecology. *Proceedings of the Royal Society B: Biological Sciences* **274**: 2769–77.

Cheeseman, C. L. & P. J. Mallinson (1981). Behaviour of badgers (*Meles meles*) infected with bovine tuberculosis. *Journal of Zoology, London* **194**: 284–9.

Cheeseman, C. L. *et al.* (1987). Badger population dynamics in a high-density area. *Symposia of the Zoological Society of London* **58**: 279–94.

Cheeseman, C. L. *et al.* (1988). Comparison of dispersal and other movements in two badger (*Meles meles*) populations. *Mammal Review* **18**: 51–9.

Cheeseman, C. L. *et al.* (1993). *Recolonisation by badgers in Gloucestershire.* In: *The Badger* (Ed. Hayden, T. J.). Royal Irish Academy, Dublin: 78–93.

Christian, S. F. (1993). Behavioural ecology of the Eurasian badger (*Meles meles*): space use, territoriality and social behaviour (PhD thesis, School of Biological Sciences, University of Sussex, Falmer, Brighton): 299.

Christian, S. F. (1994). Dispersal and other intergroup movements in badgers, *Meles meles. Zeitschrift für Säugetierkunde-International Journal of Mammalian Biology* **59**: 218–23.

Christian, S. F. (1995). Observations of extra-group mating and mate-defence behaviour in badgers, *Meles meles. Journal of Zoology, London* **237**: 668–70.

Ciampalini, B. & S. Lovari (1985). Food-habits and trophic niche overlap of the badger (*Meles meles* L.) and the red fox (*Vulpes vulpes* L.) in a Mediterranean coastal area. *Zeitschrift für Säugetierkunde-International Journal of Mammalian Biology* **50**: 226–34.

Clarke, G. P. *et al.* (1998). Effects of roads on badger *Meles meles* populations in south-west England. *Biological Conservation* **86**: 117–24.

Cleary, G. P. (2007). The diet of the Eurasian Badger (*Meles meles*) in the Republic of Ireland (PhD thesis, Dept of Zoology, Trinity College, Dublin): 179.

Clements, E. D. *et al.* (1988). The national badger sett survey. *Mammal Review* **18**: 1–9.

Clifton-Hadley, R. S. *et al.* (1995). The occurrence of *Mycobacterium bovis* infection in cattle in and around an area subject to extensive badger (*Meles meles*) control. *Epidemiology and Infection* **114**: 179–93.

Conradt, L. (1993). Food, setts and mates as factors underlying social territoriality in the European badger, *Meles meles.* Diplomarbeit, Facultät für Biologie, Universität Tubingen, Tubingen.

Corner, L. A. L. (2006). The role of wild animal populations in the epidemiology of tuberculosis in domestic animals: how to assess the risk. *Veterinary Microbiology* **112**: 303–12.

Cosivi, O. *et al.* (1998). Zoonotic tuberculosis due to *Mycobacterium bovis* in developing countries. *Emerging Infectious Diseases* **4**: 59–70.

Council of Europe (1979). Convention on the conservation of European wildlife and natural habitats. Bern: <conventions.coe.int/Treaty/en/Treaties/Html/104.htm>

Courtenay, O. *et al.* (2006). Is *Mycobacterium bovis* in the environment important for the persistence of bovine tuberculosis? *Biology Letters* **2**: 460–2.

Cowlin, R. A. D. (1967). An excavation of a badger sett in Southend. *Essex Naturalist* **32**: 70–72.

Cowlin, R. A. D. (1972). The distribution of the badger in Essex. *Essex Naturalist* **33**: 1–8.

Cresswell, P. *et al.* (1989). The badger (*Meles meles*) in Britain: present status and future population changes. *Biological Journal of the Linnean Society* **38**: 91–101.

Cresswell, P. *et al.* (1990). *The History, Distribution, Status and Habitat Requirements of the Badger in Britain.* Nature Conservancy Council, Peterborough.

Cresswell, W. J. & S. Harris (1988). Foraging behavior and home-range utilization in a suburban badger (*Meles meles*) population. *Mammal Review* **18**: 37–49.

Cresswell, W. J. *et al.* (1992). To breed or not to breed – an analysis of the social and density-dependent constraints on the fecundity of female badgers (*Meles meles*). *Philosophical Transactions of the Royal Society of London Series B: Biological Sciences* **338**: 393–407.

Da Silva, J. *et al.* (1994). Net costs of group living in a solitary forager, the Eurasian badger (*Meles meles*). *Behavioral Ecology* **5**: 151–8.

Danilov, P. I. & I. L. Tumanov (1972). *Male reproductive cycles in the Mustelidae.* In: *Biology of Mustelids: Some Soviet Research. Vol.* 2 (Ed. King, C. M.). DSIR Science Information Division, Wellington, NZ: 70–80.

Danilov, P. I. & I. L. Tumanov (1975). *Female reproductive cycles in the Mustelidae.* In: *Biology of Mustelids: Some Soviet Research. Vol.* 2 (Ed. King, C. M.). DSIR Science Information Division, Wellington, NZ: 81–92.

Davidson, A. (1999). *The Oxford Companion to Food.* Oxford University Press, Oxford.

Davies, J. M. *et al.* (1987). Seasonal distribution of road kills in the European badger (*Meles meles*). *Journal of Zoology, London* **211**: 525–9.

Davies, J. M. *et al.* (1988). The anal gland secretion of the European badger (*Meles meles*) and its role in social communication. *Journal of Zoology, London* **216**: 455–63.

Davies, R. W. (1971). The Roman military diet. *Brittania* **2**: 122–42.

Davison, J. (2007). Ecology and behaviour of urban badgers (*Meles meles*) (PhD thesis, Department of Biology and Environmental Science, University of Sussex, Falmer, Brighton): 140.

Davison, J. *et al.* (2008a). Urban badger setts: characteristics, patterns of use and management implications. *Journal of Zoology* **275**: 190–200.

Davison, J. *et al.* (2008b). Restricted ranging behaviour in a high-density population of urban badgers. *Journal of Zoology* **277**: 46–53.

de Lisle, G. W. *et al.* (2001). *Mycobacterium bovis* in free-living and captive wildlife, including farmed deer. *Revue Scientifique et Technique de l'Office International des Épizooties* **20**: 86–111.

Defra (2006). *Public Consultation on Controlling the Spread of Bovine Tuberculosis in Cattle in High Incidence Areas in England: Badger Culling – Summary of Responses.* Department of Environment, Food and Rural Affairs, London.

Del Bove, E. & R. Isotti (2001). The European badger (*Meles meles*) diet in a Mediterranean area. *Hystrix Italian Journal of Mammalogy* **12**: 19–25.

Delahay, R. J. *et al.* (2000a). The use of marked bait in studies of the territorial organization of the European badger (*Meles meles*). *Mammal Review* **30**: 73–87.

Delahay, R. J. *et al.* (2000b). The spatio-temporal distribution of *Mycobacterium bovis* (bovine tuberculosis) infection in a high-density badger population. *Journal of Animal Ecology* **69**: 428–41.

Delahay, R. J. *et al.* (2002). The status of *Mycobacterium bovis* infection in UK wild mammals: a review. *Veterinary Journal* **164**: 90–105.

Delahay, R. J. *et al.* (2006). Demographic correlates of bite wounding in Eurasian badgers, *Meles meles* L., in stable and perturbed populations. *Animal Behaviour* **71**: 1047–55.

Delahay, R. J. *et al.* (2007a). Bovine tuberculosis infection in wild mammals in the South-West region of England: a survey of prevalence and a semi-quantitative assessment of the relative risks to cattle. *Veterinary Journal* **173**: 287–301.

Delahay, R. J. *et al.* (2007b). Distribution of badger latrines in a high-density population: habitat selection and implications for the transmission of bovine tuberculosis to cattle. *Journal of Zoology* **272**: 311–20.

Delahay, R. J. *et al.* (2009). Managing conflict between humans and wildlife: trends in licensed operations to resolve problems with badgers *Meles meles* in England. *Mammal Review* **39**: 53–66.

Dixon, D. R. *et al.* (2006). Lunar-related reproductive behaviour in the badger (*Meles meles*). *Acta Ethologica* **9**: 59–63.

Do Linh San, E. (2002). *Le Blaireau.* Eveil Nature, St-Yrieix-sur-Charente, Switzerland.

Do Linh San, E. (2004). Biology and ecology of the European badger (*Meles meles*) in a low-density population (Broye, Switzerland) (PhD thesis, Faculté des Sciences, Université de Neuchâtel, Neuchâtel): 310.

Do Linh San, E. (2007). Ectoparasite categories of the European badger (*Meles meles*) in western Switzerland. *Wildlife Biology in Practice* **3**: 52–9.

Do Linh San, E. *et al.* (2003). Le Blaireau (*Meles meles* L.) dans le Jura suisse: succès de capture, parametres démographiques et ectoparasites. *Revue Suisse de Zoologie* **110**: 565–80.

Do Linh San, E. *et al.* (2007a). Socio-spatial organization of Eurasian badgers (*Meles meles*) in a low-density population of central Europe. *Canadian Journal of Zoology* **85**: 973–84.

Do Linh San, E. *et al.* (2007b). Spatio-temporal ecology and density of badgers *Meles meles* in the Swiss Jura Mountains. *European Journal of Wildlife Research* **53**: 265–75.

Domingo-Roura, X. *et al.* (2006). Badger hair in shaving brushes comes from protected Eurasian badgers. *Biological Conservation* **128**: 425–30.

Doncaster, C. P. (1992). Testing the role of intra-guild predation in regulating hedgehog populations. *Proceedings of the Royal Society B: Biological Sciences* **249**: 113–17.

Doncaster, C. P. & R. Woodroffe (1993). Den site can determine shape and size of badger territories: implications for group living. *Oikos* **66**: 88–93.

Donnelly, C. A. *et al.* (2003). Impact of localized badger culling on tuberculosis incidence in British cattle. *Nature* **426**: 834–7.

Donnelly, C. A. *et al.* (2006). Positive and negative effects of widespread badger culling on cattle tuberculosis. *Nature* **439**: 843–6.

Donnelly, C. A. *et al.* (2007). Impacts of widespread badger culling on cattle tuberculosis: concluding analyses from a large-scale field trial. *International Journal of Infectious Diseases* **11**: 300–8.

Dragoo, J. W. & R. L. Honeycutt (1997). Systematics of mustelid-like carnivores. *Journal of Mammalogy* **78**: 426–43.

Dugdale, H. L. *et al.* (2003). Offspring sex ratio variation in the European badger, *Meles meles. Ecology* **84**: 40–45.

Dugdale, H. L. *et al.* (2007). Polygynandry, extra-group paternity and multiple-paternity litters in European badger (*Meles meles*) social groups. *Molecular Ecology* **16**: 5294–306.

Dugdale, H. L. *et al.* (2008). Reproductive skew and relatedness in social groups of European badgers, *Meles meles*. *Molecular Ecology* **17**: 1815–27.

Dumartin, B. *et al.* (1989). Determination expérimentale de la croissance foetale chez le blaireau européen *Meles meles* L. *Mammalia* **53**: 279–85.

Dunnett, G. M. *et al.* (1986). *Badgers and Bovine Tuberculosis*. HMSO, London: 73.

Evans, P. G. H. *et al.* (1989). Social structure of the Eurasian badger (*Meles meles*): genetic evidence. *Journal of Zoology, London* **218**: 587–96.

Eves, J. A. (1999). Impact of badger removal on bovine tuberculosis in east County Offaly. *Irish Veterinary Journal* **52**: 199–203.

Fairnell, E. H. & J. H. Barrett (2007). Fur-bearing species and Scottish islands. *Journal of Archaeological Science* **34**: 463–84.

Fargher, S. & P. Morris (1975). An investigation into age determination in the badger *Meles meles* (Unpublished MSc thesis, Department of Zoology, University of London, London).

Fedriani, J. M. *et al.* (1998). Dietary response of the European badger, *Meles meles*, to a decline of its main prey in the Doñana National Park. *Journal of Zoology, London* **245**: 214–18.

Fell, R. J. *et al.* (2006). The social integration of European badger (*Meles meles*) cubs into their natal group. *Behaviour* **143**: 683–700.

Feore, S. & W. I. Montgomery (1999). Habitat effects on the spatial ecology of the European badger (*Meles meles*). *Journal of Zoology, London* **247**: 537–49.

Ferrari, N. (1997). Eco-éthologie du blaireau européen (*Meles meles* L. 1758) dans le Jura suisse: comparaison de deux populations vivant en milieu montagnard et en milieu cultivé de plaine (PhD thesis, Institute of Biology, Université de Neuchâtel, Neuchâtel): 260.

Fischer, C. *et al.* (2005). Exploitation of food resources by badgers (*Meles meles*) in the Swiss Jura mountains. *Journal of Zoology, London* **266**: 121–31.

Fowler, P. A. & P. A. Racey (1988). Overwintering strategies of the badger, *Meles meles*, at 57 °N. *Journal of Zoology, London* **214**: 635–51.

Frantz, A. C. *et al.* (2004). Estimating population size by genotyping remotely plucked hair: the Eurasian badger. *Journal of Applied Ecology* **41**: 985–95.

Frewin, B. C. (1976). The excavation of badger setts at Stantonbury and Milton Keynes Village. *Milton Keynes Natural History Society* **2**: 20–28.

Gallagher, J. & R. S. Clifton-Hadley (2000). Tuberculosis in badgers: a review of the disease and its significance for other animals. *Research in Veterinary Science* **69**: 203–17.

Gallagher, J. & J. Nelson (1979). Causes of ill-health or natural death in badgers in Gloucestershire. *Veterinary Record* **105**: 546–51.

Garnett, B. T. (2002). Behavioural aspects of bovine tuberculosis (*Mycobacterium bovis*) transmission and infection in badgers (*Meles meles*) (PhD thesis, Department of Biology, University of Sussex, Falmer, Brighton): 159.

Garnett, B. T. *et al.* (2002). Use of cattle farm resources by badgers (*Meles meles*) and risk of bovine tuberculosis (*Mycobacterium bovis*) transmission to cattle. *Proceedings of the Royal Society B: Biological Sciences* **269**: 1487–91.

Garnett, B. T. *et al.* (2003). Use of cattle troughs by badgers (*Meles meles*): a potential route for the transmission of bovine tuberculosis (*Mycobacterium bovis*). *Applied Animal Behaviour Science* **80**: 1–18.

Gibbons, D. W. *et al.* (2007). *The Predation of Wild Birds in the UK: A Review of its Conservation Impact and Management. RSPB Research Report no.* **23**. RSPB, Sandy, Bedfordshire: 56.

Gilbert, M. A. Mitchell, *et al.* (2005). Cattle movements and bovine tuberculosis in Great Britain. *Nature* **435**: 491–6.

Godfray, H. C. J. *et al.* (2005). *Review of Republic of Ireland 'Four Areas' Badger Culling Trial.* Defra, London.

Gorman, M. L. *et al.* (1984). Social functions of the sub-caudal scent gland secretion of the European badger *Meles meles* (Carnivora: Mustelidae). *Journal of Zoology, London* **203**: 549–59.

Gosling, L. M. (1982). A reassessment of the function of scent marking in territories. *Zeitschrift für Tierpsychologie* **60**: 89–118.

Goszczyński, J. *et al.* (2000). Diet composition of badgers (*Meles meles*) in a pristine forest and rural habitats of Poland compared to other European populations. *Journal of Zoology, London* **250**: 495–505.

Goszczyński, J. *et al.* (2005). Activity of badgers (*Meles meles*) in central Poland. *Mammalian Biology* **70**: 1–11.

Graf, M. & A. I. Wandeler (1982). The reproductive cycle of male badgers (*Meles meles* L.) in Switzerland. *Revue Suisse de Zoologie* **89**: 1005–8.

Green, D.M. *et al.* (2008). Estimates for local and movement-based transmission of bovine tuberculosis in British cattle. *Proceedings of the Royal Society B – Biological Sciences* **275**: 1001–5.

Griffin, J. M. *et al.* (2005). The impact of badger removal on the control of tuberculosis in cattle herds in Ireland. *Cattle Practice* **13**: 381–99.

Griffiths, H. I. (1990). Badger game-bag data estimates of badger (*Meles meles*) population sizes in Europe. *Small Carnivore Conservation* **1**: 9–10.

Griffiths, H. I. (1991). *On the Hunting of Badgers.* Piglet Press, Brynna, Mid Glamorgan.

Griffiths, H. I. (1993). The Eurasian badger, *Meles meles* (L. 1758) as a commodity species. *Journal of Zoology* **230**: 340–42.

Griffiths, H. I. & D. H. Thomas (1993). The status of the badger *Meles meles* (L. 1758) (Carnivora, Mustelidae) in Europe. *Mammal Review* **23**: 17–58.

Griffiths, H. I. & D. H. Thomas (1997). *The conservation and management of the European badger (Meles meles). Nature and Environment, No. 90.* Council of Europe, Strasbourg: 77.

Hancox, M. (1980). Parasites and infectious diseases of the Eurasian badger (*Meles meles* L.): a review. *Mammal Review* **10**: 151–62.

Hancox, M. (1988a). The nidicolous fauna of badger setts. *Entomologists' Monthly Magazine* **124**: 93–5.

Hancox, M. (1988b). A review of age determination criteria in the Eurasian badger. *Lynx (Praha)* **24**: 77–86.

Hancox, M. (1990). Badgers breeding above ground. *Small Carnivore Conservation* **2**: 10.

Harlow, H. J. (1981). Torpor and other physiological adaptations of the badger (*Taxidea taxus*) to cold environments. *Physiological Zoology* **54**: 267–75.

Harris, S. (1982). Activity patterns and habitat utilisation by badgers (*Meles meles*) in suburban Bristol: a radio-tracking study. *Symposia of the Zoological Society of London* **49**: 301–23.

Harris, S. (1984). Ecology of urban badgers *Meles meles*: distribution in Britain and habitat selection, persecution, food and damage in the city of Bristol. *Biological Conservation* **28**: 349–75.

Harris, S. & W. J. Cresswell (1987). Dynamics of a suburban badger (*Meles meles*) population. *Symposia of the Zoological Society of London* **58**: 295–311.

Harris, S. *et al.* (1995). *A Review of British Mammals: Population Estimates and Conservation Status of British Mammals Other Than Cetaceans.* Joint Nature Conservation Committee, Peterborough.

Harris, S. *et al.* (2010). *Eurasian badger.* In: *Urban Carnivores* (Ed. Gehrt, S. D., Riley, S. P. D. & Cypher, B. L.). Johns Hopkins University Press, Baltimore, MD.

Helgen, K. M. *et al.* (2008). The hog-badger is not an edentate: systematics and evolution of the genus *Arctonyx* (Mammalia, Mustelidae). *Zoological Journal of the Linnean Society* **154**: 353–85.

Henry, C. (1984a). Adaptation comportementale du blaireau Européen (*Meles meles* L.) à la prédation d'une espèce-proie venimeuse, le crapaud commun (*Bufo bufo* L.). *Revue d'Écologie (Terre et Vie)* **39**: 291–6.

Henry, C. (1984b). Éco-éthologie de l'alimentation du blaireau européen (*Meles meles* L.) dans une forêt du centre de la France. *Mammalia* **43**: 489–503.

Hewitt, S. E. *et al.* (2009). Context-dependent linear dominance hierarchies in social groups of European badgers, *Meles meles. Animal Behaviour* **77**: 161–9.

Hofer, H. (1988). Variation in resource presence, utilization and reproductive success within a population of European badgers (*Meles meles*). *Mammal Review* **18**: 25–36.

Hofmann, T. *et al.* (2000). Home-range size and habitat use in European badger (*Meles meles* L. 1758) in the Hakel forest. *Beitrage zur Jagd- und Wildforschung* **25**: 199–209.

Holmala, K. & K. Kauhala (2006). Ecology of wildlife rabies in Europe. *Mammal Review* **36**: 17–36.

Hoogeveen, Y. (1985). Food and habitat preference of the European badger (*Meles meles*) in central Sweden (Unpublished thesis, Ecology Department, Groningen University, Groningen): 26.

Hounsome, T. & R. Delahay (2005). Birds in the diet of the Eurasian badger *Meles meles*: a review and meta-analysis. *Mammal Review* **35**: 199–209.

Hounsome, T. D. *et al.* (2005). An evaluation of distance sampling to estimate badger (*Meles meles*) abundance. *Journal of Zoology, London* **266**: 81–7.

Huck, M. & T. J. Roper (2008). Low genetic variability, female biased dispersal and high movement rates in an urban population of Eurasian badgers (*Meles meles*). *Journal of Animal Ecology* **77**: 905–15.

Huck, M. *et al.* (2008). Predicting European badger sett distribution in urban environments. *Wildlife Biology* **14**: 188–98.

Hutchings, M. R. & S. Harris (1997). Effects of farm management practices on cattle grazing behaviour and the potential for transmission of bovine tuberculosis from badgers to cattle. *Veterinary Journal* **153**: 149–62.

Hutchings, M. R. *et al.* (2002). Is population density correlated with faecal and urine scent marking in European badgers (*Meles meles*) in the UK? *Mammalian Biology* **67**: 286–93.

Iversen, J. A. (1972). Basal energy metabolism of mustelids. *Journal of Comparative Physiology* **81**: 341–4.

Jaine, T. (1986). *Cooking in the Country.* Chatto & Windus, London.

Jenkins, H. E. *et al.* (2007). Effects of culling on spatial associations of *Mycobacterium bovis* infections in badgers and cattle. *Journal of Applied Ecology* **44**: 897–908.

Jenkins, H. E. *et al.* (2008). The effects of annual widespread badger culls on cattle tuberculosis following the cessation of culling. *International Journal of Infectious Diseases* **12**: 457–65.

Jenkins, H. E. *et al.* (2010). The duration of the effects of repeated widespread badger culling on cattle tuberculosis following the cessation of culling. *PLoS One* **5**: e9090. doi:10.1371/journal.pone.0009090

Jenkinson, S. & C. P. Wheater (1998). The influence of public access and sett visibility on badger (*Meles meles*) sett disturbance and persistence. *Journal of Zoology, London* **246**: 478–82.

Jensen, P. V. (1959). Lidt om graevlingen. *Naturens Verden* **11**: 289–320.

Jepsen, J. U. *et al.* (2005). Predicting distribution and density of European badger (*Meles meles*) setts in Denmark. *Biodiversity and Conservation* **14**: 3235–53.

Johnson, D. D. P. & D. W. Macdonald (2001). Why are group-living badgers (*Meles meles*) sexually dimorphic? *Journal of Zoology, London* **255**: 199–204.

Johnson, D. D. P. & D. W. Macdonald (2003). Sentenced without trial: reviling and revamping the Resource Dispersion Hypothesis. *Oikos* **101**: 433–40.

Johnson, D. D. P. *et al.* (2002). Environmental correlates of badger social spacing across Europe. *Journal of Biogeography* **29**: 411–25.

Kaneko, Y. *et al.* (1996). Growth and seasonal changes in body weight and size of Japanese badger in Hinodecho, suburb of Tokyo. *Journal of Wildlife Research* **1**: 42–6.

Kaneko, Y. *et al.* (2006). Food habits and habitat selection of suburban badgers (*Meles meles*) in Japan. *Journal of Zoology, London* **270**: 78–89.

Kauhala, K. (1995). Changes in distribution of the European badger *Meles meles* in Finland during the rapid colonization of the raccoon dog. *Annales Zoologici Fennici* **32**: 183–91.

Kawamura, Y. *et al.* (1989). Middle and late Pleistocene mammalian faunas in Japan. *Quaternary Research* **28**: 317–26.

Koepfli, K.-P. *et al.* (2008). Multigene phylogeny of the Mustelidae: resolving relationships, tempo and biogeographic history of a mammalian adaptive radiation. *BMC Biology* **6**: doi:10.1186/1741-7007-1186-1110.

Kowalczyk, R. *et al.* (2000). Badger density and distribution of setts in Białowieża Primeval Forest (Poland and Belarus) compared to other Eurasian populations. *Acta Theriologica* **45**: 395–408.

Kowalczyk, R. *et al.* (2003a). Annual and circadian activity patterns of badgers (*Meles meles*) in Białowieża Primeval Forest (eastern Poland) compared with other Palaearctic populations. *Journal of Biogeography* **30(3)**: 463–72.

Kowalczyk, R. *et al.* (2003b). Spatial organization of demography of badgers (*Meles meles*) in Białowieża Primeval Forest, Poland, and the influence of earthworms on badger densities in Europe. *Canadian Journal of Zoology* **81**: 74–87.

Kowalczyk, R. *et al.* (2004). Seasonal and spatial pattern of shelter use by badgers *Meles meles* in Białowieża Primeval Forest (Poland). *Acta Theriologica* **49(1)**: 75–92.

Kowalczyk, R. *et al.* (2006). Daily movement and territory use by badgers *Meles meles* in Białowieża Primeval Forest, Poland. *Wildlife Biology* **12**: 385–91.

Krebs, J. R. & the Independent Scientific Review Group (1997). *Bovine Tuberculosis in Cattle and Badgers: Report to the Right Honourable Dr Jack Cunningham MP.* Ministry of Agriculture, Fisheries and Food, London.

Kruuk, H. (1978a). Foraging and spatial-organization of European badger, *Meles meles* L. *Behavioral Ecology and Sociobiology* **4**: 75–89.

Kruuk, H. (1978b). Spatial organisation and territorial behaviour of the European badger *Meles meles*. *Journal of Zoology, London* **184**: 1–19.

Kruuk, H. (1989). *The Social Badger: Ecology and Behaviour of a Group-Living Carnivore* (Meles meles). Oxford University Press, Oxford.

Kruuk, H. & L. De Kock (1981). Food and habitat of badgers (*Meles meles* L.) on Monte Baldo, northern Italy. *Zeitschrift für Säugetierkunde-International Journal of Mammalian Biology* **46**: 295–301.

Kruuk, H. & T. Parish (1981). Feeding specialization of the European badger *Meles meles* in Scotland. *Journal of Animal Ecology* **50**: 773–88.

Kruuk, H. & T. Parish (1982). Factors affecting population density, group size and territory size of the European badger, *Meles meles*. *Journal of Zoology, London* **196**: 31–9.

Kruuk, H. & T. Parish (1983). Seasonal and local differences in the weight of European badgers (*Meles meles*) in relation to food supply. *Zeitschrift für Säugetierkunde-International Journal of Mammalian Biology* **48**: 45–50.

Kruuk, H. & T. Parish (1985). Food, food availability and weight of badgers (*Meles meles*) in relation to agricultural changes. *Journal of Applied Ecology* **22**: 705–15.

Kruuk, H. & T. Parish (1987). Changes in the size of groups and ranges of the European badger (*Meles meles* L.) in an area of Scotland. *Journal of Animal Ecology* **56**: 351–64.

Kruuk, H. *et al.* (1984). Scent-marking with the sub-caudal gland by the European badger *Meles meles* L. *Animal Behaviour* **32**: 899–907.

Kurose, N. *et al.* (2001). Low genetic diversity in Japanese populations of the Eurasian badger *Meles meles* (Mustelidae, Carnivora) revealed by mitochondrial cytochrome b gene sequences. *Zoological Science* **18**: 1145–51.

Lambert, A. (1990). Alimentation du blaireau Eurasien (*Meles meles*) dans un écosystème forestier: variations spatiales du régime et comportement de prédation. *Gibier Faune Sauvage* **7**: 21–37.

Langevelde, F. v. *et al.* (2009). Traffic mortality and the role of minor roads. *Journal of Environmental Management* **90**: 660–67.

Langley, P. J. W. & D. W. Yalden (1977). The decline of the rarer carnivores in Great Britain during the nineteenth century. *Mammal Review* **7**: 95–116.

Lankester, K. *et al.* (1991). Management perspectives for populations of the Eurasian badger (*Meles meles*) in a fragmented landscape. *Journal of Applied Ecology* **28**: 561–73.

Lanski, J. (2004). Diet of badgers living in a deciduous forest in Hungary. *Mammalian Biology* **69**: 354–8.

Leeson, R. C. & B. M. C. Mills (1977). *Survey of Excavated Setts in the County of Avon.* Ministry of Agriculture, Fisheries and Food, London.

Likhachev, G. N. (1956). *Some ecological traits of the badger of the Tula Abatis broadleaved forests.* In: *Studies of Mammals in Government Preserves* (Ed. Jurgensen, P. B.). Ministry of Agriculture, Moscow: 72–94.

Løfaldi, L. (1980). Partially albino badgers *Meles meles* from Rindal, Møre and Romsdal county, Norway. *Fauna* **33**: 144–6.

Long, C. A. & C. A. Killingley (1983). *The Badgers of the World.* Charles C. Thomas, Springfield, Illinois.

Loureiro, F. *et al.* (2007). Use of multiple den sites by Eurasian badgers, *Meles meles*, in a Mediterranean habitat. *Zoological Science* **24**: 978–85.

Lüps, P. (1983a). Gewichtsschwankungen beim Dachs (*Meles meles* L.) im bernischen Mittelland, nebst Bemerkungen zu seiner Biologie. *Jahrbuch des Naturhistorisches Museum Bern* **8**: 273–89.

Lüps, P. (1983b). Daten zur morphologischen Entwicklung des Dachses *Meles meles* L. *Kleine Mitteilungen Naturhistorisches Museum Bern* **11**: 1–11.

Lüps, P. & T. J. Roper (1988). Tooth size in the European badger (*Meles meles*) with special reference to sexual dimorphism, diet and intraspecific aggression. *Acta Theriologica* **33**: 21–33.

Lüps, P. & T. J. Roper (1990). Cannibalism in a female badger (*Meles meles*): infanticide or predation? *Journal of Zoology, London* **221**: 314–15.

Lüps, P. & A. I. Wandeler (1993). Meles meles *(Linnaeus, 1758) – Dachs.* In: *Handbuch der Säugetiere Europas* (Eds Niethammer, J., Krapp, F. and Stubbe, M.). AULA-Verlag, Wiesbaden: 856–906.

Lüps, P. *et al.* (1987). Stomach contents of badgers (*Meles meles* L.) in central Switzerland. *Mammalia* **51**: 559–69.

Lynch, J. M. (1996). Postglacial colonization of Ireland by mustelids, with particular reference to the badger (*Meles meles* L.). *Journal of Biogeography* **23**: 179–85.

Macdonald, D. W. (1980). The red fox, *Vulpes vulpes*, as a predator upon earthworms, *Lumbricus terrestris*. *Zeitschrift für Tierpsychologie* **52**: 171–200.

Macdonald, D. W. (1983). The ecology of carnivore social behaviour. *Nature* **301**: 379–84.

Macdonald, D. W. & C. Newman (2002). Population dynamics of badgers (*Meles meles*) in Oxfordshire, UK: numbers, density and cohort life histories, and a possible role of climate change in population growth. *Journal of Zoology, London* **256**: 121–38.

Macdonald, D. W. *et al.* (2002). No evidence of social hierarchy amongst feeding badgers, *Meles meles*. *Ethology* **108**: 613–28.

Macdonald, D. W. *et al.* (2004a). The distribution of Eurasian badger, *Meles meles*, setts in a high-density area: field observations contradict the sett dispersion hypothesis. *Oikos* **106**: 295–307.

Macdonald, D. W. *et al.* (2004b). Increasing frequency of bite wounds with increasing population density in Eurasian badgers, *Meles meles*. *Animal Behaviour* **67**: 745–51.

Macdonald, D. W. *et al.* (2004c). Encounters between two sympatric carnivores: red foxes (*Vulpes vulpes*) and European badgers (*Meles meles*). *Journal of Zoology, London* **263**: 385–92.

Macdonald, D. W. *et al.* (2008). Male-biased movement in a high-density population of the Eurasian badger (*Meles meles*). *Journal of Mammalogy* **89**: 1077–86.

MacNally, J. (1970). *Highland Deer Forest.* Dent, London.

Madsen, S. A. *et al.* (2002). Seasonal food of badgers (*Meles meles*) in Denmark. *Mammalia* **66(3)**: 341–52.

Madurell-Malapeira, J. *et al.* (2009). Oldest European occurrence of *Meles* (Mustelidae, Carnivora) from the Middle Pliocene (MN16) of Almenara-Casablanca-4 Karstic site. *Journal of Vertebrate Paleontology* **29**: 961–5.

MAFF (1979). *Third Report on Bovine Tuberculosis in Badgers.* MAFF Publications, London.

Marassi, M. & C. M. Biancardi (2002). Diet of the Eurasian badger (*Meles meles*) in an area of the Italian prealps. *Hystrix Italian Journal of Mammalogy* **13**: 19–28.

Marmi, J. *et al.* (2004). Phylogeny, evolutionary history and taxonomy of the Mustelidae based on sequences of the cytochrome b gene and a complex repetitive flanking region. *Zoologica Scripta* **33**: 481–99.

Marmi, J. *et al.* (2006). Mitochondrial DNA reveals a strong phylogeographic structure in the badger across Eurasia. *Molecular Ecology* **15**: 1007–20.

Martín, R. *et al.* (1995). Local feeding specialization by badgers (*Meles meles*) in a Mediterranean environment. *Oecologia* **101**: 45–50.

Matthews, A. J. & C. J. Wilson (2005). *The Management of Problems Involving Badgers (*Meles meles*).* Defra Rural Development Service, Bristol.

Maurel, D. *et al.* (1984). Seasonal reproductive endocrine profiles in two wild mammals: the red fox (*Vulpes vulpes* L.) and the European badger (*Meles meles* L.) considered as short-day mammals. *Acta Endocrinologica* **105**: 130–8.

Maurel, D. *et al.* (1986). Seasonal moulting patterns in three fur-bearing mammals: the European badger (*Meles meles* L.), the red fox (*Vulpes vulpes* L.), and the mink (*Mustela vison*). A morphological and histological study. *Canadian Journal of Zoology* **64**: 1757–64.

Maurel, D. *et al.* (1987). Thyroid and gonadal regulation of hair growth during the seasonal moult in the male European badger, *Meles meles* L. *General and Comparative Endocrinology* **65**: 317–27.

Maynard Smith, J. & D. Harper (2003). *Animal Signals.* Oxford University Press, Oxford.

McNab, B. K. (1979). The influence of body size on the energetics and distribution of fossorial and burrowing mammals. *Ecology* **60**: 1010–21.

Melis, C. *et al.* (2002). Food habits of the Eurasian badger in a rural Mediterranean area. *Zeitschrift für Jagdwissenschaft* **48**: 236–46.

Mellgren, R. & T. J. Roper (1986). Spatial learning and discrimination of food patches in the European badger (*Meles meles* L.). *Animal Behaviour* **34**: 1129–34.

Milner, C. (1967). Badger damage to upland pasture. *Journal of Zoology, London* **153**: 544–6.

Mitchell-Jones, A. J. *et al.* (1999). *The Atlas of European Mammals.* T. & A. D. Poyser, London.

Moore, J. A. H. & T. J. Roper (2003). Temperature and humidity in badger *Meles meles* setts. *Mammal Review* **33**: 308–13.

Moore, N. *et al.* (1999). Survey of badger *Meles meles* damage to agriculture in England and Wales. *Journal of Applied Ecology* **36**: 974–88.

More, S. J. & M. Good (2006). The tuberculosis eradication programme in Ireland: a review of scientific and policy advances since 1988. *Veterinary Microbiology* **112**: 239–51.

More, S. J. *et al.* (2007). Does reactive badger culling lead to an increase in tuberculosis in cattle? *Veterinary Record* **161**: 208–9.

Mouchès, A. (1981). Variations saisonnières du régime alimentaire chez le blaireau Européen (*Meles meles* L.). *Revue d'Écologie (Terre et Vie)* **35**: 183–94.

Mulder, J. L. (1996). Reintroducing the badger *Meles meles*: stories of failure and success. *Lutra* **39**: 1–32.

Neal, E. (1948). *The Badger.* Collins, London.

Neal, E. (1977). *Badgers.* Blandford Press, Poole, Dorset.

Neal, E. (1986). *The Natural History of Badgers.* Croom Helm, London & Sydney.

Neal, E. & C. Cheeseman (1996). *Badgers.* T. & A. D. Poyser, London.

Neal, E. G. & R. J. Harrison (1958). Reproduction in the European badger (*Meles meles* L.). *Transactions of the Zoological Society of London* **29**: 67–131.

Neal, E. & T. J. Roper (1991). The environmental impact of badgers (*Meles meles*) and their setts. *Symposia of the Zoological Society of London* **63**: 89–106.

Newman, C. *et al.* (2005). The function of facial masks in midguild carnivores. *Oikos* **108**: 623–33.

NIAO (2009). *The Control of Bovine Tuberculosis in Northern Ireland.* The Stationery Office, Belfast.

Nichol, D. *et al.* (2003). Application of ground-penetrating radar to investigate the effects of badger setts on slope stability at St Asaph Bypass, North Wales. *Quarterly Journal of Engineering Geology and Hydrogeology* **36**: 143–53.

Nolan, A. & J. W. Wilesmith (1994). Tuberculosis in badgers (*Meles meles*). *Veterinary Microbiology* **40**: 179–91.

Nolet, B. A. & C. A. Killingley (1987). The effects of a change in food availability on group and territory size of a clan of badgers *Meles meles* (L. 1758). *Lutra* **30**: 1–8.

O'Mairtin, D. *et al.* (1998). The effect of a badger removal programme on the incidence of tuberculosis in an Irish cattle population. *Preventive Veterinary Medicine* **34**: 47–56.

O'Donoghue, P. *et al.* (2008). Can non-intrusive geophysical techniques assist in mapping setts of the Eurasian badger? *In Practice* **December**: 17–20.

Obidzinski, A. & R. Glogowski (2005). Changes of forest flora composition in vicinity of dens of red fox and setts of Euroasian badger. *Polish Journal of Ecology* **53**: 197–213.

Ostler, J. R. & T. J. Roper (1998). Changes in size, status, and distribution of badger *Meles meles* L. setts during a 20-year period. *Zeitschrift für Säugetierkunde-International Journal of Mammalian Biology* **63**: 200–9.

Ozolinš, J. & V. Pilāts (1995). Distribution and status of small and medium-sized carnivores in Latvia. *Annales Zoologici Fennici* **32**: 21–9.

Page, R. J. C. *et al.* (1994). Seasonality of reproduction in the European badger *Meles meles* in South-West England. *Journal of Zoology, London* **233**: 69–91.

Paget, R. J. & A. L. F. Middleton (1974). Some observations on the sexual activities of badgers in Yorkshire in the months December–April. *Journal of Zoology, London* **173**: 256–60.

Palphramand, K. L. & P. C. L. White (2007). Badgers, *Meles meles*, discriminate between neighbour, alien and self scent. *Animal Behaviour* **74**: 429–36.

Palphramand, K. L. *et al.* (2007). Spatial organization and behaviour of badgers (*Meles meles*) in a moderate-density population. *Behavioral Ecology and Sociobiology* **61**: 401–13.

Pelikan, J. *et al.* (1983). Mammals in the urban agglomeration of Brno. *Acta Scientiarum Naturalium Brno* **17**: 1–49.

Pertoldi, C. *et al.* (2000). Allozyme variation in the Eurasian badger *Meles meles* in Denmark. *Journal of Zoology, London* **252**: 544–7.

Pertoldi, C. *et al.* (2005). Present and past microsatellite variation and assessment of genetic structure in Eurasian badger (*Meles meles*) in Denmark. *Journal of Zoology, London* **265**: 387–94.

Petter, G. (1971). Origine, phylogénie et systématique des blaireaux. *Mammalia* **35**: 567–97.

Phillips, C. J. C. *et al.* (2003). The transmission of *Mycobacterium bovis* infection to cattle. *Research in Veterinary Science* **74**: 1–15.

Pigozzi, G. (1987). Behavioural ecology of the European badger (*Meles meles* L.): diet, food availability and use of space in the Maremma Natural Park, central Italy (PhD thesis, Department of Zoology, University of Aberdeen, Aberdeen).

Pigozzi, G. (1989). Digging behaviour while foraging by the European badger, *Meles meles*, in a Mediterranean habitat. *Ethology* **83**: 121–8.

Pigozzi, G. (1991). The diet of the European badger in a Mediterranean coastal area. *Acta Theriologica* **36(3–4)**: 293–306.

Pigozzi, G. (1992). Frugivory and seed dispersal by the European badger in a Mediterranean habitat. *Journal of Mammalogy* **73(3)**: 630–39.

Pitt, F. (1935). The increase in the badger (*Meles meles*) in Great Britain during the period 1900–1934, with special reference to the Wheatland area of Shropshire. *Journal of Animal Ecology* **4**: 1–6.

Pocock, R. I. (1911). Some probable and possible instances of warning characteristics amongst insectivorous and carnivorous mammals. *Annual Magazine of Natural History* **8**: 750–57.

Poole, D. W. *et al.* (2002). Effectiveness of an electric fence to reduce badger (*Meles meles*) damage to field crops. *Crop Protection* **21**: 409–17.

Poole, D. W. *et al.* (2004). The effects of fence voltage and the type of conducting wire on the efficacy of an electric fence to exclude badgers (*Meles meles*). *Crop Protection* **23**: 27–33.

Pope, L. C. *et al.* (2006). Isolation by distance and gene flow in the Eurasian badger (*Meles meles*) at both a local and broad scale. *Molecular Ecology* **15**: 371–86.

Pope, L. C. *et al.* (2007). Genetic evidence that culling increases badger movement: implications for the spread of bovine tuberculosis. *Molecular Ecology* **16**: 4919–29.

Powell, R. A. (1979). Mustelid spacing patterns: variations on a theme by *Mustela*. *Zeitschrift für Tierpsychologie* **50**: 153–65.

Reichman, O. J. & S. C. Smith (1990). *Burrows and burrowing behavior by mammals*. In: *Current Mammalogy, Vol.* 2 (Ed. Genoways, H. H.). Plenum Press, New York: 197–244.

Remonti, L. *et al.* (2006). Range of the Eurasian badger (*Meles meles*) in an agricultural area of northern Italy. *Ethology, Ecology and Evolution* **18**: 61–7.

Revilla, E. (2003a). What does the Resource Dispersion Hypothesis explain, if anything? *Oikos* **101**: 428–32.

Revilla, E. (2003b). Moving beyond the resource dispersion hypothesis. *Trends in Ecology and Evolution* **18**: 380.

Revilla, E. & F. Palomares (1999). Changes in the behaviour of a male Eurasian badger: evidence in favour of the anti-kleptogamy hypothesis? *Acta Theriologica* **44**: 471–6.

Revilla, E. & F. Palomares (2001). Differences in key habitat use between dominant and subordinate animals: intraterritorial dominance payoffs in Eurasian badgers? *Canadian Journal of Zoology* **79**: 165–70.

Revilla, E. & F. Palomares (2002a). Does local feeding specialization exist in Eurasian badgers? *Canadian Journal of Zoology* **80**: 83–93.

Revilla, E. & F. Palomares (2002b). Spatial organization, group living and ecological correlates in low-density populations of Eurasian badgers, *Meles meles*. *Journal of Animal Ecology* **71**: 497–512.

Revilla, E. *et al.* (1999). Physical and population parameters of Eurasian badgers (*Meles meles* L.) from Mediterranean Spain. *Zeitschrift für Säugetierkunde-International Journal of Mammalian Biology* **64**: 269–76.

Revilla, E. *et al.* (2001a). Edge-core effects and the effectiveness of traditional reserves in conservation: Eurasian badgers in Doñana National Park. *Conservation Biology* **15**: 148–58.

Revilla, E. *et al.* (2001b). Characteristics, location and selection of diurnal resting dens by Eurasian badgers (*Meles meles*) in a low-density area. *Journal of Zoology, London* **255**: 291–9.

Reynolds, D. (2006). A review of tuberculosis science and policy in Great Britain. *Veterinary Microbiology* **112**: 119–26.

Rodríguez, A. & M. Delibes (1992). Food habits of badgers (*Meles meles*) in an arid habitat. *Journal of Zoology, London* **227**: 347–50.

Rodríguez, A. *et al.* (1996). Space use and activity in a Mediterranean population of badgers *Meles meles*. *Acta Theriologica* **41**: 59–72.

Rogers, L. M. *et al.* (1997). The demography of a high-density badger (*Meles meles*) population in the west of England. *Journal of Zoology, London* **242**: 705–28.

Rogers, L. M. *et al.* (1998). Movement of badgers (*Meles meles*) in a high-density population: individual, population and disease effects. *Proceedings of the Royal Society of London Series B: Biological Sciences* **265**: 1269–76.

Rogers, L. M. *et al.* (2003). The role of setts in badger (*Meles meles*) group size, breeding success and status of TB (*Mycobacterium bovis*). *Journal of Zoology, London* **260**: 209–15.

Roper, T. J. (1987). Have you got badgers? *Grape Press* **57**: 24–8.

Roper, T. J. (1992). Badger *Meles meles* setts: architecture, internal environment and function. *Mammal Review* **22**: 43–53.

Roper, T. J. (1993). *Badger setts as a limiting resource*. In: *The Badger* (Ed. Hayden, T. J.). Royal Irish Academy, Dublin.

Roper, T. J. (1994a). The European badger *Meles meles*: food specialist or generalist? *Journal of Zoology, London* **234**: 437–52.

Roper, T. J. (1994b). Do badgers, *Meles meles*, bury their dead? *Journal of Zoology, London* **234**: 677–80.

Roper, T. J. (1999). Olfaction in birds. *Advances in the Study of Behavior* **28**: 247–32.

Roper, T. J. & I. Kemenes (1997). Effect of blocking of entrances on the internal environment of badger *Meles meles* setts. *Journal of Applied Ecology* **34**: 1311–19.

Roper, T. J. & P. Lüps (1993). Disruption of territorial behaviour in badgers *Meles meles*. *Zeitschrift für Säugetierkunde* **58**: 252–5.

Roper, T. J. & P. Lüps (1995). Diet of badgers (*Meles meles*) in central Switzerland: an analysis of stomach contents. *Zeitschrift für Säugetierkunde-International Journal of Mammalian Biology* **60**: 9–19.

Roper, T. J. & E. Mickevicius (1995). Badger *Meles meles* diet: a review of literature from the former Soviet Union. *Mammal Review* **25**: 117–29.

Roper, T. J. & J. A. H. Moore (2003). Ventilation of badger *Meles meles* setts. *Mammalian Biology* **68**: 277–83.

Roper, T. J. *et al.* (1986). Scent marking with faeces and anal secretion in the European badger. *Behaviour* **97**: 94–117.

Roper, T. J. *et al.* (1989). *Badgers as pests in English vineyards*. In: *Mammals as Pests* (Ed. Putnam, R. J.). Chapman and Hall, London: 661–9.

Roper, T. J. *et al.* (1991). Excavation of three badger (*Meles meles* L.) setts. *Zeitschrift für Säugetierkunde-International Journal of Mammalian Biology* **56**: 129–34.

Roper, T. J. *et al.* (1992). Structure and contents of four badger (*Meles meles* L.) setts. *Mammalia* **56**: 65–70.

Roper, T. J. *et al.* (1993). Territorial marking with feces in badgers (*Meles meles*) – a comparison of boundary and hinterland latrine use. *Behaviour* **127**: 289–307.

Roper, T. J. *et al.* (1995). Damage by badgers *Meles meles* to wheat *Triticum vulgare* and barley *Hordeum sativum* crops. *Journal of Applied Ecology* **32**: 720–26.

Roper, T. J. *et al.* (2001). Sett use in European badgers *Meles meles*. *Behaviour* **138**: 173–87.

Roper, T. J. *et al.* (2003). The process of dispersal in badgers *Meles meles*. *Mammal Review* **33**: 314–18.

Rosalino, L. M. *et al.* (2003). Food digestibility of a Eurasian badger *Meles meles* with special reference to the Mediterranean region. *Acta Theriologica* **48**: 283–8.

Rosalino, L. M. *et al.* (2004). Spatial structure and land-cover use in a low-density Mediterranean population of Eurasian badgers. *Canadian Journal of Zoology* **82**: 1493–502.

Rosalino, L. M. *et al.* (2005a). Dietary shifts of the badger (*Meles meles*) in Mediterranean woodlands: an opportunistic forager with seasonal specialisms. *Mammalian Biology* **70**: 12–23.

Rosalino, L. M. *et al.* (2005b). Resource dispersion and badger population density in Mediterranean woodlands: is food, water or geology the limiting factor? *Oikos* **110**: 441–52.

Sadlier, L. M. J. *et al.* (2004). Methods of monitoring red foxes *Vulpes vulpes* and badgers *Meles meles*: are field signs the answer? *Mammal Review* **34**: 75–98.

Scheppers, T. L. J. (2009). The socio-spatial organisation of the Eurasian badger (*Meles meles*) in relation to population density: a non-invasive genetic analysis (PhD thesis, Biology & Environmental Science, University of Sussex, Falmer, Brighton): 128.

Scheppers, T. L. J. *et al.* (2007). Estimating social group size of European badgers by genotyping remotely plucked single hairs. *Wildlife Biology* **13**: 195–207.

Schley, L. (2000). The badger *Meles meles* and the wild boar *Sus scrofa*: distribution and damage to agricultural crops in Luxembourg (PhD thesis, Department of Biology, University of Sussex, Falmer, Brighton): 284.

Schley, L. *et al.* (2004). Distribution and population density of badgers *Meles meles* in Luxembourg. *Mammal Review* **34**: 233–40.

Schmid, P. & P. Lüps (1988). Zur Bedeutung von Wespen (Vespidae) als Nahrung des Dachses (*Meles meles* L.). *Bonner Zoologische Beiträge* **39**: 43–7.

Seiler, A. (2003). The toll of the automobile: wildlife and roads in Sweden (PhD thesis, Department of Conservation Biology, Swedish University of Agricultural Sciences, Uppsala).

Seiler, A. *et al.* (2004). Road mortality in Swedish mammals: results of a drivers' questionnaire. *Wildlife Biology* **10**: 225–33.

Service, K. M. *et al.* (2001). Analysis of badger urine volatiles using gas chromatography-mass spectrometry and pattern recognition techniques. *Analyst* **126**: 615–23.

Shepherdson, D. J. *et al.* (1990). Diet, food availability and foraging behaviour of badgers (*Meles meles* L.) in southern England. *Zeitschrift für Säugetierkunde-International Journal of Mammalian Biology* **55**: 81–93.

Simms, E. (1957). *Voices of the Wild*. Putnam, London.

Skinner, C. A. & P. J. Skinner (1988). Food of badgers (*Meles meles*) in an arable area of Essex. *Journal of Zoology, London* **215**: 360–62.

Skinner, C. *et al.* (1991). The past history and recent decline of badgers *Meles meles* in Essex – an analysis of some of the contributory factors. *Mammal Review* **21**: 67–80.

Skoog, P. (1970). The food of the Swedish badger, *Meles meles* L. *Viltrevy* **7**: 1–115.

Sleeman, D. P. (2006). Records of otters (*Lutra lutra* L.) and badgers (*Meles meles* L.) from built-up areas in Ireland. *Bulletin of the Irish Biogeographical Society* **30**: 3–6.

Sleeman, D. P. *et al.* (1997). Investigations of an association between the stinkhorn fungus and badger setts. *Journal of Natural History* **31**: 983–92.

Sleeman, D. P. *et al.* (2003). Flies (Diptera) trapped at a badgers' sett in Co. Cork, Ireland. *Entomologist's Gazette* **54**: 167–70.

Sleeman, D. P. *et al.* (2009). How many Eurasian badgers *Meles meles* L. are there in the Republic of Ireland? *European Journal of Wildlife Research* **55**: 333–44.

Smal, C. (1995). *The Badger and Habitat Survey of Ireland.* National Parks and Wildlife Service and Department of Agriculture, Food and Forestry, Dublin.

Smith, G. C. (2002). The role of the badger (*Meles meles*) in rabies epizootiology and the implications for Great Britain. *Mammal Review* **32**: 12–25.

Smith, G. C. & D. Wilkinson (2002). Modelling disease spread in a novel host: rabies in the European badger *Meles meles. Journal of Applied Ecology* **39**: 865–74.

Smith, G. C. *et al.* (1995). Modelling bovine tuberculosis in badgers in England: preliminary results. *Mammalia* **59**: 639–50.

Smith, L. A. *et al.* (2009). Livestock grazing behavior and inter- versus intraspecific disease risk via the fecal–oral route. *Behavioral Ecology* **20**: 426–32.

Smith, N. H. *et al.* (2006). Bottlenecks and broomsticks: the molecular evolution of *Mycobacterium bovis. Nature Reviews Microbiology* **4**: 670–81.

Sommer, R. & N. Benecke (2004). Late- and post-glacial history of the Mustelidae in Europe. *Mammal Review* **34**: 249–84.

Starck, R. *et al.* (1987). Gastrointestinal anatomy of the European badger (*Meles meles* L.) with reference to diet and taxonomic status. *Zeitschrift für Säugetierkunde-International Journal of Mammalian Biology* **52**: 88–95.

Stewart, P. D. & D. W. Macdonald (1997). Age, sex and condition as predictors of moult and the efficacy of a novel fur-clip technique for individual marking of the European badger (*Meles meles*). *Journal of Zoology, London* **241**: 543–50.

Stewart, P. D. & D. W. Macdonald (2003). Badgers and badger fleas: strategies and counter-strategies. *Ethology* **109**: 751–64.

Stewart, P. D. *et al.* (1999). Individual differences in den maintenance effort in a communally dwelling mammal: the Eurasian badger. *Animal Behaviour* **57**: 153–61.

Stewart, P. D. *et al.* (2002). Behavioural mechanisms of information transmission and reception by badgers, *Meles meles*, at latrines. *Animal Behaviour* **63**: 999–1007.

Stirling, E. A. & R. J. Harper (1969). The distribution and habits of badgers on the southern outskirts of Durham city. *Bulletin of the Mammal Society* **32**: 5–6.

Stocker, G. & P. Lüps (1984). Qualitative and quantitative aspects of food consumption of badgers *Meles meles* in Swiss midlands. *Revue Suisse de Zoologie* **91**: 1007–15.

Stuart, L. J. (2009). The reproductive cycle of the male and female Eurasian badger, *Meles meles* (PhD thesis, Department of Zoology, Trinity College, Dublin).

Stubbe, M. (1971). Die analen Markierungsorgane des Dachses (*Meles meles*). *Zoologische Garten (N.F.)* **40**: 125–35.

Tanaka, H. (2006). Winter hibernation and body temperature fluctuation in the Japanese badger, *Meles meles anakuma. Zoological Science* **23**: 991–7.

Tanaka, H. *et al.* (2002). Spatial distribution and sett use by the Japanese badger *Meles meles anakuma. Mammal Study* **27**: 15–22.

Tavecchia, G. (1995). Data on urban badger activity in south Wales: a brief study. *Hystrix Italian Journal of Mammalogy* **7**: 173–6.

Teagle, W. G. (1969). The badger in the London area. *London Naturalist* **48**: 48–74.

Thornton, P. (1988). Density and distribution of badgers in south-west England: a predictive model. *Mammal Review* **18**: 1–23.

Tolhurst, B. A. *et al.* (2008). The behavioural responses of badgers (*Meles meles*) to exclusion from farm buildings using an electric fence. *Applied Animal Behaviour Science* **113**: 224–35.

Tolhurst, B. A. *et al.* (2009). Behaviour of badgers (*Meles meles*) in farm buildings: opportunities for the transmission of *Mycobacterium bovis* to cattle? *Applied Animal Behaviour Science* **117**: 103–13.

Trewby, I. D. *et al.* (2008). Experimental evidence of competitive release in sympatric carnivores. *Biology Letters* **4**: 170–72.

Tuyttens, F. A. M. *et al.* (2000). Spatial perturbation caused by a badger (*Meles meles*) culling operation: implications for the function of territoriality and the control of bovine tuberculosis (*Mycobacterium bovis*). *Journal of Animal Ecology* **69**: 815–28.

Vicente, J. *et al.* (2007). Social organisation and movement influence the incidence of bovine tuberculosis in European badgers as a case study. *Journal of Animal Ecology* **76**: 348–60.

Vink, J. *et al.* (2008). Defragmentation measures and the increase of a local European badger (*Meles meles*) population at Eindgooi, the Netherlands. *Lutra* **51**: 75–86.

Virgos, E. & J. G. Casanovas (1999). Badger *Meles meles* sett site selection in low-density Mediterranean areas of central Spain. *Acta Theriologica* **44(2)**: 173–82.

Virgos, E. *et al.* (2004). Food habits of European badgers (*Meles meles*) along an altitudinal gradient of Mediterranean environments: a field test of the earthworm specialization hypothesis. *Canadian Journal of Zoology* **82**: 41–51.

Wandeler, A. I. & M. Graf (1982). Der Geschlechtszyklus weiblicher Dachse (*Meles meles* L.) in der Schweiz. *Revue Suisse de Zoologie* **89(4)**: 1009–16.

Wandeler, A. I. *et al.* (1974). Rabies in wild carnivores in central Europe. I. Epidemiological studies. *Zentralblatt für Veterinaermedizin B* **21**: 735–56.

Ward, A. I. *et al.* (2008a). Deterrent or dinner bell? Alternation of badger activity and feeding at baited plots using ultrasonic and water jet devices. *Applied Animal Behaviour Science* **115**: 221–32.

Ward, A. I. *et al.* (2008b). Survey of badger access to farm buildings and facilities in relation to contact with cattle. *Veterinary Record* **163**: 107–11.

Weber, J.-M. & S. Aubry (1994). Dietary response of the European badger, *Meles meles*, during a population outbreak of water voles, *Arvicola terrestris. Journal of Zoology, London* **234**: 687–90.

Whelan, R. & T. J. Hayden (1993). *The reproductive cycle of the female badger* (Meles meles *L.) in East Offaly*. In: *The Badger* (Ed. Hayden, T. J.). Royal Irish Academy, Dublin: 64–77.

White, P. C. L. *et al.* (1993). Badgers (*Meles meles*), cattle and bovine tuberculosis (*Mycobacterium bovis*): a hypothesis to explain the influence of habitat on the risk of disease transmission in southwest England. *Proceedings of the Royal Society B: Biological Sciences* **253**: 277–84.

White, P. C. L. *et al.* (2008). Control of bovine tuberculosis in British livestock: there is no 'silver bullet'. *Trends in Microbiology* **16**: 420–27.

Wiertz, J. (1993). Fluctuations in the Dutch badger *Meles meles* population between 1960 and 1990. *Mammal Review* **23**: 59–64.

Wijngaarden, A. v. & J. v. d. Peppel (1964). The badger, *Meles meles* (L.), in the Netherlands. *Lutra* **6**: 1–60.

Wilkinson, D. *et al.* (2000). The effects of bovine tuberculosis (*Mycobacterium bovis*) on mortality in a badger (*Meles meles*) population in England. *Journal of Zoology, London* **250**: 389–95.

Wilson, C. J. (1993). Badger damage to growing oats and an assessment of electric fencing as a means of its reduction. *Journal of Zoology, London* **231**: 668–75.

Wilson, C. J. & R. G. Symes (1998). *The Management of Problems Involving Badgers* (Meles meles). Farming and Rural Conservation Agency, London.

Wilson, G. *et al.* (1997). *Changes in the British Badger Population, 1988–1997.* People's Trust for Endangered Species, London.

Wilson, G. J. & R. J. Delahay (2001). A review of methods to estimate the abundance of terrestrial carnivores using field signs and observation. *Wildlife Research* **28**: 151–64.

Wilson, G. J. *et al.* (2003). Estimation of badger abundance using faecal DNA typing. *Journal of Applied Ecology* **40**: 658–66.

Wölfel, H. & E. Schneider (1988). Beobachtungen zum Nestbauverhalten des Dachses (*Meles meles*). *Zeitschrift für Jagdwissenschaft* **34**: 47–9.

Wong, J. *et al.* (1999). Vocal repertoire in the European badger (*Meles meles*): structure, context, and function. *Journal of Mammalogy* **80**: 570–88.

Woodroffe, R. (1993). Alloparental behavior in the European badger. *Animal Behaviour* **46**: 413–15.

Woodroffe, R. (1995). Body condition affects implantation date in the European badger, *Meles meles*. *Journal of Zoology* **236**: 183–8.

Woodroffe, R. & D. W. Macdonald (1993). Badger sociality – models of spatial grouping. *Symposia of the Zoological Society of London* **65**: 145–69.

Woodroffe, R. & D. W. Macdonald (2000). Helpers provide no detectable benefits in the European badger (*Meles meles*). *Journal of Zoology* **250**: 113–19.

Woodroffe, R. *et al.* (1993). Dispersal and philopatry in the European badger, *Meles meles*. *Journal of Zoology, London* **237**: 227–39.

Woodroffe, R. *et al.* (2006a). Culling and cattle controls influence tuberculosis risk for badgers. *Proceedings of the National Academy of Sciences* **103**: 14713–17.

Woodroffe, R. *et al.* (2006b). Effects of culling on badger *Meles meles* spatial organization: implications for the control of bovine tuberculosis. *Journal of Applied Ecology* **43**: 1–10.

Wright, A. *et al.* (2000). Predicting the distribution of Eurasian badger (*Meles meles*) setts over an urbanized landscape: a GIS approach. *Photogrammetric Engineering and Remote Sensing* **66**: 423–8.

Yalden, D. (1999). *The History of British Mammals.* T. & A. D. Poyser, London.

Yamaguchi, N. *et al.* (2006). Female receptivity, embryonic diapause, and superfetation in the European badger (*Meles meles*): implications for the reproductive tactics of males and females. *Quarterly Review of Biology* **81**: 33–48.

Young, R. P. *et al.* (2006). Abundance of hedgehogs (*Erinaceus europaeus*) in relation to the density and distribution of badgers (*Meles meles*). *Journal of Zoology* **269**: 349–56.

Zabala, J. *et al.* (2002). Habitat selection and diet of badgers (*Meles meles*) in Biscay (northern Iberian Peninsula). *Italian Journal of Zoology* **69**: 233–8.

Zagorodniuk, I. V. (2003). Wild mammal fauna of Kyiv city and its vicinities, and trends in its urbanization. *Vestnik Zoologii* **37**: 29–38.

Zande, L. v. d. *et al.* (2006). Genetic structure within and among regional populations of the Eurasian badger (*Meles meles*) from Denmark and the Netherlands. *Journal of Zoology* **271**: 302–9.

Zee, F. F. v. d. *et al.* (1992). Landscape change as a possible cause of the badger *Meles meles* L. decline in the Netherlands. *Biological Conservation* **61**: 17–22.

Zuckerman, S. (1980). *Badgers, Cattle and Tuberculosis*. HMSO, London.

Index

Permissions and Credits

Figure 8 reproduced by permission of the editors of the *Russian Journal of Theriology*, from Abramov, A. V. (2002). Variation of the baculum structure of the Palearctic badger (Carnivora, Mustelidae, *Meles*). *Russian Journal of Theriology* **1**: 57–60. Figure 11 © Societas Europaea Mammalogica, reproduced with permission from Mitchell-Jones, A. J. *et al.* (1999). *The Atlas of European Mammals*. T. & A. D. Poyser, London. Figure 13 reproduced by permission of the Finnish Zoological and Botanical Publishing Board, from Bevanger, K. & Lindstrom, E. R. (1995). Distributional history of the European badger *Meles meles* in Scandinavia during the 20th century. *Annales Zoologici Fennici* **32**: 5–9. Figure 21 reproduced by permission of Wiley-Blackwell, from Davies, J. M. *et al.* (1987). Seasonal distribution of road kills in the European badger (*Meles meles*). *Journal of Zoology* **211**: 525–9. Figure 34 reproduced by permission of A. V. Abramov from Abramov, A. V. (2003). The head colour of the Eurasian badgers (Mustelidae, *Meles*). *Small Carnivore Conservation* **25**: 5–7. Figure 55 © Michael Clark, reproduced by permission of the artist. Figure 59 © Wiley 1978, reproduced by permission of Blackwell Publishing Ltd, from Kruuk, H. (1978). Spatial organisation and territorial behaviour of the European badger *Meles meles*. *Journal of Zoology* **184**: 1–19. Figure 66 reproduced by permission of Wiley-Blackwell, from Roper, T. J. (1992). Badger *Meles meles* setts: architecture, internal environment and function. *Mammal Review* **22**: 43–53. Figure 68 reproduced by permission of Wiley-Blackwell, from Moore, J. A. H. & Roper, T. J. (2003). Temperature and humidity in badger *Meles meles* setts. *Mammal Review* **33**: 308–13. Figure 73 reproduced by permission of Koninklijke Brill NV, from Roper, T. J. *et al.* (2001). Sett use in European badgers *Meles meles*. *Behaviour* **138**: 173–87. Figures 74 and 75 © Mammal Research Institute, Polish Academy of Sciences, reproduced with permission from Kowalczyk, R. *et al.* (2004). Seasonal and spatial pattern of shelter use by badgers *Meles meles* in Bialowiecza Primeval Forest (Poland). *Acta Theriologica* **49**: 75–92. Figure 91 © Mammal Research Institute, Polish Academy of Sciences, reproduced with permission from Pigozzi, G. (1991). The diet of the European badger in a Mediterranean coastal area. *Acta Theriologica*. **36**: 293–306. Figure 93 reproduced by permission of Elsevier, from Mellgren, R. & Roper, T. J. (1986). Spatial learning and the discrimination of food patches in the European badger (*Meles meles* L.). *Animal Behaviour* **34**: 1129–34. Figure 98 reproduced by permission of Elsevier, from Garnett, B. T. *et al.* (2003). Use of cattle troughs by badgers (*Meles meles*): a potential route for the transmission of bovine tuberculosis (*Mycobacterium bovis*). *Applied Animal Behaviour Science* **80**: 1–18. Figure 99 reproduced by permission of Elsevier, from Roper, T. J. & Lüps, P. (1995). Diet of badgers (*Meles meles*) in central Switzerland: an analysis of stomach contents. *Zeitschrift für Säugetierkunde – International Journal of Mammalian Biology* **60**: 9–19. Figures 104 and 107 reproduced by permission of The Royal Society, from Cresswell, W. J. *et al.* (1992). To breed or not to breed – an analysis of the social and density-dependent constraints on the fecundity of female badgers (*Meles meles*). *Philosophical Transactions of the Royal Society of London Series B – Biological Sciences* **338**: 393–407. Figure 113 reproduced by permission of Koninklijke Brill NV, from Fell, R. J. *et al.* (2006). The social integration of European badger (*Meles meles*) cubs into their natal group. *Behaviour* **143**: 683–700. Figure 129 © Michael Clark, reproduced by permission of the artist. Figure 132 reproduced by permission of Wiley-Blackwell, from Davies, J. M. *et al.* (1988). The anal gland secretion of the European badger (*Meles meles*) and its role in social communication. *Journal of Zoology* **216**: 455–63. Figures 133 and 138 reproduced by permission of Koninklijke Brill NV, from Roper, T. J. *et al.* (1986). Scent-marking with faeces and anal secretion in the European badger. *Behaviour* **97**: 94–117. Figure 136 reproduced by permission of Elsevier, from Kruuk, H. *et al.* (1984). Scent-marking with the sub-caudal gland by the European badger *Meles meles* L. *Animal Behaviour* **32**: 899–907. Figure 153 © Mammal Research Institute, Polish Academy of Sciences, reproduced with permission from Kowalczyk, R. *et al.* (2004). Seasonal and spatial pattern of shelter use by badgers *Meles meles* in Bialowiecza Primeval Forest (Poland). *Acta*

Theriologica **49**: 75–92. Figure 155 © Mammal Research Institute, Polish Academy of Sciences, reproduced with permission from Kowalczyk, R. *et al.* (2000). Badger density and distribution of setts in Bialowiecza Primeval Forest (Poland and Belarus) compared to other European populations. *Acta Theriologica* **45**: 395–408. Figures 157 and 158 reproduced by permission of Elsevier from Ostler, J. R. & Roper, T. J. (1998). Changes in the size, status and distribution of badger *Meles meles* L. setts during a 20-year period. *Zeitschrift für Säugetierkunde – International Journal of Mammalian Biology* **63**: 200–09. Figure 151 reproduced by permission of Elsevier from Shepherdson, D. J. *et al.* (1990). Diet, food availability and foraging behaviour of badgers (*Meles meles* L.) in southern England. *Zeitschrift für Säugetierkunde – International Journal of Mammalian Biology* **55**: 81–93. Figure 162 reproduced by permission of the publisher from Kowalczyk, R. *et al.* (2006) Daily movement and territory use by badgers *Meles meles* in Bialowiecza Primeval Forest, Poland. *Wildlife Biology* **12**: 385–91. Figure 164 reproduced by permission of Elsevier, from Goszczyński, J. *et al.* (2005). Activity of badgers *Meles meles* in central Poland. *Mammalian Biology* **70**: 1–11. Figure 168 reproduced by permission of Elsevier, from Macdonald, D. W. *et al.* (2004). Increasing frequency of bite wounds with increasing population density in Eurasian badgers, *Meles meles. Animal Behaviour* **67**: 745–51. Figure 171 © Zoological Society of London, reproduced with permission, from Harris, S. (1982). Activity patterns and habitat utilisation by badgers (*Meles meles*) in suburban Bristol: a radiotracking study. *Symposia of the Zoological Society of London* **49**: 301–23. Figure 172 reproduced by permission of Wiley-Blackwell. from Davison, J. (2008). Restricted ranging behaviour in a high-density population of urban badgers: *Journal of Zoology* **277**: 46–53. Figure 174 reproduced by permission of the Mammalogical Society of Japan, from Tanaka, H. *et al.* (2002). Spatial distribution and sett use by the Japanese badger *Meles meles anakuma. Mammal Study* **27**: 15–22. Figure 178 reproduced by permission of Wiley-Blackwell, from Kruuk, H. & Parish, T. (1982). Factors affecting population density, group size and territory size of the European badger, *Meles meles. Journal of Zoology* **196**: 31–9. Figures 179 and 181 reproduced by permission of Elsevier, from Brøseth, H. *et al.* (1997). Spatial organization and habitat utilization of badgers *Meles meles*: effects of food patch dispersion in the boreal forest of central Norway. *Zeitschrift für Säugetierkunde – International Journal of Mammalian Biology* **62**: 12–22. Figure 206 reproduced by permission of Nature Publishing Group, from Smith, N. H. *et al.* (2006). Bottlenecks and broomsticks: the molecular evolution of *Mycobacterium bovis. Nature Reviews Microbiology* **4**: 670–81. Figure 215 reproduced by permission Public Library of Science, from Jenkins, H. E. *et al.* (2010). The duration of the effects of repeated widespread badger culling on cattle tuberculosis following the cessation of culling. *PLoS One* **5**: e9090. doi:10.1371/journal.pone.0009090

The New Naturalist Library

1. *Butterflies* — E. B. Ford
2. *British Game* — B. Vesey-Fitzgerald
3. *London's Natural History* — R. S. R. Fitter
4. *Britain's Structure and Scenery* — L. Dudley Stamp
5. *Wild Flowers* — J. Gilmour & M. Walters
6. *The Highlands & Islands* — F. Fraser Darling & J. M. Boyd
7. *Mushrooms & Toadstools* — J. Ramsbottom
8. *Insect Natural History* — A. D. Imms
9. *A Country Parish* — A. W. Boyd
10. *British Plant Life* — W. B. Turrill
11. *Mountains & Moorlands* — W. H. Pearsall
12. *The Sea Shore* — C. M. Yonge
13. *Snowdonia* — F. J. North, B. Campbell & R.Scott
14. *The Art of Botanical Illustration* — W. Blunt
15. *Life in Lakes & Rivers* — T. T. Macan & E. B. Worthington
16. *Wild Flowers of Chalk & Limestone* — J. E. Lousley
17. *Birds & Men* — E. M. Nicholson
18. *A Natural History of Man in Britain* — H. J. Fleure & M. Davies
19. *Wild Orchids of Britain* — V. S. Summerhayes
20. *The British Amphibians & Reptiles* — M. Smith
21. *British Mammals* — L. Harrison Matthews
22. *Climate and the British Scene* — G. Manley
23. *An Angler's Entomology* — J. R. Harris
24. *Flowers of the Coast* — I. Hepburn
25. *The Sea Coast* — J. A. Steers
26. *The Weald* — S. W. Wooldridge & F. Goldring
27. *Dartmoor* — L. A. Harvey & D. St. Leger Gordon
28. *Sea Birds* — J. Fisher & R. M. Lockley
29. *The World of the Honeybee* — C. G. Butler
30. *Moths* — E. B. Ford
31. *Man and the Land* — L. Dudley Stamp
32. *Trees, Woods and Man* — H. L. Edlin
33. *Mountain Flowers* — J. Raven & M. Walters
34. *The Open Sea: I. The World of Plankton* — A. Hardy
35. *The World of the Soil* — E. J. Russell
36. *Insect Migration* — C. B. Williams
37. *The Open Sea: II. Fish & Fisheries* — A. Hardy
38. *The World of Spiders* — W. S. Bristowe
39. *The Folklore of Birds* — E. A. Armstrong
40. *Bumblebees* — J. B. Free & C. G. Butler
41. *Dragonflies* — P. S. Corbet, C. Longfield & N. W. Moore
42. *Fossils* — H. H. Swinnerton
43. *Weeds & Aliens* — E. Salisbury
44. *The Peak District* — K. C. Edwards
45. *The Common Lands of England & Wales* — L. Dudley Stamp & W. G. Hoskins
46. *The Broads* — E. A. Ellis
47. *The Snowdonia National Park* — W. M. Condry
48. *Grass and Grasslands* — I. Moore
49. *Nature Conservation in Britain* — L. Dudley Stamp
50. *Pesticides and Pollution* — K. Mellanby
51. *Man & Birds* — R. K. Murton
52. *Woodland Birds* — E. Simms
53. *The Lake District* — W. H. Pearsall & W. Pennington
54. *The Pollination of Flowers* — M. Proctor & P. Yeo
55. *Finches* — I. Newton
56. *Pedigree: Words from Nature* — S. Potter & L. Sargent
57. *British Seals* — H. R. Hewer
58. *Hedges* — E. Pollard, M. D. Hooper & N. W. Moore
59. *Ants* — M. V. Brian
60. *British Birds of Prey* — L. Brown
61. *Inheritance and Natural History* — R. J. Berry
62. *British Tits* — C. Perrins
63. *British Thrushes* — E. Simms
64. *The Natural History of Shetland* — R. J. Berry & J. L. Johnston

65. *Waders* — W. G. Hale
66. *The Natural History of Wales* — W. M. Condry
67. *Farming and Wildlife* — K. Mellanby
68. *Mammals in the British Isles* — L. Harrison Matthews
69. *Reptiles and Amphibians in Britain* — D. Frazer
70. *The Natural History of Orkney* — R. J. Berry
71. *British Warblers* — E. Simms
72. *Heathlands* — N. R. Webb
73. *The New Forest* — C. R. Tubbs
74. *Ferns* — C. N. Page
75. *Freshwater Fish* — P. S. Maitland & R. N. Campbell
76. *The Hebrides* — J. M. Boyd & I. L. Boyd
77. *The Soil* — B. Davis, N. Walker, D. Ball & A. Fitter
78. *British Larks, Pipits & Wagtails* — E. Simms
79. *Caves & Cave Life* — P. Chapman
80. *Wild & Garden Plants* — M. Walters
81. *Ladybirds* — M. E. N. Majerus
82. *The New Naturalists* — P. Marren
83. *The Natural History of Pollination* — M. Proctor, P. Yeo & A. Lack
84. *Ireland: A Natural History* — D. Cabot
85. *Plant Disease* — D. Ingram & N. Robertson
86. *Lichens* — Oliver Gilbert
87. *Amphibians and Reptiles* — T. Beebee & R. Griffiths
88. *Loch Lomondside* — J. Mitchell
89. *The Broads* — B. Moss
90. *Moths* — M. Majerus
91. *Nature Conservation* — P. Marren
92. *Lakeland* — D. Ratcliffe
93. *British Bats* — John Altringham
94. *Seashore* — Peter Hayward
95. *Northumberland* — Angus Lunn
96. *Fungi* — Brian Spooner & Peter Roberts
97. *Mosses & Liverworts* — Nick Hodgetts & Ron Porley
98. *Bumblebees* — Ted Benton
99. *Gower* — Jonathan Mullard
100. *Woodlands* — Oliver Rackham
101. *Galloway and the Borders* — Derek Ratcliffe
102. *Garden Natural History* — Stefan Buczacki
103. *The Isles of Scilly* — Rosemary Parslow
104. *A History of Ornithology* — Peter Bircham
105. *Wye Valley* — George Peterken
106. *Dragonflies* — Philip Corbet & Stephen Brooks
107. *Grouse* — Adam Watson & Robert Moss
108. *Southern England* — Peter Friend
109. *Islands* — R. J. Berry
110. *Wildfowl* — David Cabot
111. *Dartmoor* — Ian Mercer
112. *Books and Naturalists* — David E. Allen
113. *Bird Migration* — Ian Newton